PUBLIC POLICY ANALYSIS AND DESIGN

About the Author

V.K. Agnihotri, an IAS Officer of the 1968 batch, belongs to Andhra Pradesh cadre of the service. Born on 25 August, 1945, he obtained his Masters degrees in English Literature and Political Science from the University of Allahabad, Allahabad. He was the recipient of several awards and honours during his distinguished academic career. Before joining the IAS, he served on the Faculty of the Department of English, University of Allahabad. He has held several positions with the State and Central Governments. His previous substantive assignment was Development Commissioner for Handloom in the Ministry of Textiles, Government of India, prior to his joining the Lal Bahadur Shastri National Academy of Administration, Mussoorie, as its Joint Director and Coordinator of Public Administration Faculty. He is also the Chairman of the Core Group of the Centre for Micro-Planning and Regional Studies as well as SOFTRAIN at the Academy. He has been a Visiting Fellow to the Queen Elizabeth House, University of Oxford in 1991-92. He has extensive experience in development administration and public policy making. His current area of research is public policy analysis and design. He has published several articles and books. He has recently co-edited the book *Environment and Development.* Author book entitled *skills for Effective Administrators* is being published by Vikas.

PUBLIC POLICY ANALYSIS AND DESIGN

Edited by
VIVEK K. AGNIHOTRI, I.A.S.
Joint Director
Lal Bahadur Shastri National Academy of Administration
(Government of India)
Mussoorie

Foreword by
Prof. A.M. Khusro
Editor, Financial Express
New Delhi

CONCEPT PUBLISHING COMPANY, NEW DELHI 110059

ISBN 81-7022-561-2

First Published 1995

Published and printed by
Ashok Kumar Mittal
Concept Publishing Company
A/15-16, Commercial Block, Mohan Garden,
NEW DELHI - 110059

DEDICATED

TO

THE SPIRIT OF ACADEMY

WHICH

INSPIRED AND MADE THIS WORK POSSIBLE

FOREWORD

It occurs to me that if a well-designed and clearly definable policy did emerge in any realm, the chances are that some one must have designed it—either a group or an individual policy-maker. Now for such a designing of policy, perfect or imperfect, however, elegant of crude, what is required is a knowledge of the relevant milieu or environment for which this policy is to be made, a knowledge of the problems in that area and the deteriorations that are taking place which might necessitate a policy correction to change the deteriorating environment. Moreover, an awareness is required as to what is happening in similar situations elsewhere and how other policy-makers have solved some of these problems. All this means a horizon about that area and then some new thinking, some initiative to evolve a new policy. Who does all this, is not clear to me at all. Do things happen this way in our country or is it a hit and miss process. Things do happen sometimes because somebody has some leadership quality; things happen in committees, things happen randomly or things happen because some situations deteriorate so much that something has to be done about them and the response to those situations is policy. Thus policies emerge in many ways and it may well be difficult to single out a particular manner in which policy evolution or policy change actually taken place. The Seminar will reveal much more about how policies are made and how changes take place in policy.

Policy need not be made by governments only, but in this country policy has been made almost wholly by governments. It may be because other segments, sector and socio economic agents in the country—the private industrial sector, the commercial sector and the social sector have been weak and are in the throes of a slow developmental process, they will acquire a degree of resilience and a policy-making capability later. But to begin with they are weak. And therefore, it fell to the lot of Central and State Governments to make policies and programmes during the last 40 years. Who can deny that very major thrusts on policy have been made by the governments and that incidentally many of them have served well. I am not one of those who believe that when new policies are launched the old policies can be said to have failed. Policies, even good policies, fulfil their destiny and have to be replaced by other policies. I would say that after 1951 a period of 20 years had passed in this country when many policies were imaginatively conceived and successfully launched and did their job commendably. But as time went by and as the structure of the society and the economy began to change, those policies became less relevant, in some cases irrelevant and ineffective, and later on counterproductive. That is why major changes had to be brought about in the recent past.

I am talking basically of the area of economic policies at this moment. Now, governments have been making these policies and they have had some competence to make policies. But it is often found that governments respond sooner or later to a deteriorating environment and policies come as a response to problems that arise. And why not? Such a policy response is very legitimate. But it must be conceded that in this country governments can be credited with some initiatives too. Not just response but initiatives — and that was clearly very true in the time of Mr Nehru and even in that time of later Prime Ministers. New ideas were conceived and policy initiatives were taken which no intellectual group, no academic group, no chamber of commerce, no industrialist group etc. undertook to propose or adopt. It was nearly always the State and the government. Clearly a lot of credit for policy initiatives and even implementation in this country goes to the governments. What is the internal process of policy-making in government? How is policy made — very often responding to and occasionally initiating the change? We will come to know the answer in due course through the seminar.

Land Reforms and Economic Planning

One of the major policies adopted in this country, namely Land Reforms, is the gift of the administration. It may not have worked too well. But nobody can say it didn't work anywhere. It worked in Kerala, West Bengal, Uttar Pradesh for sometime, the Decan (Hyderabad) area, Bombay presidency and elsewhere. There are large pockets of the country where the policy reform gave dividends but the conception of that is not the work of economists like V.M. Dandekar or M.L. Dantwala or myself. No, it was the work of governmental agencies. Sometimes it was the driving force of politicians like the Chief Minister of Hyderabad, Borgul Ram Kishen Rao, the famous lawyer who launched the Land Reforms Programme and pushed it with high energy. There have been politicians and there have been administrators who launched this programme and in some pockets of this country carried it long distance.

Similarly the whole idea of economic planning and the policies that went with planning, is the gift of the Nehru regime. No thinking had been done on this subject baring the Bombay Plan that was made by some industrialists and baring the People's Plan. They are of course some initial exercises and some individual thinking, but making the grand design of economic planning and working out the accompanying policies has been a gift of politics and administration to this country.

When you think of the Nehruvian team including C.D. Deshmukh, V.T. Krishnamachari, Tarlok Singh, J.J. Anjaria, Pitambar Pant and others, you take your hat off to that group for initiating a major change in policies and programmes leading to economic growth. But, other than the governmental circles which have borne larger responsibilities, the general bureaucracy and government seems to have been an agent of change as well as of stickiness. Along with right policies they have also made wrong policies and often-times have failed to change the policies in time. But in initiating the change, the governments have to be given the credit. How did they do it and what is the internal mechanism? The seminar will reflect on that too.

Resistance to Change

Apart from governmental work, academic and social analyses have certainly played a larger role in policy-making. Here I talk of not only academics, economists, political scientists, social psychologists and other social scientists, but also of the captains of industry and Chambers of Commerce and Industry who have been battering the administration for the last forty years with new ideas, particularly those of change from a controlled economy to a relatively free economy. The Federation of Chambers of Commerce and Industry typically invited the Prime Minister every year, except in the most recent times, to discuss industrial and trade policy. Mr Nehru, Mrs Gandhi, Mr Lal Bahadur Shastri, Mr Morarji Desai and Mr Rajiv Gandhi were all invited to the FICCI and other Chambers in an annual ritual when the President of the Chamber told the Prime Minister that while industry is doing its best and thing are going on well, the over-controlled and over-administered system is not working and that it is creating black money and inefficiency. So they pleaded for a change in terms of freedom from excessive controls. But each time the response of successive Prime Ministers was more or less negative. They told the Chambers to hold their horses. It is not jut the decontrol of the economy that is important but it is the direction of investment in different cannels that must be determined appropriately, as the government has to guarantee the welfare of the people that industrialist and men of commerce should therefore, bear with the administration. Some freedoms are there and one can do many things within the controlled framework. Thus, there was always a resistance on the part of the Prime Ministers to bringing about a change in the control system and suggestion from trade and industry were typically ignored. But, after 40 years an effective change has become visible in the recent past.

Weak Agents of Change

In all these past years, academics, social analysts, chambers of commerce and industry and consumer organisations have shown themselves to be very weak in influencing the policies and have hardly played a role. The non-government organization have recently emerged as an important category which thinks of policies and influences the government to some extent. This group will have a large say in the future because the day of deregulation and relative withdrawal of the governments from economic matters and social affairs has arrived. It has arrived all over the world and it has arrived here too. Governments everywhere are announcing their withdrawal and even if they do not withdraw in absolute terms, they stay put while the other sectors of economy, the private sector, the cooperative sector and the NGOs sector are going to grow phenomenally and nobody can stop that tendency in the future. Such a trend will lead to a shift in the share of policy-making away from the government and in favour of the other economic agents of the society—the consumers, the producers, the traders, the institutions and the NGOs. These are the individuals, groups, corporations and other non-government bodies that will undertake policy changes in the future. These are the individuals, groups corporations and other non-government bodies that will undertake policy changes in the future. The government's role will shrink relatively and the role of other agencies will expand in comparison.

Now the impact of these non-governmental organizations is very weak so far. The new agencies and organizations the academics, the social analysts, the people in industry and trade and the NGOs have emerged only recently. They do come out with new ideas and new formulations of policy, but sometimes are listened to and sometimes not. I don't really know how much influence they have : that depends upon the realm that we are talking about. Governmental policy-making often proceeds through committee work which is sometimes necessary and even effective but at other times inefficient and counter-productive. As has been general remarked, committees and sub-committees produce camels! The camel, a somewhat distorted structure, is said to be an animal which was put together in a committee! The suggestion is that the kind of thing that emerges in policy making, through committee work is less than the best and often turns out to be a crudity. But, at the same time, committees do provide a mechanism for moving forward and non-dictatorial decision-making, seem to have no substitute.

Indian governments certainly get credit for major policy initiatives and policy reforms in areas like and reforms, economic planning and anti-poverty programmes. These areas are very crucial and substantive in nature and with all their difficulties and failures, these developmental programmes such as the IRDP, the NREP and Nehru Rozgar Yojana, like the earlier programmes of Community Development, Intensive Agriculture District Programmes etc. have done a great deal of good. Each programme has had some failure at the margin but each has made some dent in an otherwise frozen situation. And what is more, the sum total of those bits and pieces of success which each programme has had in different degrees and the cumulative effect of those partial successes has altogether made an impact and the country which has moved on from a 1 per cent growth rate in the first half of this century to a 31/2 per cent growth rate from 1951 to 1975 and to a 5 per cent growth rate thereafter. True that a 5 per cent growth is the weakest in Asia but is impressive nevertheless, compared to 1 per cent, 2 per cent or 21/2 per cent in Europe, the United States and Japan. Indian progress in economic uplift is to a great extent the sum total of the aggregative macro-effects of small successes in many realms. This brings up an important point about policy analysis. We may analyse the impact of a given policy but we can seldom isolate the impact of other policies on this area of a given policy and the impact of this area on the other policies. Policy analysis is an interactive study of different policies and the effect or impact that we see, while studying a given policy, is actual the cumulative effect of various (possibly) mutually reinforming policies.

I have already stated that non-governmental organizations (NGOs) that could make policies are still weak, but that they are emerging slowly. There are NGOs like Policy Initiatives or Policy Alternatives, etc. and there are the associations of industry and trade. Many people in the private sector of industry and trade, the cooperative sector, the NGO sector, the social sector and the intellectual sector are beginning to think of many policy areas and it is certain that their role will increase with time.

Leadership and Policy Initiative

Very often, apart from committee work and governmental initiative, a critical factor in the emergence of new policies is leadership. More often then not, new policies emerge through the work of a leader, even as institution-building often takes place under the auspices of effective leadership. We know a good deal about how institutions grow and how they work. There may be a situation in which a certain individual with an idea, organizational ability and a driving force sets up a mission, motivates people and galvanizes his followers. He may stay for 40 years with the institution and formulate policies for it. He may even get governments to make appropriate policies. When he is gone, the institution may decline or it may not. In social analysis, it often turns out that the role of leadership is crucial. And in like manner, in institution-building and policy formulation the role of leadership is undeniably crucial. When I think of the role of an effective leader in a certain area of policy-making, I think of Shri S.K. Dey, in the community development field. I don't think that if the Maharajas had been there, economic planning and development would have been the same. However, much we may decry economic planning today, it had its innings and its heyday. The planning mechanism worked — it worked in the Second, the Third, the Fourth, the Fifth and the Sixth plan periods, and even in the Seventh Plan — and the credit goes to the leadership, the institution building and the galvanizing personalities.

However much we might discredit the nationalisation and socialisation of banks today — though I should hesitate to do so — the job was done well, when it was done. The banking system was reformed; and extended it was not thrown out of the window. I think this system has done big things during the seventies and the eighties, and I don't think that banking would have reached the general populace in this country, particularly in the rural/agricultural areas, the way it has done, had not Indira Gandhi, whether for her own political reasons or out of conviction, forced the banks to move into the countryside.

Designing of Policies

Now, apart from all the paraphernalia of policy designing, intellectual work, interactions, committee work etc., I think the role of a leader in policy making has generally been and is very crucial. Once the leader sets the pace and the big idea gets going, designing comes from behind. More often than not, you don't design first on the part of some body and then move on to the details of designing and implementation. Of course, the opposite is also possible and must have happened. But generally it is the thinking on the part of leadership in a particular area of policy-making, followed by a sharing of the idea with others to get a large and critical group interested in it; then getting the designers to come from behind and make the design for a forward movement of this policy, and finally working towards the generation of some compelling forces in society to push the new policy to the stage of implementation - that seems to be the sequence in the generality of cases.

Be that as it may, I believe that good policy designing is important for sustainability. The brilliance of a leader or the brilliance of the new policy idea that has been initiated, supported and launched, may go some distance for some time. But, if this policy is to be sustained beyond what the leadership has done, then a proper designing is required. Without an appropriate design, I think a given policy would collapse. Thus, even though designing comes from behind, it is critically important. Similarly, monitoring and evaluation of policies is crucial too; or else how will policy change? It is the monitoring that brings into the open the non-fulfilments and fulfilments. It is evaluation that brings out the defects in policies and may be it is evaluation that leads to new ideas about changing the path of policy later on. So, I would say leadership is crucial, designing must follow for reasons of sustainability, and then monitoring and evaluation must be the accompanying processes which would lead to future change.

Vested Interests

Very often policies get bogged down in what are called vested interests. As I reflect on this, it occurs to me that first we have to decide who is deciding the policies and who are the vested interests. But it may be that in the democracies some processes exist which isolate the vested interests. There can be two kinds of vested interests. Some want to preserve and retain the prevailing policies as these are sanctioned by the wisdom of the ages. They think that many of things that are happening, institutionalised or non-institutionalised, are the right things that should probably go on. One thinks of the preservation of environments by tribals and one thinks of a general preservation of environment. There are lots and lots of our people who, in line with their present culture, would not allow a tree to be cut down. Policy has to take advantage of such positive cultural factors which rightly want to preserve the good institutions and healthy social conventions and make supportive arrangements, lows and rules.

Thus, on the other side, there are the interest groups which want to change the approaches and policies followed conventionally, because the conventional wisdom has run its full course and the conventional institutions have fulfilled their destiny. Policy makers, alert as they must be to changing times and needs, must decide early enough when to switch over to the new approaches and become supportive of the new interests.

And then, there is a very important group of vested interests who have a stake in the existing system and would not like a change. They would dig their feet deeply and would obstruct the new policies. To take one or two examples, it voting rights were given to women of to the illiterate or less literate people, embedded interests would laugh at it and oppose the change. Similarly they would reject a new economic policy if it aimed at liberalization or decontrol.

I remember that when I was posted in Germany, there was a very competent man, who is regarded as a wise man in Germany. This was Ambassador Gunther Diehl, who had been the Ambassador of Germany for six years in India. Gunther Diehl was sitting with some German friends and a few Indian friends when I was also present. Discussion turned on the need for literacy and education as a precondition to participation in democratic elections. Most Germans were wondering how a country like India, can have a voting system when literacy rates are so poor 40 per cent, 35 per cent, 30 per cent or whatever. How can people select their government with 40 per cent literacy? What do they know about the issues? What do they know about who will be able to tackle those issues? How can the illiterate decide? The general feeling in that group was that an illiterate country cannot really run a democratic voting system. Gunther Diehl objected to this and addressing me, he said, "Mr. Ambassador, I know your country very well as I have been there for six years. I disagree with my German friends here. Yes, India is an illiterate country, but in your country there are millions of educated people who have never been literate!" In other words, Gunther Diehl was saying: literacy or illiteracy, there is a wisdom of the ages in the hearts and minds of people which is their mainstay and conservatives and no-changers would not recognize that wisdom, nor give the people their due. Yes, there are always some obstructionists who would obstruct new policies; they would resist change because the benefit from the present policies and hence want to sustain these. But policies do need to be changed at a certain point of time and these interests stand in the way.

For 40 years, we ran a system in India which I would attempt to describe to you in a moment — an economic system, a policy set or a policy frame which, taken together, can be termed a strategy of economic development. This strategy seems to have worked well for about 15 to 20 years, but thereafter it became counter-productive and then somebody had to think to change it. When the economy landed in a series of economic crises in 1989-91, the prevailing policies which relevance were at one time, were seen to be irrelevant. Now a U-turn must take place, the old order must change, yielding place to new. And hence, phenomenal policy changes came in 1991, 1992 and 1993.

But, by this time, our industrial class and commercial class had got used to the older hackneyed system in which there was no innovativeness, no grand designs for change, no competitiveness, no cost reduction and not even sustainability. In the older system or policy set-up, there was very little efficiency, no exportability and very little profitability. The system did not admit of new technology. Forgetting all these desirable things and leaving them aside, the main concern of the industrial and commercial class in the 1970s and the 1980s came to be to by-pass the system of controls, restrictions and licensing, or, through public-relationing to bend the system in ones favour. How to get a bit industrial licence for onself and how to prevent the other fellow in the queue from getting another licence in that same field, so that one remained either a monopolist or an oligopolist.

That is to say, one should do everything to be the only seller or one of the very few sellers of the particular product. Policy mechanism should be bent in order to disallow fresh entries and an oligopolistic situation should not be converted into a competitive one. Such vested interests in India have concentrated their energies on bending or by-passing the policies rather than going on toe the main thrusts of technological upgradations, managerial improvements, cost cutting and efficiency orientation.

One, however, feels happy that when policy change began to come in the early 1990s, these vested interests could not stop it and did not emerge as a major factor of resistance. Captains of industry and commerce have generally come around to accept the new policies. I think, it should be an important aspect of policy designing and implementation as to how to contain and deflate these vested interests and bring them around to favour the new policies and demonstrate these to be good for them as well as good for their sector of enterprise and for the country.

At this point, there is another thing that occurs to me. In policy-making and implementing, there is also a band-wagon effect. As policy moves from one posture to another, say from socialism to the market economy, and the slogans of the day change, everybody begins to jump on the bandwagon of the market economy as that is the only "in-thing". Policy-designers, policy-makers, analysts and implementors are all busy with the new designs and new slogans and you cannot allow this situation to by pass you; you cannot be left out of the advantages. But it is important to note that the bandwagons of market-dominated and private-sector-oriented policies are likely, in due course, to undergo a change. The thesis of the controlled or command economy is being replaced, by the antithesis of the market economy. But then, there is bound to be a synthesis of the two. That key part of socialism which had to do with the elimination of poverty and the uplift of the poor will remain or come back and reassert itself. But the other, more superficial, part of socialism in which had to do with the control of prices and foreign exchange rates, intervention sin and suppression of the markets in the belief that the market mechanism does not function equitably, and yet another pertaining at called commanding heights of the economy through the operation and extension of a monolithic public sector those parts of socialism might disappear.

I do not see that working without the market mechanism with a set of bureaucratic public enterprises is an essential part of socialism at set of all. Thus, there are the non-essential parts of socialism as well as the essential part and in a poor economy it is the lifting up of the poor, even if it be through the market forces, and bringing into the market all those which remains a key objective. Millions of people are virtually working outside the market system under very primitive and miserable circumstances and have to be aided and assisted to enter the market economy through certain policies and programmes. If poverty remains in this country in absolute terms for fifty more years, the anti-poverty mechanism of socialism would have to stay for those 50 years. I think this discernment among policy formulators is very important. They must understand what is on and what is not.

Moreover, the policy-makers as well as the people on the policy bandwagon must understand what this market economy is. We mean by the term market economy a competitive economy where a healthy competition exists between producers and producers, traders and traders, between one firm and another and one agency and another. In such a freely competing economy, efficiency is maximized, profits are normalised innovativeness is encouraged and the 'invisible hand' of nature determines the price through supply and demand. But the actual market economy that is now emerging threatens to be something else. It may be a non-competitive market economy, a set of oligopolies or market-dominant firms, an economy of monopolistic competition.

Among market-dominating firms, monopolies or oligopolies which bend the economy to their purpose, compromise quality, make abnormal profits and possibly exploit the consumers, we need not single out the multinational in particular. Domestic firms can also do the same thing. Multinations can be competitive but they can also be part of an oligopolistics structure of a few major firms dominating a certain line of product. So can be the domestic enterprises — either functioning in a competitive market or being part of a structure in which a few major firms dominate the economy or a sector. So it is not the privilege only of the multinations that they are oligopolistic. They can be and so can be the locals. It is by definition the oligopolies - whoever they are, foreign firms or locals — who are the market-dominant sellers, who bend the market in their favour, fix prices at their own behest, share the market as they like, avoid competition, and differentiate the products as they think fit. For instance, three or four manufacturers of cars may collude with each other: they look like competitors, but they are not. They may sit together around a table and decide things hand in glove: "you make a four seater car, I make a five seater and he makes a six seater — so there is a product differentiation: we don't produce the same thing and we don't compete. After all, the man who wants a four seater car is not a customer in the six seater market generally. So your market is your own without competition. Then, again, you sell in the West, I sell in the North and South and you sell in the East." This kind of thing has been going on in the automobile industry and many other industries, of course. Oligopolies do exist and while the policy-makers must understand and take account of the phenomenon, the new fangled admirers of the market bandwagon need not accept the market economy unthinkingly as a panacea for all evils. On must do a lot more of analytical policy work to advise the government or to influence policy in the right direction.

Recent Changes in Economic Policy

For the last forty years in this country, we continued with a set of policy prescriptions which together constituted a strategy. Basically, as a I see it, the main pillars of this strategy were as follows:

There should be a Planning Commission which should decide in which sectors and sub-sectors the new investment must flow. The assumption was that the Planning Commission knows better than the individual entrepreneurs what direction and volume is better for the country. All kinds of arguments were advanced in support of this decision. An individual industrial producer knows only his own line and his own business. But there are many others who are working in this line. The Planning Commission knows who is producing in Gujarat and who in Karnataka and in Kerala is also doing the same thing. The Commission has the knowledge of the totality. The are wise people who know more about investment in this line which is not visible to others and if it is not going to be profitable for them and the country they would not allow it. This may have been true 40 years ago, but it turned out, after forty years, that the entrepreneurs know better than the Planning Commission. The Commission should only undertakes indicative planning and tell the decision-makers what the prospects are for investment, production and profitability in one line and another. In the new approach, investment would not be denied but if you still want to invest in a given line after the Planning Commission has given the indication, it is your business to accept or not to accept it. That is one plank of economic policy which has undergone a change.

The second plank of policy was a public sector in which nearly all the infrastructural items will be produced. Infrastructures, like capital goods, are goods which produce more goods: but they have the additional attribute that they enter into a whole range of production. The public sector was used to produce the infrastructures on the plea the private producers would charge very high prices for infrastructural goods and services and that won't be affordable by the people. Hence, it came about that steel, coal, electricity, railways, airways, irrigation and fertilisers etc. came to be in the public sector. Private sector would not only over price the infrastructures for the sake of profits but also it may not have the huge volume of capital required. But, in these forty years, the capabilities of the private sector have improved and a world horizon has been acquired by the private entrepreneurs. They are now capable of doing big things and can even set-up and run very large infrastructural industries. The new policy purports to change this plank and hopes to allow the private sector considerable participation in infrastructure building.

The third plank of policy was a private sector of enterprise to produce all kinds of consumer goods, agricultural products and a great many capital goods, many of these under a licensing system. Here again the presumption was that the licensing authority knows better than the producers and the consumers what was good for the economy. This presumption prevailed for more than 30 years but finally had to be given up when the policy reforms arrived in 1991. By that time, the licensing system had actually begun to put a brake on the supply system of India. The economy had been reduced to a mere demand-managed and demand-controlled economy with all its implications for supply shortages, black money, corruption and serious distortions. But all that required to be changed and the licensing system had to be removed or dilated.

The fourth plank of policy was price controls. The poorer section of the population, 40 per cent or more in the sixties and the seventies, could not buy such essentials at rice, wheat and jawar at market prices. So the prices of essentials must be lower, rice, wheat, kerosene, drugs and pharmaceutical etc. must sell at controlled prices lower than the market prices and a system of prices control must be operated. By the end of the Second plan (1961) there might have between only about 10 key commodities under price control. But 10 years later when you look back over your shoulder, you find that may be 200 commodities are under control. Besides commodity price controls there had emerged a plethora of foreign exchange controls, important controls, capital goods controls, licensing controls and a whole lot of things which had come under one form of control or another. Now whenever there are two prices for a given commodity; a free market price and a controlled price, every seller wants to sell at the higher free market price and hides this activity as it is illegal to sell at any but the controlled price. The under gain is black money over the last 25 years. Nevertheless price controls have been one of the key elements of policy, thoughtlessly continued too long and thoughtlessly expanded too much. Such policy interventions and controls should have been terminated long ago. The world bank and the IMF took this position but many Indian analysts, thinkers and even policy-makers also thought so and advised accordingly. Dr. Manmohan Singh too had taken a position against the over regulated economy. Incidentally, he and I taught together at the University of Delhi and I happen to know his mind. He and I were among the early protesters against the extensive control system that had lived too long. But there were other protesters even within the government such as Abid Hussain and Arjun Sen Gupta and many others who were recommending a policy change.

Yet another plank of policy was an extensive subsidization of the economy. The argument was that poor people cannot buy the essential commodities without subsidy and small producers cannot produce cheaply without subsidy. Thus the items carrying a subsidy and the volumes of subsidy were expanded unduly, covering the target as well as the untargeted populations of consumers and producers. The subsidized regime became enormous and the subsidy on two major items of food and fertilizer came to be Rupees seven thousand crores when the budget deficit of the Central Government itself was Rupees seven thousand crores. What kind of economies was it that in order to subsidize the prices of two commodities — foodgrains and fertilizers — the government ran a subsidy scheme — Rs. 7000 crore — deficit of same magnitude which inflated all commodities in the economy! This policy was a total economic nonsense; it put people on crutches, it subsidized the under living and it led to a colossal wastage and inefficiency.

Another plank of policy was import substitution. This was designed to make at home what was being hitherto imported or would be imparted in the future. I think that there was a lot of merit in this as infant industries did need some protection for some time from the highly efficient and established producers. To run a strategy of import substitution this country, many others, had to raise tariff walls to protect the domestic producers for say five to seven years. This was an infant industry tariff, but alas it was kept too long — for 25 or 30 years or more. Inefficient production behind the tariff walls became the order of the day and perhaps none of the so-called import substituted enterprises became exporters even after 25 years. They could not compete in the external world. Subsequently this policy of import substitution had to be replaced by something else say by a policy of export generation.

Yet another plank of our policy was a fixed external value of the rupees determined by the Reserve Bank of India rather than the market. Various advantages were claimed for a fixed value, say Rs. 16 to a dollar. Exporters would know how much they would earn in rupees for an export sale of a given number of dollars. Importers would know, how much a machinery or a commodity in dollars would cost in terms of Indian rupees. It did not matter what rate, in terms of dollar, the market was offering for say a Rs. 1000.

All these policies were actually well-conceived when they were first put into operation. Indeed, they worked well for some years and gave dividends. As everyone knows the growth rate of the economy which used to be approximately 1 per cent per annum in the first half of the century got raised to 3.5 per cent after 1951 when most of these policies were adopted and it got further enhanced to 4.5 per cent after 1975. However, as the structure of the economy began to change, each one of these policies begin to lose its cutting edge and, in due course, became not only unproductive but counter-productive. By the middle of the '60s and beyond, several vested interests had emerged which had a stake in the continuation of this set of policy and they worked towards consolidating it and not allowing it to change. There were, of course, agents of change among the academics and also in the private industrial and commercial sectors as well as the NGO sector but they did not seem to have been strong enough to influence the Government and the bureaucracy to change the policies. And so things went on until the end of the '80s when the first symptoms of change began to emerge. Mrs. Gandhi's government did initiate some change but there was a lot of haziness about the thought pattern of change. It was Mr. Rajiv Gandhi who, in 1985 and early 1986, spelt out a new policy approach with courage and conviction but he soon got involved in other matters and could not reach the stage of detailed designing of the policies he wanted to pursue — the policies of liberalisation, deregulation, decontrol and globalisation.

By the end of the 1980s, in the face of emerging crises — a crisis of foreign exchange, a crisis of government's budgetary resources and a crisis of accessive controls and regulations affecting the supply side of the economy — several political parties, except those on the Left, began to talk of policy reform and on the even of elections in 1991, nearly all of them committed themselves in their manifestoes or liberalisation, competitiveness, technological change and a market-oriented as well as globalised economy.

From July 1991 onwards, the Government of Mr. P. V. Narasimha Rao, under the economic leadership of Dr. Manmohan Singh, introduced a powerful and comprehensive economic policy package which focused on correcting the external value of the rupee, liberalising and debureaucratising the import licensing system, eliminating export subsidies, cutting the budget deficit, reducing the other subsidies, especially the one on fertilizers, delicensing the industrial sector and raising the administered prices of various commodities under the control of the Government. This policy began to give dividends and still continues to do so but it appears that the policy reached a plato, at any rate for the time being, and stopped short of extending liberalisation and deregulation to many other sectors of the economy such as the educational sector, urban ceiling and agricultural land ceiling, urban and rural rent controls, the financial sector, the cooperative sector and several others. In other words, the horizontal extension of liberal policies virtually came to a hault. Moreover, the vertical implementation of the new policies slowed down as the state governments and the lower civil service became a stumbling block in proceeding with the new policies. Today we get two alternative views from people who are directly affected by liberalisation. Some say that implementation has slowed down but others believe and state that it is proceeding quite well. If industry is not extending rapidly and taking advantage of the delicensed set-up, in terms of rapid expansion, it is because of the high rates of interest in the banking system which do not make many projects worthwhile. Recent reductions in the rates of interest, however, are perhaps changing the attitude of the private sector towards investment and expansion. It is not clear why the party in power at the Centre does not tell those state governments which are being run by the same party that the decisions taken at the Centre are the results of the party's acceptance of the new ideas and that the state governments, wherever they are of the same party, are obliged to adopt the same policies. It is clear that in policy matters, leadership proposes but the vested interest disposes. However, it is comforting to know that the obstructionists will not have their say for all times and that the industrial sector of the Indian economy which could have feared the competitiveness emerging from the new policies, has not actually opposed these policies but has generally cast its vote in favour of the new policies.

Despite a good beginning, the new policy machine has had to slow down and political considerations seem to have come in the way of further extension. The policy of subsidy reduction has not been continued with any conviction. An exit policy, though talked about, has not been adopted for fear of adverse reactions from the labour force and the trade unions, deregulation of the many remaining sectors of the economy has not been proceeded with and cuts in government expenditure and the elimination of government departments, which are in the nature of sixth finger, could not be brought about. Nevertheless, enough seems to have been done on the policy front to make the economy self-propelling so that it does not depend any more on the fortunes of a particular government or a given political party. When policy formulation and implementation reaches that stage, one would say that great success has been achieved and that the vested interests holding the policy back can be said to have been virtually defeated.

PROF. A.M. KHUSRO

ACKNOWLEDGMENTS

I gratefully acknowledge the wide and varied contributions made by the participants of the Seminar on PUBLIC POLICY ANALYSIS AND DESIGN organised by Lal Bahadur Shastri National Academy of Administration from 23 to 25 August, 1993, which made the publication of this book possible. Some of the papers presented at the Seminar could not be included in this book for copyright reasons.

I am also beholden to other contributors who helped enrich the coverage of various public policy areas by acceding to my request to prepare articles on certain commissioned topics.

I am extremely grateful to Prof. A.M. Khusro for agreeing to write the Foreword for this book based on his inaugural address delivered at the Seminar.

The assistance from and support and active participation in the Seminar of the faculty and staff of LBS National Academy of Administration, Mussoorie, and particularly its Training I Section and the Centre for Micro-Planning and Regional Studies, are thankfully acknowledged. I am extremely grateful to my Senior Personal Assistant, Sri M.D. Bahukhandi, for shouldering the responsibility to organise the Seminar during the initial stages. Special mention must also be made of the painstaking efforts made by Sri Anil Kumar Dimri in putting together the material for publication. Special thanks are due to Ms. Uma Mahadevan, trainee-officer, for her remarkably professional editorial help.

I would also like to acknowledge the gracious permission extended by the editor and copyright holder of *The Administrator,* to incorporate in this book the articles published in the Journal's Special Issue on Public Policy (Volume XXXIX, No.1, January-March, 1994).

My ultimate gratitude is reserved for Vijay, my wife, whose patience and encouragement at all times, even at considerable personal inconvenience, made working on this book an exciting venture.

V.K. AGNIHOTRI

CONTENTS

LIST OF TABLES

LIST OF FIGURES

LIST OF CONTRIBUTORS

Agnihotri, V.K.
Joint Director, Lal Bahadur Shastri National Academy of Administration, Mussoorie-248 179.

Alagh, (Dr.) Yoginder K.
Vice Chancellor, Jawahar lal Nehru University, New Delhi-110067

Ayyar, (Dr.) R.V.Vaidyanatha
Joint Secretary, Ministry of Human Resource Development, Department of Education, Government of India, Shastri Bhavan, New Delhi-110 001.

Batra, S.K.
Senior Consultant, Tata Consultancy Services, Gulab Bhavan, Rear Block, 6, Bahadur Shah Zafar Marg, New Delhi-110 002.

Behura, S.
Joint Secretary, Ministry of Industry, Government of India, Udyog Bhavan, New Delhi-110 001.

Bjorkman, (Prof.) J.W.
Professor of Public Policy and Administration, Institute of Social Studies, P.O. Box 90733, 2509 LS the Hague, (Netherlands).

Cameron, (Dr.) Ahmed
Head, National Informatics Centre Training Unit, Lal Bahadur Shastri National Academy of Administration, Mussoorie-248 179.

Dey, S.C.
Additional I.G. of Forests, Ministry of Environment and Forests, Paryavaran Bhavan, CGO Complex, Lodi Road, New Delhi-110 003.

Dharmarajan, K.
Joint Secretary, Ministry of Urban Development, Government of India, Nirman Bhavan, New Delhi-110 011.

Dimri, Anil Kumar
Research Officer, Centre for Micro-Planning and Regional Studies, Lal Bahadur Shastri National Academy of Administration, Mussoorie-248 179.

Dutta, S.S.
Consultant, Town and Country Planning Organisation, New Delhi.

Gaur, S.K.
Faculty of Engineering, Dayal Bagh Educational Institute, Dayal Bagh, Agra-282 005.

Giridhar, (Prof.) G.
Indian Institute of Health Management, 1, Prabhu Dayal Marg, Sanganer Airport, Jaipur-550 065.

Juyal, (Dr.) R.P.
Lecturer, Shri Guru Ram Rai, Post Graduate College, Dehradun-248 001.

Karki, (Dr.) Rajnish
Reader, Faculty of Management, Lal Bahadur Shastri National Academy of Administration, Mussoorie-248 179.

Khusro, (Prof.) A.M.
Editor, Financial Express, Express Building, 9-10, Bahadur Shah Zafar Marg, New Delhi-110 002.

Mohapatra, (Prof.) Pratap K.J.
Department of Industrial Engineering and Management, Indian Institute of Technology, Kharagpur-721 302.

Mehta, (Dr.) Dinesh
Director, National Institute of Urban Affairs, 11, Nyaya Marg, Chanakyapuri, New Delhi-110 021.

Mishra, D.S.
Faculty of Engineering, Dayal Bagh Educational Institute, Dayal Bagh, Agra-282 005.

Misra, V.K.

Joint Secretary, Department of Science and Technology, Technology Bhawan, New Mehrauli Road, New Delhi-110 016.

Rajan, (Dr.) Y.S.

Adviser, Department of Science and Technology, Government of India, Technology Bhavan, New Mehrauli Road, New Delhi-110 016.

Razdan, Rajni
Joint Secretary, Department of Programme Implementation, Government of India, Sardar Patel Bhavan, New Delhi-110 001

Saikia, Ashok
Joint Secretary, Ministry of Agriculture, Government of India, Krishi Bhavan, New Delhi-110 001.

Satsangi, (Prof.) P.S.
Director, Dayal Bagh Educational Institute, Dayal Bagh, Agra-282 005.

Saxena, (Dr.) J.P.
Director, National Council for Building Material, H-14-D, DDA Flats, Saket, New Delhi-110 017.

Saxena, (Dr.) N.C.
Director, Lal Bahadur Shastri National Academy of Administration, Mussoorie-248 179.

Subhash, (Dr.) C.
Reader, Department of Futurology, Devi Ahilya Vishwavidyalaya, Indore.

Sushil, (Prof.)
Department of Management Studies, Indian Institute of Technology, Hauz Khas, New Delhi-110 016.

Vij, (Dr.) A. K.
Manager, Computers and Systems Engineering, Engineers India Ltd., 1, Bikaji Cama Place, New Delhi-110 036.

Vizayakumar, (Prof.) K.
Associate Professor, Indian Institute of Technology, Kharagpur-721 302.

EDITOR'S NOTE

— V. K. Agnihotri

I. PUBLIC POLICY AND METHODOLOGIES

Uses of the Word 'Policy'

In the broadest sense we use the word 'policy' to elicit or comment on the presence or absence of a pattern or logic in human or organisational behaviour. Thus one may talk of a person having a definite policy about the upbringing of his children or an organisation having a clear cut policy about developing its human resources. Having failed to identify any underlying pattern in the person's approach to application of his resources, one may conclude that he does not have an investment policy. Similarly, after observing erratic behaviour on the part of an organisation to meet social needs one may be forced to ask the question: 'Does it have a social policy?'

In the field of public policy, the word 'policy' is used in a variety of different ways (Hogwood and Gunn, 1984, pp. 13-19). The most common usage is in the context of broad statements about a government's 'economic policy', 'social policy' and so on. Within these broad labels, there may be more specific references to government's policy towards small-scale industries or housing. What is being described here are 'fields' of governmental activity and involvement. To illustrate the point further one may look at the usage of the word in the newspapers, on the one hand, and the policy statements of the Government of India, on the other. The field of activity considered could be quite narrow as in:

"New Policy on blood transfusion likely" (*The Hindu,* 1.12.92).

"New Policy framework to improve wool quality" *(Times of India,* 1.12.1992).

"Government to continue policy on edible oil" (*Times of India,* 1.2.1993).

Or very comprehensive in its coverage as in:

> "Integrated policy urged to uplift people in villages" (*The Hindu*, 28.10.1992).
>
> "New look by J.D. at socio-economic policies" (*The Hindu*, 17.10.1992).

It may refer to a specific policy document of the government:

> "Loopholes in national forest policy" (*Indian Express*, 8.9.1992).
>
> "Endorsement of Centre's industrial policy by states" (*Times of India*, 17.10.1992).

Or simply to what the Government is supposed to be doing:

> "Pranab blasts Govt.'s policy on disinvestment of PSUs", (*Indian Express*, 17.10.1992).
>
> " Opium control policy successful in M.P." (*Economic Times*, 13.10.1992).

Very often the word policy is also loosely used for programmes, schemes, directives and strategies of the Government.

Often policy is an expression of general purpose or desired state of affairs. It outlines the broad purpose (or 'ends') of governmental activity in a particular field. For example, consider the following prescription in the National Forest Policy (Ministry of Environment and Forests, 1988) of the Government of India:

> "The basic objectives that should govern the National Forest Policy are the following:
>
> Maintenance of environmental stability through preservation and, where necessary, restoration of the ecological balance that has been adversely disturbed by serious depletion of the forests of the country...".

Or the following provision in the Textile Policy (Department of Textiles, 1985):

> "...the main task of the textile industry...is to increase the production of cloth of acceptable quality at reasonable prices to meet the clothing requirements of a growing population."

The policy of the Government may also find expression in a specific scheme e.g. the Jawahar Rojgar Yojana for rural employment or the

Janata Cloth Scheme for the handloom industry. The policy may come to be embodied in a formal authorisation such as an Act of Parliament or the State Legislature or more broadly in a programme which is defined as a package of legislation, organisation and resources, e.g. Panchayati Raj.

On a more practical plane, policy is sometimes seen as what the government actually delivers (i.e. policy as output) as opposed to what it has promised or has authorised through legislation. Another way of looking at policy is in terms of its outcome, that is, what is actually achieved or the impact of policy. For example, supply of subsidised seeds and fertilisers to the farmers, making available credit for their agricultural operations, support price for their produce, etc. are the outputs of the Indian Government's agricultural policy; the outcome is the increase in the foodgrain production, if any.

Above all, policy could be seen as a process (often a cyclical one) over a period of time. A rather simplistic description of the working of the policy process model may be as follows. A social or economic problem arises, it is debated in various forums and attracts government's attention. The government in turn examines various alternative solutions and chooses to implement one of them. It satisfies some but hurts others, giving rise to a fresh problem and the cycle is again repeated.

From the consumer's point of view again, public policy, in effect, is not really what policy statements/documents issued by the government from time to time would have us believe, but the government's pattern of behaviour over time. As Griffin (1975) has perceptively observed: "Rather than assume that governments attempt to maximise social or national welfare but fail to do so, it might be more suitable to assume that that governments have quite different objectives and generally succeed in achieving them. Rather than criticising governments for failing to attain, or offering advice on how to attain a non-goal, it would be instructive if more time were devoted to analysing what governments actually do and why."

Features and Characteristics of Public Policy

In the context of these varied usages and understandings of the term 'policy', there is need to look at some of the more definitive features and characteristics of public policy.

In a very broad sense, policy can be defined as a general statement or understanding devised to guide the thinking and decision-making process in an organisation. A more focused definition of public policy is provided by Anderson (1979, p. 3):

"A purposive course of action followed by an actor or set of actors in dealing with a problem or matter of concern".

A very comprehensive definition of public policy is provided by Hogwood and Gunn (1984, pp.23-24) outlining the following salient features of public policy:

(1) It is subjectively defined by an observer.
(2) It comprises a series of patterns of related decisions.
(3) The policy-making process involves many sub-processes and may extend over a considerable period of time.
(4) It has a purpose which may change over time and, in some cases, may be defined only retrospectively.
(5) It is concerned with policy-makers' intentions (i.e. broad purpose or 'end') as well as behaviour (i.e. outputs and outcomes).
(6) It involves action as well as inaction. Thus "a policy can consist of what is not being done" (Helco, 1972).
(7) It involves intra- and inter-organisation relationships with a key, but not exclusive, role for public agencies.

Some of the distinguishing characteristics of public policy and its processes in democratic societies are worth noting (El Sherif, 1990):

(1) Public policy is characterised by involvement of many participants. The stakeholders in public policy comprise the policy-makers (political executive and bureaucracy), those affected (the public and their interest groups) and those interested (specialists, experts and media).
(2) As a consequence of the variety of stakeholders, public policy making requires conflict resolution and consensus building.
(3) It has to deal with many constraints (e.g. technology, resources) and assumptions (e.g. those concerning reactions of interest groups).
(4) It is also ill-structured insofar as the objectives are often ill-defined and vague and the relationship among them is not always evident.

Public policy making process is, therefore, highly polyarchal and diffused (Pai Panandiker, 1988). The problems of public policy are "wicked" (Webber and Rittle, 1973), "squishy" (Strauch, 1974) or "messy and complex" (Phillips, 1989). Dror's (1989, pp. 188-99) following description of public policy, in this context, is worth quoting:

"Public policy is the product of a complex, dynamic interrelationship between many sub-policies, decisions, and sub-decisions, each of which is itself reached by a complete decision-making process that is in turn composed of sub-decisions, and so on, down to single decisions made by an individual acting nominally on his own. These multiple decisions are made by various social units and individuals who are distributed over many different social structures and points in time.

The nominal outcome of the interactions...between these social units and individuals.....is the public policy, while the aggregating process is the public-policy making process."

From the systemic point of view, the public policy making system, with many sub-systems within it, is itself a part of the political system which in turn is subsumed within the overall societal system. At another level, it dynamically intersects the decision-making system and the administrative system. Looked at from yet another point of view, public policy making is one of the ways in which societal problems are sought to be resolved and as such is part of the problem solving activity of the society as a whole (Dror, 1989, pp. 173-174).

Public Policy Making Process

The range and scope of public policy has been growing the world over, especially in the developing democratic societies, on account of market failures and the increasing compulsions of administering the welfare state. As policy spaces have tended to become more crowded, public policy has come under greater scrutiny from the public as well as the academicians. Perceived inadequacies in government's policy responses to chronic problems has led to an increased interest in policy orientation or policy focused analysis with a view to improve public policy (Hogwood and Gunn, 1984, p. 32).

There are several approaches available for improving public policy, such as:

(i) improve policy making competence of policy-makers;
(ii) improve policy making institutions;
(iii) improve policy making process; and
(iv) improve policy delivery systems.

Of critical and immediate concern among these is the policy making process itself. In order to upgrade the policy making process, various stand alone as well as packages of methodologies have been developed for policy support. However, as pointed out by Dror (1989), the major problem with contemporary public policy making is the constantly widening gap between what is known about policy making and how policy is actually made. Contemporary societies, faced with critical problems whose solutions require the best human skills, rely on outmoded policy making machinery (Dror, 1989, p.3). He lists several shortcomings in the contemporary policy making process, important among them being absence of meta-policy making, inadequate feedback, very little systematic and explicit determining of policy strategies, insufficient elaboration of operational goals, very little search for policy alternatives, inadequate development of rational as well as extra-rational components of public policy, sub-optimally qualified manpower, inadequate knowledge and information about policy making and so on (Dror, 1989, pp. 121-122). In brief, to borrow Lasswell's (1970) phrase, it is a case of inadequate knowledge of as well as knowledge in policy making process.

Warfield (1976, pp. ix-x) has also pointed out that the rate of change in society is faster than the rate at which people can perform effectively. In order, therefore, to bring the future more under control, there is need to increase the rate at which people can perform effectively in complex situations.

Policy Making Process in India

Two distinct, although not mutually exclusive, tendencies in public policy making are currently identifiable in India. They could be classified as structured and unstructured. The structured approach to policy making results in outputs variously termed as national policies, policy statements, policy resolutions, policy measures, action plans and so on. At the last count more than a dozen policy documents were available ranging from sports to industry to telecommunications, and another half a dozen of them were at various stages of formulation. Unstructured policy making is the normal and universally practised method wherein policy making proceeds from problem identification to selection of a suitable policy alternative to solve that problem.

The institutional framework for policy making at the Central Government level in India (Pai Panandiker, 1985) has the Council of Ministers or the Cabinet headed by the Prime Minister at its apex. For facilitating its work the Cabinet makes use of the committee system comprising standing committees which are assigned specific areas like

Cabinet Committees on Political Affairs, Economic Affairs, Appointments, Accommodation, Natural Calamities, Minorities' Welfare, Trade and Investment, Expenditure, Infrastructure, Drug Abuse and so on as well as ad hoc committees which are constituted to investigate and report on specific issue as and when the need is felt e.g. Cabinet panel set up to draft the white paper on Ayodhya. However, the actual functioning of the cabinet system largely depends on the leadership style of the Prime Minister and, in recent times, the holders of this office have tended to be the principal decision-makers supported by their independent secretariat. The creation of Prime Minister's secretariat in 1965 was an institutional innovation of far reaching consequences with regard to the policy making process in India. Over a period of time the Prime Minister's Office (PMO), headed by a Secretary, has tended to become a super-Ministry of officials who are accountable only to the Prime Minister. In addition, the Prime Minister often enlists the support of experts as advisers to assist him in the discharge of his policy making functions in certain areas e.g. science and technology. In some ways the National Development Council (chaired by the Prime Minister and *inter alia* comprising Central Government ministers and the chief ministers of the State Governments) is the highest policy making body in the country. It is, in effect, a forum for arriving at a consensus on major policy issues. The other "super" policy making body is the Planning Commission which too is chaired by the Prime Minister.

At the ministry level, the Secretary to the Government of India is the highest policy making functionary in his field. He is normally assisted by a Joint Secretary for coordinating policy related matters. Several ministries, especially the economic and technical ones, have policy advisers attached to them. Thus we have advisers in the ministries of Commerce, Industry, Finance, Health and Family Welfare, Science and Technology and so on. In addition, several other functional institutions have been set up with specific policy related advisory roles, such as, Agricultural Prices Commission, Bureau of Industrial Cost and Prices, Export Promotion Councils and so on.

Last but not least, the Government of India has constituted ad hoc committees and bodies from time to time with a specific policy advisory task. As a matter of fact the structured policy making process normally starts with the setting up of an expert committee or panel with specific terms of reference to inquire into a particular problem or field-area. This is a time tested device dating back to Royal Commissions and Inquiry Committees of the pre-independence era. For example, the process of preparing the *Statement on Textile Policy* of June 1985 (Department of

Textiles, 1985) started with the setting up of an Expert Committee on Textile Industry, the report of which formed the basis of the Statement.

The policy making process itself is necessarily polyarchal. However, two broad categorisations could be made, namely, political and administrative, which ultimately merge in the final policy output. In some cases, however, they are simultaneously in operation. By and large, the political process is more complex and originates from diverse sources but most importantly from the political parties which do not always have a policy-orientation. Their role in policy making comes into focus at the time of the general election when important ones among them publish their manifestoes. The election manifesto of a party is traditionally the policy framework for its governmental decision-making. However, these manifestoes, to a large extent, do not get translated into specific policies, programmes and schemes when the party comes to power. Although, the policy documents of Government of India do often read like political manifestoes. The political process also comprises the role of interest groups and lobbies, press and academia or the "policy community" (Pai Panandiker, 1988) in policy making. A newly emerged breed influencing this process is that of "policy entrepreneurs" (Pai Panandiker, 1988) who are willing to invest their resources, time and energy to pursue a particular policy alternative. On the periphery is the policy engineering function performed by a closed set of actors taken from "policy community", "policy entrepreneurs" and bureaucracy.

This leads to a discussion on the administrative policy process which is comparatively straight forward (Pai Panandiker, 1988). The two major sets of policy actors in this process are provided by the political executive and the government bureaucracy. Of these, the bureaucracy in India has traditionally been the source of policy thought and action. Immediately after independence, with political stalwarts having a closer feel of the pulse of the people than most of the contemporary bureaucrats brought up in maintenance-of-law-and-order-administration-of-justice-revenue collection culture, the political executive had the upper hand in the traditional democratic policy-making model of alternative-suggesting-policy-implementing bureaucracy and policy-making politicians. Gradually, the bureaucracy came to have a greater say in policy making, specially with the growing centralisation of the process built around the Prime Minister's Office. Over a period of time, the fluctuations in the policy-making role of bureaucracy have been partly due to its own failings and partly on account of the pressures created by the growing selfish urgency of its masters.

On the whole, the polyarchal process of public policy making in

India is largely due to its federal polity, diversity of the country and the growth of plural policy initiating forces. The mega-policy making still originates a great deal in the macro-political system while the more specific policy or sub-policy making remains the domain of the bureaucracy. The policy-making capabilities of the Indian system vary from "reasonable competence" or even "sublime" to the "ridiculous". In some fields like planning, the systems tends to be reasonably rational, even if tortuous, whereas in several other fields it tends to be capricious and even hollow (Pai Panandiker 1985, 1988).

Policy Methodologies

There are obvious problems with the policy making process. It is easy to put the blame for this at the door steps of policy makers for their failure to utilise optimal policy analysis methodologies in policy-making. However, in all fairness, the policy scientists should also share the onus for designing packages of practices which would be acceptable to and operable by the policy-makers, given their characteristics and predilections and an honest desire to improve public policy. For better acceptability, the methodologies have to be more user-oriented rather than consultant-oriented.

The two most important policy making units in democratic states are the political executive and the government bureaucracy. The screening mechanism for advancement into highest policy making positions puts a premium on the individual's ability to get votes and/or build coalitions. These abilities depend largely on extra-rational processes. The political executive also, naturally, tends to weigh policies in terms of their political feasibility. Progressively, political feasibility is getting equated with ability to generate consensus. The government bureaucracy, on the other hand, based as it is in these countries on the "merit system" and "career service", favours experience and intuition which decide administrative feasibility (Dror, 1989, pp.93-95).

One way of improving public policy, therefore, is to design policy support methodologies which attempt to integrate and build on these special dispositions of central policy actors and cater to the need for creating policy on the basis of a broad consensus among various stakeholders. Such methodologies have necessarily to be simple in design, utilise experience and extra-rational capabilities of the main policy actors and not only generate policy options through consensus building but also appear to be doing so.

Further, a systemic method of dealing with complex issues has distinct potential in terms of improving our approach to problem solution. Very often lack of understanding of the structure of the system misdirects our search for solutions to societal problems. Technology is no doubt important to the solution of such problems, but successful application of technology to societal problem areas must consider three levels (Chen, Ghansi and Sage, 1975), namely, symptoms, institutions and values. Too often we approach problems only at the level of symptoms. Attacking problems at the level of institutions would allow the design of new institutions to make full and effective use of technologies. Also of vital importance is the need to deal with societal problems at the level of values. It is important to appreciate the significance of values and identify basic issues in term of conflicting values (Sage, 1977).

In order to cope with complexity in societal systems, the substantive aspects which need to be understood are a broad perspective arising from identification of elements of the problem situation and the relationship among them, developing a shared understanding among stakeholders who have different perspectives and values, presenting such understanding in an informed, organised and effective manner so as to generate plans, policies and decisions having a bearing on the future of the society (Warfield, 1976, p.ix).

In order, therefore, to be able to solve complex problems, the system requires ways to deal successfully with (Sage, 1977, p.3):

* problems involving many considerations, and inter-relations;
* areas in which there are far-reaching and controversial value judgements;
* problems the solutions to which require knowledge from several disciplines;
* problems in which future events are difficult to predict; and
* problems in which structural and institutional elements are given full consideration.

Systems engineering possesses these necessary characteristics, having not only a large-scale perspective but also an understanding of needs and values. Some of the policy analysis and design methodologies that address and incorporate these concerns are those generically categorised as consensus methodologies and inter alia comprise Nominal Group Technique, Interpretive Structural Modelling, DELPHI, Analytic Hierarchy Process, Fuzzy Set Evaluation Technique and so on.

II. PUBLIC POLICY ANALYSIS AND DESIGN

In the context of the foregoing discussion on public policy and methodologies, the Seminar on Public Policy Analysis and Design was structured around two themes. The first one concentrated on an informed discussion on several Public Policy areas namely Agriculture, Forestry, Environment, Industry, Population, Health, Urban Sector, Education, Science and Technology, Energy, and Computers. The second theme attempted to highlight appropriate methodologies for public policy analysis and design in the context of the concern for systemic and consensus approaches mentioned earlier. The methodologies explored, suitably illustrated with reference to some of the public policy areas listed above, were Ideawriting, Nominal Group Technique, Interpretive Structural Modelling, Options Field Methodology, Options Profile Methodology, Fuzzy Set Evaluation Technique, System Dynamics, Viable System Modelling, DELPHI, Analytic Hierarchy Process, Flexible Systems Methodology, Logical Framework Approach, Logical Processual Framework and so on. Several of these are new and innovative as well as multi-dimensional, multi-criteria and multi-person decision-making techniques. Understandably, the two themes were not dealt with independently or in isolation and often tended to merge with each other, creating a supportive synergy.

This book has been accordingly, somewhat arbitrarily, divided into two parts, namely, SECTORAL POLICIES and METHODOLOGIES: although, as already stated, the two parts basically differ in terms of their approach and perspectives rather than in substantive coverage of policy areas. In some cases, even this demarcation is considerably blurred. With a views to interpret and put in perspective the themes explored in the book, the Proceedings of the Seminar on Public Policy Analysis and Design have been provided at the end.

In Part I dealing with SECTORAL POLICIES, the papers are arranged in a somewhat hierarchical fashion, starting with the primary activity, namely, Agriculture, and ending with superconductivity. We move from economic and environmental concerns to social aspects and graduated to science and technology.

In Chapter 1 on EVOLUTION OF AGRICULTURE POLICY IN INDIA, Ashok Saikia seeks to analyse evolution of agriculture policy in India since 1926 with the establishment of Royal Commission on Agriculture. An attempt has also been made to focus on major issues having a bearing on agricultural development strategy during various plan periods. Finally, some useful suggestions have been made in respect of issues to be addressed in order to sustain economic development of the country.

Chapter 2 on POLICY ISSUES IN FORESTRY by Dr. N.C. Saxena first focuses on the shortcomings of the India forest policy of the past, which was primarily market-oriented and based on the plantation of high value commercial species. It unambiguously points out that in order to meet fuelwood and timber needs of the people, plantation through social forestry on village and private lands is significant not only to ensure people's participation but also to strengthen joint forest management. An attempt has also been made to review policies regarding privatisation of forest land and leasing out of such land to the user industries. The author is of the opinion that the poor would be greatly benefited if opportunities of collection of fuelwood from forest and public land are enhanced.

Chapter 3 on CONSERVATION OF BIOLOGICAL DIVERSITY by S.C. Dey deals with the concept of bio-diversity with regards to the position of comprehensive as well as managed protected area, which preserve the greatest amount of world's biotic species. An analytical framework of the protected areas of the developing regions of the world reflects unlimited diversity of life. It also seeks to analyse how the protected areas make a vital contribution to the conservation of world's natural and cultural resources. It concludes that the conservation strategy should tackle the human problem through employment and resources built up in the vicinity of the protected areas so that they could be sustained and preserved.

Chapter 4 on INDUSTRIAL POLICY—HISTORICAL PERSPECTIVES by S. Behura deals with the evolution of industrial policy in India since 1945. To ensure economic independence and sovereignty, importance of industrialisation and promotion of industrial infrastructure has been clearly recognised. The paper also traces the role of central government to accelerate industrial growth and speed up industrialisation. In the light of the main objectives of industrial development, the industrial policy legislation and regulations have been amended. Finally, it focuses on the implications of recent radical changes that have been brought about in the form of New Economic Policy, laying emphasis on liberalisation.

Chapter 5 on PLANNING AND MARKET by Dr. Y. K. Alagh deals with the role of the price-based planning policies, both for the industrial and agricultural sectors of the Indian economy. However, the need for integrating objectives of industrial policy with the development objectives of the country through the process of structural adjustment is given priority. It also reflects how tariff and price policy protect the industries, particularly the industries in the priority sector. An attempt, therefore, has been made to explore the possibility of the use of economic models with emphasis on empirical testing of propositions.

Chapter 6 on POPULATION POLICY IN INDIA by Dr.G. Gridhar reviews the evolution of population Policy in India beginning with 1952, when India became the first country to have an official population control programme, its implementation experiences and institutional arrangements which reflected the increasing complexity of the programme and continue to be a major challenge to the planners, policy makers and researchers. To ensure the success of population policy, emphasis is laid on integrated programme activities and decentralisation of planning and implementation as well as people's participation.

Chapter 7 on POPULATION POLICY by Rajni Razdan seeks to analyse the objectives of Central Government's population policy, its success and failure since Family Planning and Welfare Programmes have been initiated in the country. The main objective of the paper is to focus on the nexus between population and poverty. It tries to portray the reality, which confronts the demographer, as obtained from the statistics of the 1991 census and the perceptions of the policy-makers. In this process it underscores the importance of achieving harmony between what is and what should be with regard to India's population.

Chapter 8 on DEVELOPMENTAL LESSONS OF SRI LANKA'S HEALTH SYSTEM: INSTRUMENTS AND OPTIONS IN "HEALTHY" IMPLEMENTATION by Dr. J.W. Bjorkman examines Sri Lanka's record in health care management and results within the context of emergent universals about the policy implementation process. It identifies changes in empirical achievements among selected health status indicators; centre/periphery problems in the inter-governmental system; and supportive social policies in the generation of human capital. Among the explanatory factors are internal arrangements of operational administrative agencies, hierarchical versus lateral arrangements for control, and political support among relevant publics. By discussing mechanisms for the practices of public accountability of professional providers of health services, the paper concludes with potential lessons about sustainable development in the health sector. Comparisons have also been drawn from health systems in other South Asian countries.

Chapter 9 on URBAN POLICY REFORMS IN INDIA by Dr. Dinesh Mehta traces the evolution of urban policy. The author is of the opinion that urban sector has been regarded as wealth of a nation and engine of growth, and continues to perform this role in the context of economic development. It further focuses on the perceptions such as rapid urbanisation, increasing rural-urban migration, problems of slum dwellers which are necessary in order to understand the issue's in policy reforms. While dealing with the policy objectives, details of specific policy actions have been presented. It underscores that the urban sector has to find a place in national economic policy formulations, and that this is extremely important to ensure structural adjustment with a human face.

Chapter 10 on NATIONAL URBAN POLICY FOR INDIA: SOME ISSUES by K. Dharmarajan and S.S. Dutta similarly emphasises the urgent need to articulate systemic and integrated national urban policy. The authors, having underscored the complexities in the emerging urban scenario, point out the inadequacies in policy and programme initiatives of the Central Government and focus on certain recent developments including the 74th Constitutional Amendment. They go on to suggest a framework for National Urban Policy.

Chapter 11 on DEMOGRAPHIC PRESSURE AND URBANISATION: A CASE OF DEHRADUN URBAN AGGLOMERATION IN GARHWAL HIMALAYAS by Anil Kumar Dimri and Dr. R.P.Juyal analyses the pressure of population on the growth of urbanisation with reference to Dehradun Urban Agglomeration, which happens to be largest Urban Agglomeration in the Himalayan region. The paper further deals with the conditions which are necessary for the growth and development of this peculiar urban agglomeration. The diversification of economic base of the region which offers opportunities of income and employment to a large number of people has also been dealt with. The authors have also attempted to focus on the problems resulting from haphazard urbanisation and suggested remedies to overcome them.

Chapter 12 on POLICY-MAKING-IN EDUCATION by Dr.R.V.V. Ayyar stresses the importance of studying not only the substance of policy, but the processes underlying the formulation of the policy. In the context of processes in educational policy making he analyses the respective roles of Central and State Governments. In policy-making, however, the design of instruments which influence the behaviour and functioning of the grassroots functionaries who implement the policy very often tend to be ignored. The author concludes that the design of instruments, goals and strategies should be considered together.

Chapter 13 on ISSUES RELATING TO SCIENCE AND TECHNOLOGY POLICY by Dr.Y.S. Rajan deals with various issues regarding the historicity of technological resolutions and its effect on the society as a whole. The paper further comments on the role of technology in the policy issues before the nation, simultaneously throwing light on the interconnectivities of science and technology with micro and macro economic policy. An assessment of what should be contained in such a policy provides a framework for understanding the prevailing scenario. A draft paper on technology policy has also been provided, in which various issues relating to human skills have been addressed. An attempt has also been made to identify new thrust areas.

In Chapter 14 on HOW A MAJOR PUBLIC POLICY INITIATIVE CREATES IMPACT: THE CASE OF INDIAN COMPUTER HARDWARE INDUSTRY (1984-1990), Dr. Rajnish Karki and Dr. Ahmad Cameron propound that policy announcements by governments are indicative of their will to attain the national objectives. The '80s saw a phenomenal growth in the Information Technology Sector at the global level. Government of India took a number of initiatives for the development of the Information Technology Sector in the country. New Computer Policy of November 1984 was one such landmark. The authors attempt to examine the interaction between the contents and objectives of the New Computer Policy, and six key variables which impact the computer industry and constitute a system. A systems analysis approach is applied to understand the resulting interactions.

Chapter 15 on EMERGING LONG-TERM ENERGY POLICY FROM THE BROADER NATIONAL GOALS AND PRIORITIES IN THE S & T POLICY OF INDIA by Dr. C. Subhash deals with the long-term energy policy of India. There are three major policy options available in this context viz. Conservation, Augmentation and Substitution. How at present these policies are being formulated and implemented by the Government Departments and Ministries has been discussed in detail. The energy policy has strong roots in the broader science and technology policy of the country. Linkages have also come to the fore with the emergence of hydrogen as an energy vector and the rocket technology of Cryogenic Engines. It is quite likely that the research that has been imposed on the Indian scientists and technologists to develop hydrogen related Cryogenic Engines may pay off dividends in the long-term materialization of hydrogen as an energy vector.

In Chapter 16 on SOME EMERGING TECHNOLOGIES INCLUDING SUPERCONDUCTIVITY: AN INTERNATIONAL COMPETITIVENESS AND SUPPORT SCENARIO, V.K. Misra makes the proposition that technology support by the Governments and Industries in many countries take different forms depending upon the technological and industrial level advancements and balance of payment situations. Traditionally, science has been treated as international and technology, particularly its application, local. Now with changing world-order and emphasis on IPR etc., this situation is changing fast where both advanced science and technologies have become immensely competitive and cooperative; both implying a high degree of capability building and strategic alliances. This situation is generally seen as such in many illustrative areas of Emerging/Critical Technologies and superconductivity. Some illustrative promising areas in the Indian context for blending of traditional wisdom, resource base and craftsmanship/ innovativeness and modern emerging scientific and technological tools and information have been discussed.

Part II of the book, concerned with METHODOLOGIES, deals with several methodological applications for public policy design.

Chapter 17 is the first part of a two past article on application of consensus methodologies to analysis and design of industrial policy. The chapter entitled INTEGRATED DESCRIPTIVE AND NORMATIVE INDUSTRIAL POLICY FOR INDIA: A HIERARCHICAL STRUCTURE by Dr. S.K. Gaur, Dr. D.S. Mishra and Dr. P.S. Satsangi reports on an exercise of developing interpretive structural models (ISMs) for the compiled list of descriptive and normative industrial policy objectives for the growth of the Indian industrial environment and rank ordering these objectives using nominal group technique (NGT).

Chapter 18 entitled ALTERNATIVE INTEGRATED POLICY DESIGNS FOR INDIAN INDUSTRIES, by S. K. Gaur, D.S. Mishra and P. S. Satsangi, attempts to focus on a complete exercise of developing alternative policy designs for descriptive integrated national policy objectives of the Indian industrial environment, using interpretive structural modelling, options field methodology and fuzzy-set evaluation technique. Seven policy design alternatives formulated are fuzzified for determining their relative dominance under pessimistic and modified mean aggregation procedures. The policy alternative, which has the achievement of growth with social justice for the Indian Industrial policy as the only mission level objective, ranks as the most dominant policy alternative under pessimistic as well as modified mean aggregation methods, followed by others, thereby showing the robustness of such a policy design.

Chapter 19 on SYSTEM DYNAMICS MODELLING FOR PUBLIC POLICY ANALYSIS by Dr. Pratap K.J. Mohapatra presents system dynamics as a methodology for public policy analysis. The paper first discusses the broad features of the methodology and it then provides an example of how expert opinion, which can help in delineating the problem areas, making event forecasts, and listing policy alternatives, can be a bad assessor of dynamic consequences. The paper then highlights the use of system dynamics modelling for scenario generation for the energy requirement in the Indian transport sector.

In chapter 20 on ENVIRONMENTAL POLICY ANALYSIS:

SYSTEM DYNAMICS APPROACH by Dr. K. Vizayakumar, system dynamics has been proposed as a method of environmental policy analysis, using the coal sector as a case study. Environment protection has taken an important place in the activities of every government in the world. Almost all countries, including India, have made several legislations to protect the environment and are undertaking several policy measures to achieve the goal. Unless the policies are analysed for their effect over a time horizon and we visualize the possible effects or scenarios, the attempts in environmental protection only lead to a trial and error approach and, due to long delays in environmental activities, hamper achievement of the goal of better environment. The paper discusses the utility of system dynamics methodology for environmental policy analysis. While discussing the abilities of system dynamics, it briefly presents the methodology involved. Two examples of environmental policy analysis are discussed. One, a macro-level analysis, modelling and analysing environmental policy making at the national level, and two, a micro-level analysis modelling and analysing the environmental impacts in a coal mining area.

In Chapter 21 on POLICY ANALYSIS AND DESIGN USING FLEXIBLE SYSTEMS METHODOLOGY, Dr. Sushil postulates that analysis and design of public policy needs a sound methodological framework that can cater to diverse considerations, perspectives, nature and requirements at different levels. Flexible systems methodology provides a spectral and integrative paradigm, which is pragmatic and can be effectively used to synthesize available systems based techniques in a cohesive framework. It can help in overcoming the limitations of different techniques by suitably interfacing them, at a deep philosophical level, that can be used for formulating policies at different levels. Two case studies are overviewed; one in the area of agricultural waste management and the other in energy policy, utilizing two different kinds of integration.

In Chapter 22 on GUIDELINES FOR POLICY ON VOCATIONAL TRAINING IN ADVANCED TECHNOLOGY, S.K. Batra emphasises the need for a policy document in each country for training in advanced technology areas. Owing to socio-political, economic and cultural differences amongst various countries, it is not practicable to design a single policy document applicable across all countries. However, it is possible to formulate broad policy guidelines which can be used to develop country specific policy documents. Basing its elaboration on Stafford Beer's Viable System Model, the paper highlights the important characteristics of 'policy'. The key components of policy include Institutional Framework, Resources, Co-ordination and Dissemination of

Information, Monitoring and Control, Quality, Research and Development and Innovation. Other features, which a policy document should provide include the background, objectives, definitions, philosophy, strategies, linkage with other policies in related areas and conformity with international norms and conventions. It should also be ensured that legislative support, levies, obligations, restrictions, concessions, incentives, preferences and subsidies etc. are specifically and explicitly covered, if provided for as a part of the policy framework of the country.

In Chapter 23 on ANALYSIS OF OPTIONS FOR ENERGY CONSERVATION POLICY IN INDIAN CEMENT INDUSTRY, Dr. J.P. Saxena profound that the main sources of energy in cement industry in India are coal and power. The average energy consumption in the Indian Cement Industry is about 20 to 30 per cent higher as compared to some of the advanced countries. Designing an energy conservation policy for the Indian cement industry will, therefore, go a long way in achieving the desired result. The paper discusses the DELPHI methodology for identification of Energy Conservation Options (ECOs) and Energy Performance Indicators (EPIs). The important ECOs and EPIs are selected for detailed analysis. Analytic Hierarchy Process has been used in deciding the importance of various EPIs. The Hierarchy of energy conservation options is determined by applying multi-criteria multi-persons decision making technique. The ECOs, when studied together in a hierarchy, present a policy for energy conservation in Indian Cement Industry.

Chapter 24 on ROLE OF MODELS IN PUBLIC POLICY ANALYSIS AND DESIGN by Dr. A.K. Vij deals with the key research trends in public policy modelling, with special emphasis on the integration of system methodologies. The study has been conducted against the backdrop of the Indian energy scene. It also describes an Indian case study, where the input-output approach has been successfully integrated with physical systems theory and system dynamics to analyse the energy issues of the Indian economy in a dynamic, multi-sectoral framework. The integrated model has helped in exploring many inter-related issues of the Indian economy cohesively, which would not have been possible if these issues were analysed in an isolated manner.

In Chapter 25 on AN INTEGRATED APPROACH TO PUBLIC POLICY DESIGN, the author refers to the increasing penchant of the Government of India for structured public policy making which has resulted in a profusion of "statements" on public policy in recent years. Taking note of the important shortcomings of these policy statements in general and the statement on Textile Policy in particular, and the significance of objectives in designing public policy, a new approach to public policy design has been formulated. This new approach, based on objectives paradigm, is a Logical Processual Framework comprising a step by step procedure for designing and redesigning public policy statements. The process is both iterative and cyclical. The prescription has been illustrated with reference to the textile policy of the Government of India in general, and the handloom policy in particular.

The book thus provides a wide coverage of public policy issues from different perspectives. It should, therefore, be of interest to experts, academician, practitioners, researches as well as students and observes of public policy phenomenon. It should satisfy the palate of those concerned with different sectors of public policy as well as others interested in the policy making process.

REFERENCES

Anderson, J.E. (1979) *Public Policy Making*. New York: Holt, Rinehart and Winston.

Chen, K., Ghansi, M., Sage, A.P. (1975) 'Social Systems Engineering : An Introduction', Special Issue on Social Systems Engineering, IEEE Proceedings, 63:3, pp. 340-343 (General).

Department of Textiles (1985) Statement on Textile Policy, New Delhi: Ministry of Supply and Textiles, GOI.

Dror, Y. (1989, Third Printing) *Public Policy Making Reexamined*. New Brunswick/Oxford: Transaction Publishers.

El Sherif, H. (1990) 'Managing Institutionalization of Strategic Decision Support for Egyptian Cabinet', *Interface*, 20:1, pp. 97-114.

Griffin, K. (1975) *Political Economy and Agrarian Change*. London: Macmillan.

Helco, H. (1972) 'Policy Analysis', *British Journal of Political Science*, 2, pp. 83-108.

Hogwood, B.W. and Gunn, L.A. (1984) *Policy Analysis for the Real World*. Oxford: Oxford University Press.

Lasswell, H.D. (1970) 'The Emerging Conception of the Policy Sciences', *Policy Sciences*, Vol. 1, p. 3.

Ministry of Environment and Forests (1988) *National Forest Policy*. New Delhi: GOI.

Pai Panandiker, V.A. (1985) *Policy Making in India*. New Delhi: Centre for Policy Research.

Pai Panandiker, V.A. (1988) *Policy Sciences and Policy Making in India*. New Delhi: Centre for Policy Research.

Phillips, L.D. (1989) *Decision Analysis in the 1990s*. London: Decision Analysis Unit, London School of Economics.

Sage, A.P.(1977) *Methodology for Large-Scale Systems*. New York: McGraw-Hill.

Strauch, R.E. (1974) A Critical Assessment of Quantitative Methodology as a Policy Tool, p-5282. Santa Monica: The Rand Corporation.

Warfield, J.N. (1976) Societal Systems: Planning, Policy and Complexity. New York: Wiley. (Reprinted, Salinas, CA: Intersystems, 1989).

Webber, M.N. and Rittle, H.W.J. (1973) 'Dilemmas in a General Theory of Planning', Policy Sciences, 4:2, pp. 155- 169.

PART-I

SECTORAL POLICIES

1. EVOLUTION OF AGRICULTURE POLICY IN INDIA

Ashok Saikia

Agriculture Policy in India in the beginning of the century had a colonial bias. Emphasis was laid on Agricultural Research and Education only after the Report of the Royal Commission on Agriculture in 1928. In January 1946, the Government issued a Statement on Agriculture and Food Policy in India. The main goal of this Policy was to move the country away from the menace of famine to a new vigour and prosperity. A series of policy initiatives in different sub-sectors of agriculture were taken after the Independence to promote the development of agriculture and achieve self-sufficiency in foodgrains. These had a salutory impact on the growth of agriculture in last 45 years.

Of late, the agriculture sector has become very complex. There has emerged a multiplicity of approaches and philosophies for remedying the distortion in growth and planning future development of this sector. In October 1989, the then Prime Minister announced an Agricultural Package, reiterating that the highest national priority must be given to the farmers, to farming, to food and agriculture as the cornerstone of our economy. The package identified specific areas for development to achieve these objectives.

In March 1990, the then Finance Minister in his Budget speech announced the intention of the government to bring out an Agricultural Policy Resolution. A preliminary draft of Agricultural Policy prepared by the Government was considered in a National Seminar held in New Delhi in June 1990 and a modified draft was prepared by the Government in March 1991 and circulated.

Consequent upon the decision of Government to liberalise the economy, a new draft of Agricultural Policy was prepared by the Government to lay down the broad framework of policy initiatives, at macro level, to accelerate all-round development and economic viability of agriculture. After elaborate consultations, this Policy was placed on the Table of both Houses of Parliament in May 1993.

The Policy initiative includes a clear orientation to reduce current support measures, promotion of infrastructural development, providing benefits to agriculture at par with industry without subjecting it to regulatory and tax collection machinery of the Government, promotion of peoples' institutions/cooperatives, development of post-harvest technologies and value addition facilities, and creation of an economic environment for increasing farmers' own investments and efforts.

1. This paper seeks to review the evolution of Agricultural Policy in India since appointment of the Royal Commission on Agriculture (RCA) in 1926 and proceeds to describe the main ingredients of the new Agriculture Policy formulated by the Government in the context of recent trends in the agricultural situation.
2. Agricultural policy in India as has been already indicated, in the beginning of the century had a colonial bias. The emphasis was on production, primarily with the intention of export of food and raw material for industries in Great Britain. The increase in production during the period was almost exclusively through bringing more land under cultivation and extension of irrigation facilities. Little attention was paid to the need for increasing productivity through research and extension.
3. Setting up of the RCA in 1926 under the Chairmanship of Marquess Linlithgow marked the first major effort to examine the conditions of agriculture and of the rural population. RCA gave a comprehensive report covering agriculture research, crop production, animal husbandry, forestry, fisheries, cooperation, village development, agriculture finance, communication, marketing, education and public health. It is necessary to note here that land tenancy and reforms were subjects beyond the scope of the RCA. A significant outcome of the RCA report was the establishment of the Imperial Council of Agricultural Research in 1929. The Council, subsequently renamed as the Indian Council of Agricultural Research (ICAR), with its network of 46 Central Institutes, 20 National Research Centres and 27 State Universities, is now at the vanguard of the agricultural research system in the country and the apex organization to coordinate and conduct agricultural research and education in the country. Although the report of RCA was accepted as the basis for future development of agriculture its implementation has such financial implications which were beyond the resources available with

provincial government.

4. Unfortunately, before the recommendations of RCA could be effectively implemented, there came the Great Economic Depression (1929-33). The Depression affected India's market for raw and manufactured jute and indirectly the demand for other raw material exports. Precipitous fall in the prices of agricultural commodities hit the rural population hard. Even cultivators of sound means found it difficult to meet their liabilities. The condition of small farmers, who even in normal times depend on private money lenders for meeting their pre-harvesting food requirements, became precarious. The agricultural indebtedness which was estimated at Rs. 900 crores in 1929 by the Central Banking Inquiry Committee, doubled between 1929 and 1936. Many agriculturists turned into agricultural labourers.
5. The Government of India Act, 1935 which provided for autonomy and responsible Government in the provinces transferred subjects like agriculture, land, irrigation, forest, fisheries, education etc., under control of provincial governments. States were, however, left without adequate financial support for making even reasonable progress in these directions. The provincial autonomy became effective after elections in 1937. During their short tenures, the popular ministries brought about legislative actions to regulate money lending and reduce the burden of indebtedness, tenancy legislations were passed or amended, some actions were initiated for consolidating holdings, strengthening of credit structures, creating basic infrastructure of marketing, etc. Enactment of Agriculture Produce (Grading and Marketing) Act, 1936, establishment of the Central jute Committee in the same year, and adoption of the Policy of Discriminating Protection are other important landmarks of provincial autonomy which lasted only two years.
6. World War-II was the turning point for Indian Agriculture. The immediate effect of the war was that commercial crops like jute, cotton and groundnut lost their export market and the demand for foodgrains increased manifestly, pushing up prices. The agricultural situation became grim. The loss of Burma to the Japanese forces deprived India of a dependable supplier of foodgrains. This compelled the Government to launch the Grow More Food (GMF) campaign, 1942. Its immediate objective was to increase food production by increasing area under foodgrains

crops—even by diverting areas from cotton, jute and other non-food crops, extension of irrigation, use of inputs like improved seeds, manure and fertilizer. In the wake of Bengal Famine, the Government of India assumed higher responsibilities with regard to food production—a field so far with the provincial Governments. The GMF campaign started being directed from Delhi with provision of higher resources.

7. The World War II years and after saw the formation of institutions at the Centre in quick succession to take care of agricultural development. In 1942, the Department of Food was created; in 1944 posts were created to supervise GMF campaign; in 1945, the Department of Agriculture was created.; in 1946 the Central Tractor Organization and the Directorate of Plant Protection, Quarantine and Storage were established. For giving research support to agriculture, four Commodity Committees for sugarcane, tobacco, coconut and oilseeds, the Central Rice Research Institute at Cuttack and Institutes of Inland and Marine Fisheries Research were established.

8. After the World War II, in June 1946 the Government issued a statement on Agricultural and Food Policy in India. According to the Statement:

   The All India Policy is to promote the welfare of the people and to secure a progressive improvement of their standard of living. This includes the responsibility of providing enough food for all, sufficient in quantity and of requisite quality. For the achievement of these objectives, high priority will be given to measures for increasing food resources of the country to the fullest extent and in particular measures designed to increase the output per acre and to diminish dependence on the vagaries of nature. Their aim will be not only to remove threat of famine but also to increase the prosperity of cultivator, raise the level of consumption and create a healthy and vigorous population.

   The major policy objectives of the Policy Statement include (i) increase in production of foodgrains; (ii) improvement in methods of production and marketing; (iii) stimulating production of raw material for industry and exports; (iv) securing remunerative prices for the producers and fair wages to the agricultural labourers; (v) ensuring fair distribution of the food produced; and (vi) promoting nutritional research and education.

9. The period after Independence and Partition was marked by distribution of irrigation and other resources between India and

Pakistan and new problems that arose with regard to supply of cotton and jute. GMF campaign was placed on a planned basis from 1947-48. Subsequently in 1950-51, the campaign was reoriented to "intensive cultivation areas", areas possessing fertile lands and assured irrigation. "Integrated Production Programme" was launched in 1950 to cover jute and cotton for providing adequate raw material to Indian industry.

10. A GMF Inquiry Committee was also constituted under the Chairmanship of Shri T.T. Krishnamachary whose recommendations for establishment of a National Extension Organization, speeding up implementation of irrigation programmes and provision of credit, seed and other inputs were accepted in toto by the Government. Simultaneously, agrarian reforms, e.g. zamindari abolition and tenancy reforms were introduced.
11. The new Constitution of the Republic of India originally assigned only a limited role to the Central Government in the sphere of agriculture. The centre's jurisdiction was limited to regulation and development of inter-State rivers, fishing beyond territorial waters, national institutions for scientific research and education. The Third Amendment to the Constitution put Agriculture on the Concurrent List and widened the scope of action by the Central Government.
12. The First Five Year Plan is a watershed in the history of Indian agriculture. The major objectives of the First Five Year Plan in the field of agriculture were to correct the imbalances caused by Partition in the supply of foodgrains and commercial crops, particularly cotton and jute and improve infrastructure facilities. Agriculture, including irrigation and power, was therefore accorded the highest priority. Efforts to improve agriculture were spread over the entire country and every village was to be involved in it through the Community Development Programme. A land policy aimed at eliminating exploitation and extending security of tenancy was also announced.
13. In the Second Plan, agriculture was accorded somewhat lower priority vis-a-vis industry. The shift in priorities was due to: (a) the smooth performance of agriculture during the First Plan period; (b) the possibility of financing economic development through foreign aid; and (c) heavy industry being considered as the leading sector of economic development. Towards the close of the Second Plan a new approach to agricultural development based on selectivity of area and concentration of efforts gained

acceptance. Accordingly, under the Third Plan, Intensive Agricultural Development Programme (IADP) and the Intensive Agricultural Areas Programme (IAAP) were launched. The main objectives of the Third Plan were to achieve self-sufficiency in foodgrains and increase in agricultural production to meet the requirements of industry and export. A number of new institutions were set up to extend support to development activities in different fields; these included the Food Corporation of India, the National Seeds Corporation, the Fertilizer Corporation of India and the Agricultural Refinance and Development Corporation. However, the implementation of the Third Plan was hindered by three unexpected events; the Indo-Chinese War in 1962, the Indo-Pakistan War in 1965 and the drought of 1965 and 1966.

14. In 1966-67, a new strategy of agricultural development was launched. Its main planks were the High Yielding Varieties Programme and the Multiple Cropping Programme, both based mainly on the exotic, high yielding and short duration crop varieties. The other elements of the strategy were use of modern inputs, e.g. fertilizers, the new concepts of irrigation and water management, adaptive research and price guarantee to producers. While most of the programmes adopted under the new strategy were continued in the Fourth Plan (1969-74) a new orientation was imparted to agricultural policy. To achieve growth with social justice, a built-in-bias was introduced in agricultural programmes to help the weaker and vulnerable sections and backward areas. The role of technology as a major input in agriculture was accorded explicit recognition.

15. The strategy of agricultural development launched in 1966-67 was continued during the Fifth Plan. The development strategy in the Fifth Plan focused greater attention on application of dry farming over larger areas, development of irrigation commands, development of small and marginal farmers and promotion of horticultural programmes.

16. The strategy of agricultural development during the Sixth Plan emphasised consolidating the gains already achieved, accelerating the pace of implementation of land reform and institution building, extending the benefit of new technology to more farmers, cropping systems and regions and promoting greater farm management efficiency and promoting scientific water use patterns. The plan aimed on safeguarding the interests of both producers and consumers by attending the needs of production,

conservation, marketing and distribution in an integrated manner. A three-pronged strategy to improve the economic well-being of small and marginal farmers and share croppers was launched during the Sixth Five Year Plan based on (i) improving productivity and income from small holdings through detailed advice on land and water use based on the criteria of ecology, economics, energy and employment, (ii) promoting farmer "own" organisations for storage and marketing and (iii) diversification of opportunities for income through introduction of subsidiary occupation.

17. The Seventh Plan (1985-90) sought to emphasise/policies and programmes which will acclerate the growth in foodgrains production, increase employment opportunities and raise productivity. It aimed at broadening the agricultural growth and modernisation through infrastructural development, i.e., irrigation, drainage, roads, markets and credit institutions in the less developed regions, extension of new technology, particularly breakthrough in dryland farming, afforestation and appropriate price and procurement policies for crops were accorded priority for accelerating the growth of agricultural output, reducing annual fluctuations in output and for correcting inter-regional, inter-crop and inter-class disparities.

18. Some major initiatives were taken in the Seventh Five Year Plan (1985-90) to expedite the pace of growth. A Special Foodgrains Production Programme was launched in 1988-89 following the severe drought of 1987 and 1988. The Special Rice Production Programme launched in the Sixth Plan in Eastern India was merged with the Integrated Programme for Rice Development. The coverage of the SFPP was expanded. A Technology Mission on Oilseeds launched in the Sixth Plan in Eastern India was on Oilseeds was launched in 1986 with objective of attaining self-sufficiency in edible oils. An Integrated Oilseeds Policy was adopted in 1989 to support the farmers with technology, inputs and remunerative price for their produce. It was decided to bring pulses also under the Technology Mission on Oilseeds in 1990-91. A new Seed Policy was announced in 1988 permitting the import of high quality seed and planting material after verification of performance in Indian conditions. A National Watershed programme was also taken up in mid-eighties for the rainfed areas. These measures yielded good results. The annual compound rate of growth for agricultural commodities between 1980-81 to

1990-91 increased to 3.3 per cent against 2.4 per cent in the preceding decade.

19. In October, 1989 the then Prime Minister announced an Agricultural Package, reiterating that the highest national priority must be given to the farmers, to farming, and to food and agriculture as the corner-stone of our economy. Some of the major initiatives proposed in the Agricultural Package related to the methodology for determining the support price for farm produce, extension of institutional credit, more efficient management of land and water resources, strengthening of research support, encouragement of agro-based industries, promotion of agricultural export, etc.

20. The strategy for agricultural development in the Eighth Plan aims at not only achieving self-sufficiency in food but also generating surpluses of specific agricultural commodities for export. The Plan endeavours consolidating the gains from the base built over the years in agricultural production, sustaining improvements in productivity and production to meet the increasing demand of the growing population, enlarging the incomes of farmers and raising country's production for stepping up agricultural exports.

21. The strategy for agricultural development in the Eighth Plan focuses on

— diversification of agriculture and development of horticulture, fisheries, etc.
— accelerated growth in North-Eastern and Hill Region through improvement in productivity levels
— increasing productivity of oilseeds and pulses
— rationalisation of subsidies
— revitalisation of cooperatives
— development of post-harvest technologies

The agriculture sector is expected to grow at an average annual rate of over 4 per cent in terms of gross value of output during the Eighth Plan period.

22. A substantial growth of foodgrains output is an outstanding achievement of India's economy in last 45 years. A study of the absolute increase in foodgrains output between the triennia ending 1951-52 and 1992-93 shows that the quantum increase

in absolute terms has far exceeded the level of foodgrains output in the initial triennium:

TABLE 1.1: Changes In Output of Selected Groups: 1949-50 to 1992-93

Crop	Average-Annual-Output (Million tonnes/Bales)		Increase-in-Output Absolute terms	
	1949-50 to 1951-52	1990-91 to 1992-93*	Million Tonnes/ Bales	% increase
(1)	(2)	(3)	(4)	(5)
Rice	21.81	73.28	+ 51.47	236.0
Wheat	6.34	55.71	+ 49.37	779.0
Other Cereals	16.10	31.92	+ 15.82	98.0
Total Cereals	44.25	160.91	+116.66	263.60
Pulses	8.33	13.67	5.34	64.10
Total Foodgrains	52.58	174.58	+122.00	132.0
Oilseeds	5.14	19.36	+ 14.22	276.7
Sugarcane	56.28	243.10	+186.82	331.9
Cotton	3.02	10.50	+ 7.48	247.7
Jute & Mesta	3.71	9.03	+ 5.32	143.4

* Based on anticipated estimates for 1992-93.

23. The growth of production of foodgrains and all agricultural commodities during different periods is given in Table 1.2 It would be seen that there has been a consistent increase in the rate of growth of productivity. The growth rate of foodgrains production in India during the longer time-frame of 1949-50 to 1991-92 was 2.69 per cent. The rate of growth in productivity of foodgrain crops during this period was 2.13 per cent, whereas growth of productivity during the more recent period was 3.23 per cent.

24. The decade of eighties witnessed a perceptible acceleration in agricultural growth which played an important part on sustaining the economy on a higher growth path. Agricultural performance in the decade was a source of confidence and self-respect and it helped keep the rate of inflation in check. However, the development at the macro-level is characterised by marked

TABLE 1.2: Annual Compound Growth Rates of Foodgrains and All Agricultural Commodities

(Percent per annum)

	Foodgrains			All Commodities		
	Area	Production	Productivity	Area	Production	Productivity
1949-50 — 1964-65	1.41	2.93	1.52	1.61	3.13	1.50
1967-68 — 1980-81	0.38	2.39	1.99	0.54	2.38	1.83
1980-81 — 1991-92	0.26	2.95	3.23	0.05	3.21	3.16
1949-50 — 1991-92	0.55	2.69	2.13	0.64	2.70	2.05

disparities in both research and production, across regions and crops. The level of foodgrains production itself tended to be sluggish and fluctuated around 175 million tonnes. A major cause for this is deceleration in public and private sector investments in agriculture. Table 1.3 gives the trends in gross capital formation in agriculture.

25. The thrust in investment in agriculture in recent years has been on optimising benefits from investments already made, rather than making fresh starts with large investment. This affected the volume of investment. Absorption of a large proportion of available resources by current expenditure also affected capital formation in agriculture. The decelerating trends, however, need to be arrested to sustain the pace of growth.

26. In this context formulation of new agricultural policy has become very complex. The main challenge is to create a favourable economic environment for farmer's own efforts and investment to step up agricultural growth. A muitiplicity of approaches and philosophies has emerged for remedying the past distortions in growth and planning the future development of this sector. In March 1990, the then Finance Minister in his Budget speech announced the intention of the Government to bring out an Agricultural Policy Resolution. A preliminary draft of agricultural policy prepared by the Government was considered in a National Seminar held in New Delhi in June 1990 and a modified draft was prepared by the Government and circulated to all States/ Union Territories for their comments in March 1991 and was also released for public discussion. The draft identified eight major objectives/challenges facing agriculture and discussed in detail the policy aspects relevant to various sub-sectors/ programmes. The draft is broadly a reiteration/and reorientation

TABLE 1.3: Gross Capital Formation in Agriculture

(At 1980-81 price)
(Rs. in Crores)

Year	Gross Domestic Capital Formation			Gross Capital Formation in Agriculture			Percentage		
	Total	Public Sector	Private Sector	Total	Public Sector	Private Sector	Col. 5 as of Col.2	Col.6 as of Col.3	Col.7 as of Col.4.
1	2	3	4	5	6	7	8	9	10
1960-61	11775	4805	6970	1668	589	1079	14.2	12.3	15.5
1970-71	16550	6984	9566	2758	789	1969	16.7	11.3	20.6
1978-79	28144	12519	15625	5246	1697	3549	18.6	13.6	22.7
1980-81	25794	11767	14027	4636	1796	2840	18.0	15.3	20.2
1985-86	38258	18216	20042	4322	1516	2806	11.3	8.3	14.0
1990-91	48773	21613	27160	4642	1221	3421	9.5	5.6	12.6
1991-92*	41662	18734	22928	4580	1043	3437	11.0	5.6	15.4

* Quick Estimates

of existing programmes/policies rather than any major policy pronouncement.

27. The draft, however, succeeded in generating a public debate on the components of agriculture policy. Some people felt that there were grave errors in the policies followed in the past and overriding priority should now be given to agriculture in the allocation of financial, physical and other resources. It was proposed that subsidies may be aimed directly at the consumer and there should be a guarantee that the agricultural prices should cover the comprehensive cost of production and be divorced from the movement of non-agriculutral prices, to be ensured by supplementary system of market intervention through Commodity Management Boards. A concern was also for increasing the minimum wages for agricultural labour at par with the service sector through a time-bound programme. These formulations tended to be heavily and at places exclusively influenced by the concern for the interest of agricultural producers. An ad-hoc and isolated approach without considering the problems of agricultural development in the context of the total economy could lead to contradictions and distortions in economy.

28. Consequent upon the decision of the Government to liberalise the economy, a new draft agricultural policy was prepared by the Government after elaborate consultations to lay down the broad frame work of policy initiatives at macro-level to accelerate all round development and economic viability of agriculture. This was discussed in a meeting of Chief Ministers on 5th March 1993. They have broadly endorsed the thrusts and policy initiatives of the draft resolution. Copies of the draft Resolution, after incorporating important suggestions made by the States during the Chief Ministers' Conference have been placed in Parliament on the 14th May 1993.
29. The Central theme of the Policy draft is on increasing capital formation in agriculture. The draft clearly stipulates that the resource allocation regime in agriculture sector will be reviewed with a view to rechannelising available resources from current support measures towards capital formation and infrastructure building.
30. The Agriculture Policy seeks to create a favourable economic environment for growth and to induce the farmers to intensify their efforts and investments in agriculture through a favourable price and trade regime. Agriculture has to be a profitable and worthwhile occupation and not just subsistence. The agriculture sector has to be commercially and economically viable. The draft resolution attempts to free the farm sector from the artificial support system to make agriculture profitable so that both the nation and the farmers benefit by pursuing farming as a means of livelihood.
31. Like the industrial sector, the agriculture sector has to have the needed flexibility to switch over to other activities with greater returns. For promoting the growth of agriculture in a long-term perspective, it is essential that this sector should generate income comparable to other sectors so that the farmers continue to have interest in farming. The objective of government policy will be to develop effective systems and bestow similar benefits on agriculture as exists in industry, without subjecting the agriculturists to the regulatory and tax collection machinery of the Government. This will provide an inducement to the farmers to put in greater efforts and raise their income level. The aim is to enable the farm sector to register higher growth in income levels vis-a-vis other sectors. The Policy is thus attempting what is called social engineering in the field of agriculture.

2. POLICY ISSUES IN FORESTRY

N.C. Saxena

1. Genesis of the Problem

Till the mid-seventies forest policy in India was to plant non-browsable and market oriented timber trees and increase state revenues. Right from the First Plan in 1952, emphasis was laid on the conversion of "low" value mixed forests into "high" value plantations of commercial species like teak and eucalyptus. The National Commission on Agriculture (NCA) put its stamp of approval on this approach in the following terms, "There should be a change over from the conservation oriented forestry to more dynamic programme of production forestry. The future production programme should concentrate on clear felling of valuable mixed forests, mixed quality forest and inaccessible hard wood forests and planting these areas with suitable fast growing species yielding higher returns per unit area." This deprived millions of poor of the livelihood goods that they used to get from mixed forests. Neglect of people's demands during 1960-80 exacerbated biotic pressure which made regeneration of natural forests further difficult. The ratio of firewood to foodgrain price doubled in 1975-85 which made cutting wood for sale an attractive economic activity. Almost all important NTFPs were nationalised, that is, these can be sold only to government agencies. Nationalisation reduces the number of legal buyers, chokes the free flow of goods, and delays payment to the gatherers, as government agencies find it difficult to make prompt payment. This results in contractors entering from the back door, but they must now operate with higher margins required to cover uncertain and delayed payments by government agencies, as well as to make the police and other authorities ignore their illegal activities. All this reduces gatherers' collection and incomes.

Social forestry: By the mid-seventies the realisation became clear that if peoples' demands were not met it would be impossible to save forests. This was to be achieved through social forestry on village and private lands. It is significant that social forestry was not tried on forest lands, as such lands were sought to be used for producing timber and peoples' participation on such lands was not encouraged. Thus social forestry was seen as a programme which would release industrial forestry from social pressures. But in order to keep people out, it was necessary to make them produce what they consumed free of charge, using community and private lands to draw off the pressure on forest lands.

Social forestry on village lands failed to take off because local people were not involved; village councils are multi-village bodies which do not inspire confidence in every constituent village; and there is no tradition of management (meaning protection, fresh planting and punishment to fresh riders) of common lands. The area available as village lands was also far less than anticipated at the project stage. Besides these structural constraints, there were shortcomings in the way the programme was conceptualised and implemented, leading to a marked divergence between the stated objectives of social forestry and the actual outcomes.

First, market oriented trees were planted which did little to improve consumption within the village. Fodder trees were generally ignored. Close spacing to accommodate more trees affected grass production. Second, as projects did little to meet the demand of the poor for fuelwood and fodder, pressure on forest land continued. Third, as deforestation was perceived to be due to fuelwood and fodder demands of the people, it was assumed by the policy-makers that given government help, people would willingly invest their labour and capital in raising fuelwood and fodder trees. However, as fuel and fodder were often collected free, farmers preferred income-generating trees, and continued to collect branches, twigs, leaves and grasses from forests as before. Thus the assumption in Social Forestry about how village farmers would react to a given crisis was totally untenable. Producers were interested in increasing their income, and not in the national objective of providing fuelwood and fodder to the poor. Fourth, as state funds got locked to meet the matching contributions required for external assistance for social forestry projects, forest lands got starved of funds, with several adverse effects. The neglect of forest lands hurt forest dwellers and tribals. It reduced timber supplies to the markets, resulting in price escalation, which further increased smuggling from forest lands. Fifth, species selection and spacing were considered technical questions, and hence were not examined carefully at the project stage. Benefits which could flow to the poor from species yielding intermediate products were not properly appreciated. The value of a tree was linked in the minds of foresters with the final product obtained through felling. Thus production of grasses, legumes, fodder, fruit and MFPs was neglected.

Spacing has often been reduced to avoid intermediate management operations, to reduce plantation cost, and to cut down on staff supervision time. As a consequence, spacing, thinning and pruning which could have produced intermediate yields of grass and tree products for the people have not been made use of. Technology with which the foresters were familiar for large scale plantations for markets within forest areas was applied to small scale village woodlots, where the need was more for fodder and subsistence than for timber.

Privatisation of forest lands: The present policies regarding government forests have neither led to improved productivity, nor to improved welfare of the people. Several alternatives have been suggested, including leasing of forest lands to user-industries.

The demand by paper industry in the country can easily be met from plantations on 2 million ha. As against this there is 141 m.ha of cultivated land, 60 per cent of which is owned by rich and affluent farmers, who are market oriented, and can be trusted to fulfil the requirements of the industry. Since the overall demand of the industry is limited, and if it is allowed to be met by leasing out lands to industries, this would necessarily reduce the size of the markets for farmers. Leasing of forest lands will thus adversely affect the farm forestry programme, which is one of the cheapest and most sustainable method of producing wood. It is worth mentioning here that industry requires eucalyptus or bamboos, which can be easily produced in 5-8 years time, hence is eminently suitable for farm forestry.

It may be mentioned here that industry was offered desert lands of Rajasthan, and ravines of M.P., but they refused, as they wanted better quality lands. Thus the contention of the industry they wanted wastelands only is not true. Even if they are to be allotted marginal but cultivable lands, what is the guarantee that they would not manoeuver to get better quality forest lands allotted to them through corruption?

Then, most degraded lands have extreme biotic pressure, and often have rights of the people recorded on such lands. It will be impossible to extinguish such rights, or to reduce biotic pressure. Already, in many protected areas reserved for biodiversity and wild life, government is finding it tough to deal with people's rights of access. If land is given to industry (which is a less legitimate cause than preservation of wildlife), such problems will be many fold, and will attract attention of the NGOs and press, who will get a ready made battle field to fight and criticise government.

In addition to large industry, forest raw material is also needed by saw mills. If paper industry is given land, there is going to be a scramble of such demands by construction industry, contractors and saw millers. If given teak and sal forests, they may be tempted to raise short-term and quick growing species, thus changing land-use pattern. Its ecological implications need to be taken into consideration. Lastly, if lands are to be given to industry, why not to efficient farmers, who can produce raw material cheaply, as their overhead costs are lower than that of industry. They exploit their own and family labour (which is unpaid), and therefore can produce wood cheaper than industry. Thus leasing to industry is not advocated.

2. Possible Solutions

The poor would be greatly benefited if opportunities for collection from forest and public lands are enhanced. This would require:

- a change in the silvicultural practices of managing forests;
- a change in the nature of species being planted on public lands from timber to usufruct based trees;
- promoting Joint Forest Management; and
- a change in outlook to facilitate the above.

Silvicultural practices: Forests have been looked upon as a source of revenue and not as a means of meeting the genuine needs of the people. That is why the entire thrust of forestry has been towards the high forest system, which calls for felling and ruthless cutting back of all growth, except the species chosen for dominance. This has the major defect of creating a bias in favour of coppice origin plants which, in the long run, are more amenable to biotic and climatic factors than the seedlings, and secondly, the removal of all the material which could serve nistar needs. The high forest system has resulted in pure forests being created, but with nistar falling a causality in the process. It is in this context that a major policy change is required.

A start could be made by deciding that nistar is a legitimate and genuine expectation of the people and that if they do not get it they will treat the forests with hostility. What is now termed as biotic interference, i.e., foraging for fuel and fodder, grazing, removal of bamboo and small timber, should be looked upon as a logical and appropriate working of the forests. This calls for an abandonment of the existing silvicultural practices, not so much to achieve high forest as to restore to the forests an admixture in which the appropriate level of vegetation would be available to meet nistar needs. An immediate identification of quick growing shrubs with high calorific value, with their retention in the forest to serve fuel requirements, the development of pastures, i.e., giving over adequate forest land to grasses, and the development of massive fuelwood plantations around centres of high consumption and encouragement of silviculturally sensible exploitation of fuelwood species would also be important components of the new policy.

Only over-mature, mal-formed, dead or dying trees should be removed, with no particular reservation by species. Ground flora and the understorey should be largely left undisturbed, except for the improvement of hygiene of the forest flora through removal of noxious weeds. Particular attention should be paid to the elimination of lantana and parthenium. Adequate fire protection works should also be carried out so that fire can be contained within a block and not allowed to spread. Under-stocked or ecologically fragile areas should be brought under full protection and there would be no felling, except for the maintenance of forest hygiene. In a reasonably well-stocked area, there would be a simultaneous upsurge of all the species naturally growing there, without any bias for coppice origin plants. There would also be no bias for any species, with the result that over time the forest would become reasonably well mixed in plant species. There would be an overwood of the best species such as teak, sal, saj, bija, tinsa, etc. but there would also be a substantial middle and understorey, together with ground flora. The crop would be representative of all age groups because no attempt would be made to achieve an uniform crop in terms of variety or age. In those areas where teak and sal are the naturally dominant species, they would continue to predominate even without silvicultural intervention to achieve an uniform crop. However, because of age and species mix the forests would be able to maintain a continuous supply of miscellaneous small timber and fuelwood for use in nistar. Commercial working would taper off because clear felling by blocks would be totally abandoned, but there would be some production of timber from the over mature trees that would be felled.

Change in Species on degraded lands: Social forestry concepts should be extended to degraded reserved and protected forest lands by changing the nature of species from teak and eucalyptus to usufruct based trees, such as neem, mahua, bamboo, and tamarind. These should be supplemented with grasses, legumes, shrubs and bushes to yield fuelwood and fodder in the shortest possible time. This would strengthen the access of the poor to forests, and therefore benefits would be directly appropriated by them. Unlike commercial timber species, relatively low value non-rotational trees for recurrent products would not so much attract the attention of powerful panchayat leaders and contractors.

This requires a complete reversal of the recommendations of the

National Commission on Agriculture, 1976 which favoured commercial plantations on forest land, and trees for consumption and subsistence on private land (Saxena 1990). Our recommendation is that subsistence and consumption should be met from forest and common lands, and market demand should by and large be met from private land. For quick benefits to the poor, long gestation trees would be supplemented with an understorey of bushes and shrubs so as to satisfy immediate needs of the poor. "Scientific" forestre should therefore mean that environmental benefits, MFPs, grasses, leaves and twigs become the main intended products from forest lands and timber a by-product from large trees like mahua and sal. The reverse has been the policy for the last 100 years.

Primacy of Rights: As already pointed out, the rights of the poor of access and their right to collection of forest products are restricted, vague, or not known to them. Sharing arrangements in Joint Forest Management or community forestry schemes are ill-defined or not publicised, or poorly implemented. Therefore, we suggest that outside each forest coupe or social forestry plantation, there should be a notice board publicising what rights people have as regards collection. A simple notice that "these trees belong to the community, and not to Government", may in itself, change peoples' attitude towards village plantations.

Similarly, nationalisation of MFPs, justified in the name of preventing tribal exploitation, creates excellent opportunities for private traders and bureaucracy to extract 'suitable' rents for "services rendered". Practical considerations point out that Government is incapable of effectively administer complete control. It is better for Government to regulate private trade, and to act as a watchdog rather than try to eliminate it. Monopoly purchase by Government requires sustained political support and excellent bureaucratic machinery. It is difficult to ensure these over a long period and hence nationalisation has often increased exploitation of the poor. The solution is to set up promotional Marketing Boards, as distinct from commercial corporations (which are inefficient, and hence demand nationalisation), with responsibility for dissemination of information about markets and prices to the gatherers. The Boards would help in bridging the gap between what the consumers pay and what gatherers get. We would be quite happy if government organisations could compete in the open market, as in the wheat purchase scheme, but government should never acquire a monopoly. Setting up of processing units within the tribal areas is also to be recommended.

3. Joint Forest Management and Ecodevelopment

Ecodevelopment is based on the belief that if foresters support village development in the broadest way — resources, cattle, veterinary inputs, schools, health, water, roads, etc. then the people will appreciate the role of forests and help its protection. This is reminiscent of the older social forestry philosophy that creation of fuelwood reserves outside forest lands will make people give up gathering from forest lands. This assumption too may prove in future to be rather naive. Empirical evidence linking prosperity with reduction in gathering is not very conclusive. By itself, poverty alleviation does not reducc dependence on open resources. Besides, there may be other problems if ecodevelopment is made the main programme for forest regeneration, such as —

a: overall cost per ha. — ecodevelopment may turn out to be very expensive, Rs 10,000 to 25,000 per ha. of forest lands;
b. appropriateness of the Forest Department for carrying out some schemes, for which they are not trained, and there are other administrative departments to do that job better than the Forest Department. It is not clear whether the Finance Department of the state would permit the Forest Department to undertake livestock development or carry out irrigation works; and
c. viability of schemes — as the landless and poor farmers depend more on forest resources than other categories of people, for ecodevelopment to be effective, the economic programmes must be targeted to improve the income of this class of people. The experience of the last twenty years of rural development schemes (starting with Marginal Farmers and Agricultural Labourers Programme of the late 1960s) shows that it is very difficult to concieve of programmes on a large scale for this target group. Besides, there is no evidence that the Forest Department is aware of the past mistakes made by the development blocks in implementing these schemes. In the absence of this knowledge, Forest Department may be 're-inventing the wheel' and repeat the same mistakes made by the Rural Development department.

Present Status of Joint Forest Management (JFM) : Several states have introduced JFM. We discuss below the policy regarding JFM in one state, MP. The state government order enabling JFM in Madhya Pradesh was issued in December, 1991, and is thus more than a year old. The following specific problems/ deficiencies in its implementation have been noticed:

1. Although some DFOs on their own initiative have formed committees, there is no monitoring of their number, of progress

or no lessons learnt from the implementation, and no communication sent from the headquarters to other field officials. Thus JFM is still not high on the agenda of a supervising officer. Similarly, no evaluation seems to have been done of the pilot experiments tried in the state (the only study done of Harda by the IIFM is more in the nature of a PR exercise — that too has not been widely circulated), with the result that a field officer desirous of initiating JFM has to reinvent the wheel every time. A JFM cell at the headquarters perhaps could be the beginning.

2. Both ecodevelopment and Joint Forest Management are not yet supported by the state Forest Department's plan outlay, indicating that these activities are not considered priority items by the state government, or that other activities are considered to be giving greater returns. Forest Department should therefore indicate immediately in no uncertain terms how ecodevelopment and Joint Forest Management activities are to be financed.

3. In Madhya Pradesh, communities already have considerable rights over forest produce under Nistar agreements. Joint management agreements, while claiming to give usufruct, are thus not giving any thing extra. Therefore, one needs to address the question as to how to provide greater security to communities that they will benefit from protection related work. Some workable suggestions are therefore:

   a. give full nistar requirements of building material etc. to the protecting village, not from the depot, but from the protected area itself, and that too free;
   b. include bamboo in the category of NTFP, and give its full production (and not merely 30%) to the people;
   c. change silvicultural practices to improve understorey and production of grasses and underwood;
   d. formalise and sign agreements with the community within three months of the forming of the community, and keep its copy with the village, so that the credibility of the Forest Department improves;
   e. incorporate in such agreements the fact that people from other villages have no right of entry in the earmarked forest coupe. Each proposed patch for protection should have a well-defined and recognised user-group. Admitting the rights of the entire population of that region will make forests open-access lands, leaving no incentive to the protecting village.

People of other villages will have to be given other coupes, in order to make the scheme workable and politically acceptable; and

f. This will also require a cluster approach, as opposed to 'one range-one village' proposal that has been mooted so far.

4. The present formula of giving a share out of net income should be replaced by a share of gross income. which is easily understandable by the people. The village communities should have the freedom to decide whether this will be individually distributed or deposited in the village fund. Para 3 of the government order under the heading 'Responsibility and Duty of the Forest Department' provides for detailed instructions to be issued by the department, but this has still not been done.
5. The instructions provide that 30 per cent of the net income obtained from the nationalised MFPs will be given to the committee, but to my knowledge, nowhere has a share out of tendu leaf or bamboo or sal seeds income been given to the people.
6. There are no funds at present for training of village communities, nor of their visits to the successful areas.
7. In a state-level meeting held on 25-8-92 that was presided over by the Principal Secretary, Forests, it was stated by the Principal Secretary that Forest Protection Committees can be given a share from revenues only after approval in each individual case from the Finance Department of the government. This is strange, and such a tedious bureaucratic procedure has not been prescribed by any other state in India. This will cause great delay, and will surely inhibit peoples' enthusiasm as it makes flow of benefits to them uncertain. Rather than announce uncertain benefits, it is much better to give only a few but certain and well publicised benefits. The minutes of the meeting also mentioned almost all 300 village societies, purported to be formed by the field officials, were only on paper. Principal Secretary, Forests commented that most field officers did not understand the difference between Village Forest Committee and Forest Protection Committee. Obviously, if officers do not understand the difference, the people will be even more confused.

4. Farm Forestry

Agriculturally developed areas: First, restrictive laws on cutting and selling privately owned trees should be abolished. Second, government should stop subsidies on government supply of wood to industries, thereby forcing industry to buy from the farmers at a remunerative price. The new Forest Policy endorses this suggestion, but in many states, subsidies still continue. Third, it should also initiate schemes for linking farmers with industries, in ways similar to the linking of poplar growing farmers with a Swedish match factory in north India. Fourth, the subsidy on seedlings is unnecessary. The main thrust of government's intervention in seedlings should be to ensure that pedigree seed is used in regard to all species selected. Free distribution leads to bogus reporting too.

And last, temporary nurseries are able to supply only such seedlings which can be raised in a short time of three/four months. Many high value trees, like teak or fruit species, require seedlings to be at the nursery stage for a longer period. Hence, temporary nurseries should be replaced by permanent nurseries.

Agriculturally backward areas: The agrarian structure of subsistence regions in the eastern and tribal India is characterised by heavy dependence on grain production, smaller holdings, low overall incomes, a less marketed surplus, imperfect credit markets, more dependence on the village merchant for marketing the small surplus, inter-locked credit and output markets, less monetisation, less diversity of rural incomes, greater debt bondage, a less developed infrastructure for the supply of agriculture inputs, greater insecurity of land tenure, and on the whole poor human capital as far as enterprise is concerned. These conditions can at best promote low intensity tree growing strategies for home consumption, and are not conducive to market oriented high intensity tree planting.

This is not to deny the need for generating cash incomes for the poor farmers in this region. But given the nature of markets, which are more exploitative in subsistence areas, generating cash requires a technology which is highly profitable, so that even after meeting market costs, some profits accrue to the poor. Perhaps fruit species may meet both the subsistence needs as well as market needs of the farmers.

Farmers in these regions follow several traditional age-tested agroforestry practices, but what has been emphasised in the farm forestry programme is growing short duration trees in place of annual crops for market. In such cases trees compete with annual crops for land, unlike the traditional practices where trees complement agricultural production. Constraints operating on the farming systems of these regions are non-monetary in nature, and cannot be overcome easily by giving financial incentives. Hence, while planning for these regions, one should have modest targets for trees. However, these are the areas where a lot of degraded land is available, both with farmers and government. The focus should therefore be on pilot projects, complementary agroforestry and watershed development.

Unlike annual crops in which crop decisions are autonomous of similar decisions by other families, a farmer's decision to plant trees in a mono-cropped village has to take into account herding practices in the village, availability of irrigation, distance of the fields from his hut, and the cropping pattern of other farmers. Conditions prevailing outside the farm become as important as simple costs and benefits from the preferred landuse options. In double-cropped villages, planting or not planting trees is an individual decision, just as is the selection of a cropping pattern, but in monocropped villages, a group consensus is necessary if trees have to be protected during the long fallow season. Hence it is better to concentrate on a few villages in which almost all farmers plant trees, than to take up a large number of villages, and expect a few plant trees in each village.

It is difficult to rehabilitate degraded lands without introducing moisture conservation and water harvesting measures. Such measures are needed for all rainfed areas put to biomass production. One should adopt insitu moisture conservation practices through planting of suitable grasses and trees which may also provide sufficient protection against erosion.

5. Change in Attitudes

One problem which will be encountered, if the suggestions contained in this paper are to be implemented, is the attitude of IAS and IFS officers, who associate "development" with spending of money, or with setting up of new organisations (which they head, of course!). Changes in policy or nature of species or laws are not seen as integral part of the development process because these have no direct financial implication. Non-monetary inputs in policy have unfortunately no ready acceptability in government. The Indian civil servant has still to learn the difference between planning and budgeting. S/he is looking for a scheme rather than a new policy framework. The question, however, is whether we wish to help hundreds through projects, or millions through changes in policy.

This is possible only when 'productivity', 'yield', and 'economic value' are redefined in terms of multipurpose utilisation and satisfying basic human needs. This requires a new outlook and a new strategy, in which the poor's interests, of secure rights of gathering, would be paramount. Livelihood needs of the poor are preconditions for sustainability of natural resources.

3. CONSERVATION OF BIOLOGICAL DIVERSITY

S.C. Dey

Bio-diversity is a term for the diversity of eco-system, species and genes that make up the variety of nature. In other words, bio-diversity encompasses the variety of abundance of plants, animals and micro-organisms as well as the eco-system and the ecological process to which they belong.

As a concept, bio-diversity conservation gained currency from concern for threatened species, built-up and fostered by IUCN since the 1960s through its red data book. But it has got much wider connotation now covering diversity beyond the species level and addressing genetic erosion as well as extinction.

The conservation principle accepts the position that setting up comprehensive and well managed protected area system is likely to be the most practical way to preserve the greatest amount of world's biological diversity. For this reason, it suggests that the initial efforts ofbio-diversity conservation should aim at establishment and maintenance of protected area systems by making policy changes, involving local people in the protected are management and mobilizing financial resources for conservation and protection.

The world conservation strategy lays down that considering the stress on environment the countries should aim at earmarking 10 per cent of their land area for bio-diversity conservation. Whereas in some heavily populated countries it may not be possible to earmark so much of land area by depriving or evicting the existing population. But in countries where population density is still low, specially the countries in Africa and South America, the scope of preserving 10 per cent of the land area for conservation of bio-diversity is still there.

Unfortunately, however, the biological diversity all over the developing countries is subjected to serious threat, some countries being unable to control the growth of human population and use, overuse or abuse of their forest for day to day sustenance, and other countries not attaching sufficient priorities to conservation and by their attempt to improve their life style through rapid resources use to imitate otherwise glamorous, but unsustainable and profligate, life style practiced in the West.

An analysis of the Asia-pacific region indicates that although the protected area coverage is about 3.8% of Asia's total land area but it varies from 0% in Combodia, Lao P.D.R., Maldives and Solomon islands to 38.9% in Kiribati. Out of the larger countries China has got 2.9%, India 4.2%, Thailand 10.7%, Indonesia 10%, Pakistan 4.5% of the land area under protected area system. The said percentage with respect to Bhutan stands at 19.4%, Sri Lanka 11.9%, Republic of Korea 7.7%, Malaysia 4.4.%, and Nepal 8%. For Africa the protected area cover is 3.4% of the total land area of the continent and for South America the said figure is 6.1%. The overall human population density in South America is about 16 persons per sq.km., Africa 20 persons per sq.km. and in Asia (excluding Russia) 70 persons per sq.km.

The unlimited diversity of life form of India is most remarkable, but rapid industrialisation, urbanisation, population pressure and extension of agriculture have created a serious pressure on the human eco-system, and the natural balance which is necessary for proper human development, has reached a perilous stage. Destruction of forest has resulted in shrinkage of wildlife habitat leading to the disappearance of many valuable species of wildlife which dominated the surface of the earth in earlier era. With the reduction of various species of wildlife, flora and micro-organism which form a complex cycle in the human eco-system, there has been serious damage to the environment leading to varied complication of flood and drought up-rooting the rural poor, particularly landless labour families, from their traditional homes.

Bio-geographically India has got floral and faunal diversity ranging from Alpine pasture in the high Himalayas to the coastal mangrove along sea delta and from tropical rain forest in the North East to the Arid desert in the Rajasthan in western India. There are 10 bio-geographical zones representing distinct forest eco-system harbouring plants and animals species characteristic for such areas. The 10 bio-geographical zones are given below which are further subdivided into biotic province, regions and the biomes depending upon the dispersal barriers, different land forms and ecological unit.

The 10 bio-geographical zones with 25 provinces in India area as follows:

1. Trans-Himalayas with 1 province

2. The Himalayas with 4 provinces
3. The Indian Desert with 2 provinces
4. The Semi-Arid Zone with 2 provinces
5. The Western Ghats with 2 provinces
6. The Deccan Peninsula with 5 provinces
7. The Gangetic Plain with 2 provinces
8. North East India with 2 provinces
9. The Islands with 3 provinces
10. The Coasts with 2 provinces

The first attempt of global bio-diversity conservation was crytallized when IUCN was founded in 1948 as a membership organization comprising governments, non-governmental organisation, research institutions and conservation agencies of the world. At present there are about 120 countries representation in the IUCN. In the initial years of conservation, however, the response received from the world community as such was limited, and in the 1972 Stockholm United National Conference on human environment which was designed to appreciate Man's special responsibility to safeguard the heritage of wildlife and habitat, only 2 countries were represented by the heads of the government, one was the host nation and the other was India. Subsequent years saw lot of conferences taking place in various countries on the issue but inspite of that 1984 UNEP assessment showed 4.5 billion ha, that means 35 per cent of earth's land surface, being threatened by desertification and about 12 million ha, of forest land in the tropical zone being lost every year; and in developed countries forest continued to deteriorate under stresses of air pollution and acid rains. In 1987 as much as 8 million ha of virgin forest was burned in Brazilian Amazon alone. The changed concern of the world community was seen when in the Earth Summit in Rio last year nearly 160 heads of states were present to deliberate on Environmental Conservation.

Protected areas make a vital contribution to the conservation of world's natural and cultural resources. It helps to maintain environmental stability of surrounding region, maintain fertility of marginal land, preserve the wide diversity of genepool resources, maintain the quality of water, serve as carbon sink for proper maintenance of gaseous exchange reducing depletion of ozone layer which results in global warming. These preserved sited provide scenic and aesthetic surroundings and offer facilities for recreation and tourism.

Ten categories of protection areas have been identified by IUCN for proper management of wildland resources of any nation. Of these main protected areas are national parks, wildlife sanctuaries, Nature reserves, protected landscape, biosphere reserves and world heritage sites.

India has got about 14 million ha of land under protected areas which contain 75 National Parks and 421 Wildlife Sanctuaries comprising 4.2 per cent of the country's land area and about 15 per cent of country's recorded forest areas. Our target is to preserve atleast 4.6 per cent of the country's land area in protected area system with adequate representation in each of the biotic province and biomes. We are thus, not very far from our physical target for the country though the representation of protected areas in the Trans-Himalayas and the Gangetic Plain is very less.

Considering the high density of human population in India, which as per 1991 census is 267 per sq.km, reserving 4.2 per cent of the land area is not an easy task; equally difficult it is to increase the area further. Such areas though protected by law are often not properly protected, under managed, lacking in proper infrastructure, leading to certain infringement of protected area concept.

Factors which are required to be looked into in the proper management of protected area system are the following:

1. Proper legal framework;
2. Institutional structures for implementation of work programmes;
3. Financial resources to back up the action plans;
4. Political commitment for conservation priority;
5. Human Resource Development; and
6. Involvement of NGOs and the local people in park management.

The investment in the management of the protected area vary from country to country. Whereas it is broadly felt that for proper management, money available for protected area should be about US $ 500 per sq. km. but depending upon the size of the protected area and the human population density around the protected areas the required cost may vary from US $ 200 to $ 800 per sq. km. The actual investment position in most of the countries for management of these protected areas are, however, considerably low. For example, in India we have got 1,40,000 sq. km. of protected area covering 74 National Parks and 421 Wildlife Sanctuaries, but the total investment available for management of the protected area is only Rs. 100 crore annually, including central assistance, state plan scheme and non-plan expenditure. This works out to US $ 240 per sq. km. which on an average is half the amount required for proper management of the protected areas. There is, therefore, immediate necessity of increasing the investment in the management of protected areas but for which it will be impossible to conserve the protected areas over a longer time frame for the benefit of the posterity.

Preserving biological diversity is important to development because of the economic potential of species that are currently undiscovered, undervalued or unappreciated. Many previously unknown or obscure and threatened species have turned out to have major economic benefit. Wildlands perform "Environmental services" such as improving water supply for agriculture, industry and human consumption; reducing sedimentation of reservoirs, harbours and irrigation projects; minimising floods, landslides, droughts and coastal erosing; providing ideal nursery for development of fishery. Mechanised and fast city life is putting great stress on human mind causing physical and mental fatigue. To remove this stress and strain people go to nature for solitude where the sight of playing wild animals refreshes human mind and enables them to start their next day's work afresh with increased vigour and healthy mind.

The earth is one but the world is not. Each community strives for survival and prosperity with little regards for its impact on others. Some consume earth resources at a rate that will leave very little for others or future generations. Others consume for too little and live with hunger, squalor, desease and early death. Reversing deforestation and destruction of wildlife, which is the primary cause of environmental degradation, require political will and leadership, and appropriate policy changes to support the community level initiative. Our strategy for conservation development should, therefore, be tackling of human problems through employment and resource built up in the fringes adjoining conservation areas so that demarcated conservation areas are sustained and maintained. The key ingredient is the active participation of the millions of people living in the forest fringe — who regularly uses forests, its trees and their wild denizens for meeting their daily needs. Our future development plan should, therefore, be drawn in such a manner that this will not bring misery to the people in the long run by destruction of wildlands but will be aimed at rejuvenation of environment of the country and far beyond it.

4. INDUSTRIAL POLICY : Historical Perspective

S. Behura

During the British Raj, there were very few instruments of Government policy which could be considered as any kind of industrial policy. At the time of Independence, the industrial sector was extremely under-developed: there was a lack of infrastructure industries; the structure of ownership was highly concentrated; technical and managerial skill were in short supply; since most export industries such as tea, jute, etc. were in colonial hands, it was felt that export orientation had been against the country's interest and finally the lack of Government intervention in favour of industrial sector was seen as an important cause of under-development.

The national consensus, therefore, was that economic development must lay emphasis on economic independence and economic sovereignty. The need for rapid industrialisation and promotion of industrial infrastructure was clearly recognised. The Indian industrialists were seen as having served the national cause in the face of colonial adversity. They, therefore, deserved protection. Discrimination of the Indians by the British in all economic activities and social and cultural life as well as positions in the Government and the private sector laid the basis for rapid indigenisation and general antipathy towards foreign trade and foreign investment.

The beginning of all thinking in key Industrial Policy Resolutions can be traced to the Statement of Industrial Policy, 1945. The idea of Government participation in certain sectors of industry was included in this Industrial Policy Statement. The concept of industrial licensing was considered as an instrument for dispersal of industries and to prevent establishment of excess capacity in industry. The contribution of the Second World War in the development of regulatory apparatus governing Indian industry has also been no less. The Statement on Industrial Policy, 1945 explicitly noted the relevance and importance of developing industry in order to make the country better prepared for defence. In fact, powers of the Central Government over industry were first brought into effect under rule 81 of the Defence of India Rules, promulgated in 1939 under the Defence of India Act, which was enacted after the out-break of the Second World War. Rule 81 had a blanket provision for "regulating or prohibiting the production, treatment, storage, employment, transport, distribution, disposal, acquisition, use or consumption of articles or things of any description whatsoever," Under Rule 84, the Central Government was also empowered to prohibit or restrict the import or export of all kinds and to control purchase of foreign exchange and to make restrictions on payments, etc. Some of the main instruments of the Capital Issues (Continuance of Controls) Act and others which came into being after Independence were essentially extensions of Defence of India powers acquired by the Central Government during the Second World War.

The powers of the Central Government to regulate industrial development is derived from the Industrial (Development and Regulation) Act, 1951. Prior to this Act, the development of industries was a provincial subject. The original intention of the I (D&R) Act was that licensing provision would be used on the basis of knowledge concerning different industries and according to indepth surveys and reports that would be prepared on a regular basis. The intention behind licensing was indeed developmental. This is evident from the Statement in the First Plan, that is, with the coming into force of restriction and licensing procedures laid down under the I (D&R) Act, a lot of valuable information pertaining to scheduled industries will become available and it is necessary that arrangements be made for the systematic and expeditious analysis of the same. There was a need for coordination of industrial planning with the formulation of other economic policies such as customs and excise tariff structure, import and export policy, investment and technology policy, monetary and financial policy. The second and the subsequent plans have been increasingly concerned with the allocation of public resources and much less with instruments and policies to direct the whole economy in desired directions.

The system of industrial licensing has operated in the country with simultaneous operation of similar Government allocations and controls such as Five Year Plan documents, import and export controls, control of capital issues, control of foreign exchange, price control, allocation of raw-material, credit, etc. This means that the policy makers in India felt the need for a wide variety of instruments and controls for the industrial development of the country in a desired direction. While the original intention of licensing was to use this power selectively for the promotion of selected important industries, it later became a tool to control almost all industries as a result of which regulation rather than development became the more important feature of the system.

The Industrial Policy Resolution of 1956 has been the basis for all subsequent industrial policies. The main objectives of this Resolution were to accelerate industrial growth and speed up industrialisation and in particular develop heavy industries and the capital goods sector, expand the public sector and to build up a large and growing cooperative sector. The state was to assume direct responsibility for the industries of basic and strategic importance and public utilities in consonance with the goal of a socialistic pattern of society and the use of planning as an instrument of development. The industries were classified into 3 categories on the basis of the intended role of the State. Schedule A to the Resolution listed industries exclusively reserved for the State. The list of industries in Schedule B to the Resolution was one in which the State would take the initiative but the private sector was also expected to supplement the efforts of the State. The third category consisted of the remaining industries, the development of which was left to the initiative and enterprise of the private sector.

The division of industries into separate categories was strictly not in water-tight compartments. For instance, the policy resolution did not prevent the expansion of existing private sector units operating in industries reserved for the State (Schedule A). Similarly, the State could start an industry not included in Schedule A or B when the need for it was so felt. Thus, the Resolution underlined the inter-dependence between the private sector and the flexibility of the classification of industries. While subjecting private sector to controls and regulations in terms of the I (D&R) Act, the Government recognised that such undertakings should be allowed to develop with as much freedom as possible consistent with overall national objectives. It also stated that in terms of policy there would be fair and non-discriminatory treatment to units in the State in the private sector in the same industries. It had recognised the need for accelerated industrial growth and tried to formulate an industrial policy to achieve the national objectives. The underlying philosophy enunciated in this Resolution is as valid today as before.

In the historical sense, therefore, the subsequent Industrial Policy Statements announced by the Government in 1973, 1977 and 1980 are within the broad framework of the Industrial Policy Resolution of 1956. The Statement of 1973 specified areas which are generally open to MRTP/ FERA companies as specified in the Appendix-I of the Statement. These industries in Appendix-I of the statement are the core industries of importance to the national economy, industries which have long-term export potential and industries of critical and strategic importance. The Policy Statement also laid emphasis on the growth of small and cooperative sector and specified the policy in regard to the joint sector.

The Industrial Policy Statement of 1977 was for effective promotion of small and cottage industries widely dispersed in rural areas and towns. The list of items reserved for small scale sector was substantially expanded. On the other hand, the Industrial Policy Statement of 1980 emphasised on promoting competition in the domestic market, technological upgradation and modernisation, laying the foundation for increasingly competitive export bias and encouraging foreign investment in high technology areas and for exports.

Regarding foreign investment, Government's policy was selective and was designed to channelise investments into areas which required sophisticated technology or where it was felt critical production gaps exist or that it would increase the country's export potential. Normal ceiling for foreign investment was 40 per cent of the paid up capital of the Indian company. A higher percentage was rarely allowed. There was a negative list of industries where generally no foreign collaboration, financial or technical, were ordinarily permitted. In short, the policy was restrictive and was very much a part of the Licence-Permit Raj.

The fact that the control system was not working well in directing investments had been felt in the early sixties. The Government appointed one Committee after another in the sixties to examine the industrial licensing system (The Swaminathan Committee, 1964; the Dutt Committee Report, 1969). The finding of most of these Committees was that the licensing mechanism was not serving its purpose of channelising investments into desired directions. Despite all this evidence regarding unsatisfactory performance of the licensing system, there was a persistent reluctance to change. One reason could be the linkage of industrial licensing to foreign exchange allocations. Inter-linkages within the control system were such that it was practically difficult to make changes.

The stagnation of the industrial production between sixties and late seventies induced some new thinking. There emerged a growing consensus in early eighties that Indian industry was exhibiting a slow down in industrial growth due to low productivity, poor quality of production and obsolete technology. There was an increasing realisation to substitute physical and quantitative controls by fiscal and other macro economic management and the need for measures to enhance productivity, efficiency and modernisation.

Consequently, a number of regulatory controls were gradually removed in the '80s. The Government introduced a number of schemes such as delicensed industries, exempted industries, broad banding of capacities, fixation of minimum economic scale of production and re-endorsement of capacity as a result of modernisation, technological upgradation, etc. The idea was to by-pass the licensing system.

Thus, the number of policy and procedural changes introduced in the late '80s resulted in increasing productivity, reducing costs and improving quality. The accent was on opening domestic market to increased competition and prepare our industry to stand on its own in the face of international competition. But this did not result in simplification of procedures or dismantling of the licence-permit raj. In fact, policies and procedures became even more complicated than they were before, requiring a large number of approvals.

A comprehensive review of the existing industrial policies and procedural work undertaken from 1990 onwards resulted in a Statement on New Industrial Policy (NIP) being tabled in both Houses of Parliament on 21 July 1991. The Statement reviewed all the Industrial Statements made since 1948 and restated the objectives of the country and of industrial development in the present day context. In pursuit of these objectives Government announced a number of major policy decisions relating to industrial licensing, foreign investment, foreign technology agreements, public sector and the MRTP Act. The major objective of the New Industrial Policy package, as the statement says, would be to build on the gains already made, correct the distortions or weaknesses that may have crept in, maintain a sustained growth in productivity and gainful employment and attain international competitiveness. Government's policy would be continuity with change.

The most important consequence of the New Industrial Policy was unshackling of the Indian industrial economy from the cob-webs of unnecessary bureaucratic control. These measures were subsequently complemented by the series of measures in the areas of trade policy, exchange rate management, fiscal policy, financial sector reform and overall macro economic management.

The salient features of the New Industrial Policy are as follows: industrial licensing was abolished for all projects except for a short list of 18 industries related to security and strategic concerns, social reasons, hazardous chemicals and over-riding environmental reasons and items of elitist consumption. Industries reserved for the small scale sector were continued to be so reserved. Areas where security and strategic concerns predominate were continued to be reserved for the public sector (list reduced from 17 to 8). In respect of cities with population of 1 million, industries other than those of non-polluting nature such as electronics, computer software, printing were to be located outside 25 kms of the periphery except in prior designated industrial areas and for locations other than such cities there would be no requirement of obtaining industrial approvals from the Central Government except for industries subject to compulsory licensing. The immediate procedural consequence of this was abolition of all registration schemes namely, De-licensed Registration, Exempted Industries Registration, DGTD Registration, etc. Entrepreneurs were required only to file an Information Memorandum on new projects and substantial expansions of industries not subject to compulsory licensing. This is required for statistical purposes and is not insisted upon. In practice, units prefer to file such a Memorandum.

Regarding foreign investment the New Industrial Policy provides for approval to be given for direct foreign investment upto 51 per cent foreign equity in high priority industries. There would be no bottle-neck of any kind in this process. The same would be given automatically by the Reserve Bank of India. Provision for automatic permission is also available for foreign technology agreements in high priority areas up to a lumpsum of Rs. 1 crore, 5 per cent royalty of domestic sales and 8 per cent for exports. No permission would henceforth be necessary for hiring of foreign technicians and foreign testing of indigenously developed technology.

On the public sector front, the Statement said that the portfolio of public sector investments would be reviewed to focus the public sector on strategic hi-tech and essential infrastructure. Some reservation for the public sector was retained. There would henceforth be no bar for areas of exclusivity to be opened up to the private sector selectively. Secondly, public sector enterprises which are chronically sick and which are unlikely to turn around will, for the formulation of rehabilitation, revival schemes, be referred to the Board for Industrial and Financial Reconstruction. A social security mechanism would be created to protect the interest of workers likely to be affected by such rehabilitation packages. In order to raise resources and encourage wider public participation, a part of the Government shareholding in the public sector would be offered to mutual funds, financial institutions, general public and workers.

Finally, the restrictions for any MRTP company requiring prior approval of Central Government for establishment of new undertaking, expansion of undertaking, merger, amalgamation, take-over and appointment of directors were removed.

The policy has undergone further changes. For example further reduction in the list of industries for compulsory licensing came down from 18 to 15, reduction in the areas reserved for public sector from 8 to 6, etc. The New Industrial Policy announced in July 1991 heralded a new beginning. The enactment of the I (D&R) Act, 1951 was complemented by a plethora of other regulatory measures in other related sectors such as trade and finance, thereby creating the licence-permit raj. The New Industrial Policy, 1991 was a precursor to similar policy measures in trade and financial sectors to end this raj.

5. PLANNING AND MARKET

Y.K. Alagh

In this next phase of development, it is increasingly clear that structural adjustment policies will call for increased reliance on markets.[1] This paper attempts to explore the use of economic models to empirically graft market policies in a structural adjustment programme. The illustrations are from India, although the validity may be more general.

In the earlier phase of Indian planning, the "rules" of the game were setting in allocative terms, arising from a plan model. "Controllable" fiscal policy assumptions were used to justify the neglect of prices and "behavioural" relations in the process of planning. The Seventh Plan expressed a concern for moving over from "physical" to "financial" and "fiscal" controls. Does this mean that the economy has to be tuned to follow the "laws of the market" and to some " the laws of the world market" or can planning rules be blended with the market to give a sense of direction to the economy. We discuss the role of price based planning rulcs both for the agricultural and the industrial sector of the Indian economy. The emphasis is on empirical testing of propositions. Assume an economy which follows a central planning paradigm. Investment or capacity creation, location, output, price and use and earning of foreign exchange are controlled at the firm level. This was for example applicable to most firms in the large scale corporate sector at one stage in India. Reform can follow many paths.[2] At one extreme there could be the abolition of most quantitative controls, a floating exchange rate and reduction of spread and level of tariff rates (this is the so-called SAP of international financial institutions). At the other end quantitative restrictions at the firm level could be replaced by industry level financial, tax, tariff and pricing rules. Referring to the present author's description of such a system in India, Taylor classifies it as a Multifaceted Pricing Strategy (MPS).

There are two somewhat sharply differentiated views on industrial policy being advocated in India. The differing views concern alternative prescriptions on trade policy including protection, technology and investment policies including pricing and fiscal or monetary policies, licensing policies and special policy objectives like regional development.[3] According to one view, the objective of policy should be to first align the Indian industrial economy with the international economy by reducing the dispersion of rates of protection and then reducing the average rate. Second, licensing including for MRTP and FERA companies, should be abolished apart from a negative list of industries which are presumably polluting industries or those with significant external dis-economies. Third, all kinds of pricing, fiscal or quantitative restriction should be removed. Fourth, objectives like regional development should not be followed through the industrial route. In the alternative view, however, Indian industrial policy has to be more closely integrated with planning policies. This does not mean a reliance only on quantitative allocation regimes. Fiscal and trade policies and investment allocation policies have all to be used and to the extent market forces lead to higher level of efficiencies and provide economical methods of achieving objectives, these should most certainly be adopted, but the central objectives of industrial policy have to be related with the development objectives of the nation. Given the need of structurally modernizing the Indian economy in as quick a period as possible, industrialisation related with improvement in the provision of and spread of infrastructure will need priority. Agro-based industrialisation which integrates employment and value-added generation with a more efficient use of land based products is another focus which will become important as the land constraint becomes more severe. Policies which at the margin encourage improvements in productivity, particularly in core intermediate and infrastructure industries which have significant downstream effects will need highest priority. Apart from a major emphasis on exports, at the current stage of development, policies which provide for an integration of the manufacturing sector with design of the development of backward areas, particularly by encouraging the development of selected growth centres, will need to be encouraged.[4] The point, however, being made is that industrial policies will have to be related with a development strategy and apart from macro policies, will also have to be industry specific. It is at that level that the priorities of a development strategy unfold themselves. Some industries have to be given higher priority than others. In the high priority sectors, technical change has to be strongly supported. Fiscal and trade policies have to orient themselves to this overall framework. Thus, there is an intimate connection between micro-economics and macro-economics. It is not that supply and demand elasticities or effective rates of protection of theories of market clearance, have no relevance in an economy like India. As we shall see, these concepts have to be related with development policy objectives and priorities, rather than being applied in an uncritical neo-classical framework.

If this understanding of industrial developmental problem is correct, public policies will be increasingly concerned with the accentuation of processes of structural and technical change in the Indian industrial growth in lagging regions. The country now has the capability of making a decisive attack on the remaining problems of backwardness and much faster structural change can be expected. Public policies will have to integrate with wider processes of faster and more dispersed growth and technical change. Indian industrial policy cannot, therefore be oriented to mechanical adjustment to world prices and the approximation of free markets. Policy has to be integrated with the objectives of planning through processes of structured adjustment.

Tariff and Pricing Policies

An adjunct of the policy of structured liberalisation through delicensing and abroad banding, has been increased reliance on tariff policies for affective protection and price regulation; as contrasted to direct price control measures. The approach, therefore, has not to be that of mechanical adjustment to international prices but of studies which provide for structured adjustment in priority sectors. Some examples are given below to illustrate such policies.

The Narasimham Committee and recently the Chelliah Committee also suggested an approach towards selected processes of substitution of quantitative restrictions by tariffs. Indian industries which have already achieved a comparative advantage internationally and can face competition can be put on tariff and these tariffs need not be high. The Narasimham Committee also states that there is another group of capital producing units which can survive without very high tariff protection provided they are free from the impact of negative protection. In such cases, initially tariff levels would be high and could be regulated downwards as their handicaps are removed. There are also other important questions of sequencing and phasing. For example inter-related sectors have to be subjected to reform simultaneously and some can be left along at the early stages of reform, since technological support may be of low priority to them. In the case of complex goods, for example, inter-related commodity baskets and their inputs have to be placed in a simultaneous and inter-connected reform strategy. In machine tools and electronics the BICP developed such strategies for product categories (say a type of machine tool) and inputs (special alloys and electronic components). If this is not done firms with conversion efficiency which is internationally competitive could be priced out of the market.

Price Policy and Monopolistic Profits

The purpose of the tariff policy reforms is first to ensure that monopoly profits are not left hindered by a lack of a policy to control them and to give a reasonable degree of effective protection to the domestic industry, particularly in the priority sectors. Take the case of tyres where in the recent import policy, a policy on tariff regulated imports has been suggested. Here the thrust of imports was means to control curtilization behaviour.

The case of the capital goods industry mentioned earlier illustrates the thrust of the policy. Studies, amongst others by the CEI and the World Bank have documented the domestic resources cost (DRC) efficiency of a number of Indian capital goods manufacturers. Domestic resource cost of 19 items of capital goods has been estimated at between 0.91 to –0.87 apart from three cases which ranged between 2.08 to 2.12 (Table 5.1). BICP has published estimates giving most DRCs of capital goods between 0.9 to 1.82. Only in one item is it above 4. [See Rows 1 to 4 of (Table 5.2). However, on account of tariff policies and administered pricing regimes, the Indian capital goods manufacturers according to the World Bank and CEI, buy inputs like steel, special steels and components at higher prices than foreign manufacturers and hence the effective rate of protection is sometimes even negative ranging between 0.99 to –0.78. The implicit tariff on inputs was as high as 95 per cent and in many cases ranged between 50 to 60 per cent. In the light of these findings, and given the fact that cost reduction in sectors like the steel industry takes time, the nominal rate of tariff protection on major machine tool items announced at 85 per cent in the recent budget implies lower effective protection rates. If the disadvantage in terms of input purchases is in the range estimated above, this nominal rate of protection would boil down to effective protection rates between 25 to 50 per cent. The domestic industry will, however, also get the advantage of reduced duty on imports of special quality steels and components of capital goods. More important, import duty on project imports has been raised. It may be noted that other developing countries give high protection to capital goods. For example, work by Edquist and Jacobsson showed that South Korean capital goods manufacturers got high rates of protection.[5]

TABLE 5.1: Price Policy and Allocative Efficiency in Static Framework

(World Bank Estimates of Domestic Resource Cost of Indian Capital Goods)

Cement Mill Crusher	(DRC = 0.73)
Complete 1000 t.p.d. Cement Plant	(DRC = 0.36)
Pulp and Paper Machinery	(DRC = from 0.60 to 0.53
Sugar Manufacturing Machinery	(DRC = from 0.81 to 0.45
Complete sugar plant of 1250 tops	(DRC = from 0.29 to 0.56
Stainless Steel Splitting Column	(DRC = 0.60
Stainless Steel Absorption Tower	(DRC = 0.91
Separator Vessel	(DRC = 0.91
210 MW Boilers	(DRC = 0.84

Source: The World Bank, India : Non-Electrical Industrial Machinery Manufacturing—A Subsector Study (August, 1994).

Another interesting case where tariff protection has been used to regulate domestic prices, is Soda Ash. Here, tariff rates had been broadly regulated so that the efficient domestic manufacturers make a normal rate of profit. The new projects here are in the joint sector.

Price Policy and Technical Change

The general approach to tariff reform in the Indian case, seems to be work out a tariff regulating mechanism at a level such that the efficient Indian producer is given a normal rate of profit and then to nudge industry to move towards efficiency improvements through cost reducing technical change. In that sense, the existing experiments may be conceived of as the first round of continuing policies. It does not seem to be the intention of the policy-makers to cause very large dislocation by policies formulated entirely with a *priori* principles without any consideration of relocation and adjustment costs. This approach can also be illustrated with recent policy changes towards thermoplastics, aluminum, etc. Take thermoplastics as an instance. Recent indepth surveys have estimated the rural consumption of LDPE per caput of the population while lower than in urban areas, is fairly widely distributed amongst different sections of the population ranging around the equivalent of 1 kg. of resin per caput in 1983-84. Similar trends were observed in PVC. Given the population distribution, aggregate rural consumption is roughly equal to urban consumption. Technical change is taking place in the industrial sector and the use of feedstock for the production of ethylene has declined by 10 to 15 per cent

TABLE 5.2: Domestic Resource Cost Ratio

		D.R.C. Ratio
1.	Machine Tools Radial Drill, Surface Grinder, Gear Hobber and C.N.C. Lathe	1.48 — 1.82
2.	Electrical Machinery Boiler 210 MW, Turbo Generator Set, Hydro Turbine and Auto Transformer	1 — 1.32
3.	Mining Machinery Shovel, Crusher 1750, Crusher 1350, Dragline and 0.8 Drill Sash	1.3— 4.8
4.	Fertilizer Machinery Reactor, Heat Exchanger and Iron Ore	0.9 — 1.77
5.	Synthetic Rubber PBR, SBR	
	— (Alcohol route)	2.65 — 1.78
	SBR (Naptha Route)	1.66 — 2.94
6.	Thermo-Plastics	
	LDPE (Film Grade)	0.41 — 0.97
	PP (Injection Moulding)	2.75 — 4.50
	VAM (Actual)	6.27 — 7.55
	GAM (Normative)	1.56 — 1.71
7.	Jute Goods Carpet Backing, Hessian, Sacking, Others, Overall Jute Products	0.78 — 1.16
8.	Truck Tyres	0.80 — 1.25
9.	Mini Steel	1.5
10.	Electronic Capacitors	0.95 to 1.93
11.	Medical Instruments Medical, X-Ray, Industrial X-Ray, Graphic Arts and Roll Films	1.22 — 6.30

Source : S.N. Kaul, Cost Competitiveness of Indian Industry in I.C.W.A.I., Industrial Development Prospects and Retrospect, 1983.

unit of output and by 1 to 4 per cent at subsequent stages of production. Reduction of tariff protection would, therefore, force the domestic suppliers to reduce prices for the very widespread and decentralised thermo-plastics processing centres and should lead to lower prices for consumers. Price elasticity of demand is 1.1. As such, very poor consumers would benefit from this policy. Recent policy changes in this direction can be seen as part of a long-term strategy. The new project producing resin in the public sector Nagotane would be 40 to 50 per cent more efficient in energy use than existing facilities and real costs and prices could, therefore, fall. Let us look into these arguments in some details.

Estimates of income elasticities of demand shown in Table 5.3.

TABLE 5.3: Per Capita Income Elasticity (Cross-Section Data)

Sl. No.	Type	Rural Poverty Line		Urban Poverty Line	
		Above	Below	Above	Below
1.	LDPE	0.893	0.578	0.409	0.457
2.	HDPE	0.805	0.392	0.455	0.601
3.	PP	0.718	0.301	0.424	0.491
4.	Total	0.743	0.391	0.423	0.569
	Total Average		0.567		0.496

Demand for thermoplastics shows low elasticity with respect to income for all resins and all area. The elasticity is highest for the category of Non-Poor Consumers in Rural Areas.

Demand for the resins is probably price-elastic. To estimate the price effects on demand, both time-series and cross-section data can be pooled. Taking the income elasticity of demand figures as given, a new set of per capita consumption of resin figures can be worked out washing out the income effect. The effect of prices of these estimates can be worked out as follows:

1_n (Per Capita Demand = -1.339 $\quad -1.10)_n$ Relative Price
(-0.61) (-1.31)

$R^2 = 0.15$ (Figures in brackets are *t* values)
Relative Price = Price of LDPE — Price of Substitute Products

Price effects, therefore, matter. The price elasticity demand for resins in also brought out by earlier studies which have indicated that the use of reprocessed material for the manufacture of resins is inversely related with the price. Thus, it is quite obvious that the demand for the virgin resin would depend upon the price.

On the supply side, equally dramatic changes are taking place. To begin with, note that the capacity utilisation in the industry is improving. There is also evidence to suggest that the existing producers have invested in energy utilisation investments for the industry and it is quite likely that improvement in energy use to the extent of 15 to 20 per cent per unit of production has already taken place.

The central question is that the expansion of capacity that now in place will be viable and will be realised in the market only if attempts are also made to bring about cost reduction and pass on the benefits of such cost reduction to the consumer. Otherwise, given the income and price elasticities of demand and the behaviour of the Indian consumer, there will be a realisation problem of the scale of petrochemical products in the market only if attempts are also made to bring about cost reduction and past on the benefits of such reduction to the consumer. Recent policy has very correctly stated that the tariff policies for the thermo-plastics sector should be seen as a part of a medium-term policy trend. In short, the attempt is to keep on placing pressure so that the industry benefits low income consumers and the price of this intermediate does not arise.

The thermoplastic processors are a high dispersed industry. It is very important that apart from attempts at technological upgradation, efforts are made to provide the resin to these processors which runs into tens of thousands in sufficient quantity and at a reasonable price. The technological planning of the MGCC and other large projects and the tariff and pricing policies have to be seen as steps in this direction.

Selective liberalisation and structured change of the kind discussed above requires adjustment and strengthening of planning procedures. The emphasis may shift from details of desegregated target shifting to greater concentration on policy issues, but the focus on analysis of policy and strategy options would be more pronounced. Questions of tariff, pricing, licensing and related issues will need to be synchronised with investment planning for core sectors with a major emphasis on modernisation programmes in the Plan. We have already discussed methods like domestic resource cost, effective rates of protection or demand elasticities and the use of numerical magnitudes of these concepts with comparative static policy design. However, it is of importance to appreciate that our policy and developmental problems are essentially of a dynamic nature involving investment and technology choice questions.

Tariff and pricing policies will, therefore, need to be linked up with investment and planning policies. The plan first gives the indications of the differential rates of growth expected from different sectors on account of developmental priorities. Tariff and pricing policies have to be oriented to the achievement of these targets in an efficient manner. Normative pricing is a method of achieving this. But the capital cost of either the expansion of existing plant or of new plants on optimal scale, has to be provided for.

Prices of industrial products must be fixed on the basis of reasonable norms of efficiency and enterprises must be given incentives to internalise the benefits of raising productivity and innovations for reducing costs. The return on capital employed should be determined on the basis of the level required to generate and attract investment funds. This in essence is the concept of the long range marginal cost pricing (LRMC) which is now being strongly endorsed.

A few clarifications may be in order. LRMC pricing takes explicit cognizance of the cost reducing aspect of modernization of fresh 'green field' investments. Second LRMC is not always determined by 'green field' investments, but incremental output arising from modernisation which is in many cases a cheaper option. Third, since this is an economic method of pricing, investments costs are considered inreal terms and returns provided on the basis of the estimated life of the project, rather than financial methods alone being used. Finally the cash flow requirements of servicing borrowing requirements have to be explicitly provided for.

Pricing: Equity and Efficiency — An Example

It would be incorrect to infer that LRMC prices would always be higher. Pricing based on efficient technologies, leads to savings on real costs and paradigms which rely on such methods, would reflect this feature. The real price of cement today in many locations is lower than it was in early 1982. However, LRMC pricing to be made effective in a market economy would need economic policy interventions through tariff policies, taxation policies and even dual pricing schemes. The use of dual pricing would require that the 'free' and 'controlled' market proportions could be regulated in such a manner as to cover the long range marginal cost of an efficient producer. This would neatly provide incentives to producers to expand output to the levels 'planned' for and also permit equity objectives to be not on consumer side.

It is therefore being advocated that the stage has now been reached far more actively integrating pricing and tariff policies with the development plans. In fact questions of technology policies are one aspect of this question. Let us return back to the cement example. The economist needs to study technical factors more closely. The large differences between energy consumption between wet and dry plants in terms of G/cal per tonne of OPC through different technologies are shown in Table 5.4.

The pricing policy for cement developed in 1982 provided that the realization to the cement producer should cover the LRMC of the dry process plants either through modernization, expansion or fresh investment. Note that the LRMC is fact in a Supply Curve. If the demand price elasticities are correctly specified, it will always be possible to work out a levy/non-levy share, so that the producer covers the LRMC. The elasticity of energy consumption to capacity utilization was estimated as

TABLE 5.4: Variation of Wt. Av. Consumption of Thermal Energy

Sl. No.	Process Employed	Variation of Wt. Av. Consumption of Thermal Energy (G. Cal/t) through time					
		1978-79	1979-80	1980-81	1981-82	1982-83	1983-84
0	1	2	3	4	5	6	7
1.	Wet	1.652	1.683	1.662	1.591	1.666	1.657
2.	Dry	1.069	1.083	1.079	1.005	1.079	1.977
3.	All Plants	1.390	1.414	1.393	1.313	1.298	1.330

–0.6 with from level data for the period 1981-1983. Thus a 10 per cent increase in capacity utilisation leads to a 6 per cent fall in energy use.

Notice that with this pricing mechanism, there is a powerful incentive to increase capacity utilisation since realisation at the margin (open market price) will be higher than the average (determined by levy price). Capacity utilisation increase led to tremendous improvement in energy use. In the GICP energy audit, for all plants taken together that relationship is econimatrically estimated as follows:

(i) Log Electrical Power (kWh)/tonne = 9.3848-1.083 Log (Capacity Utilisation %)

(ii) Log Thermal Power (G. Cal)/tonne = 3.125 -0.6431 Log (Capacity Utilisation %)

Thus a 10 per cent increase in capacity utilisation leads to a 10.28 per cent decrease in electrical power consumption per tonne of cement. If the power rate is 60 paise per unit, this means a saving or Rs. 28.07 crore to the economy with an estimated cement production of 35 million tonnes. Similarly a 10 per cent increase in capacity utilisation leads to a 6.43 per cent decrease in thermal power consumption to the economy. Improved capacity utilisation is a powerful tool of energy conservation. A 10 per cent improvement in capacity utilisation will lead to a saving of 85 MW of power capacity and 7.12 lakh tonnes of total annually.

In this dual pricing alogorithm, however, if the shape of levy and non-levy demand curves are known, the levy/non-levy proportions can be set to ensure the LRMC realisation on the average. Radhkrishna has estimated econometrically that in the model:

$$\log D = \log a + b \log y + c \log p$$

where
D = Demand for cement
Y = Income
F = Price

the price elasticity of demand was in the range —(0.35 to 0.37), for non-levy cement.

The impact of capacity utilisation on energy efficiency in 17 fertilizer plants was also econormatrically rested. To estimate variation in energy consumption with the variation in capacity utilisation, six equations, given below were fitted:-

1. $Y = A + B x$
2. $Y = A + B \log x$
3. $Y = A + B/x$
4. $\text{Log } Y = A + B \log x$
5. $\text{Log } Y = A + B x$
6. $\text{Log } Y = A + B/x$

whereby
Y = Energy consumption in million kilo calories, and
x = Capacity utilisation in percentage. Data of Energy consumption and capacity utilisation and quarter for the period 1978-79 to 1982-83. Plant-wise results are shown in Table 5.5.

For the fertilizer, industry feedstock variation capacity use can be expected to be the major cost discriminating categories. Also to properly discriminate for annual input price changes, time dummies were introduced for each of the years for which cost data was collected. The variables Dm to Dp were introduced below to take care of the years 1978-79 to 1981-82. The statistical relations which best discriminated the cost behaviour of the plants studied in to homogeneous categories could be stated as follows:-

$$
\begin{array}{lllll}
VC = & 2432.92 & + \; 941.26\,Dp & + \; 708.26\,DN + & 773.64\,DC \\
 & (14.77) & (5.98) & (6.28) & (3.05) \\
 & -\; 10.28Cu & -\; 1384.59\,D_m & -\; 1357.89\,Dn & \\
 & (4.93) & (10.12) & (10.48) & \\
 & -\; 901.97\,Do & -\; 299.63\,Dp & & \\
 & (6.94) & (2.50) & & \\
 & R^{-2} & = \; 0.76 & & \\
IC = & 4351.24 & + \; 1518.46\,DF & + \; 774.45\,DN + & 3305.88 \\
 & (22.11) & (4.42) & (3.15) & (5.98)
\end{array}
$$

TABLE 5.5:Energy Use and Capacity Utilisation in 17 Fertilizer Plants

	Best Fitted Equation			r	Equation
	(1)			(2)	(3)
1.	Log Y	=	3.320-0.006x	0.56	5
2.	Y	=	40.06-5.749 Log X	0.81	2
3.	Log Y	=	3.261-0.005 X	0.61	5
4.	Y	=	18.840-2.132 Log X	0.78	2
5.	Log Y	=	3.065 + 21.72/x	0.95	6
6.	Y	=	44.234-6.772	0.94	2
7.	Log Y	=	4.149.0.340 Log X	0.55	4
8.	Log Y	=	2.673-0.102 X	0.52	5
9.	Log Y	=	5.051-0-5 Log X	0.58	
10.	Y	=	39.20-23 Log X	0.40	
11.	Y	=	38.827-618 LogX	0.96	
12.	No Relation				
13.	Log Y	=	3.187.0.007 X	0.58	5
14.	No Relation				
15.	Y	=	54.526-8.829 Log X	0.94	2
16.	Y	=	16.389-0.0556 X	0.85	
17.	Log Y	=	2.39+34.05	0.75	6
	X				

Note : Though we have chosen equation with highest value of r^2 it does not mean that other equations do not fit well. In many cases we are getting values of r^2 which are in the close range. We have chosen the one which gives the highest value of r^2.

— 27.58 Cu	— 1700.40 Dn	1708.41 Dn	– 1012.14 Dn
(6.07)	(5.69)	(6.02)	(3.57)
— 627.68 Dp		DF 20.70	
(2.40)			

The base case herc in gas based plants for 1982-83. Notice both the relations and each one of the variable is highly significant.

TC = Total Cost /Rs. per tonne of ammonia, Dn = 1 for 1978-79 onc = O, otherwise. Similarly Dn = 1 for 1979-80, Do = 1 for 1980-81 and Dp = 1 for 1981=82. Thc base case is gas based for 1982-83. (VC is Variable Cost/Rs. per tonne of amounts, DF=1, for fuel oil plants, and = 0 otherwise similarly DR=Dummy for naphtha, DC=Dummy for coal gassification, D=Dummy for partial oxidation, Ca=Capacity levels, Cu=Capacity utilisation rates.

In fertilizers, thermoplastics, fibers and the related inputs (DMT, Caprolactum, etc.) reform has been slow on account of the inability of the policy-makers to bit at the super profits of domestic monopolists. It is easier to cut fertilizer subsidies to farmers than to curtail the profits of large companies. Similarly reform in industries like sugar has been non-existent although will designed packages exist and has been slow and hesitant in agro-input industries.

Agricultural Price Policy

There are four questions to which we address ourselves. We note, to begin with, that the basic objective of agricultural price policy in India will be to provide support to the farmer in improving productivity and output growth, particularly in lagging regions and to balance this with the interest of the por households who are puchasers of cereals. The dilemmas this leads to are addressed elsewhere and I do not propose to go through them here. The first point we note is the need to bring quality considerations into play in agricultural price policy. The second consideration is the whole question of agricultural price policy in deficit regions. The third aspect is the need to support commercialisation of agriculture in dry land areas. Finally, there is the question of input price rationalisation. We briefly comment on each.

It is heartening to note that the Government has accepted the recommendation of the APC and later the CACP to increase the price differentials in paddy. In some States of India, more than 40 per cent of the area is under high yielding superfine paddy (PR series). Market price differentials were over 60 per cent but the procurement price was only marginally higher than that of coarse varieties. The farmer must benefit from demand patterns of this products and must be rewarded for such efforts.

As regards inter-regional price differentials, a proposal on the APC needs serious consideration. It is as follows:

"A peculiar feature of the wheat economy is the localised nature of supply particularly marketable surplus, in relation to demand. The Commission reiterates that a uniform national procurement price needs to be continued as creation of a national market encourages crop specialisation and optimal use of nation's land resources. The price structure of wheat indicates that in the deficit regions the worwed between the farm harvest and lean season prices is much higher than in the surplus regions. Transport cost only explain a part of these differences which in no small measure are due to the weakness of public marketing agencies in ensuring purchase channels, marketing support and other infrastructural facilities which are least developed in these regions. To ensure price support to the farmer in the peak marketing season, to even out inter-seasonal price differentials (the advantage of which presently accrue to private trade) and to increase the possibilities of enhancement of public stocks, the Commission recommends that the feasibility of public sector agencies conducting market operations in the deficit regions should be examined by the Government".[7]

An aspect of Indian agriculture which needs to be more carefully studied is the fact that some dry land agriculture regions are showing relatively high value added per worker. Thus after Punjab and Haryana, States like Gujarat and Karnataka which have very low irrigation intensities are showing relatively high value added per worker. These regions have benefited from concentrating on "high valued" crops. Behind these "trends" however, is probably organisational and institutional systems, which have led to successful commercialisation of agriculture, including relatively successful cooperative marketing systems. Improved price support operations for commercial crops and strengthened marketing systems, are important aspects of the strategy of reducing the uncertainty of dryland agriculture and internalising the benefits of the available technologies. These policies will have to be an important part of the overall strategy as Indian agriculture moves over to a more regionally diversified phase, from its earlier favoured crop-region pattern.

The Task Force on the Special Foodgrains Production Programme recommended pricing strategies to meet the objectives of cheaper inputs to farmers, rather than direct subsidies. In inputs like pesticides and seeds, subsidies can become a method of supporting inefficient production units (high cost technical grade manufacturers or formulators) or high cost distributors in cooperative, state or private sectors, and the benefit may not go to the farmers. Thus subsidies can support high cost pesticide supply or seed prices say higher than Rs. 450 per quintal. With a price rationalisation scheme the farmer gets[8] the benefit straight away. Thus the agricultural sector now needs to get the same kind of policy attention that the industrial was getting in the early years of the Seventh Plan in terms of policy and delivery system reform.

Conclusion

The essence of Indian planning methodology is a search for strategies and instruments for growth and redistributive justice. Apart from the quantitative dimensions of the work, the strategic aspects have related to the perception of dominating constraints and available opportunities in a sequential development process. The essence of the search of the early Indian planners for development strategies which would relocate resources to preferred sectors and regions still has to continue since low productivity employment is a part of the Indian economic configuration. Yet the increasing complexity of the economy and its development process in the agricultural and industrial sectors is calling for more disaggregated and detailed sectoral planning and policy strategies. Our main emphasis has been that pricing policy should be a part of a planning strategy and that both go together. The challenge of policy is to harmonise the two.

REFERENCES

1. See Lal Jayawaradena, Director, World Institute of Development Economic Research's Preface to Yoginder K. Alagh, *Indian Development Planning and Policy,* Vikas, 1991, for a statement of the problem. Also see Lance Taylor's description of this aspect in *Ibid,* p. 15.
2. For a description of alternative paths in the late Eighties, see Lance Taylor, *The Rocky Road to Reform,* M.I.T., 1992.
3. For a description of alternative views on Indian industrial policy, see I.J. Ahluwalia, 'The Role of Policy in Industrial Development', in P.R. Brahmananda and V.R. Panchmukhi (ed.), *The Development Process of the Indian Economy,* Bombay, Himalaya, 1987, pp. 388-419.
4. See S. Gangopadhyay and O. Goswami, *Capital Goods and Project Imports,* CEI, 1986.
5. C. Edquist and S. Jacobsson, 'Production of Hydraulic Excavators and Machining Centres in India and the Republic of Korea: State Policies, Firm Performance and Firm Strategies'. ICSSR/SAREC Symposium, New Delhi, 1985, pp. 44, in Y.K. Alagh (ed.), *Industrialisation and Technological Alternatives,* New Delhi ICSSR, Forthcoming.
6. IC = Total Cost/Rs. per tonne of ammonia, Dm=1 for 1978/79 one = 0, otherwise. Similarly Dn = 1 for 1979/80, Do = 1 for 1980/81 and Dp = 1 for 1981/82. The base case is *gas based* for 1982/83. VC is Variable Cost/Rs. per tonne of ammonia, DF=1, for fuel oil plants, and = 0 otherwise similarly DN=Dummy for naphtha, Dc=Dummy for coal *gassification,* DF=Dummy or *partial oxidation,* Ca=Capacity levels, Cu=Capacity utilisation rates).
7. APC, Government of India, *Report on Price Policy for Crops Sown in the 1982/83 Season,* p. 23.
8. Based on the recommendation of the Task Force, the Finance Minister in the Budget Speech of 1989 indicated that "government is going to ask the fertilizer companies, in both public and private sectors, to give a discount of 7.5 per cent over notified prices for coming Kharif and Rabi sowings. This will reduce the price of a bag of Urea by around eight rupees and eighty paise. The companies should be able to absorb the cost of this

discount through better inventory managment." The Finance Minister in 1989 indicated full exemption from excise duty for a large number of pesticide intermediates. Further, reduction of customs duty in respect of a number of pesticides and pesticide intermediates from the existing levels of 100 per cent and 147 per cent to 70 per cent and 60 per cent *ad valorem.*

Similarly, import of fungicides, weedicides and insecticides was permitted uner OGL as recommended by the Task Force. This covers Isoproturon, Benzene Hexachloride, Endosulfon, Malathion, Dimethoate, 2, 4-D, Managanese Ethylene, Bis Dithicarbarmate (Maneb), Methyl Parathion, Monocrotophos, Phorate, TMT (thiram), Dithane, Butachlor and Benthocarb. These could be imported by Indian Farmers Fertilizer Cooperative (IFFCO), Krishak Bharati Cooperative (Kribhco) and State Agro Industries Corporation, for stock and sale. Industry pressure reversed these policies in 1990 and they have again been introduced in a milder form in the 1992 budget, indicating the pressure of interest groups.

6. POPULATION POLICY IN INDIA : A Review

G. Giridhar

1. Introduction

Public policy on population cannot ignore the micro-level socio-economic and cultural conditions and processes governing decision-making on family size. Population growth takes place in households and hence macro-level orientation does not help us understand the factors influencing family size decisions. Families have a certain number of children which they determine as suitable and necessary for them. Population policies, translated into programme activities, can enable families to change this number and achieve the desired size.

Broadly two types of public policies are formulated—(a) influencing policies, and (b) responsive policies. Since family formation practice is very personal to the couple, it was recognised that the influencing policies should be built on principle of voluntarism and not coercion. Where deep-rooted convictions prevail, the task is very challenging. In such a scenario, public policies give a broad framework in support of efforts to develop family size norms.

India has a long history of introducing public policy interventions to influence households to plan their family size. Starting from 1952, when India became the first country to have an official population control programme, a number of developments have taken place in terms of infrastructure, programme coverage, mix of methods, modes of service delivery etc. With increasing complexity of the programme, its implementation continues to be a major challenge. It is argued that piggy-backing family planning programme with the health centres is an efficient infrastructure but has resulted in unnecessary medicalisation of our approach.

This paper reviews the evolution of India's population policy. This is followed by a review of implementation experiences and institutional arrangements. Some suggestions on future course of action are also made. Throughout this paper, the emphasis is on management of population programme, and not on recounting quantitative performance levels. Also, the context of Population Policy in this paper is limited to family planning only.

2. Origin of Population Policy

Individuals and groups have contributed to India's population policy over last several years. In 1916, Prof. P.K. Wattal published a book titled *The Population Problems in India,* Prof. Karve opened the first ever birth control clinic in Pune. The Family Planning Society was formed in 1940 and Family Planning Association of India in 1949. The National Planning Committee, in its resolution in 1940 said, "In the interest of social economy, family happiness and national planning, family planning and a limitation of children are essential and the state should adopt a policy to encourage these". The Bhore Committee in 1943 also advocated deliberate limitation of family size.

The First Five-Year Plan (1950-55) called for an explicit population policy and considered family planning as a step towards improvement in health of mothers and children. All subsequent five-year plans continued to emphasize the need to reduce population growth rates. In fact, from Fourth plan onwards, quantitative targets with respect to birth rate have been indicated for the plan period. In 1979, a Working Group on Population Policy set up by the Planning Commission, recommended the goal of Net Reproduction Rate of one, to be achieved by 1996 for the country as a whole and by 2001 in all states. This translates to (a) average family size of 2.3 children (from 4.2 in 1978); (b) birth rate of 21 (from 32); (c) death rate of 9 (from 14); (d) Couple Protection Rate of 60 per cent (from 21 per cent) and (e) Infant Mortality Rate of 60 per 100 live births (from 129 in 1978). The expert committee pointed out that, if all of the above can be done, our population will be around 900 million by the turn of the century and will stabilize at 1200 millions by A.D. 2050.

A National Population Policy statement was released by the government in April 1976 which emphasised that reducing population growth rate is the top national priority. It further stated that to wait for education and economic development to bring about a drop in fertility is not a practical solution and that public opinion was favourable to accept stringent measures for family planning. The aftermath of compulsory sterilization drives linked to the above policy statement is a distinct point in the country's population policy scenario.

In June 1977, the new government formulated a revised Population policy, stressing the voluntary nature of the programme and viewing it as an integral part of education, health, maternal and child health etc. During this time, the name of the programme also changed from Family Planning to Family Welfare. The 1977 policy should not be seen as an effort to water-down our emphasis on family planning. In fact it reiterated the programme thrust, minus any form of compulsion. The 1977 statement endorsed the previous policy on increasing age at marriage, allocation of central funds to the states based on fixed population figures and family planning performance. The birth rate target of 25 per 1000 population was also reaffirmed.

The Expert Committee recommendation (NRR=1 by A.D. 2001) still remains the guiding number for our population programme. Over the years, the time horizon kept shifting backwards, based on actual performance of the programme since the committee made its recommendations. The National Health Policy of 1982 has also formally adopted these recommendations as the long term demographic goal of the country. The 1986 version of India's Population Policy views family planning in a broader perspective of child survival, women's status and employment, literacy and anti-poverty efforts. The policy calls for increasing age at marriage, postpone the birth of the first child, increasing birth intervals and concentrating on child survival.

In 1991, the Ministry of Health and Family Welfare decided to impart a "new dynamism" to the programme by devising innovative strategies. This led to the development of an Action Plan for revamping family welfare programmes in India. The Plan emphasises the need to improve the quality of services and to devise special area-specific strategies. It calls for micro-level planning; priority filling of vacant positions, construction of subcentres and ICDS centres; improved management training and active involvement of district administration.

Specifically, the Action Plan consists of the following elements:

1. National consensus backed by political commitment, supported by religious and other opinion leaders at different levels,
2. Improvement of the quality and outreach of services, leading to consolidation of existing infrastructure, improved motivation, training and supervision,
3. Special strategy for 90 lagging districts with special efforts in micro-level planning, filling up of vacant posts, priority for

construction of service centres, intensive training, effective communication efforts, linkage with other related agencies and more active involvement of district administration,

4. Improved coverage of younger age couple with spacing methods; removal of certain incentive schemes which tend to distort the programme and design an innovative package of incentives and disincentives and community-based incentives are to be encouraged,
5. Promoting a wider contraceptive method-mix social marketing and community-based distribution systems will be developed and free distribution system will be gradually curtailed and new method introduction and related research efforts will be encouraged,
6. UIP and MCH services need to be strengthened, through active surveillance, effective investigation of adverse reactions from vaccines, better supervision and cold chain maintenance, improved diarrhoea management and implementation of CSSM programme,
7. Attention to urban schemes, involvement of NGOs to provide services in urban slums and better management of urban institutions,
8. Recruitment of female health guides and if this is not feasible, there will be a need to examine other alternatives,
9. Thorough review of ANM/LHV training schools and gradual phasing out of non-functional units, and net working arrangements of training institutions at different levels will be developed,
10. Revitalisation of IEC inputs; strengthening of Mahila Swasthya Sangh; more attention to folklore, traditional art fairs, field publicity, decentralised production of media material and training of IEC staffs (a specific mention of Rajasthan efforts in this direction has been made),
11. Active involvement of voluntary organisations, cooperatives, trade unions, Zilla Parishads, municipal corporations, panchayats and other organised sector institutions, and
12. Development of institutional mechanism for intersectoral coordination. Population Commissions may be set up at central, state and lower levels to facilitate it.

3. Scope of Population Policy

Policy is usually a broad statement of intentions. The Population Policy, however, goes beyond intentions and specifies levels of achievement by a certain specified period. Hence this is both time-bound and target oriented. Subsequent documents such as 5-year plans and the Action Plan to revamp the programme have given several implementation guidelines as well. In addition, implementation of other policies on age at marriage, child labour, compulsory education and social welfare are essential complements to the population policy. The National Health Policy is administratively and substantively related to the population policy since fertility and health of mother and child are directly related and family planning and health policy is administratively and substantively related to the population policy, since fertility and health delivery systems are integrated at the operational level.

Experience in implementation of MCH/FP services indicates that larger allocations are required to run the programme more effectively. A large part of the budget goes for non-plan expenditures, including staff salaries, leaving very little for enhancement of delivery systems. External assistance in the form of Area Development Projects have been extremely useful in supplementing government resources. At present 67 districts in 15 states are covered under these projects, with a total outlay of about 1000 crores. These projects have also suffered due to several administrative bottlenecks and lack of strong implementation mechanism.

Policy-making, however, should not be limited to broad statements of intentions. It should address several interrelated activities such as population data collection, research, dissemination, policy formulation, policy planning, policy implementation and evaluation (Fig. 6.1). Data collection and analysis relevant for policy revisions have always a scope for improvement in India. Utilization of research to formulate policies and activities have also lagged behind. It has been argued that government is not sufficiently interested in promoting or encouraging policy analysis and does not attempt seriously to act upon the results of analysis. There are also arguments that the academic community is ignorant of working of the government and tend to make impractical suggestions. Perhaps the truth lies in between.

Policy planning involves application of population information and research findings by policy-makers to improve or design new policies. Knowledge of efficacy of different kinds of population interventions is basic to policy planning. Implementation experiences and evaluation of interventions are necessary for this purpose. For this reason, it is often said that if policy makers are closely familiar with field realities, their policy interventions are likely to be the most appropriate.

The gap between policy intentions and implementation realities has

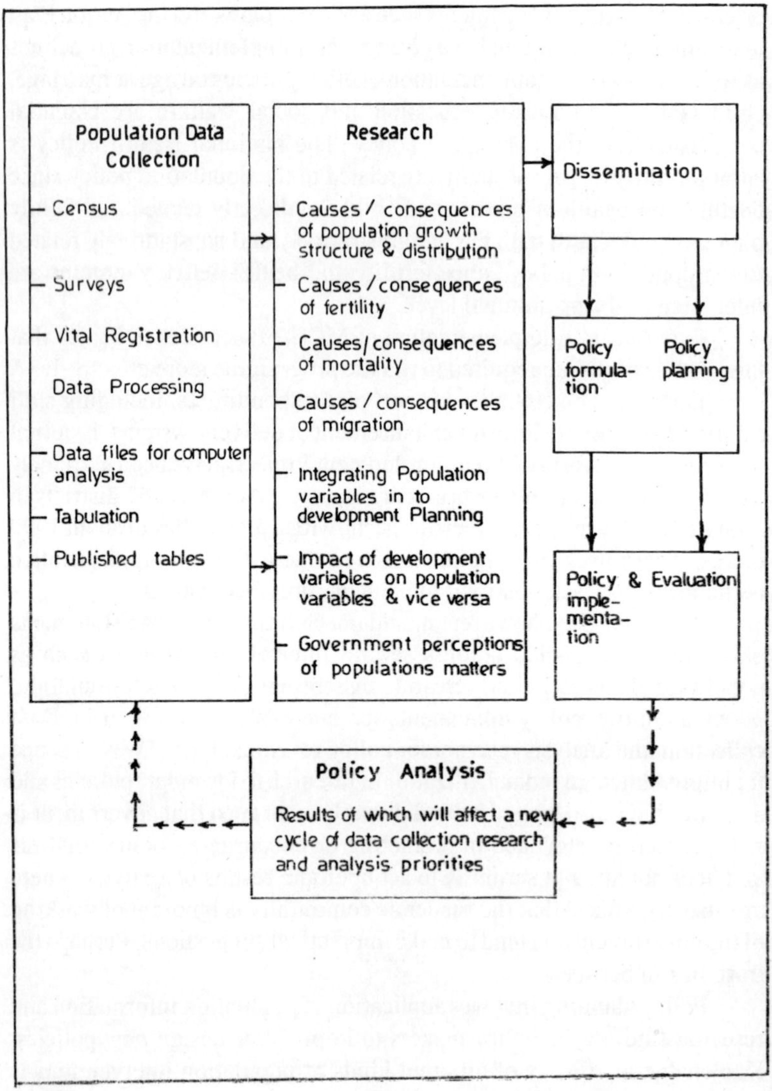

FIG. 6.1 : Inter Related Activities in Population-making

to be closely watched and minimized by the implementing agencies. It is often not practical to assume that the Department of Family Welfare of MOHFW is solely responsible for family planning performance. This department is administratively responsible but it is difficult to put the entire burden on one department, particularly when education, employment, social welfare and status of women are crucial influencing factors.

The Action Plan points out that the government departments of Health and Family Welfare essentially supply family welfare services. The demand for these services is, however, influenced by female literacy, age at marriage, status of women, their gainful employment, social security etc. All of these are beyond the scope of activities of the departments of Family Welfare. Therefore, a mechanism for inter-sectoral coordination of relevant departments needs to be built-up through a suitable institutional mechanism.

4. Programme Infrastructure and Strategy

The programme strategy included in various five year plans was directed towards increasing the quantity of services and at the same time decreasing regional imbalances. During the Fifth Five Year Plan (1974-79), a package of minimum services was introduced and at the same time the objective was decreasing regional imbalances. During the Fifth Five Year Plan (1974-79), a package of minimum services in rural areas was evolved, consisting of health, education, rural housing, rural roads, nutrition, public distribution system and primary health care services. The norms of health infrastructural facilities are:

1. One village health guide for every village for an average of 1000 rural population,
2. One trained dai for every village by training indigenous practising dais, with ultimate objective to train all the Traditional Birth Attendants (dais) in rural areas,
3. One sub-centre with one male and one female MPW for every 5000 rural population in general and for every 3000 population in hilly and tribal areas,
4. One male and one female health assistant for supervising the work of every four sub-centres,
5. One PHC either by conversion of the existing rural dispensary or establishing new units for every 30,000 rural population in general and for every 20,000 population in tribal and hilly areas, and

6. One Community Health Centre for 10,00,000 population by providing additional inputs either in one of the existing primary health centres or in the referral hospitals already functioning below district level.

As of March 1992, the country had 130,219 subcentres functioning, of which 53,822 (41%) have constructed buildings. Of these buildings, 10,993 (20%) were constructed under Area Projects. In early 1950s, India had only 725 Primary Health Centres and no subcentres. Over the years, the infrastructure has increased several folds.

In spite of these developments, we are still below the norms of infrastructural facilities indicated above. A large number of subcentres function without a female worker and some PHCs operate without full-time doctors. There is a need to pay more attention to staff recruitment, placement, training and human resource development.

The Indian population programme is predominantly target oriented. Targets are set centrally by the Planning Commission, in consultation with the Ministry of Health and Family Welfare. They are then systematically broken down to the states, districts, Primary Health Centres and Subcentres. Every worker is given a target quota for sterilization, other spacing methods, immunization and other MCH care. A large part of programme performance is achieved through special campaigns mostly for sterilisations. Incentives are given to service providers, motivators and acceptors. About 15 to 20 per cent of family welfare funds go towards incentive payments.

The delivery system has a 3 tier structure starting with subcentres in villages, Primary Health Centres in blocks and Community Health Centres in districts. Through these centres, all demand generation activities and contraceptive delivery take place. Demand generation is dependent on IEC inputs, which require communication needs' assessment, audience research, creation, motivation and acceptance process. The demand generated by these efforts has to be met with a good quality of service that attracts people to begin to use and continue to use. Studies indicate that for spacing methods, continuation of use is often more important than recruitment of new users. And there is no better motivator than a satisfied user. Judith Bruce (1990)[1] defines quality in family planning programmes with respect to the following six elements:

1. Choice of methods
2. Information given to clients
3. Technical competence of the providers

4. Interpersonal relations between the providers and clients
5. Mechanisms to encourage continuity, and
6. Appropriate delivery of services that are convenient and acceptable to clients.

Using the above framework and available information on quality, Anrudh Jain (1992)[2] makes the following five propositions which have substantial policy implications:

1. Providing choice of methods will increase effectiveness of family planning programmes.
2. Providing choice of methods will increase contraceptive prevalence.
3. Taking individuals' needs and preferences into account while prescribing a method can increase its continuity of use.
4. Recruiting a small number of acceptors and taking good care of them is a better strategy than trying to recruit a large number of acceptors whose needs can not be met by the programme.
5. Follow the individual/women/couple and not any particular method.

5. What is Ahead

A Policy is a general statement of intent, but is often identified by its effect rather its intent. Policy statements are expected to guide allocation of resources, give directions for action and instruments necessary to achieve desired objectives. The process by which policies are formulated and suggested is one aspect of intent. The other is the programme thrust and the project activities from which policy-makers are responsible. Programming starts with a situation analysis. This will help identify priority problems and broad lines of action. This is followed by specific activities needed, their coverage, targets, timing etc. so that necessary resources can be estimated and allocated.

The Policy, the programmes, and various projects are all linked to each other. For example, the Area Development Projects are derived from the Model Plan which in turn is an expression of the policy thrust in increasing accessibility of service centres. This linkage may need review and strengthening.

In spite of massive budgetary support and infrastructural development, the performance of family welfare programme has not improved at a commensurate pace and level. While contraceptive prevalence has increased, the expected decline in birth rate has not occurred. Heavy emphasis on sterilisation and improper selection of acceptors are two possible reasons for lack of demographic impact. In recent years, the government has indicated a shift in its implementation policy from excessive emphasis on terminal method to more balanced method mix, focussing on younger couples and on spacing. This top level shift has not created much impact at the implementation level. The Eighth Plan Directional Paper (approved by National Development Council) includes the following:

a) Convergence of services provided by various social services by pooling resources from other related schemes, integrating them structurally and evolving mechanisms for planning, implementing and monitoring such integrated programme activities,
b) Decentralised planning and implementation, based on area-specific needs and targets will be fixed and monitored at district level, with a process of building from below,
c) Greater involvement of people through Panchayati Raj systems and limiting Centre's role to general policy formulation, coordination and providing technical inputs,
d) Increased attention on younger couples, spacing methods, child survival and safe motherhood, and
e) Improved quality of services.

A policy statement should also include the "how" part in broad terms. Details can be worked out later, in conformity with the policy guidelines. Specific areas for study may be identified, to be conducted by Task Forces appointed for this purpose. These may be short studies to suggest policy options, all of which can be coordinated and deliberated upon by a larger body.

REFERENCES

1. Bruce, Judith (1990), "Fundamental Elements of Quality of Care: A Simple Framework", Studies in Family Planning, 21, 2: 61-91.
2. Jain, Anrudh (1992), Definition and Impact of Quality, Kumarian Press.

7. POPULATION POLICY

Rajni Razdan

From ancient times numbers have been important, especially as agriculture was labour intensive and manpower extremely important. With civilizations industrializing and modern medical science growing, the decline in the death rate without a concomitant decline in the birth rate brought the warnings of population as a public policy issue. However, most countries of the world do not have a population policy agenda for themselves.

India was one of the earliest countries to launch an officially sponsored fertility control programme in the First Five Year Plan in 1951. Thereafter, every successive Plan has had greater fund allocation for Family Planning with a larger target group being covered. The 1871 census showed a growth rate of 2.25 per cent and the 1981 census showed that between 1971-81, the growth of population in India was the highest ever recorded in the history of the country.

In June 1975, there was emergency in the country. The 20-Point Programme was introduced giving prominence to population control. The Constitution of India was amended by the 42nd Amendment to include Family Planning in the Concurrent List. Family Planning was compulsorily enforced by the administration, by the political masters and the number of sterilizations rose from 1.3 million in 1974-75 to 2.6 million in 1975-76 to 8.1 million in 1976-77 (Shah Commission Third Report, 1978:207), a level which has never been attained or attempted since. The electorate reacted sharply and the Congress party lost badly in the 1977 Lok Sabha elections. Thereafter, successive Governments in power at the Centre have tackled the population policy with extreme caution. Though the population of India continues to soar, yet the population control policy remains in a low key and shows more failure than success.

Today in India the population explosion is perhaps the single most pressing problem. The ever growing population has eroded to an extent the achievements on the economic front. While the availability of better health services and improved nutritional standards have helped bring down the death rate considerably, the birth rate continues to be high. The need for a determined effort to bring down the birth rate cannot, therefore, be over-emphasised.

India's population which was 342 million in 1947 has touched 846.3 million according to the 1991 census. On 2.4 per cent of the land area, India is supporting more than 16 per cent of the world population. The population of India is increasing by about 17 million every year. Such a large population would be virtually unmanageable despite the best efforts as it would put great strain on all the public utilities, land and foodgrains.

The average annual exponential growth rate in 1981-91 came down to 2.14 per cent (Table 7.1). The latest available Sample Registration System (SRS) data indicates the annual natural growth rate of 1.95 per cent in 1991 (See Annexure).

TABLE 7.1: Average Annual Exponential Growth Rate

Census Period	Average Annual Exponential Growth Rate (%)
1901-11	0.56
1911-21	(-) 0.03
1921-31	1.04
1931-41	1.33
1941-51	1.25
1951-61	1.96
1961-71	2.20
1971-81	2.22
1981-91	2.14

The long-term demographic goal according to the National Health Policy (1983) is to achieve a Net Reproduction Rate of Unity (NRR-1) by the year A.D. 2000. This corresponds to achieving a birth rate of 21 per thousand, death rate of 9 per thousand and natural population growth rate of 1.2 per cent. The National Health Policy also envisages reducing infant mortality rate to below 60 per thousand live births by the turn of the century.

The Seventh Plan Document visualised that the goal of reaching NRR-1 may be achievable only by 2006-11 A.D. The table below indicates the current levels of achievement with reference to the demographic goals for the Seventh Plan and long-term goals enunciated in the National Health Policy (1983) (in Table 7.2).

TABLE 7.2: Demographic Goals for Seventh Plan and Long-term Goals Enunciated in the National Health Policy 1983

	Indicator	Goals End of 7th Plan (1989)	2000 A.D.	Achievement 1984 (prior to 7th Plan)	Achievement 1991
a)	Crude birth Rate (per 1000 popn)	29.1	21.0	33.9	29.3
b)	Crude death Rate (per 1000 popn)	10.4	9.0	12.6	9.8
c)	Natural Growth Rate (%)	1.87	1.2	2.13	1.95
d)	Infant mortality (per 1000 live births)	90	below 60	104	80
e)	Couple Protection Rate (%)	42	60	31.3 (31.3.85)	43.5 (31.3.92)

As stated in the Eighth Five Year Plan Document the NRR-I would be achievable only by A.D. 2011-16.The goals set for the Family Welfare Programme under the Eighth Plan are as under:

TABLE 7.3: The Goals Set for the Family Welfare Programme Under the Eighth Plan

	Indicator	Goals to be achieved by the end of the 8th plan
a)	Crude Birth Rate (per 1000 population)	26.0
b)	Infant mortality Rate (per 1000 live births)	70
c)	Couple Protection Rate	56%

By A.D. 2035 India's population would be 1.545 billion as against China's population of 1.516 billion (Medium Variant Projection by U.N., assuming NRR-1 for India by A.D. 2020-25). According to this projection, India's population would stabilize at the size of 1.949 billion by A.D. 2150. China would have 1.389 billion, indicating that China's population is expected to decline after reaching 1.521 billion in A.D. 2025. A statement showing the projected population for India, China and the world up to A.D. 2150 is given in Table 7.4.

TABLE 7.4: Comparative Population Projection

Year	Projection Population (Millions)		
	India	China	World
1950	358	555	2518
1990	853	1139	5292
2000	1042	1299	6261
2025	1442	1513	8504
2050	1699	1521	10019
2075	1820	1451	10840
2100	1870	1405	11106
2125	1931	1395	11391
2150	1949	1389	11543

(*Source:* World Population Projections, Two centuries of population Growth, 1950-2150; U.N. 1992)

Even though the Family Planning/Welfare Programme has been pursued in the country since 1951, there are marked variations in its impact from State to State. States like Goa, Kerala and Tamil Nadu with crude birth rates of 16.8, 18.1 and 20.7 respectively have performed well. On the other hand, the crude birth rates in Assam (30.9), Bihar (30.5), Haryana (33.1), Madhya Pradesh (35.8), Rajasthan (34.3) and Uttar Pradesh (35.1) are higher than the national average of 29.3 per thousand population in 1991. Similar variation are seen in respect of the infant mortality rates. At one end of the spectrum, Kerala has on IMR only 17 per thousand live births whereas it is as high as 122 in Madhya Pradesh and 126 in Orissa. The total fertility rates in Bihar (5.1), Haryana (4.4), Madhya Pradesh (4.7), Rajasthan (4.7) and U.P. (5.2) are significantly higher than the All-India average of 3.9 (SRS:1989). Therefore, the poor performing States would have to make special efforts to bring about improvement in their performance and improve the quality of health and family welfare services.

The death rates have declined over the last 90 years from over 40 per thousand population to 9.8 in 1991. The IMR at 80 per thousand live births in 1991 is still comparatively high though it has declined from 110 in 1981. Life expectancy at birth has shown a remarkable increase from 32 years in 1941-51 to 58.6 years in 1986-91. Undoubtedly the massive investments in health, sanitation, water supply etc. have directly contributed to this steep fall in the death rate.

The achievement in fertility reduction has been significant. The Total Fertility Rate (TFR) is 3.8 (1990 SRS) children per woman as against 5.97 in 1951-61. However, fertility decline is not fast enough to offset the decline in mortality. As a consequence, the growth rate still remains above 2 per cent per annum.

The social and cultural milieu of India has long favoured early marriage for women. The proportion of married women in the 10-14 age group was that 22 per cent girls were married in the rural areas and 6.8 per cent in the urban areas in 1961, by 1981 these percentages fell to 7.7 and 2.4 respectively. The singulate mean age at marriage of women which remained at about 12 to 13 till about 1931 has increased gradually to 18.3 years in 1981. The Child Marriage Restraint Act, 1978 statutorily increased the minimum age at marriage to 18 years for girls and 21 years for boys. The Government's efforts at raising the status of women by providing education and economic activities contributed to increase the mean age at marriage over the years.

Migration is yet another component affecting the growth of population. In-migration from neighbouring countries and out-migration to other countries disturb the development of identified geographical areas. The development of backward and hilly areas, rural development programmes and special programmes for tribal areas have some impact on the spatial mobility trends. There must be a check on migration.

There is a concern of urbanisation. In 1991 the localities classified as urban was only 26, out of town dwellers numbered 218 million (more than the population of all countries except China, India and the USA). This urban population, according to the 1991 census, is spread over 3768 urban agglomerations/towns. The decadal growth rate declined significantly during 1981-91. In India, one third of the population lives in 23 metropolitan cities. Three mega cities have a population of more than eight million and the other 20 cities have population ranging from one to eight million. All the cities continue to grow, mainly through natural increase (and to a lesser extent because of the net rural-urban migration). The provisions for basic infrastructure like water supply, sanitation and sewerage, housing, transportation, health, education continue to lag behind acceptable norms.

Population Policy Perceptions

The National Family Welfare Programme is the main instrument for bringing about population stabilization in the country. The Family Welfare Programme seeks to promote on a voluntary basis planned parenthood through voluntary and free choice of family planning methods best suited to individual acceptors. It has evolved over the years into an integrated programme of Family Planning and Mother and Child Health Care.

There is great need to respond to the demographic and environmental challenges — today's consumption of the earth's resources are far greater than in Malthus's day. The assault of man on nature has greatly increased. If our population stubbornly persists to grow at 17 million per annum, we would never be able to render social and economic justice to the poor. The Eighth Plan also recognises the environmental degradation associated with unchecked population carrying with it the "inherent risk of natural calamities and disasters" (Planning Commission, Eighth Five Year Plan, Vol. 2, p.331). Therefore, slowing down the rate is a must (Ibid., p. 336) and is considered the pivotal point for the success of all developmental efforts (vol.1, p.10).

These concerns were shared by the Committee on Population set up by the National Development Council in December 1991. They have also endorsed the plea for enunciating a Population Policy to be approved by Parliament.

For ensuring strong political commitment, the Seventy-Ninth Constitution Amendment Bill, 1992, in the Rajya Sabha on 22.12.1992 has been introduced in Parliament with a view to incorporating promotion of population control and the small family norm, within the framework of Article 47 dealing with the Directive Principles of State Policy and including in the list of Fundamental Duties (Article 51-A), a clause enjoining the citizens of India to promote and adopt the small family norm. As the elected representatives need to set an example and act as role models for the population they represent. The Bill proposes to add an additional schedule under which a person shall be disqualified from being elected as Member of either House of Parliament or of legislature of State, if he/she has more than two children on the date of commencement of the proposed amendment or within a period of one year of such commencement. Rajasthan amended its Rajasthan Panchayat Act which disqualifies a person having more than two children to hold elected office in Panchayati Raj Institutions in the State.

It is widely recognised that the population growth is essentially a function of poverty. The nexus between poverty and population and environmental degradation is great. Thus the challenge has two factors — poverty and environmental degradation. The removal of poverty is an integral part of an environmentally sustainable development strategy. It is towards this goal that several efforts are underway. These are environmental initiatives - not merely of Government at various levels but of the people and organisations outside the Government.

Policy Framework

The population policy in India since 1950 has been to decrease the fertility rate so that the population is stabilized as soon as possible. The Family Welfare Programme seeks to promote on a voluntary basis, responsible and planned parenthood through voluntary and free choice of family planning methods, best suited to individual acceptors. People's participation is sought through local self-government institutions, voluntary organisations and opinion leaders at different levels. Imaginative use of mass media and inter-personal communication is made for highlighting the benefits of the small family norm and removal of socio-cultural barriers for its adoption. As a result of this approach the number of acceptors of various methods of family planing have been registering a progressive increase over the years.

The policy has been governed so far by essentially negative considerations of reducing fertility. This has meant larger investments in fertility control, more family planning centres, promotion of contraceptive technology and even compulsory sterilization. Fertility would decline not by family planning programmes and plans, but by economic and social transformation. In the west, the families are small because of a structural transformation from agricultural to industrial societies. Social development is essential, especially education of women. This is not to belittle our family planning programmes but to emphasise the importance of female literacy, age at marriage, employment opportunities for women and their status in society. These are as important as achieving a reduction in infant mortality, improving health and nutrition of pre-school children and providing a comprehensive package of maternal health care services.

In spite of massive efforts, budgetary support and infrastructure development, the performance of the family welfare programme has lagged behind in the northern States of Bihar, Madhya Pradesh, Rajasthan and Uttar Pradesh which continue to be characterised by high birth and total fertility rates. Efforts for containment of population growth have to be intensified. This calls for an integrated approach and concerted efforts through both Government and non-government organizations besides social and political commitment to make it a national movement. Along with a proper supply of family planning services, the country must move towards a positive policy of development of educational skills of its fertile target group. These programmes should be supported with matching investments in the industrial and tertiary sectors.

Urbanisation and the changing role of women contribute to demographic transition, but the quickest way to stabilize family size is to adopt measures to reduce conception in the first place.

There are solutions to this ominous problem but the people and the politicians are equally reluctant to implement changes which cause short-term personal costs to secure long-term general benefits.

Issues for Consideration

1. In view of empirical evidence of the co-relation between high female literacy and lower birth rates, it is imperative that the educational status of girls and women must improve at a much faster rate. It must also be ensured that the dropout rate of girls from schools is brought to a very low level.
2. The Child Marriage Restraint Act must be strictly enforced. The States/UTs may be consulted if the Act needs amendment for enforcement of its provisions.
3. All States/UTs must either frame Acts or amend their relevant Acts and Rules relating to Urban Local Bodies and Panchayati Raj Institutions to include the duty of 'promoting Population Control' for these institutions if no such provision already exists.
4. The quality and outreach of family welfare services must improve by timely supply of family planning aids. These should be distributed to all centres throughout the year and not dumped to complete targets.
5. Funds must be made available to States/UTs on the basis of reduction of actual birth rates. New improved contraceptives must be made available through the Public Distribution System.
6. There must be an intensification of the 'Small Family Norm' by communication through the Press, Radio, Television, Schools, Colleges, Universities, non-formal education centres, Adult Education Programmes and Vocational Training Centres. Women from the villages should be made to promote the message in their areas.
7. The Family Welfare staff in the States/UTs must be revitalised and asked to motivate and counsel the target groups. Trained psychologists could be appointed for changing the mind-set of the people. There should be emphasis on reorientation of information, education and efforts to focus on the quality of life

issues.

8. Religious heads, voluntary and non-governmental organisations should be involved in a big way to promote active community participation in the programme.
9. There should be a system of disincentives which would directly influence fertility behaviour like stoppage of increments, normal commercial rate of interest for a house building advance for employees of the Central Government and PSUs and if possible States/UTs. For the rest of the public not employed by the Government if they exceed the two-child norm, they should be made to pay a higher tax rate, disallowed use of the Public Distribution System, withdrawal of free education and free medical care, etc.
10. All incentives should be withdrawn to Central Government employees, PSU employees and employees of States/UTs, if feasible, in cases where employees have more than two children.
11. Couples in the reproductive age group, living below the poverty line, who are unable to sustain themselves without any proper and steady means of livelihood, should be compulsorily sterilized after they have produced two children irrespective of their sex.
12. Pilot studies should be carried out by independent agencies to evaluate the success or failure of the various Family Welfare Programmes. The availability and acceptability of the different birth control methods to the target groups and their results should help in formulating future policy and its thrust areas.
13. Since high mortality rate among children acts as a disincentive, the coverage of Child Health Care Programmes such as immunisation targets be made more effective.
14. The doctors should not discourage parents who want to adopt the terminal method immediately after the birth of the second child.

ANNEXURE

SAMPLE REGISTRATION SYSTEM

Estimated Live Birth Rates for States and Union Territories 1991

Final

States/Union Territories	Combined	Rural	Urban
INDIA:	29.5	30	24.3
Bigger States			
Andhra Pradesh	25.0	26.5	24.4
Assam	30.9	31.7	21.3
Bihar	30.7	31.3	25.5
Gujarat	27.5	28.2	25.9
Haryana	33.1	34.7	27.2
Himachal Pradesh	28.5	29.2	18.6
Karnataka	26.9	27.9	24.0
Kerala	18.3	18.4	18.1
Madhya Pradesh	35.8	37.3	29.7
Maharashtra	26.2	28.0	22.9
Orissa	28.8	29.6	21.6
Punjab	27.7	28.5	25.6
Rajasthan	35.0	36.0	30.3
Tamil Nadu	20.8	20.8	20.8
Uttar Pradesh	35.7	37.2	29.0
West Bengal	27.0	30.3	18.5
Other States & Union Territories			
Arunachal Pradesh	30.9	31.6	24.0
Goa	16.8	16.7	16.9
Manipur	20.1	20.7	18.0
Meghalaya	32.4	35.4	18.7
Nagaland	18.5	20.4	10.1
Sikkim	22.5	24.2	14.4
Tripura	24.4	25.4	15.5
A&N Islands	20.0	21.5	15.2
Chandigarh	13.9	19.2	13.5
Dadra & Nagar Haveli		31.1	
Daman & Diu	27.9	34.6	17.0
Delhi	24.7	30.2	24.2
Lakshadweep	27.1	30.0	23.8
Pondicherry	19.2	20.5	18.1

Excludes Jammu & Kashmir

Estimated Death Rates for States and Union Territories 1991

Final

States/Union Territories	Combined	Rural	Urban
INDIA:	9.8	10.6	7.1
Bigger States			
Andhra Pradesh	9.7	10.5	6.7
Assam	11.5	11.8	6.9
Bihar	9.8	10.2	6.3
Gujarat	8.5	8.8	7.9
Haryana	8.2	8.5	6.8
Himachal Pradesh	8.9	9.1	5.2
Karnataka	9.0	9.8	6.9
Kerala	6.0	6.2	5.3
Madhya Pradesh	13.8	14.9	9.2
Maharashtra	8.2	9.3	6.2
Orissa	12.8	13.5	6.5
Punjab	7.8	8.5	5.7
Rajasthan	10.1	10.6	7.7
Tamil Nadu	8.8	9.6	7.6
Uttar Pradesh	11.3	12.0	8.3
West Bengal	8.3	8.9	6.7
Other States & Union Territories			
Arunachal Pradesh	13.5	14.5	3.5
Goa	7.5	8.0	6.4
Manipur	5.4	5.4	5.7
Meghalaya	8.8	9.9	4.0
Nagaland	3.3	3.9	0.8
Sikkim	7.5	8.5	3.0
Tripura	7.6	7.7	6.4
A&N Islands	5.8	6.2	3.8
Chandigarh	4.6	6.4	4.5
Dadra & Nagar Haveli		11.4	
Daman & Diu	9.0	10.5	6.5
Delhi	6.3	8.0	6.2
Lakshadweep	4.7	6.4	2.7
Pondicherry	6.6	7.4	6.0

Excludes Jammu & Kashmir

8. DEVELOPMENTAL LESSONS OF SRI LANKA'S HEALTH SYSTEM: Instruments and Options in "Healthy" Implementation

J.W. Bjorkman

1. Introduction

Few problems are more complex and intractable than finding effective ways to implement development objectives that seek betterment of life-chances and the human condition. These problems become even more daunting when the objectives acknowledge the limits of state intervention, yet seek sustainable growth. Pressures of population and resource constraints further compound implementation problems; so the search for effective methods and efficient systems challenge policy activists and analysts alike. Given that experience is often the best teacher, careful examination of reputable "success stories" could provide some practical guidelines on what to do as well as what to avoid. As health policy in Sri Lanka has been characterized by exceptionable results despite conditions of economic scarcity, its experiences may contain lessons about how to achieve sustainable development as well as what should be avoided.

At a general level, policy science literature has been long on deductive logic but short on empirical evidence about its own nomothetic foundations. Attempts to apply the analytic components of health services systems revealed formidable problems of attempting to link design with practice (Bjorkman, 1986b). During the 1980s, public sector management began to focus seriously on issues of implementation rather than only on policy-making *per se.* Thirty years earlier, the emergence of public policy as a field of disciplined study had signalled the integration of normative concerns into behavioural social science. However, after several decades of perennial emphases on values, goals and "what is to be done" by public agencies under governmental guidance, little had been achieved beyond sketching the stages of the policy process. In a seemingly ceaseless cycle of prophylaxis, normative goals were reiterated time and again amidst profuse pleas for more and "better" policy design, but empirical results as well as explanatory models of causality were conspicuously absent. Like medieval scholasticism, policy analysis had become characterized (and even caricatured) by increasingly arcane refinements of diminishing utility.

Nonetheless, from the nondisciplined world of practical politics and economic realities came a self-corrective questioning about so what? why? and how? Such questions — despite their messy and perhaps unanswerable nature — provoked a few scholars into trying to account for what had happened (or, more often, had not happened) within the so-called policy process. Beginning with the seminal work by Pressman and Wildavsky (1972), issues of implementation entered policy debates. While these implementation issues did not displace concern for policy formation nor obviate the need for better design, a new terminology has emerged which signals a new perspective on public policy (Brown, 1992).

This article reviews emergent universals of the implementation process as well as problematic features of centre/periphery relations, and then examines the Sri Lankan health system within the context of those issues. Potential lessons are derived about sustainable development in the health sector or, phrased more modestly, hunches and hypotheses are posed which merit exploration and future research. When appropriate, comparisons are drawn with health systems in other South Asian countries.

2. Perspectives on Implementation: An Underdeveloped Field

Implementation spans the process by which policy decisions are carried out by actors and organisations. Influenced by internal and external pressures at various levels of government, numerous public and private entities translate national objectives into concrete outputs such as discrete goods and services. Depending on the mission of an agency, its format, and its professional, bureaucratic or technocratic nature, these organizational activities are subject to environmental stresses as well as to internal strains.

Despite common practice, implementation designs and capabilities cannot be assumed nor deductively derived. Empirical mapping of such arrangements and interdependencies among public bureaucracies, between public and private bureaucracies, and at different levels of government, are important research tasks. While some interdependencies are highly stable and exclusive, others clearly are not; and some may be relatively unstable because of changes in policy goals and means *per se*. Therefore, interactive coexistence among, rather than exclusively of, multiple actors and organisations characterizes the implementation process.

Comparative studies of implementation in the health sector start by mapping actors, structures and contextual environments as preconditions for generalizations. Individual country studies describe basic features of the political and health care systems. Then for selected policy issues, the informal functional and structural macroprocesses and interdependencies are mapped that involve decision-making on planning, financing, operating and evaluating health care.

The study of social policy implementation is difficult, however, because social services are delivered by diverse local organizations like hospitals, clinics, and health care centres that are relatively independent of central control. Each level (central and local) has its own implementation problems, so the implementation of national public policy consists of at least two separate classes of problems. A Central Government must execute its policy in order to persuade local delivery organizations to behave in desired ways; this is the macro-implementation problem. And in response to those Central Government actions, the local organizations must devise and execute their own internal policies; this is the micro-implementation problem. "Essential differences between the processes of micro-implementation and macro-implementation arise from their distinct institutional settings. Whereas the institutional setting for micro-implementation is a local delivery organization, the institutional setting for macro-implementation is an entire policy sector" (Berman, 1978: 164).

Implementation analysis involves the study of why authoritative decisions (laws, policies, and plans) do — or, more likely, do not — lead to expected results. Such analyses go beyond the aspirations of the policy goal *per se* because, to paraphrase a biblical admonition, a goal ("faith") without action ("works") is dead. Policy exists only as it is implemented and, therefore, the "goodness" of most ideas cannot be tested apart from their implementation. Thus, the two relationships — a policy's technical validity and its implementation effectiveness — cannot be divorced. Taken together, they constitute the domain of implementation analysis.

Although normative theories of administrative law assume top-down automatic obedience, models of policy implementation indicate that the process requires continuous reciprocal interaction between the setting of objectives and the actions geared to achieving them. Twenty years ago Pressman and Wildavsky (1972) observed that the study of implementation involves tracing the paths of decision points all the way from the national policy-making level down to the level of the service manager, who often makes the final decision. The study of implementation also involves an examination of the network of clearances at each decision point as well as a study of those actors involved at each point. Delay in implementation is viewed, in part, as a function of the number of actors involved.

Research throughout the world on the implementation of health policies has reinforced the validity of the Pressman-Wildavsky observations. Although their conclusions dealt with implementation in a highly competitive, pluralistic, and heterogeneous political and administrative system (the USA), their propositions about implementation also apply when the best of all circumstances prevail— when, for example, the following exist:

(1) a hierarchically structured administrative system;
(2) a uniform and codified body of legal rules and norms;
(3) civil servants and service managers with the same training; and
(4) considerable homogeneity in national, regional, and local politics.

Even under these circumstances, the delay encountered in the implementation process is directly related to the number of decision and clearance points and to the different views— to the refinements and the nuances, if you will—held by diverse actors who intervene in the implementation of a programme.

The circle of relevant actors is much larger than administrative law suggests. Conceptual formulations based on public law and administrative law treat the governmental sector as a monolithic entity, but organization theory shows that the governmental sector instead consists of numerous competing governmental segments. bureaus and agencies are just as competitive in a highly centralized system of the "administrative state" as they are in a more open American system; and the competition is even more intense in resource-poor systems of the Third World. One reason for opposition from below, from the periphery, is that field officials and field service managers have to be as attentive to the requirements of local and regional politicians, as well as interest-group pressures, as they have to be obedient to central instruction from above.

The conclusions to be drawn from these observations on the theory of implementation for health and social development are clear. Implementation largely depends on the functioning of multi-institutional, multi-actor, and multi-level systems. Sometimes these complex systems already exist; sometimes they have to be set up by national mandate.

Almost all arrangements for health planning, for example, require such multi-segmented implementation networks. The initial assumption, of course, which derives from normative theories of implementation, is that national programmes require a unified integrated approach. Inevitably, however, a highly complex network that includes multiple, competing actors will develop for implementing the preferred goals.

3. Centre-Periphery Problems: Classic Dilemmas

Tensions and conflicts exist in all polities. Problems in setting, financing and implementing policy priorities emphasize the need to clarify relationships within the intergovernmental system as well as inter-dependencies among governmental and non-governmental organizations. The degree and quality of these linkages are vital areas of research not only on component parts of federal and quasi-federal systems but also a policy management and implementation in any political system.

A recent concern among policy-makers is building the capacity of regional and local governments to manage policy problems, a concern which derives from different streams of thought, perspectives and research activities. Regardless of their different methodologies and levels of abstraction, both the research community and the policy actors share a common concern about policy analysis. Their shared concern centres around a desire to better understand the dynamics of the intergovernmental system as it affects the implementation of national objectives, to propose and test hypotheses about causal linkages in the implementation process, and to develop a reliable framework for predicting policy impacts in future programs based on assessment of alternative administrative arrangements.

Less prompted by theory than by practice, a new appreciation of intergovernmental relations as an evolutionary process and a pragmatic art of governing federally structured political systems has emerged. Gaps often appear between the proclamation and the achievement of policy goals because governmental mechanisms are often wasteful, duplicative and archaic. Current infatuation with management-by-contract, privatization, and other "market solutions" will eventually yield to concerns about inequitable coverage as well as variable results that deviate from acceptable standards. At minimum, issues of government regulation—both externally imposed standards and internally determined self-regulation—will arise. In all cases, domestic policies necessarily rely on the intergovernmental system for allocation of responsibilities if not direct implementation and thus produce greater interdependencies among all public and private components of any national system.

In order to translate policy demands into tangible benefits through effective, efficient and equitable implementation, three requirements are necessary. First, economic resources must be available. Second, both governmental and non-governmental organizations are needed to supply the administrative framework. And third, skilled and experienced personnel must be on tap to carry out policy goals. Each set of resources has a different impact on the implementation of government policies.

Furthermore, the relative presence or absence of these resources stimulates conflict within the inter-governmental system. Tensions occur if one partner has disproportionate economic resources, or more organizational resources at a particular point in time, or better human capital skills in either the public or private sectors; and the ensuing conflicts produce important sources of governmental change. Modernizing nations repeatedly attempt to reconcile such tensions over these three sets of variables. Consequently, a network of inter-organizational and intra-organizational relations has emerged and enlarged; the texture of interactions among organizational personnel changed; and public and private governance became increasingly complex. Although countries are usually a really organized, the dynamic effects of economic resources, organizational mechanisms and professional-bureaucratic relations transcend territorial boundaries.

The increasing interdependence of territorially organized governmental arenas is reflected in an ever larger share of central funds in regional budgets and a larger share of state funds in local government budgets. Ironically, unless carefully monitored, downward flows of funds generate increasing dependency as well as pronounced reluctance to raise local revenue (e.g. taxes). Agencies at various levels of government, however, are not the only organizational options available for implementing policies. Many non-governmental organizations (NGOs) also perform public functions with public funds through (whether explicitly designated or not) government-by-contract. In the past decade, these NGOs have increased considerably in number and significance of policy implementation.

In addition to economic and organizational resources, skilled and experienced people are vital for implementation. Consistuency-building and coalition formation within highly specialized public and private bureaucracies are well-known phenomena. Functional specialists appear in all areas of human activity, and similar training and skills facilitate communication among the inter-governmental professional guilds and with their peers in private organizations. Communications facilitate the permeation of the political system by the interests of diverse professional groups. Such patterns of communication transcend any boundaries set up by bureaucratic and/or jurisdictional hierarchies.

In an era when burgeoning numbers of social problems appear on public agendas and when state interventions increasingly occur across a range of substantive policies, the findings of intergovernmental research ventures are both sobering and challenging. Contemporary governments seek to marshall resources in order to change events, conditions and/or the environment in a preferred direction. Because Third World governments have comparatively limited capacity, they naturally conclude that centralizing power is the most realistic way to achieve specific ends with scarce resources. When development policies are defined to include redistribution of power and resourccs, this bias toward centralized authority is even greater.

Although the argument for centralized power is initially appealing and perhaps even compelling, it is flawed both logically and empirically. Since development also concerns power-sharing and responsiveness to popular interests, a strong central authority easily overwhelms the process; centralized authority becomes heavy-handed and, rather than encouraging participation and growth, breeds dependency and unresponsive stagnation. The literature, is replete with example after example of well-intended (and, sometimes, not so well intended) centralization producing counterproductive results. While nation-building as well as resource management requires some degree of centralization and control, it has become clear (at least to analysts and consultants) that development requires a strong component of local control—even when local control generates decisions, acts and behaviour incongruent with central preferences (Bjorkman, 1992).

Despite the abiding interest in and justification of decentralization, however, centre-periphery relations throughout the world reveal a privileged role for central authority. This empirical trend derives from three factors of particular relevance to the Third World. First, Central Governments retain most of the formal constitutional powers. Second, given their control (both formal and informal) over the few resources available, Central Governments are the most visible welders of authority. And third, deriving from the previous factors, citizens usually accord much more legitimacy to central governments than to local or regional levels.

Reinforced by their colonial heritage, Third World states unsurprisingly locate most of their formal powers at national level. For obvious reasons, colonialism was predicated on dominance by central authorities. More recently, donors and international institutions have reinforced this centralizing trend because they prefer to deal directly with single sources of authority—even if the "unity" of a single source is often more apparent than real. When central authorities receive loans and grants, such resources make them all the more visible to the general public. Though attempts have been made to counter this tendency, donors still largely channel aid through central governments.

Throughout South Asia, centre-periphery relations demonstrate a marked pattern of decidedly centralized government. While the British Raj formally espoused "indirect rule" and thereby encouraged local government, in practice the central government made most of the decisions—and often as much from London as from New Delhi. Although the post-independence constitutions of Pakistan and India established quasi-federal systems of government, and although the Indian Constitution of 1950 incorporated a strong Gandhian commitment to decentralization and participation, the respective central governments have flourished at the expense of both provinces (states) and localities. Since the 1960s, despite much publicized experiments with decentralized local government (Panchayati Raj in India, Basic Democracy in Pakistan), regional and local authorities have become more and more subservient to the national government. Local resources remain meager; local decisions are frequently over-ruled, if they are even taken at all (Bjorkman and Chaturvedi, 1993).

The centralization evident in all five of South Asia's major countries derives not only from structural realities but also from a political rationale. When both resources and manpower are perceived to be scarce (which, ironically, is a misperception that serves to validate once again W. I. Thomas' dictum that "what is perceived to be real is more real than what is real"), it seems only logical to manage these scarce resources within a centrally directed framework in order to use them more effectively and efficiently. Since ethnic diversity also generates tensions and occasionally overt conflict, central government has an additional reason to expand its power and to maintain control over regional and local agencies.

Nonetheless, actual development activities occur at local level where humans live and work. Apart from a few (admittedly very notable and important) major infrastructural projects that require "lumpy investments" and centralized coordination (e.g. dams; power-generation plants; trunk-roads; national defense facilities), actions occurs at the proverbial crossroots which (horticultural imagery notwithstanding) include towns and cities as well as farms and rural villages. Hence, national governments have devised and deployed various methods to exercise central control over local activities. The most common method is to provide services through projects or programmes of a regular line agency or ministry centralized directives are conveyed through a chain of bureaucrats and administered by agents at the local level. Alternatively, special project units or semiautonomous institutions are sometimes established whose managers, however, under fiscal or some other form of central control.

During the past several "development decades", a third device for managing development projects had appeared: the so-called "integrated" approach which seeks to reintegrate the many required functions that become highly fragmented and specialized under line departments. Since poverty (whether urban or rural) is a seamless web of interrelated problems, and since projects of line agencies can address only single aspects of them, development activities must address multiple aspects simultaneously. The integrated approach established yet another layer of agencies at regional level which were intended both to coordinate services of several central agencies and to channel them to local users.

While the underlying logic would seem compelling as a method to bridge the gaps among fragmented services, the integrated agencies at regional levels suffered the worst of both worlds. Central line agents were loathe to cooperate with these new institutions (which, to make matters worse, were staffed almost invariably with bureaucrats on secondment who retained their original loyalties to parent agencies) while local users did not readily recognize, much less acknowledge, the authority of autonomous new units. Despite such flaws as well as disappointing results, these so-called integrated agencies persist.

Whether operated through line agencies, autonomous units or regional conduits, centrally directed development programmes in practice suffer a variety of chronic problems. Not only are they often ineffective in terms of high rates of recidivism; audits and scandals have regularly revealed that resources are frequently wasted while local views are ignored. Flows of information among levels are often blocked, both top-down and bottom-up; and evaluations indicate with depressing frequency that the poor are neglected while the middle classes and well-to-do benefit disproportionately). In short, despite the best of initial intentions and their obvious merits in deductive logic, centralized programmes regularly fail to achieve objectives. Their major accomplishment (in itself, not insignificant politically) is visible symbolic evidence that "governments" are "trying" to do "something" — but without evident success. So-called intervention by a state agency is more often than not symbolic and ephemeral rather than substantive and effective.

Given the empirical problems of centralized control (long before its recent loss of ideological underpinning made criticism not only easier but also fashionable), decentralization to the periphery was advocated as an important factor in development policy. Without here elaborating their distinctions, proposals for decentralization took two forms: administrative decentralization is usually lebelled deconcentration, which involves the delegation of some (for almost all) powers of implementation to local levels while initial decisions about goals are retained at the center in order to assure standardization of at least criteria; and political decentralization is known as devolution, which empowers local and regional actors to decide authoritatively about not only the deployment of assigned resources but also the modification of objectives. The most well-known form of devolution is probably the federalist system in which different levels of government have specific powers and jurisdictions—or, put otherwise, where citizens have rights and owe duties to several governments simultaneously. Perhaps needless to add, for reasons adumbrated above, most examples of decentralization are instances of deconcentration rather than of devolution—even in nominally federal states. Decentralization in practice almost always concerns administrative delegation of responsibility among different levels of government, which divide and share power with a clear pattern of superordinate units overruling subordinate ones.

The empirical record of decentralized development policies is underwhelming, no matter how appealing the strategy *per se* as compensation for excessive centralization. Nearly two decades ago, Caiden and Wildavsky (1974:82) identified the "myth of decentralization" which, when disabused of its halo-effect about the virtues of shared (read: dispersed) responsibility, notes that local elites almost always reap the major benefits of development projects. Derthick (1975) reports a similar pattern in American welfare programs in which decentralization erodes administrative and political power so that organizations cannot carry out their policies as intended. Consequently, project resources become vulnerable to expropriation by external interests (usually local elites) which are better organized than the implementing agency. This evident tendency reinforces the importance of centralization— an importance made even greater in so-called "soft states" which have little authority in the first instance, and so must jealously guard and conserve whatever is available.

Clearly, therefore, center-periphery problems occur whether a state opts for centralized or decentralized strategies of development. Since neither strategy can be automatically prescribed as appropriate policy, one must examine the particular circumstances in which services are sought or are to be implemented before selecting and applying an appropriate degree of (de) centralization. These circumstances necessarily include types of services *per se,* political contexts, governmental structures, human resources, and information. Stated in terms of five discrete yet interlinked hypotheses, it seems likely that centre-periphery problems will be minimized while desired policies will be implemented (a) when services are simple but effective, (b) when the political climate is supportive, (c) when intragovernmental linkages are clear and coordinated, (d) when adequate human capital is available, and (e) when information is abundant. Without a favourable profile framed on this laundry-list of enabling factors, centre-periphery problems will flourish while government services (much less development policies) will remain largely symbolic and, even worse, incapable of meeting legitimate human needs for a reasonable quality of life.

4. Health Policy in Sri Lanka: Elements and Parameters

Based on earlier writings (Bjorkman, 1985, 1988, 1991) as well as several recent in-depth reports (Wolffers, 1987; Silva, 1992; Lodder, 1993), the following section sketches the development of health policy in Sri Lanka and discusses aspects of its implementation raised above. General knowledge of Sri Lanka's society, history and contemporary politics is presumed, but a brief outline of its health system will be presented for the nonspecialist reader. Also, given my explicitly politico-administrative theme within the general category of health systems research, it should be noted that Sri Lankan health care can be divided into so-called modern (allopathic) and traditional (largely Ayurvedic) sectors. Because of overwhelming government investment and involvement in the former, this report focuses on the modern sector, but this focus should not obscure the fact that contemporary Sri Lanka displays a relative acceptance and mutual respect (albeit sometimes grudging) among the different traditions of medicine.

5. Basic Parameters: Administrative and Organizational Design

Along with the state of Kerala in India, Sri Lanka has been known for high rates of overall health status and literacy amidst relatively low per capita income. This situation has raised puzzling questions about the factors that facilitated such social development. Certainly it is universally agreed that per capita GNP is an inadequate indicator to measure social development, although it does roughly indicate the level of wherewithal available for basic needs and discretionary choices. Other composite indicators have been devised as meaningful measures of development, namely the Physical Quality of Life Index (PQLI) and the Human Development Index (HDI). Nonetheless, the striking issue remains about how a very poor, pluralistic, democratic society obtained such solid and impressive improvements in health measures and social welfare.

Initial parameters to examine are administrative arrangements for organizing health services. Sri Lanka's have access to and received allopathic care in medical institutions throughout the country although an urban bias remains evident in the pattern of distribution. Curative care institutions are organized in a hierarchical network in terms of the scale and scope of services provided, the extent to which they provide specialist care, and the criterion of inpatient versus outpatient treatment. Hospitals in Colombo head the hierarchy because they are the largest in size and provide the most specialized care. At regional level, provincial and base hospitals each cater to an entire administrative division. At district level are District Hospitals, each directed by a District Medical Officer. Finally, smaller institutions provide general medical care, either through out-patient clinics or a combination of inpatient/ambulatory services. There are peripheral units, rural hospitals and central dispensaries as well. Medical care follows the principle of referral; patients begin their treatment at the lowest unit of the hierarchy and, as necessary, are referred to more specialized institutions of health care.

In terms of overall areal organization of health care Sri Lanka is divided into nineteen health divisions, each headed by a Superintendent of Health Services who is responsible for curative and preventive services in the division. The main task of preventive medicine, of course, is the promotion of good health and the prevention of disease. To the chagrin of public health advocates, however, preventive health care has never occupied an important place within the totality of health care provisions in Sri Lanka. This underemphasis remains true today although, as always, there are claims about imminent change in the near future. Schools play a role in the dissemination of such preventive information, but there are contradictory assessment about their effectiveness.

Below divisional level, the country has been divided into 104 health units, each headed by a Medical Officer of Health with responsibility for promoting family health, environmental health, school health and family planning. These areas are further subdivided into territories for Public Health Inspectors and for Public Health Midwives. In addition, on a countrywide basis, there are five specialized health campaigns for combating specific diseases, namely malaria, filaria, tuberculous, leprosy and venereal diseases.

Despite its privileged status *vis-a-vis* traditional approaches, Sri Lanka's modern health care sector has many problems. None of these is exceptional, but all merit brief review. First, there are financial problems.

Given the persistent economic recession, it is increasingly difficult to maintain health care services at their present levels, let alone to extend them. Although absolute expenditures are increasing, investment in health care has diminished in recent years both in terms of relative budget share and per capita expenditures in constant rupees (Lodder, 1993) which, by implication, must erode the development standards achieved thus far. This shortfall is occurring just when, ironically, population pressures require more rather than less assured health services in order to complete the demographic transition successfully. It is argued (or perhaps hoped) that past experience with the evident value of health services will induce Sri Lanka's well-educated population to finance more of their own health care needs through health insurance or through out-of-pocket payments rather than via the public purse. Certainly this goal is one of the three major recommendations of the recent World Development Report entitled Investing in Health (World Bank, 1993:11).

Secondly, there is a shortage of medical personnel. The problem is particularly acute in the supply of doctors but also other para-medical helps as well. The issue of health services personnel is very complicated, and involves questions of incentives and status as well as skills per se. Some argue, the example, that the situation is caused mainly by the migration to foreign countries of well-qualified medical workers (especially doctors) after being educated in Sri lanka— largely, although not entirely, at state expense. Others argue the supply is artifically restricted at its entry point because the state-financed medical schools seek to monopolize training and obstruct competition.

Oddly enough, India and Pakistan have much more favourable physician/population ratios than Sri Lanka which, in this instance, more resembles Bangladesh. There is need to explore both distribution and types of health care personnel since, paradoxically, evidence indicates under-employment and even unemployment of urban-located physicians in Pakistan and India who refuse rural postings which lie vacant. Interestingly, Sri Lanka has a four fold advantage over India and Pakistan in availability of hospital beds (and 15-fold over Nepal and Bangladesh) so perhaps the quality (as compared to the quantity) of physicians produces medical services that are both efficient and effective. Unwelcome as the medical community might regard this formerly unthinkable hypothesis, it may be that under certain conditions a lower supply of physicians is preferable to an oversupply.

Then, there are classic organizational problems, one being the division between curative and preventive services mentioned above. Another concerns the location of curative institutions. Outpatient clinics and other peripheral units for ambulatory care are relatively well distributed throughout the island. But, given the need for economies of scale, hospitals are rarely placed in thinly populated rural areas so access to their services remains problematic despite otherwise admirable systems of communications and transport. As a certain point, of course, there is an irreducible "grumble factor" among people about all service sector activities; and one can wryly observe that "where one stands depends on where one sits" (or, rather, resides). In any case, almost all specialists, most of the facilities, and the best medical care services are found in Colombo.

For towns as well as the countryside, Primary Health Care (PHC) provides the principle strategy in Sri Lanka. Clearly antecedent to (and, in part, an inspiration for) 1978's Alma Ata Conference that boldly (albeit naively) proclaimed "Health for All by the year 2000." this strategy is rooted not only in a spirit of social justice but also in a spirit of self-reliance. In contrast to the dependency bred by top-down delivery of medical services, PHC expects that people can and will self-determinedly help themselves... with perhaps a bit of initial "pump-priming" initiative from external sources. Without delving further into assumptions about human nature and relative autonomy, PHC seeks to provide the first level.of contact of individuals, family and community with the national health system; it thus brings health care as close as possible to where people live and work while it simultaneously constitutes the first element of a continuing interlinked health care process. Although a universally agreed definition of PHC and its components exists, a meaningful approximation might be "democratization of health care" (van der Geest et al., 1990: 1033).

Consonant with its own policies, Sri Lanka formally signed the "Health Charter" in 1980 and officially adopted PHC as its key approach. Again without listing the myriad components and suggested nuances of this strategy, PHC requires extensive community participation in planning, organizing and managing services in order to attain self-reliance. Although its programmatic evaluation may still be somewhat premature, assessments of these efforts indicate that PHC is likely to be most effective (1) when it employs means that are understood and accepted by the community, (2) when it employs health workers (including traditional practitioners) who reside in the community they serve, and (3) when it operates at a cost that the community can afford. Such conditions are not easily achieved, and Sri Lanka continues to confront problems concerning accessibility as well as participation. In order to be able to comment on the effectiveness of Sri Lanka's PHC strategy, detailed research must be conducted at village and ɔcal level. Given experiences with PHC elsewhere in the world, there also re rich opportunities for comparative studies based on the three pragmatic ropositions presented above.

. Instrumental Elements: Legacies, Luck and Investments

3eyond administrative structure and PHC strategy, other specific arameters of Sri Lanka which have facilitated implementation can be ummarized under five headings, namely (a) colonial experiences; (b) nvestments in human capital; (c) universal suffrage, participation and ompetitive politics; (d) accessible tax-base; and (e) compact geography. 'he contributions of inter-governmental relations to the implementation f health policies are more ambiguous, although tantalizing for their nixed record and incomplete results, and will be assessed in the third ubsection below.

(a) Sri Lanka had a long colonial history dominated successively by he Portuguese, the Dutch and the British. On their arrival European ulers introduced health care facilities for their own benefit, but only in nid-20th century were the real foundations laid for an extensive and xtendible system of modern health care facilities. Free (that is, free to an mmediate user) health care combined with free education, subsidized ood and selected social measures became major elements of post-ndependence government policy in which the social and medical well-eing of almost all Sri Lanka's received high priority.

It should be recalled that 19th century British administrators had nitiated a rudimentary public health system in Sri Lanka that was based n the prevailing European concepts of "western" medicine. The colonial ower was understandably committed to protecting its expatriate dministrators from epidemic disease; it also wanted to protect the health f its local administrative officials as well as those employed in the roductive plantation sector. Such a public health programme was ntirely in harmony with a general colonial outlook that aimed at ninimizing governmental intervention in matters not directly connected vith commercial interests. In fact, such a utilitarian attitude was not very lifferent in practice from the policies that Britain adopted towards its own itizens in the United Kingdom. Thus, the rudimentary public health ystem provided only partial coverage of the health needs of the island, and t unequally distributed its services between the rich and the poor, between rban and rural areas, between foreign plantation labor and indigenous 'illagers.

Nevertheless this rudimentary system of preventive and curative health measures was effective enough to begin a process of reducing mortality and morbidity. These reductions raised life expectancy at birth in Ceylon from less than 30 years at the turn of the century to about 45 years by World War II. Probably the most dramatic demonstration of the effectiveness of preventive health measures in coping with the problems of communicable diseases came in 1945 and thereafter in the massive malaria eradication campaigns (Seneviratne, 1980).

(b) Among the domestic policies historically favoured by Sri Lankan governments has been education. Investments in education began early in Sri Lanka and were regularly expanded (de Silva, 1982). Through competitive politics among several political parties, education became an important policy instrument for reducing socio-economic inequality. The investments in educational infrastructure produced dramatic changes in literacy rates; and literacy among women in particular has important cascade impacts on home hygiene, nutrition practices, infant mortality and life expectancy. Such investments in human capital extend beyond building schools or promoting adult education to the training and deployment of skilled personnel where and when needed. In 1927 for example, partly stimulated by Rockefeller funds, a primary health care infrastructure based on the services of state-trained village midwives and public health nurses was established and subsequently expanded. In the 1930s, expansion of medical education led to the establishment of an extensive network of rural dispensaries, maternity homes, and cottage hospitals. This rural network has become so accessible and acceptable that today three-quarters of all births now occur in these institutions under the supervision of trained midwives (recently renamed Family Health Workers). It is estimated that a state-supported health care facility of one type of another is located at an average maximum distance of three miles from any habitation. Indeed, by including all practitioners of traditional medicine, Wolffers (1987:53) argues that "within a radius of 0.8 miles some form of health care service is available to everyone."

(c) After the introduction and initial expansion of health measures in the 19th and early 20th centuries came another innovation in Sri Lanka. In 1931 the British introduced universal adult suffrage into Ceylonese politics and gave locally elected politicians responsibility for formulating and implementing domestic policies. The universal franchise (16 years before India gained the same and only two years after the United Kingdom itself extended the vote to women) provided the basis for competitive party politics. In the two decades before 1948 and in the 45 years since independence, democratic participatory politics have stimulated other public investments in what broadly is labelled human capital. Yet another example of pre-and post-colonial social policies that enhanced human capital formation and all its down-stream benefits were food subsidies. While the level of subsidy has waxed and waned, and while the universal entitlement to a food ration has been retrenched, there is little doubt that participatory politics have contributed to nutritional status in Sri Lanka.

Such politics have stimulated other public investments that synergistically enhance human capital. Without detailing them in full, related policies include communication systems, all-weather (hard-surfaced) roads throughout the island, subsidized state-bus fares (in contrast to better-quality commercial traffic), land reform expedited by the massive Mahaweli rural development and reclamation programmes, and resettlement schemes. These reforms have provided some security of tenure to the tenant cultivators who comprise the bulk of the Sri Lankan peasantry of rural Sri Lankans now use approved methods for disposing of human wastes, while 30 per cent of them have access to safe drinking water. Today some four out of five urban Sri Lankans can rely on supplies of relatively pure water.

(d) A fourth feature long of advantage to Sri Lanka is its accessible and modestly elastic tax-base which has helped to finance social investment. Its well-developed plantation economy has relatively easily monitored productive assets from which to extract revenue for allocation to government programmes. Because peasants engaged in subsistence farming are by virtue of their condition unable to produce a surplus of free-floating resources to use elsewhere, plantations for tea, rubber and coconut have been proverbial "milch-cows" for generating revenue. During the 1970s all these plantations were nationalized and, to shift the metaphor, the goose over time laid fewer eggs. Nonetheless a type of low-level security of predictable revenues permitted governments to allocate adequate resources to the health sector and other social programmes. In terms of real health expenditures (that is, in so-called constant rupees that have been corrected for inflation), spending has barely kept pace with population growth; and inconsistencies among reported financial figures cause one to recall the book entitled *Lies, Damn Lies and Statistics.* Given the semi-cynical adage that "budgeting is the art of letting someone else pay for your benefits," here is a complicated subject for further research.

There is, however, an emergent downside to Sri Lanka's impressive achievements in social well being. In common with welfare states elsewhere in the world, Sri Lanka has begun to experience over faces that will escalate the costs of health services as well as limit the magnitude of future change. As prevenable diseases are controlled and as acute infectious diseases are replaced by chronic diseases that are much more costly to treat or contain. Successful development along the lines envisioned by most government planners necessarily introduces new causes of morbidity and even mortality, such as industrial injuries, agro-chemical poisoning, environmental pollution, addition-related disorders, stress-induced illness, traffic accidents, and iatrogenic disease.

(e) As the penultimate parameter in the short list of factors that have facilitated (although not ensured) implementation of health policies in Sri Lanka, its compact size and geography make access to medical care (through placement of clinics and referral services) easier in rural areas. Given reasonably quick communications and transportation networks, curative services and preventive information are within easy reach of a literate population. The island is relatively small and, under normal Decentralisation-conditions, can be crossed within a day by road and within an hour by air. Even the distribution of population is advantageous with major concentrations in several regions.

7. Experiments in Deconcentration Versus Devolution

Quite clearly, Sri Lanka's record in health policy and human well-being is due to a variety of antecedent factors. In addition, a perennial problem shared throughout the world, namely the coordination of activities by governmental and non-governmental agencies, has been episodically addressed over time. In its basic constitutional format, Sri Lanka is a unitary state with classic features of centralized control of both choice of goals and administration of policy. Indeed, the major issue of political contention during recent decades has been the permissible degree of regional autonomy versus invariant standards ordained by central authority.

Since its 1931 "constitution", Sri Lanka has been a veritable laboratory for experiments in inter-governmental relations. Without reviewing this history, the establishment of District Development Councils in 1980 marked the first authentic (if limited) transfer of authority to incorporated local governments. The law's provisions included popularly elected members, revenue raising and spending powers, and the authority to make bye-laws. Prior to its passage, there had been two notable phases in the evolution of decentralized government since independence. During the 1960s and 1970s, attempts were made to coordinate activities of national government agencies involved in agricultural programmes at district level. Only cursory references were made to social and health services which were, presumably, considered adequately well-integrated and/or irrelevant.

Dissatisfaction with the fragmentation of, as well as the lack of cooperation among, national departments had led Sri Lanka's United National Party leaders in 1965 to designate the Government Agent (GA) within each district as coordinator of all national departments. Under his auspices, coordinated at the center a cabinet committee (chaired by the prime minister) coordinated national agencies. Decentralization, however, was understood only as local coordination of national functions; it was deconcentration of tasks rather than devolution of power. Evaluated in retrospect, these efforts were not very effective (Rondinelli, 1992:110-116).

With its advent to power in 1970 the Sri Lanka Freedom Party technically decentralized all development planning, implementation, monitoring and evaluation responsibilities to the district. Government Agents became responsible for formulating and implementing district plans, but again basically through the device of coordinating all national department representatives at the district level. While District Development Committees were established, appointed planning officers assisted the GA in carrying out development tasks. Divisional Development Councils served as links between the district body and community organizations, cooperatives and village committees. In addition, a Member of Parliament from the ruling party was appointed as District Political Authority) later called a District Minister) by the Prime Minister in order to expedite action and implementation. In 1974 the government established a limited district development budget that earmarked a specific amount of money annually for small-scale development activities selected by the District Development Committees.

The District Development Committee system and its limited district budgets fell short of expectations. Much of the money was used for infrastructure rather than for productive enterprises while intervention of MPs and local political leaders undermined systematic involvement of district residents in the process. Dissatisfaction with top-down coordination led to legislation in 1980 which created District Development Councils. These were composed of local citizens who were popularly elected for four-year terms along with non-local MPs again appointed by the Executive President. The Councils were empowered to raise revenue from a variety of sources and obtain loans as part of the district development fund. The Council's Executive Committee could formulate an annual development plan and monitor its implementation. In an ironic twist of fate, District Development Councils also began to centralize lower-level functions in that they could formulate, finance and implement projects previously the responsibility of village and town councils.

Although the District Development Councils introduced a degree of devolution of decision-making power into the system, ambiguities remained in design as well as allocation of tasks. Relationship between Councils and national agencies were left undefined. Likewise the Councils' administrative capacity needed strengthening in order to deal with the new responsibilities and functions assigned to them. In a sense, a major (as yet seemingly unfulfilled) reorientation of attitudes among central ministries and agencies is required that would shift the focus from control and direct delivery of services to one of supervision and support of local efforts.

During the past decade various adjustments to the system have been introduced, including a recent effort to augment inter-governmental relations with an intermediate provincial tier between centre and district. In 1989, a system of elected Provincial Councils was added in order to link local administration with a (potentially) sustainable resource base and to introduce a measure of federal devolution of power, keeping both within the Sri Lankan tradition of accountability to competitive democratic politics. Simultaneously it was an attempt to address and perhaps resolve endemic ethnic strife that periodically erupts into civil violence. It is yet too soon to judge performance, but opportunities seem cautiously auspicious. More experience and even greater experimentation are necessary before these challenges can be said to have been successfully met.

8. A Review of Lessons or How Hunches Yield Hypotheses for Healthy Implementation

The lessons to be learned from the Sri Lankan "welfare state" in an otherwise typical Third World Economy can be traced be their basic development approach, which was then augmented by local empowerment and participation by an educated populace. Well before independence, governments in Sri Lanka had launched a simple basic needs strategy, long before this approach became popular in the 1970s. Successive governments then adopted policies directed toward the achievement of social equity. Occasionally these governments over-reached their own resources; and occasionally they over-centralized control for undoubtedly the best of reasons and good intentions. Fortunately, given the relatively open society (despite its sometimes violent dimensions) and given the well-rooted tradition or public accountability through the electoral process, Sri Lankans have alternated their rulers over time.

Whether new arrangements can reinforce and deepen this important tradition remain open to scrutiny, but hope springs eternal. Certainly the governments of Sri Lanka have continued a multi-strategy approach to development that simultaneously pursues policies encouraging liberal market economics, massive state investments in development projects and continued social services for the people. Since 1978, an increasingly open economy has been promoted in which market forces of supply and demand have adjusted prices and resources; and most recently, the worldwide trend toward privatization has been evident in attempts privates the plantation sector.

Of all the factors facilitating implementation of health policies in Sri Lanka, two still stand out: universal education and competitive politics, which have an additional synergistic effect. Education contributes directly to Sri Lankan successes in establishing and utilizing a broad-based primary health system (including especially access to the services of trained midwives). Educational opportunities for women and the associated female literacy rate are especially important. The high rate of literacy, the intensely competitive political system, and the resulting politicization provide opportunities to articulate popular demands. A political and social environment has been created for a continuous dialogue. Political participation, articulation of popular demands, political awareness and mass mobilization have all lead to more distributive equity in the services provided to all Sri Lankans.

Behind the promises made by competing political parties, of course, lie diverse ideological orientations with their various value-commitments and causal logics as well as their preferred agents and modes of action. But the vigor of public participation win a competitive democratic environment has ensured that the overall pattern of a welfare system has been maintained. Social policies and programmes develop a political momentum such that social development obtains an intertial logic of its own.

Nonetheless, Sri Lanka's record of building a welfare state on an Asian economy cannot be understood without considering the cost of these achievements. Since low levels of per capita income yield little tax revenue, health services and associated investments in human capital must compete with other pressing needs and demands of development. More recently, irrational factors of ethnic pride and escalating violence have confounded efforts to promote consistent policies of social betterment. In terms of statistical reporting, these factors seem unrelated to results since thus far output and outcome indicators seem to be either improving or stable (Lodder, 1993). But commonsense as well as anecdotal evidence suggest inevitable problems. These are issues for sober reflection as well as for creative research.

Finally, this review of Sri Lankan health policies and implementation factors has revealed the need for systematic research into linkages between broadly decentralized development administration and more narrowly focused health care systems. Surprisingly, the literature and studies on the two distinct domains seem to run on parallel tracks which rarely (if ever) intersect. Perhaps this mutual exclusively derives from the fact that development administration in Sri Lanka has largely concerned self-sufficiency in food production. Despite their importance in local government, social services received second-order priority. Given official adoption of the Primary Health Care strategy in 1980 as well as the District Development Councils, the role of inter-governmental relations in Sri Lanka's health system will merit careful attention and systematic analysis as another sustainable uptown in "healthy implementation" of development goals.

"The care of human life and happiness, and not their destruction, is the first and only legitimate object of good government."

Thomas Jefferson (1809)

STATISTICAL APPENDIX I

		Bangladesh	India	Nepal	Pakistan	Sri Lanka
Crude Birth Rate	1970	48	41	46	48	29
	1981	46	36	44	44	29
	1991	34	38	41	41	21
Crude Death Rate	1970	21	18	22	19	8
	1981	20	15	20	16	7
	1991	13	10	13	11	6
Natural Increase	1981	2.6	2.1	2.4	2.8	2.2
(%)	1991	2.7	2.1	2.3	2.9	1.3
Population	1951	42	361	8	34	8
(Millions)	1960	51	442	9	50	10
	1976	81	632	13	73	14
	1985	101	762	17	99	16
	1990	107	850	19	112	17
	1991	111	867	19	116	17
	1993	123	882	20	122	18
Population	2000	131	1017	24	148	19
Projected	2025	180	1365	38	244	24

STATISTICAL APPENDIX II

		Bangladesh	India	Nepal	Pakistan	Sri Lanka
Urban Population	1951	4	17	3	18	15
(%)	1961	5	18	4	22	19
	1971	9	20	4	25	22
	1981	11	22	5	28	27
	1991	17	27	10	33	22
Infant Mortality	1960	—	146	—	147	63
(deaths/1000	1970	140	137	157	142	53
births)	1981	139	134	133	142	42
	1991	103	90	101	97	18
Life Expectancy	1960	46	47	44	49	58
(Yrs)	1991	47	50	44	51	66
	1985	48	53	46	50	68
	1991	51	60	53	59	71
Literacy Rate	1960	—	24	—	15	75
(%)	1976	25	36	19	21	80
	1980	31	40	19	32	85
	1991	33	41	21	36	86
Female/male Rates	1991	22/43	29/57	12/39	19/40	85/91

STATISTICAL APPENDIX III

		Bangladesh	India	Nepal	Pakistan	Sri Lanka
Per Capita GNP	1979	$100	$190	$130	$270	$230
(US$)	1987	164	314	154	294	402
	1991	179	350	170	365	340
	1993	220	310	180	400	550
Health Expendi-	1976	$ 1	$ 2	$ 1	$ 1	$ 4
ture (Public Per	1980	0.5	2	1	1	6
Capita)	1981	1	3	1	1	7
Population Per	1960	—	4,850	72,870	11,000	4,490
(Physician)	1976	14,208	4,106	38,265	3,814	6,241
	1980	9,780	2,910	30,780	3,630	7,220
	1991	6,219	2,522	20,356	2,086	7,253
	1993	6,166	2,075	20,234	1,987	5,516
Population Per	1976	4,901	1,336	6,512	1,927	338
Hospital Bed	1980	4,602	1,312	5,865	1,844	343
Population with	1976	19	31	8	25	56
Safe Water	1980	22	41	11	29	68
Supply (%)						

Sources : ASIAWEEK (9 June) 1993:15-17; Johnson 1983:62, 174, 215; Murphy 1981:10; MacLachlan 1986:33; Sewell et al 1980:165; Sivard 1979, 1982, 1986, 1991; World Bank 1993: 200-201, 240, 288-292, 298

REFERENCES

Altenstetter, C. and J. W. Bjorkman (1983) Planning and Implementation: A Comparative Perspective on Health Policy, *International Political Science Review* 13: 73-91.

Aluwihare, A P R. (1982) 'Traditional and Western Medicine Working in Tandem' *World Health Forum,* 3: 450-451.

Ashford, D. (ed.) (1980) *Comparative Public Policies: New Concepts and Methods,* Beverly Hills, California: Sage Publications.

Banerji, D. (1974)' Social and Cultural Foundations of Health Services Systems', *Economic and Political Weekly* (Special August Number): 1333-1345.

Berman, P. (1978) 'The Study of Micro- and Macro-Implementation', *Policy Science,* 26:157-184

Bjorkman, J. W. (1979) *The Politics of Administrative Alienation in India's Rural Development Programmes.* Delhi: Ajanta Publications.

________. (1984) 'Health Policy and Politics in Sri Lanka: Developments in the South Asian Welfare State', *Asian Survey,* 34:211-240.

________. (1985) 'Who Governs the Health Sector? Comparative European and American Experiences with Representation, Participation and Decentralization', *Comparative Politics,* 17:399-420.

_______. (1986a) (ed.) *The Changing Division of Labour in South Asia.* Riverdale, Maryland: The Riverdale Company.

_______. (1986b) 'Health Policies and Human Capital: The Case of Pakistan', *Pakistan Development Review,* 11:411-430.

_______. (1988) Comparative Health Policies: A World of Difference, *Pakistan Development Review* (Islamabad), 27:473-492.

_______. (1991) 'Grains among the Chaff: Rhetoric and Reality in Comparative Health Policy'. In *From Rhetoric to Reality: Comparative Health Policy and the New Right,* edited by C. Altenstetter & S. Haywood. London: Macmillan, pp. 281-308.

_______. (1992) ' Nation-Building and Public Administration In *Falende Overheden?' Bestuur, politiek en besluitvorming in de Derde Wereld,* edited by JJF Heins. Amsterdam: VU Uitgeverij, pp. 26-46.

_______. and H. R. Chaturvedi (1993) 'Panchayati Raj in Rajasthan: Penalties of Success'. In Schomer *et al.*

_______. and R. I. Schulz. (1981) 'On the Implementation of Change, in National Health Delivery Systems: A Model and an Application, *Journal of Health and Human Resources Administration,* 4:195-227.

_______ and G.A. Silver. (1978) 'Citizen Control of Health Services: An International Perspective on Participation, Representation, and Social Policy. *Proceedings of the Ninth World Congress of Sociology* (Uppsala, Sweden, 12-19 August). Bowden, P. 1992. NGOs in Asia: Issues in Development'. In Smith: 147-158.

Brown, P. (1992) 'Alternative Delivery Systems in the Provision of Social Services', *International Review of Administrative Sciences,* 58:201-214.

Caiden, N. and A. Wildavsky. (1974) *Planning and Budgeting in Poor Countries.* New York: John Wiley.

Commonwealth Secretariat (1982) *The Contribution of Medical Schools to National Health Development* (Report of a Commonwealth Workshop at Kandy, Sri Lanka). London: Marlborough House.

Corey, K. E. (1984) 'Deconcentrated Urbanization in Sri Lanka: A Case of Policy Serendipity', *Urban Studies Working Paper 2.* College Park: Institute of Urban Studies, University of Maryland.

Derthick, M. (1975) *Uncontrollable Spending for Social Service Grants.* Washington, DC: The Brookings Institution Elling, R. H. 1980. *Cross-National Study of Health Services: Political Economies and Health Care.* New Brunswick, New Jersey: Transaction Books.

de Silva, K M. (1982) 'The Model Colony : Reflections on the Transfer of Power in Sri Lanka', In *The States of South Asia: Problems of National Integration,* edited by A Jeyaratnam Wilson and Dennis Dalton. London: C. Hurst, pp. 77-88 and 127-133.

Evans, J. R., K. Hall and J. Warford (1981) 'Health Care in the Developing World: Problems of Scarcity and Choice', *New England Journal of Medicine,* 305:1117-27.

Fesler, J. W. and D. F. Kettl (1991) *The Politics of the Administrative Process.* Chatham, New Jersey: Chatham House Publisers, Inc.

Franda, M. (1983) *Voluntary Associations and Local Development of India.* New Delhi: Young Asia Publications.

Freddi, G. and J. W. Bjorkman (ed.) (1989) *Controlling Medical Professionals: The Comparative Politics of Health Policies,* London: Sage Publications.

Freidson, E. (1975) *The Profession of Medicine: A Study of the Sociology of Applied Knowledge.* New York: Dodd, Mead and Company.

Van der Geest, S. and J. D. Speckmann and P H Streefland. (1990) 'Primary Health Care in a Multi-level Perspective: Towards a Research Agenda', *Social Science and Medicine,* 30:1025-1034.

Golladay, F and B Liese (1980) *Health Problems and Policies in the Developing Countries.* Washington, DC: The World Bank.

Grindle, M. S. (Ed.) (1980) *Politics and Policy Implementation in the Third World.* Princeton: Princeton University Press.

Hanf, K and F W Scharpf (ed.) (1978) *Interorganizational Policy Making: Limits to Coordination and Central Control.* London: Sage Publications.

Howard, L M (1981) 'What are the Financial Resources for Health 2000?', *World Health Forum,* 2:1:23-29.

Iglesias, G. (ed.) (1976) *Implementation: The Problems of Achieving Results.* Manila: EROPA.

Jameson, K P, J H Weaver and C L Wilber. (1989) ' Strategies of Development: A Survey'. In *Development Economics: Theory, Practice, and Prospects,* T R DeGregori (eds.). Boston: Kluwer Academic Publishers, pp. 137-177.

Jeffrey, R. (1988) *The Politics of Health in India.* Berkeley: University of California Press.

Johnson, B L C (1983) *Development in South Asia.* Harmondsworth: Penguin Books, Ltd.

Kearney, R N (1973) *The Politics of Ceylon (Sri Lanka).* Ithaca, New York: Cornell University Press.

Kohn, R and K L White (eds) (1976) *Health Care: An International Study.* London: Oxford University Press.

Korten, D. (1980) 'Community Organization and Rural Development: A Learning Process Approach', *Public Administration Review,* 40:480-514.

Lee, K and A Mills (ed.) (1983) *The Economics of Health in Developing Countries.* New York: Oxford University Press.

Leichter, H. (1979) *A Comparative Approach to Policy Analysis: Health Care Policy in Four Nations.* New York: Cambridge University Press.

Leslie, C. (ed.) (1976) *Asian Medical Systems: A Comparative Study.* Berkeley: University of California Press.

Lodder, V. (1993) 'Gezondheidszorg in Sri Lanka', Report on a Rijksuniversiteit Leiden Internship at the Institute of Social Studies, The Hague.

MacLachlan, M. (ed.) (1986) *Asia 1986 Yearbook.* Hong-Kong: Far Eastern Economic Review, Ltd.

MacLachlan, G. and A. Maynard (ed.) (1982) *The Public/Private Mix for Health.* London: Nuffield Provincial Hospitals Trust.

Madan, T. N. (1987) 'Community Involvement in Health Policy: Socio-Structural and Dynamic Aspects of Health Beliefs', *Social Science and Medicine.* 25:615-620.

Mahler, H. (1977) 'Blueprint for Health for All', *WHO Chronical,* 31:491-498.

Marmor, T. R., A Bridges and W Hoffman (1979) ' Comparative Politics and Health Policies

Notes on Benefits, Costs, Limits. In *Ashford:* 59-80.

Maxwell, R. (1975) *Health Care: The Growing Dilemma: Needs V. Resources in Western Europe, the US, and the USSR,* 2nd edition. New York: Mckinsey.

______. (1981) *Health and Wealth: An International Study of Health Care Spending.* Lexington, Massachusetts: Lexington Books.

Mosher, F. (1978) 'Professions in Public Services', *Public Administration Review,* 38:144-150.

Murphy, E. M. (1981) *World Population: Toward the Next Century.* Washington, DC: Population References Bureau, Inc.

Nayer, B. R. (1972) *The Modernization Imperative.* New Delhi: Vikas Publications.

Paul, S. (1982) *Managing Development Programs: The Lessons of Success.* Boulder, Colorado: Westview Press, Inc.

Population Reference Bureau. (1984) *World Population Data Sheet.* Washington DC.

Przeworski, A. and H. Teune (1970) *The Logic of Comparative Social Inquiry.* New York: Wiley-Interscience, John Wiley and Sons.

Rondinelli, D. A. (1992) 'Implementing Decentralization Programmes in Asia: A Comparative Analysis', In *Smith:* 99-125.

Saxena, A.P. (1980) *Administrative Reforms for Decentralized Development.* Kuala Lumpur: Asian and Pacific Development Administration Centre.

Schomer, K. *et al.* (eds.) (1993) *The Idea of Rajasthan: Explorations in Regional Identity,* Two Volumes, Delhi: Manohar Publications.

Seneviratne, K. N. (1980) 'Health Politics and Social Change in Sri Lanka', *The Round Table,* No. 280 (October):387-399.

Sewell, J. W. *et al.* (1980) *The United States and World Development:* Agenda. New York: Praeger Publishers.

Silva, K. T. (1992) *Feedback from Health Social Science Research in Sri Lanka.* The Triangle Program, University of Peradeniya & University of Antwerp.

Sivard, R. L. (1991) *World Military and Social Expenditures 1991.* Leesburg, Virginia: World Priorities, Inc. (also editions of 1979, 1982 and 1986)

Smith, B. (ed.) (1992) *Progress in Development Administration.* Chichester: John Willey & Sons.

Smith, T. B. (1973) 'The Policy Implementation Process', *Policy Sciences,* 4:197-209.

Steiss, A. W. and G. A. Daneke (1980) *Performance Administration.* Lexington, Massachusetts: Lexington Books.

Uphoff, N. T. (1973) 'An Analytical Model of Processes and Performance for Developing Indicators of Administrative Capability', *Philippine Journal of Public Administration,* 17:372-395.

Virgo, J. M. (ed.) (1984) *Health Care: An International Perspective.* Edwards-ville, Illinois: International Health Economics & Management Institute.

Wallis, M. (1989) *Bureaucracy: Its Role in Third World Development.* London: Macmillan.

Walt, G. and P. Vaughn. (1981) *An Introduction to the Primary Health Care Approaching Developing Countries.* London: Ross Institute of Tropical Hygiene.

Wolffers, I. (1987) *Changing Traditions in Health Care (Sri Lanka).* Leiden State University Doctoral Dissertation.

World Bank. (1993) *World Development Report 1993: Investing in Health.* New York: Oxford University Press.

9. URBAN POLICY REFORMS FOR INDIA

Dinesh Mehta

In the recent past, there has been some attempt to review the progress of economic reforms in India. (See World Bank, 1993, Bhagwati and Srinivasan, 1993 and Ministry of Finance, 1993). The issue related to the urban sector are absent in all the papers, albeit the MOF paper makes some reference to the Urban Land Ceiling Legislation in paras 73 and 74 under the sub-heading of industrial policies!

Does one conclude that urban sector is perceived as an unimportant or low priority sector in the context of the economic reforms? Is it due to the perception that the contribution of urban sector too low in the national economic development? Or is it simply that the "urban sector" which has a distinct spatial connotation, is difficult to be put into the conventional sectoral boxes?

In this note, we argue that the apparent neglect of the urban policy reforms may have grave consequences on the entire reforms process. Urban areas, which contribute around 60 per cent of GDP, are at present in a state of crisis with inadequate basic infrastructure, transport power telecommunication, and housing. These urban centres, which should become the backbone of India's globalising economy, and invite direct foreign investments and international financial institutional investment, are no longer in a position to provide an adequate base for such a transformation.

Cities have been regarded as 'wealth of a nation' and as 'engines of economic growth'. If the Indian cities have to continue to perform this role in the context of economic reforms, it is important to initiate policy reforms in the urban sectors urgently. The political and economic consequences of inactions in this will have a far reaching impact on the whole process of national development.

The Urban Context

Popular perception and past policy making processes in India are based on perpetuation of certain myths about the process of urbanization in India. It is necessary to understand the context, before considering the set of necessary policy reforms.

Myth 1: Rapid Urbanisation in India

It is generally believed that there is rapid urbanization in India. This is largely based on the perception of one's experience of a few cities that have grown rapidly.

On the whole, however, the level of urbanization at 26 per cent is among the lowest in Asian and Latin American countries. The rate of growth of urban population has also declined significantly from 3.9 per cent per annum in 1971-81 to 3.1 per cent annum in 1981-91 decade. The urban-rural population growth differential has also declined from 2.05 per cent per annum in 1971-81 to 1.29 per cent per annum in 1981-91.

TABLE 9.1: Urban Population Projection — India 1991-2001

	Millions projected	Actual	Urbanization level as per cent of total population	
			Projected	Actual
1991	235	217	27.5	12.7
1997	—	(267)	—	(28.3)
2001	332	(307)	33.0	(30.5)

Note: Figures in bracket indicate revised projections based on 1991 Census.

Source: Eighth Five Year Plan, 1992-97, Vol. II, Government of India, Planning Commission, New Delhi.

Myth 2: Increasing Rural-Urban Migration

It is generally believed that growth in urban population occurs largely due to increasing rural-urban migration. Analysis of components of urban growth suggests that the share of rural-urban migration has been declining over time. It was around 25 per cent in 1971-81 and is likely to have reduced to around 20 per cent in 1981-91. It is often surprising to many to know that nearly 60 per cent of urban growth is due to natural increase.

Myth 3: Urban Poverty and Slums are a Result of Transfer of Rural Poverty

The popular perception is that most of the rural migrants to urban areas are poor. These migrants, who account for one in every five new urban residents are not necessarily poor. Micro-level studies of rural-urban migration show that there is a self-selectivity bias among migrants and that the propensity to migrate is in fact higher among the more educated and richer rural population. The rural poor are compelled to migrate to cities only in the event of natural calamities like floods or droughts.

Myth 4: Imbalance in Urban Structure with Rapid Growth of Large Cities and Decline of Small and Medium Towns

Many policy-makers believe that larger cities in India are growing far more rapidly and the small towns are declining. The policy prescriptions that emerge from such wrong perception attempt to curb the growth of the large cities, restrict industrial development in and around cities and promote development of small and medium towns to act as "counter-magnets" to large cities and deflect rural-urban migration.

The facts are that during 1981-91, population of large cities (cities above one lakh population), had an average decadal growth of 34.49, as compared to 31.6 for class II towns (50,000 to 1 lakh) and 29.57 for class III towns (20,000 to 50,000). In the states of Karnataka, Kerala, Madhya Pradesh and West Bengal, the class II towns on an average grew more rapidly than class I cities. Even among the 23 million plus cities of India, it is seen that over half of them have a lower rate of growth of population in 1981-91 than the previous decades.

Myth 5: Problems of Urban Areas, Such as Slums, Inadequate Supply of Serviced Lands, Water, Transport, etc are a Result of Rapid Growth of Cities

Much of the ills of urban living is attributed to the rapid growth of population in cities. However, the real causes of the urban problems relate to misdirected policies and rules and regulation at national and state levels about land and housing; the mismatch of resources and functions of Indian local governments, incapacity of the city government to remove subsidies across the board; and inadequate attention in state and national policy formulation towards urban problems.

Economy and the Urban Centres

The economic reforms package aimed at structural adjustment through trade and tariff policies, capital and financial sector reforms and industrial policy reforms, aim to encourage growth in the economy. In formulating such policies it must be recognised that the performance of macro-economy can be improved by improving the productivity of the urban sector.

Table 9.2 provides estimates of the share of the urban sector in the GDP over time. It is clear that this share has risen from 29 per cent in 1951 to 47 per cent in 1981 and is estimated to be around 60 per cent in 1991. The urban/rural per capita GDP ratio has correspondingly increased from about 2.0 in 1951 to 3.6 in 1991.

TABLE 9.2: Urban/Rural Shares of GDP

Year	GDP at factor costs at current prices (Rs. billion)			Population (in millions)		Per capita GDP (Rs.)		Ratio of Urban/ Rural per capita GDP
	Urban	Rural	Total	Urban	Rural	Urban	Rural	
1950-51	27	67	94	62	299	422	225	1.97
1980-81	673	759	1433	159	524	4222	1449	2.91
1990-91	2355	1570	3925	217	627	10844	2997	3.62

Source:(1) Planning Commission, Task force Reports on Urban Development, 1983

(2) Planning Commission, Eighth Five Year Plan, Vol. II, Ch. 13.

(3) Mulkh Raj, 'Urbanization, Infrastructure and Besieged Growth Potential' (memeo), 1993.

The severe infrastructure deficiencies, the highly regulated and controlled urban land market, limited powers and resources of the urban local governments and inadequate institutional financing of urban infrastructure are some of the key elements that limit the productivity of economic enterprises and households in urban areas. These place severe constraints on the contribution of urban economies to macro-economic growth. These constraints have undermined the ability of Indian cities to be a part of the global financial market and the world economy.

Policy Objectives

The agenda for policy reforms in the urban sector is quite large. For this brief paper it is important to identify the key objectives of such reforms. These are:

(a) Increase the efficiency of urban economy through enabling regulations and procedures;

(b) Promote equity and access of urban services to the urban poor;
(c) Strengthen the capacity of local governments to manage the cities; and
(d) Strengthen the capacity of local governments to manage the cities, use innovative instruments and tools for resources mobilisation and adopt full cost recovery of urban services.

It is necessary that the objectives of urban policy are consistent with the economic reforms policies. The National Housing Policy of May 1992 and the National Commission of Urbanization 1990, have alluded to some of these objectives. Many studies have also advocated similar policies. Notwithstanding these efforts, very little has yet been done in this regard. Urban development, being a state subject, the onus of policy formulation may have to be left to the State government. However, the national government will have to provide guidelines to the states and institute reforms. As Coter (1990) states "just as countries will inevitably have to adjust their economies to global economic forces... the cities will also have to adjust to changing circumstances of the national economy". The national government will have to take a lead and institute such reforms in the areas under their own jurisdiction like the Union Territories, and demonstrate the feasibility and operations of the policy reforms to the state governments through its own actions.

Policy Actions

In a much larger paper (Mehta, 1992), details of specific policy actions are presented. In this paper we present only a summary of these action areas.

A. *Increase Efficiency of Urban Economy*

1. Removal of Urban Land Ceiling legislation.
2. Deregulations related to land transactions and transfers.
3. Information System for Land and Housing in Local Urban areas.
4. Property registration system and tenurial rights to be improved.
5. Zoning plans and FSI (FAR) regulations to be rationalised.

B. *Increase Participation of Private Sector*

1. Reduce or eliminate bulk land acquisition by public agencies in cities.
2. Procedural reforms regarding converting of land to non-

agricultural uses.

3. Rational Master plans, zoning and development control rules.
4. Fiscal incentives for private investments in infrastructure provision and maintenance.

C. *Promote Equity and Access of Land for the Poor*

1. Creation of fund from vacant land tax for purchase of land and housing for the poor.
2. Fiscal incentives to private developers for construction of housing for the poor.
3. Promoting public-private partnerships like land sharing, land pooling, guided development, coloniser licensing for land allocations to the poor.

D. *Financing Land Development and Strengthening Capacity of Local Governments*

1. Integrate infrastructure projects with land development projects for greater flexibility of cost recovery.
2. Increase institutional financing for urban infrastructure and land development.
3. Ensure full cost recovery through user charges with targeted subsidies.
4. Use of land based financing tools such as valorisation, betterment levies, special assessment districts, barter of land for services etc.
5. Provide autonomy to urban local governments for raising local taxes, levying appropriate user charges and accessing the capital and financial market.
6. Use of Revenue Bonds financing for infrastructure and land development.
7. Build local capacity in private sector for operation and maintenance of small infrastructure.
8. Contracting out BOT, BOO, BOOT arrangements for water supply, sanitation projects.

The Task Ahead

The neglect of the urban sector in the national economic policy formulation is quite apparent. The primary task is to bring about the importance of this sector within the perspective of national economy and instil commitments for the reform from the political leadership at the national and state level.

The 74th Constitutional Amendment (Nagarpalika Act) has compelled the state governments to review their municipal legislation. It is an opportune period to usher in a few of the policy reforms suggested above through this process. The national government will have to take leadership in making this happen.

Structural Adjustment with Human Development

At a much larger policy level, the economic reforms package in the country will also have to take cognisance of the fact that many international donor agencies have already begun to look at experiences of countries under structural reforms (Moser *et al.,* 1993). The general consensus which emerges from these studies are that most nations have by and large ignored the human development dimension in their reforms and that the impact of reforms on the urban poor has been adverse in the transitional period (Squire, 1993). It is only in those countries with rapid growth of national economy, that the adverse impacts are minimal. The development paradigm, at least for the multilateral donor agencies, appear to have been shifted to focus on the human development (Colclough, 1993).

In a liberal economy, the urban centres, while contributing significantly to the process of national economic development, are also likely to induce greater inequality in access of basic services. Specific safeguards to meet the basic needs of the urban poor will have to become an integral part of the urban policy reforms package. Increasing urban violence and civic disturbances are indicative of growing expections, frustrations and disenchantment of the masses with the manner in which the cities are governed today. In the present electoral arrangement, urban population does not constitute a significant vote-bank at national level. Yet, the mass movements in recent years have largely originated in urban areas. Increasing attention of the national policy makers is imperative for inclusion of urban reforms in the national economic agenda. Inactions or delays on this front may jeopardise the entire developmental process.

TABLE 9.3 Development Paradigms 1960-90

Dominal Paradigms		Main Constraints	Strategy Proposed Paradigms	Alternative
1960-70	Maximization of growth	Absorptive capacity, Low savings	Aid Foreign investment, Human capital formation	Stages of Growth, Socialist accumulation
1970-80	Structuralism	Structural rigidities, Market imperfections,	Redistribution with growth, Basic needs,	State socialism, Dependency and

		Patterns of ownership, Domestic politics	Employment generation	neo-Marxism
1980-90	Neo-liberalism	Balance of payments, disequilibrium, Constrained markets, State as pariah, Rent-seeking	Liberalize markets and prices, Reduce role of state	Modified structura-lism, Adjustment with human face
1990-	Human development Poverty alleviation	Recession, Stagnation, Deepening poverty	Investment in basic services for human development, Labour-intensity, Safety-nets	Neo-liberalism

Source: Colclough (1993)

REFERENCES

Bhagwati Jagdish and T.N. Srinivasan, (1993) "India's Economic Reforms", Government of India, Ministry of Finance, July 1993.

Colclough, Christopher (1993), "Human Development: Towards a more integrated framework for planning in the 1990s", Discussion paper no. 3223, Institute of Development Studies, Sussex, April 1993.

Mehta, Dinesh (1993), "Economic Reforms—two years after and the task ahead—discussion paper," G.O.I. Ministry of Finance, Department of Economic Affairs.

Mehta, Dinesh and Meera Mehta (1992), "Privatisation of Municipal Services", *Urban India,* Vol. XII, No.2, July-December, 1993 pp 1-30.

Mehta, Meera and Dinesh Mehta (1989), *Metropolitan Housing Market,* Sage Publishers, New Delhi.

——————(1992), "Financing urban Infrastructure and Land Development", Theme paper, Urban Land seminar at Aurangabad, School of Planning, CEPT, Ahmedabad.

——————(1990), "Financing Urban Infrastructure and Land Development," Theme paper, Urban Land Seminar at Aurangabad, School of Planning, CEPT, Ahmedabad.

Moser, Caroline, Alicia Herbert and Roza Makonneen, (1993), "Urban Poverty in the Context of Structural Adjustment—Recent evidences and policy responses", discussion paper TWU DP No. 4, Urban Development Division, The World Bank, Washington, May 1993.

Squire Lyn, (1993), "Economic Development: Recent lessons on Lighting poverty", American Economic Association—Papers and Proceedings, May 1993, pp 377-382.

World Bank, "India-Progress and Challenges in Economic transition", Report 11761-IN, May 1993, World Bank, Washington.

10. NATIONAL URBAN POLICY FOR INDIA: Some Issues

K. Dharmarajan
S.S. Dutta

Introduction

It is ironical that even after over 40 years of planned development of the country, approach to urbanisation and urban development remains adhoc and fragmented without any coherent policy framework. Lately a number of factors have combined to bring into sharper focus the need for national urban policy:

* The paradigm of development at macro level has undergone a substantive change, inter alia, involving structural adjustment and liberalisation of industry and trade. This has necessitated a review of the role of the State in the development process in general and in urban development in particular.
* The process of urbanisation has reached a stage significant enough, in economic if not in demographic terms as well, to influence the growth of the economy and this is going to assume greater importance as structural transformation of the economy gathers momentum in the future.
* There is a growing appreciation of the role of urbanisation as a positive force in the development process and a realisation that the manner in which cities economies are run in conjunction with supporting services can have a significant effect on urban productivity and hence on the whole economy's growth.
* At the same time there is a growing realisation that urban growth has the ugly side too increasing poverty and a greater stress on the environment—raising fundamental issues of sustainability of the present urban development process.
* The latest amendments to the Constitution call for greater devolution of powers to democratic units of local self-government

which would mean a new delineation of functions and responsibilities and the need for measures to strengthen these bodies managerially and financially.

While the need for an urban policy at the national level is widely appreciated, there is no agreement on what this means, its contents, and how one goes about designing it.

The formulation of an urban policy is not as straight-forward a proposition as is the case with certain other sectoral aspects of development such as agriculture, industry, population, education etc. More important among the factors which make such a policy exercise a difficult task (and perhaps nebulous too) are:

* Unlike agriculture, industry, health etc. urban development is essentially a process of development involving various sectors and actors at different levels and hence the need for consultation with several agencies.
* The linkages of economic and spatial development, both at micro and macro level and their impact, are not clearly understood.
* Urban development is essentially a State responsibility and hence the Central Government would have little hold on its implementation.
* Decisions taken in other sectors, both at macro and micro level, can have a significant impact on urban development but neither city governments nor development authorities are consulted before these decisions are taken.

Notwithstanding the difficulties spelt out above, more than ad hoc responses, one needs a framework within which urban growth takes place. The formulation of an urban policy would at least help in starting a debate at policy level on the important issues confronting urban planners and managers.

Emerging Urban Scenario

Thanks to the economic transition effected under successive national plans, while the share of agriculture and allied occupations in GDP has declined from about 56.5 per cent in 1951 to 32 per cent in 1991—92 (at 1980-81 prices) it has not been matched by perceptible reduction in the corresponding share of work force in the sector, implying a widening of gap between per capita increase in income in agricultural and non-agricultural sectors[1]. In this background the process of urbanisation has been gathering momentum over the years with clear signs of acceleration in the Seventies. The following aspects in particular merit attention:

* Growing scale or absolute size of urban population which reached 217 million in 1991; a magnitude larger than the corresponding total in all countries in the world except China. Despite a decline in the decadal rate of growth of urban population in 1981-91 (36.2) over 1971-81 (46.1), the net addition in population was 58 million as against 50 million in the previous decade.
* Despite a fairly balanced spatial pattern of urban growth there is a marked tendency towards concentration of economic activities and population in large cities; out of a total of 3996 urban settlements in 1991, 23 million plus cities accounted for 33 per cent of total urban population. (Tables 10.1 and 10.2.)
* There is a market variation in regional pattern of urban growth. Among the states showing relatively high rate of urban growth in 1971-81 were: Haryana and Punjab (where increasing productivity and commercialisation of agriculture have forced healthy rural-urban relationship and movement of population has involved push and pull factors); Bihar (with poor performance in both agriculture and industry push factors are a major force); and Karnataka (with healthy industrial expansion but stagnant agriculture has experienced urban growth because of pull factors). In line with over all trends, majority of the states registered a decline in the decenial urban growth rate during 1981-91, a phenomena which in view of marked improvement in the performance of economy and industry, warrants deeper analysis.
* The older industrialized States (such as Maharashtra, Tamil Nadu and West Bengal), though most urbanised, were found among the most poor in terms of rural poverty; their levels of urban poverty being around average. In contrast, it is the agriculturally prosperous States like Haryana and Punjab that have the least urban as well as rural poverty levels. What is of greater interest is that these two states are found to be most successful in all spheres and this has been achieved without large scale industrial investment. Yet growth in manufacturing employment is among the highest in these states including employment in household industry which is generally declining elsewhere.[2]

TABLE 10.1: Trends of Urban Population Growth: 1901-91

Year	Total Population		Urban population Census		
	in million	Decadal growth rate	in million	Decadal growth rate	As percentage of total population
1901	238.40	—	25.85	—	10.84
1911	252.09	05.75	25.94	0.35	10.29
1921	251.32	-0.31	28.09	8.27	11.18
1931	278.98	11.00	33.46	19.12	11.99
1941	318.66	14:22	44.15	31.97	13.86
1951	361.09	13.31	62.44	41.42	17.29
1961	439.23	21.64	78.94	26.41	17.97
1971	548.16	24.80	109.11	38.23	19.91
1981	683.33	24.66	159.46	46.14	23.34
1991	846.30	23.85	217.61	36.46	25.66

Note: 1. The 1981 census was not conducted in Assam, therefore, 1981 figures for India include interplaced figures for Assam.

2. The 1991 census includes projected figures for Jammu and Kashmir as projected by the sanding committee of experts population projection (October, 1984).

Source: Census of India reports.

TABLE 10.2: Urban Growth by Size Class of Towns (1981-1991)

(Population in million)

Urban Size class	1981			1991		
	Number	Population	@Percent	Number	Population	@Percent
1000,000+	12	42.02	26.90	23	70.66	32.81
500,000-1000,000	28	18.70	11.97	30	20.94	9.72
100,000-500,000	176	38.57	21.49	247	48.13	22.35
100,000 & above	216	98.29	60.37	300	139.7	364.89
50,000-100,000	270	18.19	11.65	345	23.60	10.96
20,000-50,000	739	22.42	14.35	947	28.71	13.33
Below 20,000	2020	21.29	13.63	2104	23.30	10.82
All Urban Settlements	3245	156.19	100.00	3996	215.34	100.00

@ Excludes Jammu and Kashmir

Source: Census of India 1981 and 1991.

* Though the latest Census details on components of urban growth have yet to become available, hitherto natural increase and migration have each accounted for 40 per cent and rest attributed to reclassification of boundaries.
* Though the urban sector still constitutes a little over one-fourth of the total population; it contributes about 60 per cent of GDP; major part of this originating in cities in the upper range of the urban hierarchy.
* Growth-rate of employment in the urban areas during 1977-78 to 1987-88 has averaged at about 4 per cent per annum while that in the rural areas has declined to less than one per cent per annum, indicating strong signals that the urban areas will have to absorb larger increments to labour force in future.

Various projections indicate that India's urban population by the end of the century would be double its size in 1981 (i.e. 160 million) and that to the present 23 million plus cities another 17 or more may be added. Despite their growing contribution to the national economy one only need to recall the deficiencies and constraints affecting the functioning of all categories of cities and towns to appreciate the implications of this projected increase in urban population.

During 1981-2010, the number of potential workers will double growing almost 40 per cent faster than the population as a whole[3]. In urban areas, the number of potential workers will double even more quickly, surpassing 205 million by 2000. As such provision of adequate employment constitutes a major challenge for the economy as a whole and the urban economy in particular.

The infrastructure facilities (such as water, sanitation, transport, communications etc.) which vitally affect urban productivity and living environment, are strained beyond capacities of various cities. At least 20 per cent of the urban population is not served by piped water supply and only 30 per cent has access to sanitary severage and drainage. Inadequacies in this respect are made all the more unbearable by gross inequities in their dispensation[4]. Rapid increase in land prices and cost of construction has aggravated the problem of shelter and led to the prolific growth of slums and squatter settlements, particularly in the larger cities. Urban transport capacity has also not been keeping pace with the demand leading to severe road congestion and acute inadequacy of public transport in major cities.

In the face of such glaring deficiencies in urban services adequate mobilisation of financial resources has assumed critical importance. More than a decade ago the Planning Commission Task Force on Housing and Urban Development (1983) had estimated that during 1981-2001 an investment of about Rs. 30,000—40,000 crores would be required to provide the needed urban services to meet the backlog and replacement. While financial requirements of this order can hardly be met without sufficient assistance from the higher tiers of Government, what is disturbing is the inability of most of the local bodies to mobilise resources commensurate with their growing expenditure needs[5].

A weak financial position combined with erosion of their functional base in recent years has adversely affected the management capacity of local bodies.

In brief, it can hardly be over-emphasized that nothing short of a drastic change in policy approach and priorities would enable cities and towns to cope with the anticipated growth efficiently and equitably.

Policy and Programme Initiative

It is relevant to recall that except for certain components of urban development (such as water supply, public health and sanitation) in the state list, there is no mention of urban development as such in any of the three lists of the Seventh Schedule of the Constitution allocating functional responsibilities between Central and State Government[6]. This lack of explicit status of the subject reflects an anti-urban bias which has dominated intellectual thinking and the policy environment for the major part of planned development in the country. However, partly out of its concern for exigencies of development, especially in rapidly growing cities and towns, and partly to supplement the efforts of State Governments in this direction, the role of the Central Government in the field of urban development has expanded over the past four decades or so.

Apart from the introduction of a number of centrally sponsored schemes (e.g. water supply and sanition, housing for lower income groups, preparation of master plans, environmental improvement of slums, integrated development of small and medium towns etc.), government initiative has included formal deliberations in important policy areas such as urban land policy, augmentation of urban local bodies finances, rural-urban relationship, and development of small and medium towns. Following the appointment of the Planning Commission's Task Force on Housing and Urban Development in 1983 and the National Commission on Urbanisation in 1987, recent developments reflect a better articulation of urban policy concerns at the national level. More important among these developments which can be broadly divided into two stages, are elaborated below.

It was not until the Third Plan (1961-66) that a concern was expressed about the relationship between the policies of industrial development and the growth of major cities. However, the Third Plan, as the subsequent Fourth Plan (1969-74), perceived urban development basically as a problem of social welfare and equity rather than as an aspect of economic development. The essence of the Plans' urban strategy was balanced regional development to be achieved through a policy of industrial decentralisation. The more important among other policy initiatives in the early phase of planning until the late seventies were focused on: deceleration of the growth of metropolitan cities, development of backward regions through a number of incentives (some of these regions touching the fringes of metropolitan areas such as Delhi and Bangalore), development of small and medium town to reduce the intensity of migration to metropolitan cities, promotion of social housing schemes for different categories of low income population, direct public intervention in the urban land markets and urban land ceiling legislation to prevent concentration of land ownership and speculative tendencies.

In the sphere of shelter specifically, because of the meager impact of the above schemes, a distinct change in policy emphasis was effected in the seventies involving a shift from formal housing to 'sites and services' programmes and the scheme for Environmental Improvement of Urban slums (EIUS).

Notwithstanding the emergence of new foci of industrial activity in recent years (such as Bangalore, Hyderabad, Ludhiana, Delhi and Steel towns), extensive decentralisation of industries has not taken place. Urban Land Ceiling (Control and Regulation) Act, 1976 which failed to achieve its objectives and has instead frozen large chunks of land and other market distortions is being reviewed. Without dilating on a detailed discourse in this context, one cannot perhaps do better than cite the Task Force report on policy and programme interventions in the Sixties and Seventies:

'Policy and programme interventions have been half-hearted, loosely coordinated, to say the least, and even counter productive; spatial considerations have never received the attention they deserve. Policy has been half-hearted in as much as a few of the points at which governments might intervene to manage urbanisation and effect its course and direction have been properly tackled. It is uncoordinated in as much as national planning tends to be in terms of sectoral outlays, while urban planning has been mainly linked with physical layouts. It is counterproductive in as much as the effort has been to divert, retard, or stop urban growth and in particular to inhibit the expansion of metropolitan cities'[7].

Recent Developments

Policy developments in recent years have, to an important extent, been influenced by two major reports on urbanisation and urban development mentioned above. The Planning Commission's Task Force report, which made a refreshing departure from the past thinking, emphasised shift to positive policies in support of urbanisation and urban development as an adjunct to economic development and came up with a wide range of recommendations. Unfortunately not much has been done in follow up of the Task Force's report. The National Commission on Urbanisation (1987) set up subsequently at the instance of the then Prime Minister with fairly comprehensive terms of reference has reiterated the thinking of the Task Force on a number of policy aspects and has set out fairly detailed suggestions for improvement in more than one direction[8].

Though the leads provided in these reports have not yet been given the shape of a national urban policy framework, it is important to take note of the developments in certain substantive policy aspects in recent years. These relate to:

* formulation and approval by parliament of national housing policy in 1992;
* 74th amendment of the Constitution in April, 1993 to provide long overdue Constitutional status to urban local bodies and decentralisation of urban development; and
* high level policy dialogue on urban land management and water supply and sanitation.

The National Housing Policy, which was preceded by a fairly prolonged debate at various levels before its finalisation, sets a comprehensive agenda including a shift in the role of Government from that of a provider to a facilitator of housing and more active involvement of private sector and NGOs. With major part of action in this respect being within the purview of State Government it is yet to be seen as to how soon this exercise proceeds beyond a policy statement.

The 74th amendment of the Constitution puts on a firmer footing the relationship between the State Government and local bodies with respect to functions and taxation powers and arrangements for revenue sharing. It interalia, contemplates devolving a wide range of functions including planning for economic and social development and urban poverty alleviation to local bodies and setting up by each State of a Finance Commission to review the finances of municipalities and recommend taxes to be assigned o the Municipalities and grants-in-aid from the consolidated fund of the state.

Recognising the critical need to increase the supply of serviced urban and, USAID (India) with the active support of Ministry of Urban Development and the National Housing Bank initiated a policy dialogue hrough a series of seminars during 1991-92 to discuss in depth the key and policy issues including financing of urban infrastructure and land levelopment, access of the poor to urban land, and legal and institutional ramework of urban land management. Arising out of this dialogue, key ction areas have been identified to improve delivery of serviced urban and which broadly relate to legislative, financial and fiscal and institutional eforms.

A National Conference on Urban Water Supply and Sanitation rganised by the Central Ministry of Urban Development has, after eliberating on major policy issues, come up with an exhaustive set of ecommendations as a policy statement in this sector including:

* full cost recovery in principle;
* cross subsidisation to meet the basic minimum requirements of the poor;
* the need for cost reduction of operations;
* integrated planning and utilisation of water resources at state level;
* uniform policy and guidelines for human resource development;
* improvement in data base; and
* encouragement of low cost sanitation, especially in small and medium towns.

In this context it is necessary to make a mention of the National olicy on Environment and Development brought out by Central Ministry Environment and Forests in June, 1992 which spells out broad rategies and priorities in specific sectors including human settlements gether with supporting institutional and promotional measures.

While there is enough work to be done towards translating these eas into practice, it can hardly be denied that there has been in recent ars, a better articulation of policy concerns in urban development than therto. At the same time, these highlight the complexity of policy issues urban development.

sues in Policy Perspective

espite heavy odds in their development, cities have shown a remarkable strength in generating income and employment and that the major challenge at policy level lies in maximising such opportunities to further strengthen their role as an instrument of economic development. This policy perspective departs from the conventional thinking which hitherto concentrated on pathological aspects of urbanisation or issues of population distribution without explicit concern or social and economic development. In the nature of things, while major initiatives for policy reforms and action fall in the purview of state and local governments, there are (in view of cities being a part of national and international economies) limits to development operations at these levels without supporting action in the framework of national urban policy. Alleviation of urban poverty with its ramifications rooted in the structural conditions of the economy is a case in point. Certain important issues in formulation of a national urban policy are briefly discussed below.

Turning first to the goals of National Urban Policy (NUP), these of necessity have to be related to the emerging social and economic imperatives of development in the national context. In line with the perspective of development set out in the Eighth Plan for the next 15 years, expansion of employment and income, urban poverty, and environment constitut major goals of NUP for the next two decades or so. Though the operationa implications of these goals have not yet been fully gone into, perceived in terms of sustainability of the urban development process, these ar essentially complementary in nature.

A serious impediment to policy mediation at the national level is th lack of adequate understanding about dynamics of city growth, especiall the underlying economic forces and their impact on the spatial pattern c growth. Hitherto not much progress has been made in evaluating the effe of major economic policies on urban settlements or the effect of differer activity mix and their operational environment on the productivity c various categories of urban settlements. In the face of such limitations c knowledge, spatial allocation of resources becomes quite problematic.

There is evidence to suggest that despite significant improvement i the performance of economy during the last decade, disparities at region and inter-personal levels in urban areas have increased. While it unrealistic to think of parity in regional incomes at least in the near futur choices in specific policy options have to be made after careful assessme of their political and economic implications.

As it stands, a larger part of infrastructure and other investments a concentrated in major cities. There is no feedback whatsoever on t experience of IDSMT to work out more viable strategies of decentralis development, while the export-led growth under the new economic poli coupled with liberalisation of licensing for industries may further till the balance in favour of large cities. The experience hitherto indicates that it is easier to channelise growth in existing growth centres than to generate it on new locations. All the same, because of inability to meet the social costs of negative externalities there is a tendency for private firms to over-estimate the benefits of agglomeration economies in large cities and dependence on market forces alone may not be that conducive to realise the potential of growth in other locations.

Perhaps the greatest challenge in realisation of the above goals of NUP lies at the institutional level, especially the constraints of urban local bodies which along with certain state agencies bear the brunt of responsibilities for delivery of services at the local level. Decentralisation of urban development administration has been rightly mooted to deal with the situation. But local management of decentralised development has to be seen in a broader framework of national development - as a participatory process involving all the three levels of government.

Further, along with strengthening of urban local bodies, decentralisation has raised the issue of public vs. private provision of urban services including more active participation of NGOs and community organisations. The ground realities are rather complex to admit stereotype policy fixations and warrant a flexible response depending on the characteristic and operational parameters of various services. The 74th Amendment of the Constitution augurs well to refurbish the role of urban local bodies in urban development. However, much would depend on how the implementation of the proposed reforms for urban local bodies are combined with complementary efforts to improve their management capacities.

The recent decline in the growth rate of rural employment and casualisation of labour constitute a serious portent for the economy. Apart from a review of existing development priorities, an important issue is how best can rural-urban development on a symbiotic basis be promoted on the pattern of Punjab and Haryana.

Not the least important is the question of more effective coordination than hitherto attempted at the Central Government level itself to effectively support the goals of NUP.

Lately, the macro-economic reforms introduced as a part of the new economic policy have generated keen interest in the performance of urban economy especially the need to increase urban productivity. Constrains in infrastructure have rightly been reckoned as an important factor affecting urban productivity. But beyond that what changes are necessary in terms of investment allocations or development priorities at macro and micro levels to sustain the pace of economic growth or, for that matter, the impact of economic growth itself on urban poverty and environment, have not been spelt out yet.

All in all, stakes in efficient and equitable management of urban development have outgrown the vagaries of ad hoc policy. Choice needs to be made between piecemeal interventions (such as IDSMT, Mega Cities Scheme etc.) and a coherent policy framework as an adjunct to national economic development. Given a commitment of this nature, the ongoing debates on certain sectoral aspects of urban development could be articulated to help initiate this process.

REFERENCES

1. The proportion of workforce in agriculture and allied occupations which remained unchanged at 70 per cent over seven decades (1901-71), came down to 66.5 per cent in 1981 and further declined marginally to 64.9 per cent in 1991. Another noteworthy change in the rural sector in recent years (1977-78 to 1987-88) has been an increase in the proportion of casual labour and decline in that of self-employed.
2. Rakesh Mohan and Pushpa Thottan 'The Regional Spread of Urbanisation, Industrialisation and Urban Poverty' in *Poverty in India* Edited by Barbara Harriss, S. Guhan and R.H. Cassen, 1992.
3. This rate of growth will be even faster if the female participation rate in workforce picks up.
4. For instance, as against per capita availability of 200 litres of water per day for Delhi city as a whole that in slums is only about 20 LPCD.
5. According to a recent cross-sectional analysis of 210 municipalities by NIUA, between 1979/80 and 1983/84, while current revenues grew at an average rate of 13.8 per cent annually, current expenditures grew at an average rate of 24.3 per cent annually.
6. Industrial location which has an important bearing on growth of cities and towns is in Union list as are certain other heads of development.
7. Planning Commission, Task Force Report on Housing and Urban Development, 1983, p.118.
8. More important among the Commission's recommendations include: priority for urban economic development to maximise productive employment opportunities; enhancing the efficiency of urban physical development; more realistic standards and technologies to make efficient targeting of support to the poor; shift in the role of Government form provider to enables and facilitator; development of selected cities and towns with potential for generating economic momentum; and linking urban and rural development in regional framework.

11. DEMOGRAPHIC PRESSURE AND URBANISATION: A Case of Dehradun Urban Agglomeration in Garhwal Himalayas

Anil Kumar Dimri
R.P. Juyal

Urbanisation, specially in the developing region, is viewed as a process of diffusing innovation, science, education, art and commerce to a large hinterland. Urban centres as islands in the vast sea of rurality, offer temptation of better opportunities of population. The persisting rural-urban dichotomy and regional imbalances in the process act as catalyst for disproportionate growth of some urban centres. Simultaneously adhocism in regulating the development and creating infrastructure at micro-level and failure to integrate the process of urbanisation with overall process of development at macro level (regional level) are the main reason for the plight of urban centres, mainly on account of unprecedented population growth. Thus there is an imperative need to study and examine the problems of urban centres at intra city level and in regional perspective in relation to the demographic pressure prior to formulating policies of urban development.

In this paper a modest attempt has been made to examine the problems being faced by Dehradun Urban Agglomeration, the largest urban and industrial hub of the predominantly agrarian and industrially backward north-western Himalayan region. Incidentally Dehradun Urban Agglomeration, also happens to be the largest urban centre in the Indian Himalayan region (extending from Karakoram-Kashmir in the north west to Mizo hills in north east)[1]. Thus the conclusion reached in this paper may be of relevance in similar socio-economic settings, in the other parts of the Himalayan region.

Dehradun Urban Agglomeration, is the district headquarters of District, Dehradun, the north-western District of Uttar Pradesh.

Geographically, the Urban Agglomeration, is in the approximate middle of the Doon Valley, which is enclosed by rivers Ganga and Yamuna in the east and west respectively and bounded by the lower Himalayan ranges in the north and Siwaliks hills in the south. Situated in an up-land, the Urban Agglomeration to a large extent acts as water parting ridge of the watershed of Ganga and Yamuna. Besides, numerous rivers and torrents, though seasonal, descending from the Siwaliks and lower Himalayan ranges also have decisive impact on the physical shape and environment of the Urban Agglomeration.

The Urban Agglomeration is enclosed by two-river systems viz. Song and Tons in the east and west respectively; and a third water coarse Suswa, though not at the immediate boundary of the Agglomeration, flows southeastwards along the base of Siwaliks hills encircling the uplands, on which the Urban Agglomeration is situated. Similarly the various segments of Urban Agglomeration have been segregated by the seasonal tributaries of the above-mentioned water courses. Important among them are river Rispana and Bindal which give a triangular shape to Dehradun Municipal Area, the core of the Urban Agglomeration and the principal component of the urban fabric not only of the Doon Valley but of the district and Garhwal Himalayan Region as well.

In regional context, the hinterland of Dehradun Urban Agglomeration largely consists of the predominantly rural and subsistence economy of the Garhwal Himalayas[2]. Nevertheless the strategic location of the urban centres (i.e. in the transit-zone of plains of Uttar Pradesh and Garhwal Himalayas) amidst the fertile arable land, orchards, lush green forest and position in relation to its connectivity with major centres of industry, trade and commerce and surplus production of northern India. Because of this locational advantage, scores of settlers throng the valley and continue to make it the centre of their activities. Important among these were Sri Guru Ram Rai and his follower, who settled and made his abode (Dera) in the village "Khurbura". The town derives its nomenclature from this specific incident of settling a Dera (abode) in a valley (Doon)[3]. Later, a Gurudwara was built here around which the town got nestled.

After the annexation of the Himalayan region to the British empire in 1815, the town received a special favour from imperial rulers because of its soothing climate; consequently physical activity in the town got momentum. Gradually local self administration was introduced and cantonments[4], institutions of eminence, centres of administration got established with the improving mode of accessibility and communication[5].

After independence, the prominence of Dehradun Urban Agglomeration increased manyfolds, as institutions of national eminence and repute continued established and expand in for the affluent. The present day Dehradun Urban Agglomeration has many institutions and agencies of national and international repute. To name a few these are the Oil and Natural Gas Commission, the Wild Life Research Institute, the Centres Soil Research Institute, the Survey of India, the National Remote Sensing Agency and many other besides scores of schools and colleges drawing students from across the nation and even from abroad.

Simultaneously the abundance of non-mettalic mineral like lime-stone, marble, dolomite and phosphate deposits in the lower Himalayan ranges[6], ushered in mineral based industrialisation of the valley. After sixties, about 184 lime kilns, one cement factory, one calcium carbide and one calcium carbonate and six other chemical factories were established in and on the periphery of the Agglomeration[7]. Likewise the Govt. of Uttar Pradesh, provided many financial incentives to hotel industries to promote tourism in the Himalayan region.

These development activities, diversified the economic base of the town and offered opportunities of income and employment to a large number of people. Consequently the population of Dehradun Urban Agglomeration increased from 7316 persons as per Census of 1817 (since then accurate enumeration are available) to 3,67,411 persons in the Census of 1991. In this period the area of the Urban Agglomeration increased from 1.76 sq. kms. to 83.25 sq. kms[8]. This tremendous growth of population increased the chasm between provision and demand for civic amenities and infrastructure; consequently many maladies like - transport bottlenecks, congesation, scarcity of amenities and services and environmental degradation are being faced by the town.

The worst condition among the civic amenities is of water supply. A study conducted by Jal Nigam, Uttar Pradesh reveals that against 64 MLD demand the water supply is only 52 MLD. This available water supply can also not be distributed equitably because of the uneven topography of the town. Similar is the condition of the sewerage system. At present only one-third of the town is equipped with this facility. In many slums a large part of the population has to opt for open spaces to answer the call of nature.

It is pertinent to note that after independence the population of the Urban Agglomeration has more than doubled (increased 143% in a span of 40 years i.e., from 1951 to 1991) whereas the area has increased only 40.80 per cent. The above referred disproportionate growth of area and population is more alarming because of the fact that the number constituents of Urban Agglomeration are on the increase but largely in the form of outer growths or census towns or cantonments[9] without any urban local self- government or being incorporated in the Municipal Board, Dehradun. Likewise villages on the immediate periphery are *de facto* urban, as a significant portion of their land is used up or is being used for non-agrarian purposes like housing, para-military troops, educational institutions and developing posh colonies[10]. Another discrepancy of the physical spwarl, that is also accentuating the urban miseries, is by and large stagnant resource base of the core urban area i.e., Municipal Board, Dehradun. This, to some extent, is due to non-expansion of its limits and thereby leaving a large part of urban area out of its taxation orbit whereas the stresses on the provision of services available in the Municipal limit is ever increasing. For instance, the circulating pattern in the Municipal Area of Dehradun was devised in the early decades of the century for nearly 30,000 population, when pedestrian and slow-moving animal drawn vehicles constituted the bulk of traffic volume. But now not only the pattern of travel and transportation have changed but the population burden on road Geometry has increased more than 15 times than it was at the time of designing. Furthermore Dehradun Urban Agglomeration and adjacent centres have as much as 14 fast moving vehicles per thousand of population klins[11]. This automobile boom alongwith concentration of lime within Urban Agglomeration (at Adhoiwala outer growth) alongwith the reduction of greenary in and around the city has reduced the scope of dilution of pollutants. As a result the concentration of suspended matter particulates is six to seven times higher than the safe limit of 100 μgm[12].

The condition of other amenities is also deplorable, as the chasm between their provision and demand is rapidly increasing. Although the precise estimate and empirical studies on the inflow of the migrants, the main reason for population explosion, is not available, yet conservative estimates reveal that about 60 to 70 per cent of population of the Urban Agglomeration can be attributed to immigration. There are sufficient indications to believe that this trend is not going to be abated in the near future. Town planners are of the opinion that at the turn of this century the population of existing Dehradun Urban Agglomeration may cross the limit of 7 lakh people[13]. For this population it is estimated that about one lakh additional houses will be required[14].

This phenomenon has created tremendous pressure on financial and physical resources, thereby Urban Planning efforts and development regulations are not yielding the desired results. The land values for residential, commercial and other built up uses, are soaring sky high. Therefore, the land reserved for green and non-built up uses in the Master Plan of Dehradun is being increasingly encroached. In this process of undermining the planning and development regulation not only the unscrupulous elements are making huge profits, even government agencies are also showing little respect for the physical plan document duly approved by Government. Very often they also selects easy and convenient location for their projects, irrespective of their conformity with planning norms and regulation and thereafter get the development and planning regulations and norms modified to legalise their deeds[15]. The above-mentioned process has had multifaceted impact on the urban fabric. On the one hand, it has reduced the greenary, and encroached the fertile arable land, once famous for *basmati* rice and orchards of *litchi.* On a conservative estimate, arable land, reserved as such in the Master Plan of Dehradun, has decreased by 25 to 30 per cent since the Master Plan was enforced in the year 1985. This steady erosion in the arable land will eventually shrink the resource base of agrarian economy, which, in terms is bound to have intersectoral impact. Some indications have already started surfacing. The area under sugarcane has considerably declined in the villages situated in the vicinity of the Urban Agglomeration. Continuation of this trend will ultimately reduce supply of raw material to the principal agro-based industry i.e. Doiwala Sugar Mill, which is already facing adverse conditions. In this context it is pertinent to note that Doiwala Sugar Mill had played and still has significant role to play in the diversification of agriculture in the Doon Valley[16]. The other multifaceted impact of population induced urban sprawl is visible in the spread of slums. In 1981, there were only 25 slums in Dehradun Urban Agglomeration with a population of 45,000 accounting for 16 per cent of the total population of the Urban Agglomeration. These member has now gone up to 70 with a population of 1.2 lakhs accounting for about 30 per cent of the total population of the Urban Agglomeration. These slums have been developed on the river bed and banks. Prone to floods these are generally devoid of civic amenities. Moreover, the qualities of housing, i.e. availability of space and environment, is deplorable. In a majority of cases these slums are populated by the socially and economically weaker sections of the society. Generally the slum dwellers are engaged in urban informal sector. Carrying pavement merchandise and working as hawkers, they operate on slow moving vehicle like hand and animal drawn theals. This facet of urban economy is also responsible for degradation of urban environment. Frequent encroachment of roads by pavement activities, reduces the effective carriage way; and significant presence of slow moving vehicles retards the speed of automobiles thereby increasing pollution.

The past experience of regulating urban development has yielded little in the Doon Valley. This is not because of any fault in urban design but mainly due to the external factors that are increasing the population and causing urban sprawl in the valley. Therefore, the foremost need is of a regional policy of urbanization, which will ensure decentralised and hierarchical development of various urban centres. Simultaneously the will to execute a plan in letter and spirit is the foremost ingredient of successful planning. Past experiences provide adequate evidence that the skill of physical planning has developed significantly, but the mechanisms of implementation and monitoring have yet to sharpen their lever to function adequately.

REFERENCES

1. Dehradun Urban Agglomeration, ranks 14th and 78th in the State of Uttar Pradesh and India respectively in terms of the population as per census of 1991. It is the largest urban centre of the Himalayan region comprising parts of Uttar Pradesh, Jammu and Kashmir, Himachal Pradesh, Arunachal Pradesh, Sikkim, Meghalaya, Nagaland, Mizoram and Tripura states.
2. The Garhwal Himalayan region comprises the Garhwal Division of Uttar Pradesh. It consists of 5 hill districts viz. Chamoli, Dehradun, Garhwal, Tehri-Garhwal and Uttar Kashi situated in the extreme northern part of the State. The region spread over an area of 30090 sq. kms. accommodates 29.31 lakh persons as per the Census of 1991.

   The region has 32 urban centres in all, which account for 23.81 per cent of the total population of the region. Most of these urban centres are either District headquarters or centres of pilgrimage and tourism. They have been designated as urban merely because of their administrative importance and absence of primary activities in them. In most of the cases their functional bases are devoid of any diversification; consequently they render limited services and opportunities to their hinterland. The sole exception to this phenomena is Dehradun Urban Agglomeration which, with its heavily diversified economy, accounts for 40.80 per cent of the total population of Doon Valley i.e. virtually Dehradun Tehsil of Dehradun district), 52.57 per cent and 46.27 per cent of the urban population of Dehradun district and Garhwal region respectively.

   The total urban population of the five districts of the region alongwith the number of urban centres in them are as under:
3. The literal meaning of the word Dehradun, is Dera or Dehra (abode) in Dun (a valley enclosed by two mountains). Shri Guru Ram Rai, was son of Shri Guru Har Rai who because of difference with other leaders of community preferred to retire in the solitude of Doon. [G.R.C. Williams *Historical and Statistical Memoirs of Dehradun* (1874), reprint Natraj Publishers, Dehradun (1992) page 90.]
4. Municipal Board of Dehradun was established in 1867 and realignments of its area took place in 1876, 1878, 1891 and 1909.
5. The colonial rulers took keen interest in the development of Dehradun town and its adjacent areas, because it's climate was comparatively soothing to them. They preferred the town for setting up of cantonments and institutions. Important among them are Dehradun Cantt (1987), Clement Town Cantt, Ordinance Factory (1942), Prince of Wales Royal Indian Military Academy renamed after independence as Indian Military Academy (1922), The office of Surveyor General of India (1861), The Central Forest School which was later elevated to the status of Imperical Forest Research Institute (1878) and is now known as Forest Research Institute and college.

TABLE 11.1: Garhwal Himalaya: Districtwise Area, Population and Number of Urban Centres

District	Area in Sq. Km.	Population in Lakhs		No. of Urban Centres
		Total	Urban Pop.	
Chamoli	9168	4.41	0.37	8
Dehradun	3088	10.14	5.48	9
Garhwal	5397	6.64	0.81	7
Tehri Garhwal	4421	5.75	0.37	5
Uttarkashi	8016	2.37	0.17	3
Total	30090	29.31	6.98	32

Dehradun town got connected with the plains of India by all weather Roorkee-Dehradun-Landour Mussoorie road in the year 1823. Another important road connecting the district Dehradun to the plains of northern India was Saharanpur-Chakrata Road (1873). Another important road connecting the District with Western Himalaya, Mussoorie-Simla road, was greatly improved by the Britishers. The transportation network was connected by rail network in the year 1910.

6. The estimated reserves of lime stone and marble deposits in the lower Himalayan ranges of Doon Valley are about 5.63 crore Metric Tonnes accounting for about 70 per cent of the total national deposit (Department of Mining and Geology U.P., Dehradun).
7. Most of the lime kilns and industrial units were closed after the Hon'ble Supreme Court of India canceled many mining leases in the year 1986 on the ground of ecological environmental degradation of Doon Valley.

8. TABLE 11.2: Population Picture of Dehradun Urban Agglomeration

(Area in sq. kms.)

Year	Area	Population		
		Male	Female	Total
1872	1.76	4567	2749	7316
1881	9.76	11144	7815	18959
1891	20.20	17774	10658	47391
1901	20.20	18690	12305	30995
1911	20.20	27150	15418	42568
1921	20.20	34784	16073	50858
1931	39.63	34104	18822	52926
1941	39.63	52762	27818	80580
1951	59.13	90275	61661	151936
1961	81.01	97242	75540	178782
1971	76.77	124936	95635	220571
1981	86.48	165248	132770	298028
1991	83.25	199436	167975	367411

Source: Various Issues of Census of India, District Census Hand Book, Dehradun, Uttar Pradesh.

9. TABLE 11.3: Dehradun Urban Agglomeration —Area and Population

(Area in sq. kms. and Population in Lakhs)

	1951		1961		1971		1981		1991	
	Area	Pop.	Area	Pop.	Area	Pop.	Area	Pop.	Area	Pop.
Dehradun Municipal Board	12.00	1.16	12.00	1.26	31.08	1.66	31.08	2.11	NA	2.70
Forest Research Institute	-	-	8.24	0.02	4.69	0.03	4.69	0.04	NA	0.04
Dehradun Cantt	20.98	0.27	20.98	0.26	-	-	20.98	0.43	NA	0.42
Clement Town	7.77	0.07	7.77	0.07	7.07	0.11	7.07	0.15	NA	0.18
Raipur			12.95	0.08	12.95	0.05	14.59	0.13	NA	0.13
Adhoiwala	-	-	-	-	-	-	1.50	0.04	NA	0.13
Majra Census Town*	-	-	-	-	-	-	3.24	0.05	-	0.03

*Majra was designated as Census town in the Census 1981 but in 1991 census it was treated exclusively as rural. However considering the functional and spatial linkages of the settlement with the Urban Agglomeration, it has been treated as part of it, irrespective to its urban or rural status.

Source: Census of India, 1961, 1971, 1981; District Census Hand Book, Dehradun; Census of India 1991, provisional Totals.

10. For instance, in village Niranjanpur, in the western southern fringe of the town, a battalion of Indo-Tibetan Border Police, Industrial Training Institute, a large housing colony of Mussoorie-Dehradun Development Authority, an Agricultural product whole sale market *(mandi)*, Business Complexes, Storage, and some industrial units have come up. Similar is the core of village Kanwali—where the largest posh colony of Dehradun is located and another Housing Colony has been developed by Uttar Pradesh Housing Board. On the eastern fringe of the Urban Agglomeration, in village Jogiwala and Harawala, colonization on a very large scale is being done and a Railway yard is coming up. These uses have changed the landuse and occupation pattern of these villages considerably. They have either swelled the rank of landless labour or they have joined informal sector by becoming hawkers, pavement merchants and the like.
11. Town and Country Planning Department, U.P. "Doon Valley Special Development Area Master Plan-2001" Draft (1990).
12. Studies of U.P. Pollution Control Board reveal that at clock tower, the heart of city, the concentration of suspended matter particulate is about 600 μgm^3 and at many other places it is about 400 to 500 μgm^2.
13. Town and Country Planning Department, U.P. *op. cit.*
14. Devi Dayal, "The significance of Master Plan area under Mussoorie Development Authority in relation to development of Doon Valley", paper and resolution of the symposium on Development and Environment of Doon Valley (June, 1985).
15. The agricultural marketing committee (Mandi Samiti) has selected a lush orchard of litchi and mangoes reserved as such in the Master Plan for constructing a market complex contrary to the provision of planning policy. It was later amended and regularised. Consequently the Dehradun Master Plan has been amended six times within a span of 8 years, since its approval by Government of Uttar Pradesh in 1985.
16. Mukherjee, A, Bradly, Flamm and Juyal, R.P.: Rural Area Development Planning: Application of Tools of Economic Analysis - A Case Study of Doiwala Block, Study submitted to FAO, (Unpublished) 1992.

12. POLICY-MAKING IN EDUCATION

R.V. Vaidyanatha Ayyar

In post-independence India the first national policy on education was formulated in 1968 based on the Kothari Commission. This policy was reviewed and replaced by the National Policy on Education, 1986. The process of revision began with the publication of a candid and self-critical document *Challenge of Education.* It was the debate on this document that led to the revisions. The draft NPE was discussed first in the Central Advisory Board on Education (CABE), comprising all State Education Ministers and eminent educationists, and subsequently by the National Ministers and eminent educationists, and then by the National Development Council and later adopted by the Parliament.

NPE is comprehensive in scope and covers all aspects of education. To spell out a few features:

- Emphasis on education for women's equality,
- Shift in emphasis in elementary education from mere enrolment to retention, quality and attainment,
- Recognition that formal schools cannot reach millions of working children and girls,
- Launching of a large non-formal education programme,
- National Literacy Mission,
- Vocational Education as a distinct stream at the higher secondary stage,
- Navodaya Schools to serve rural talented children,
- Emphasis on consolidation of higher education and its protection from degradation,
- Modernisation of Technical Education,
- Teacher Accountability,
- Decentralisation of Management,

— Enlisting NGOs,
— Mobilising non-budgetary resources.

Where NPE marks a departure is in the formulation of a Programme of Action, stepping up of Plan outlays and launching major centrally sponsored schemes to support the states in priority areas. Some of the schemes like the Operation Blackboard have become household names. The Policy and its Programme of action were updated in 1992; while a few modifications were made to take note of the developments since 1986 the policy frame remained more or less intact.

Now let me turn to the general points. Most discussions on policy tend towards the substance of policy and neglect the processes underlying the formulation of a policy. Thus, we have excellent studies say on industrial policy but unlike some countries such as United States, we have few studies on the politics and processes of industrial policy. An important research agenda for a premier institution like the Lal Bahadur Shastri National Academy of Administration is to document the processes of major policies. I am reminded of what the late R.K. Hazari once observed: those who can conceptualize do not know the ropes and *vice versa.* We need to blend theoretical knowledge and practical experience. In the documentation of policies we need to emulate the armed forces in their elaborate reconstruction and documentation of battles, more for their implications for strategy and tactics than to write history *per se.* Of course, there is the quip that generals prepare for the last war, but lack of any institutional memory whatsoever is worse.

Only policy analysts in ivory towers can afford to ignore the context and the processes. This is the reason why the most fiery radicals seem to lose their fervour while in office. Politics and administration, being the art of possible, it is the process of policy formulation and the situational imperative which delimit the scope of a policy and its content. To illustrate the great importance of the situational imperative, I can refer to the Balance of Payments crisis in July 1991 which facilitated the process of economic reforms. Or to cite other illustrations, the food situation in 1966 which facilitated the launch of the Green Revolution or the launch of the Sputnik by the erstwhile Soviet Union which hurt the American pride and gave an impetus to Science and Mathematics education in the United States. A crisis is thus an opportunity. In a crisis situation the process gets shortened and the resolve to act gains ascendancy. But there are crises and crises. The problem facing policy makers in most social sectors like education is not that there is no crisis but it is a quiet crisis lacking the immediacy or the high visibility of say a default on international commitments. Therefore the momentum a quiet crisis can impart to action is less.

The process is determined by the environment—the legal environment, the political environment, the system and the actors. Education, for example, is a concurrent subject. Legally the Centre can legislate in all areas of education. However, the Centre has been relying on the consensual process to promote educational development. This is as it should be, for States are very important actors in education in terms of the magnitude of resources they expend on education and the number of educational institutions they manage. It is better that such major actors "own" the policy. It is for this reason that though the States were associated in the formulation of the Programme of Action, 1992 they were requested to formulate their own state Programmes of Action, harmonising the national document and their situational imperatives.

Central legislation is limited to maintenance of standards in higher and technical education, a subject which was vested in the Centre right from the commencement of the Constitution. I have in mind the UGC Act and the All India Technical Education Act. To be effective the implementation of these acts require the co-operation of States. Hence policy-making in education has to reckon with this historical tradition. Concurrence has to be interpreted, as the NPE, 1986 does, as meaningful partnership between the Centre and the States. As the experience with universalisation of elementary education and adult literacy has shown, the partnership has to be enlarged. It is necessary to enlist NGOs and the teaching community for the cause of education. In the CABE, set up in 1935, education has a body with a good track record, to forge the national consensus. It has played a major role in the development of every national policy and programme since its inception e.g., the Plan of Post-War Educational Development, NPE, 1968, NPE and its POA as well as their revision.

The challenge in policy formulation lies in mastering the environment, process and the actors. The beguiling temptation is to indulge in generalities and, worse, in rhetoric. While a certain degree of rhetoric is unavoidable, the more specific a policy is, in terms of objectives, strategies and instruments, the better it is. Specificity is better realised if the possible trade-off with scope of the policy is recognised. The importance of managing interest groups is acquiring greater importance. The nature of interest groups in a sector determine the elbow room available. In determining the relative importance of interest groups, what matters is not only the size of the groups but the "concentration of benefits". A policy whose benefits are diffused among the public at large can be stopped in its tracks if it meets with the resistance of a small but determined group which stands much to lose. The tenacity of the License-Control Permit Raj is not a little due to the concentrated benefits it conferred on some groups. If it has been found difficult to enforce accountability in the education system it is because the *status quo* likewise confers concentrated benefits on organised groups. In policy planning, it is necessary to take cognizance of the dynamics of these groups, steer the policy formulation towards the desired goals with the clear recognition that the process determines outcomes.

Another important aspect of policy formulation which tends to be sometimes ignored is the design of instruments to realise the policy objectives. Policy is what is done rather than what is said. What is done very much depends on the instruments and the manner in which these instruments influence the behaviour and functioning of the grassroots functionaries who implement the policy. In this sense, the teacher in the remote village and the education inspector in the field are important policy makers. Ideally the design of instruments, goal and strategies should be taken up together. In this context we have to take in the right spirit the perception that "The relationship between rhetoric and behaviour in India seems so different from in the West. Speaking of the mantras, in the West we have the impression that Indians see mantras as potent, that if they say the right words often they will change the world."

And then there is the inexorable Law of Unintended Consequences. Instrumental objectives tend to supersede ultimate objectives. To illustrate, the National Adult Literacy Programme, launched in 1978, sought to promote adult literacy by funding centres which employed local educated youth. Over a course of time, the instrumental objective of running the centres gained ascendancy over the elimination of adult illiteracy Rationality being bounded, even the best policy design cannot anticipate all the responses or the emerging "states of the world". Hence the need for open mindedness, not to be a prisoner of past mindsets or to be a victim of the "Not Invented Here" syndrome. Quick decision-making coupled with the readiness to correct errors with an open mind is to be preferred to perfectionism and paralysis by analysis. The incentive structure should facilitate such a mindset. The replacement of the centre based approach by the Total Literacy Campaigns is a good example of he benefits that accrue by giving up past strategies which might have made sense when conceived but were later found inappropriate.

13. ISSUES RELATING TO SCIENCE AND TECHNOLOGY POLICY

Y.S. Rajan

Introduction

Technology has always been born out of the ingenuity of human beings. His or her interactions with nature to understand it as well as to "master" it have led him or her to innovate new methods of living - whether it is in search of food or for making different forms of food, whether to get water or in the later years more creation and enjoyment of newer necessities of life. Well, such a technological growth has always been a part of human history. In recent years this has been at a such mind boggling pace that several major revolutionary changes are seen to take place during the life span of a person (life span itself has increased considerably/thanks to technological growth). The pace of growth of technology is best illustrated by some examples listing innovations/break throughs that changed or established trends in human history and/or prevailing attitudes (See Table 13.1). Without getting into the details of each of them one may note that the time frame in which primitive tools were made by human beings was around 1,750,000 years ago. This innovativeness has extended human capabilities. Making and using gear for hunting took place about 100,000 years ago.

Subsequent innovations were aimed at reducing the manual work or making it easier leading to subsequent innovations which facilitated easy mental work. The pace then on becomes greater. Then came items aimed at improving comforts and speedy transportation. The concept of speed further concentrated on items aimed at speeding the transfer of ideas or thoughts leading to availability of telecommunications for transfer of data and long distance voice communication and so on. These comforts and speed of actions led to the desire for further improving quality of arts and entertainment. The search and growth go on leading newer aspects of life, so qualitatively different. No doubt, of course, in doing all these there were also innovations aimed at finding newer outlets for fructifying creative

TABLE 13.1: Major Innovations/Breakthroughs that Changed Established Trends in Human History and/or Prevailing Attitudes

Epoch	Approximate time (Years from 1988)	Innovation/Breakthrough	Consequence/Reason
I Technology			
A	1,750,000	* Primitive tools	
B	100,000	* Making and using gear of hunting	
	40,000	* Making and using weapons	* Extending human capabilities
D	5,500	* The wheel	
	4,000	* Bronze and other metals	
	3,500	* Boats and Sailboats	
E	800	* The clock, compass and other measurement instruments	* Reducing and/or making manual work easier
	600	* Gunpowder	
	500	* The printed book	
	350	* Mechanical calculators	* Facilitating and/or making mental work easier
F	210	* Engines	
	180	* Rail roads	
	150	* Electricity	
	130	* Image and sound reproduction)	* Improving comfort and/or speed of transportation
G	90	* Telecommunications	
	85	* Airplanes	
	70	* Automobiles and roads	
	60	* Mass-produced chemical products	* Increasing speed and/ or availability of telecommunications
	45	* Nuclear weapons	
	40	* Computers	
	35	* Mass produced home appliances	* Improving quality of arts and entertainment
H	35	* The transistor	
	30	* Extensive use of fertilizer	

Epoch	Approximate time (Years from 1988)	Innovation/Breakthrough	Consequence/Reason
	30	* Artificial satellites	* Improving material quality of life
	25	* Lasers	
	20	* Micro technology (Microchips, biochemistry, and genetic engineering	
	20	* The moon landing	
		II Exploiting Nature's Resources/Capabilities	
	400,000	* Hunting	
A	300,000	* Harnessing of fire	* Decreasing dependence on the environment
	150,000	* Shelter	
C	20,000	* Permanent settlements	
	20,000	* Domestication of animals	* Exploiting nature's capabilities
	15,000	* Agriculture	
	10,000	* Using animals for transportation and labour	
D	3,500	* Irrigation Systems	
	3,000	* Harnessing wind power)	* Using nature's resources
	2,000	* Using horses for transportation and labour	
E	800	* Using the energy of falling water	
F	180	* Using coal and oil for energy)	* Adapting to changes in the environment

Source : Makridakis Spyros (1990): " Forecasting Planning and Strategy for the 21st Century".

tendencies of the human beings. In Table 13.2 one can look at these important events in human history in terms of pace of events following the initial industrial revolution and information (computer) revolution. Let us dwell on Table 13.2 a little more. Industrial revolution started around 1760 and a major innovation that heralded its speed was the invention of the steam engine. This invention led to a number of chain events resulting around 1930 a variety of affordable car types and models on a large scale. Now after about 50-60 years, the pace of changes in industries and services have been so much that in almost all areas we have equipment and facilities through which labour could be substituted, aided or improved. Productivity of a single human being behind these facilities is enormous. This is so in almost all sectors be it in home appliances or factories or in transportation or in entertainment.

If one were to draw a similar analogy for information revolution which started in 1946 one may take it that the invention of the transistor was an event equivalent to that of steam engine for industrial revolution. The innovation of a variety of affordable and efficient computers around 1988 heralded the large scale spread of technology which was somewhat similar to availability of automobiles in 1930. The information revolution has achieved this stage within about 48 years, whereas the time span for industrial revolution was about 175 years. If one were to use a linear extrapolation, in 2000, one can expect that the application of information technology would have reached all areas and sectors creating entirely new dimensions to human life unthinkable even two decades ago.

The above has been dealt with at some length essentially to bring out some elements of the mind boggling pace with which the technologies are being generated, commercialised, operationalised and also being made obsolete in recent years. Any attempt at science and technology policy should bear in mind this speed and the need to cope up with it. This is particularly true for our country where the work culture and ethos hardly take into account the value of time.

Issues Concerning Technology Policy

For many in India technology policy is perceived as a separate stand alone policy. The interconnectivity of technology with various aspects of human endeavour in the modern times is so high that it is no longer wise to be influenced by this obsolete outlook. In every policy formulation, it is essential to look at the role of science and technology and elements resulting from such a look should be built into these policies: be it related to foreign, urban, agriculture, health, energy or a housing policy. It is

TABLE 13.2: Important Events in Human History: The Industrial and Information (Computer) Revolutions

Industrial Revolution	Stream Engine	Rail road	Electricity	Electricity in Home Use	Motorized Airplane	Ford's T.Car	Substituted G.M.'s water cooled K.Car	Aided variety of affoordable Car types and Models	Application of Technology to all areas where labour could be or improved. These include home, factory transportation, entertainment, etc.
1060	1776	1808	1830	1880	1903	1909	1925	1930s	
									Present 1988 About 50 years
		About 175 years							

Information Revolution		The Transsistor	Computers for Business Application	Microchips	Time shared Computers	Microprocessors	Apple's Personal Computers	Micro Computers	Variety of Affordable Efficient and Fast Computer	Year 2000
1946	1948	1952	1969	1971	1973	1977	1983	Present 1988	Future	
									About 12.5 Years	

The information revolution is progressing about four times as fast as the Industrial Revolution (i.e., 175/42= 4.17, or about 4)	One can expect that it will take the information Revolution 12.5 years (i.e., one fourth of the time) to accomplish what took the industrial Revolution 50 years.

Source : Makridakis Spyros (1990): 'Forecasting Planning and Strategy for the 21st Century".

proposed to discuss some facets of such a complexity here. Basically when one considers technology in an input-output system, there are many elements which come to our attention. Typical inputs for technology development or generation or assimilation etc. are: Investments such as Finance, Tax incentives and Venture Capital loans; Human resource; Raw-Material; Machinery; and the like. The outputs which come from inputs in technology generation and the like are: Market creation; promotion of new products or protection of the earlier markets; new services; profit; new business; better quality of life; public good like national security, morale and the like. Even those who are keen on science and technology related issues often tend to look at these input and output indicators only. Technology development and its penetration in industrial processes and services sector are so complex and interrelated that it is necessary to have a closed understanding of the processes involved in transforming the inputs to outputs. Certain elements of these processes are Vision, Strategy, Targets/Goals, Motivation, Organisation including administrative and financial management of technology generation, transfer, utilisation and maintenance. One needs to influence these processes to obtain a desired level of transformation. All these three major segments namely INPUT, PROCESS, OUTPUT get affected by countervailing powers such as public accountability systems, and national commitment.

There are also various other issues like intellectual property rights, dual use considerations, technology control regimes etc. which do not allow simplistic considerations of 'market pulls' alone.

When one looks at only inputs and outputs without a good understanding of the processes of technology generation, motivations for innovation, judgement of uncertainties at early stages of technology development, and technology transfer, one may arrive at a short sighted assessment of costs and benefits which are quantifiable clearly in the early stages of the idea for technology development. This can cause considerable damage to the future potential of an organisation.

While there are many now-a-days who are ready to accept the statement that investment in technology is to be considered as an equity for future of the business and the growth of an organisation, very often decision-makers in various sectors of government undertakings as well in private business get confused when it comes to judging the risks and possibilities from technologies. They are not normally amenable to usual forms of judgement on trades or conventional production systems. Unless such an assessment takes place at the early stages of conceiving of technological possibilities, the competitive advantages are often lost. It is easy to understand the benefits at a much later stage. But often competitors may have gone much further ahead and it is not possible to hasten the technological development at one's place unless some work has been done before. Thus in modern times decision-making whether or not to pursue certain research and developmental activities, requires deeper understanding of technology management processes in addition to judgement of future business potential from these developments. This is what is meant by ability to take a long term view and to be in a position to direct the work towards well set targets and goals. This does not mean regimented planning. There has to be responsiveness for uncertainties in technology development or changing external environment and so on. However, one cannot achieve technological and commercial pre-eminence if one approaches the problems as a start-stop process or with a short sighted approach.

Technology and Inter Connections

Technology is very closely interconnected with consumption styles, external/foreign policy issues, perceptions of public good, trade and industrial policies, etc. including the means adopted in achieving the ends. Macro and micro-economic policies also influence technologies very crucially. Such inter-connectivities are not mere one way or one-shot inter-connections. They are interactive. Often instability in these policies can derail technology development process which have some fixed periods or gestation times. Technology does not interact with each of these elements separately. There are often multi-element interaction with technologies. For example, the modern day speedy information, transport system etc. bring into focus the consumption styles and other social values from different parts of the world into many segments of our society. Mere administrative mechanisms may not be able to control these. Change of consumption styles can place new demands on technologies. Take the case of introduction of television in the country. In the sixties it was considered a luxury item and various controls were placed. Following world trends were actively discouraged as a policy. Indigenous development was therefore stymied. Then there was a floodgate opened fast or burst open. See what is happening with satellite television. If properly perceived and allowed to operate the technology development for television since sixties could have been converted into a major force for unleashing technology, development for large segments of electronics in the country.

There are many other examples which can be similarly cited: automobiles, food processing, etc. Similarly many in India are now only knowing about issues such as technology control regimes thanks to the publicity about super-computers and cryogenic engines. However many developed countries have always been having a well organised technology export regime both for national security as well as for commercial repeat commercial reasons. Without understanding these issues just approaching the external/foreign policy or commercial contracts as isolated elements, or by looking at project economics of build-buy options in a myopic one-project mode as is often done, one would come up with big surprises later. In the coming years where technology has got interwoven with many of these issues, things are going to be difficult for countries which have compartmentalised thinking on policy issues and especially for those who do not try to understand the role of technologies. Suffice it to say that it is essential not to have a stand alone technology policy but a system in which science and technology issues can percolate into all other areas.

What should a Policy Paper Contain?

Very often many persons in our country expect every detail to be stated in a policy statement. How much should one or can get into the details of a policy statement? Should one refer to high speed computers, high speed communication links with some specifications of limits or make a statement merely stressing information technology? Should one spell out specific clean technologies which the country should aim at? One criticism against a general or broad statement like clean technology or information technology without specificity could lead several unfocused, thinly spread efforts, which can lead to frittering away of limited resources available for research and development (R&D). On the other hand, if the technology policy only refers to only specific five or six items it may stifle further growth for a decade till the policy statement is revised. There are some who advocate a mode in which a technology policy can envision a set of possible end scenarios e.g. interconnectivity of half the colleges with computer data links, introduction of certain percentage of vehicles with certain levels of pollution control systems etc. However it should be noted that the stated targets go beyond R&D systems (be it in national laboratory or in industry) but would depend on investments. It is not easy to find an optimal mix. Probably a science and technology policy can address the mega level leaving further details to be spelt out at sectoral levels like agriculture, fertilizers etc. with their projections of future spelt out as policies. Subsequently at the level of industry associations, firms, and laboratories micro level forecasting have to be done. Infact technology forecasting, technology assessment or research foresight or technology foresight should cover separately all these levels at the one level. It cannot be done in a single document nor in one study. Our aim should rather be to develop and internalise various methods of continuous learning to look ahead in technologies at various levels - mega to meso to micro levels - and tailor technology development and investments in industries and services (i.e. business investment) according to these trends. Ability to respond to emerging situation is an important facet of policy implementation. In other words the system should be such that looking at technological options and prepare for technology trajectories should be one of the important considerations in any governmental or business operation whether it is service sector, agriculture sector or industrial/ manufacturing sector. An important issue before the economic or industrial or trade policy maker should be to be enable that technologies are continually looked at the level of board rooms. The technology policy should be such as to assist in forward looking actions resulting from the conclusions for the board rooms. In view of the increasing liberalisation it is likely that there would be commercial pressures which will make our industries look ahead in technologies. But we should realise that it is not an automatic process because the earlier protected environment have left many linkages with technologies very weak.

Some Statistics

Now let us look at some broad statistics concerning R&D in the country. There are about 380 Central Government supported scientific institutions in the country either as autonomous societies or government laboratories (e.g. CSIR labs, Defence/Space establishments, Institutes under various ministries). Similarly in the state level there are 700 such institutions. There are about 200 universities of which at least 50 would be very active in scientific research. Public sector units have about 140 in house R&D units and private sector has 1100 in house R&D units. These are the national science and technology assets. About 0.9 per cent GNP is being annually spent on all these institutions for creation of scientific and technological knowledge. (This expenditure includes that required for salaries, administrative facility, maintenance as well as for implementation of S&T projects.) However it should be noted that about 10-13 per cent of this amount only come from private source and a bulk of the expenditure is by the government either directly for its laboratories and projects and for public sector R&D units. In Japan Government spends 20 per cent and private Industry 80 per cent; in USA Government spends about 60 per cent and private industry 40 per cent. In India too there is a need to increase considerably the investment in R&D by industry. National expenditure on R&D (Government and private) should soon reach 2 per cent of GNP. Industry should learn how to invest on R&D. It should also be enabled to do so through various forms of incentives and other measures. Management of Government laboratories should be made flexible to facilitate industry to use them in a responsive and speedy manner. Other countries have taken various such steps including exerting various forms of institutional pressures to make the importers of technology develop capabilities to absorb technologies and to develop them further and also be in a position to export some of the technologies to other countries. It is not the case that there has to be a technological self-sufficiency. However no industry or no country can only be technologically an eternal or repetitive technological importer without itself generating technologies as well. In today's competitive world such an industry or country would be swept away in the torrent of technological dynamism sweeping the world. This is an issue which technology policy would need to address.

Transition

In our country since considerable amount of government investment has taken place in a number of institutions so much so that even many impartial foreign observers have commented about India having potential to become a research super power among the developing world. This infrastructure should be utilised effectively by industry till such time its own in house capabilities for R&D are strengthened which may take a decade or more. This will however mean considerable amount of mobility of personnel in the national laboratories, industries and government institutions. This has not taken place because of restrictive, complicated and time consuming administrative rules governing personnel in Government (even in Government funded societies). Many of those rules which may perhaps be useful in other administrative service have not taken into account the demands of management of technology cycles. Best interface management for technology transfer has been proven in many countries as movement of people from R&D to production to marketing and repeated cycling without rigid rules of periods, as the gestation periods are different in different areas. In addition rigid pay scales/rules on incentives may have to be made more flexible to enable incentives for motivating individuals for innovation and for mobility. In fact the management of the transition to make the Government S&T infrastructure more responsive and timely and to make the industries technologically dynamic is going to be a challenging task in implementing the technology policy.

One other issue of detail which needs to be borne in mind is the need for attracting youth towards industrial R&D (in fact towards R&D in general). Over the past several years many Government institutions have stopped recruiting youth for R&D as well. This can lead to a situation where younger people may not opt to take R&D as a career. This trend may have serious implications in future growth of technologies in the country. It should be noted that to create persons capable of doing R&D and to innovate is not a mere question of numbers. In fact one important task should be to ensure that more and more young persons are inducted into the tasks for generating newer technologies to compete in the world market and against global actors in our own domestic markets. In other words the S&T education and learning of skills should be more tied to market oriented technological foresight processes and not necessarily come from a rigidly formed academic syllabi. Here again industries have an important role to play—to identify new areas of businesses and to place demand for S&T personnel (either new or through orientation). It is necessary for strength and technological competence.

Draft Paper on Technology Policy

To a certain extent these issues have been addressed in a draft paper for a New Technology Policy. The paper points out the social tasks under a section technology and society. Another section addresses the issues/tasks relating to technology and environment. Various specific issues relating to human skills have been addressed; some special areas requiring reorientation of human resources have been pointed out. An attempt has also been made to arrive at a few thrust areas. Specifically the role of R&D and in addition the important role of engineering to convert R&D to commercial goals have also been addressed. Under the section resources for R&D, some targets for 2000 AD have been stressed. The important issues connected with linkage of institutions not only for policy-making but also for implementation, have been brought out. A section addresses the important aspect of the continuance of monitoring and review with greater emphasis on decentralised system. A copy of the draft may be seen in the Appendix. This paper has been circulated in large numbers. Wide ranging national debates were held where industry organisations, academic institutions, state Government institutions and a number of individuals had participated and offered their comments. Considerable feed back have been received. This will help in revising the draft policy statement. The responses to the draft paper whether critical or otherwise have brought out considerable awareness about the role of technologies. This process is in itself an important element of technology policy. In fact continual focussed discussions and concerted actions on various aspects of technology policy will be essential for making our economy globally competitive, and also to make our country secure vis-a-vis both internal and external threats and dangers.

APPENDIX

A DRAFT PAPER FOR A NEW TECHNOLOGY POLICY

1. Preamble

This Technology Policy Statement of 1993 has been designed to further strengthen the Indian economy and to assist the nation in fulfilling its role in the global economic environment with confidence and a sense of urgency.

The nation's commitment to the use of science and technology as key instruments for national development has been articulated in the Scientific Policy Resolution of 1958. The present policy is aimed at giving a renewed sense of purpose to indigenous technology for its accelerated development and use in the context of the Industrial Policy Statement of 1991 and keeping in view the need to adhere to international quality systems as well as preserve the environment.

2. Technology and Society

In order to enable large sections of our society to derive the benefits from science and technology, this policy is directed to:

— achieve a greater spread in the use of technological developments;

— ensure accessibility of technological devices to all segments of the society with a special emphasis on remote and rural communities in order to improve their quality of life;

— enhance infrastructural facilities;

— upgrade traditional skills and reduce drudgery keeping in view the special needs of women and the weaker sections of society; and

— encourage industries for enhancing human skills to upgrade existing technologies to comparable international levels as well as to attain such levels for newer and emerging technologies.

3. Technology and Environment

To facilitate optimal utilisation of the finite natural resources for ensuring a sustainable benefit stream for a better quality of life, it is essential that the technology conversion process must be made as efficient as possible. This will provide a much higher output of the productive goods and services from the same material inputs and consequently reduce stage which results in pollutants in the gaseous, liquid or solid form. This policy, therefore, aims at:

- — adoption, adaptation and promotion of state-of-the-art technologies for waste prevention and reduction by lesser consumption of raw materials with special emphasis on indigenous efforts;
- — modification and upgradation of the process technologies for optimal utilisation of natural resources;
- — adoption of preventive approach for pollution control;
- — promotion and use of cleaner technologies; and
- — ensuring access to cleaner technologies available abroad.

4. Human Skills

4.1 Deliberate steps would be initiated to continuously augment the number of scientific and technical personnel in relation to the country's population. A new balance of ratios between scientific and technical personnel will also be aimed at. Towards achieving this objective, attention will be directed to further enlarge the base of polytechnics, technical and vocational institutes, and engineering institutions and launch programmes for training and retraining industrial and technical personnel in numbers significantly more than what has been attempted hitherto. Industries will be involved in this process of upgrading the human skills.

4.2 Improvement of the quality of management of R&D institutions will receive special attention. Pursuit of R&D as a career prospect will be deliberately encouraged through further concrete measures so as to attract scientists and technologists to the challenges of creative science and innovative development with a target of doubling their number in R&D by 2000 A.D. This will include innovative measures to attract and to utilise scientific and technological talents of Indians all over the world.

4.3 Specific programmes will be evolved to nurture and reward talented personnel contributing notably to technology development. Accomplishments by skilled technicians will be recognised and rewarded. The overall direction would be to create an atmosphere and opportunities to promote technological innovation and excellence.

4.4 Specific emphasis will be laid on induction of professionals fully conversant with the latest technologies in Ministries/Departments which heavily depend on crucial technology inputs.

5. Thrust Areas

5.1. Thrust areas for technology development will be related to:

a) critical technologies regardless of whether they are currently available from abroad; and
b) those aimed at new products and services and technological refinements over currently available technologies.

5.2. Keeping in view the above directions, thrust areas will include:

i) energy related technologies including those for alternative fuels, renewable/non-conventional sources, and energy conservation technologies with due weightage for domestic/local availability base;
ii) technologies for conservation of land water and energy resources and their integrated management for sustainable development leading to their ecologically balanced management and obtaining higher efficiencies in utilisation as well as those enabling availability of newer sources of water;
iii) local specific requirements of exclusive concern to our own milieu such as those based on our natural resources and characteristically indigenous industries like those in the small scale sector or based on traditional and household skills;
iv) extensive and intensive mapping and exploration of natural resources as well as estimation of reserves for optimal utilisation of such resources to include beneficiation and new applications with special emphasis on integrated R&D in the mine, mineral, metal and material chain;
v) the necessity of protecting vast sections of people against natural hazards like earthquakes, cyclones, droughts and floods;
vi) agriculture, allied services and agro-based industries including development on non-hazardous pesticides, herbicides and fungicides;

vii) technologies for provision and maintenance of health services, as well as leading to development of new drugs, medical devices and instrumentation, vaccines and their delivery systems;

viii) technologies relating to betterment of infrastructural facilities such as transport, communication and housing;

ix) areas which are relevant to a whole range of modern systems like materials development, biotechnology, electronics and communications with emphasis on new product design;

x) manufacturing sciences and technologies to improve industries, including electronification as appropriate for higher productivity and upgradation of industrial processes with due consideration for employment productivity and automation;

xi) areas where continued imports are difficult to sustain, e.g. petroleum products and capital goods (e.g. instrumentation and equipment hardware);

xii) emerging and as yet unexploited zones of resources like oceans; and

xiii) speedily enlarging areas of recognised strength like software.

5.3 Specific short and long-term programmes will be drawn up in each of the above areas through detailed analyses including techno-economic assessments.

6. Role for Research, Development and Engineering (R&DE)

6.1 Recognising the critical importance of innovative research, a far more prominent role for R&DE is envisaged in the decade ahead such as:

i) predominant role for R&DE teams in corporate and Government sectors;

ii) association of the relevant R&DE laboratory system(s) for technology acquisition particularly when these are imported since absorption, adaptation and upgradation are inescapable to obviate repetitive import of technologies;

iii) institution of measures to upgrade the efficiency and productivity of the technologies for ensuring quality and enhancing competitiveness;

iv) enlarged role of R&DE in our economy so that by the turn of the century the share of the right type of indigenous technology in total industrial production would rise markedly, targets being set by Government;

v) providing technology support and services for major export oriented areas like leather, textiles, jute, jewellery, handicrafts and agro products;

vi) providing support for substantive value addition for export in areas which may emerge due to rapidly changing global mix of technologies; and

vii) development of indigenous clean technologies which are urgently needed to preserve the environment and ensure the health and safety of our people.

6.2 It is also noted that R&DE could provide vital inputs for enabling small scale industry to grow and successfully compete with large scale industry. With emerging trend of new "scale-neutral" technologies, it could decisively influence the growth of small scale industry in future.

6.3 In view of such a predominant role being envisaged for R&DE in the coming years, continual examining and reorienting the work programmes of the R&D institutions are necessary, based upon the emerging needs of the country and the areas where large foreign investments are taking place or substantial foreign technological inputs are needed. Such actions will be more and more market oriented and focussed on applications. The linkages with industry, markets, customers and feedback for feed-forward research would become important and mechanisms to achieve these would be provided for.

6.4 Significant R&DE contributions will be rewarded by according notable recognition to team efforts and by enhancement of allocations to the institutions concerned.

'. Resources for R&DE

7.1 Noting that the Government directly invests in R&DE as well as stimulates industrial investments by both the public and private sector industries and the total R&DE expenditure is currently about 0.9 per cent only of the Cross National Product, it will be the aim of this policy to enhance and to encourage investments in R&DE especially by industry so that the targets for R&DE by 2000 A.D. can be set to reach 2 per cent of the Gross National

Product. It is also recognised that the quality of results from R&DE and their applications are equally important.

7.2 It would be endeavoured that the private sector R&DE contributions would be significantly enhanced. Towards achieving the targets for R&DE, the Government will provide for incentives and other measures to stimulate contributions from the industry based on the annual turnover.

7.3 All Government funded R&D institutions will be actively encouraged to earn revenues. Increased industrial contributions have a decisive role to play. Government would enable Government funded agencies/institutions to retain the earnings resulting from the services offered by them to Government, industries or others, as an additionality to the Government funding.

8. Linkages

8.1 The strength of our R&DE systems mainly comes from the expertise built over past few decades. The weaknesses are in the linkages with industry and time taken from the laboratory to actual applications. Implementation of this policy will endeavour to remove the weaknesses and build on strengths.

8.2 Realising that there is an urgent need to shift from localised excellence to integrated excellence, R&DE collaborations will be deliberately and actively encouraged through:

i) funding national laboratories-academic institutions through linked projects;
ii) promoting university-industry linkages by diverse means, including adjunct positions for necessary personnel;
iii) instituting appropriate systems in all the research institutions for keeping track of the needs of industries and users as well as the R&DE project undertaken by other institutions;
iv) encouraging use of national laboratory facilities and their expertise by industrial units by way of contract research projects paid for by the industry appropriately;
v) developing consortium approach involving academic institution national laboratories, including those of the mission agencies namely, Department of Atomic Energy, Space and Defence Research and Development, wherever feasible, and the user industry for goal oriented programmes and new

product development;

vi) enabling joint R&DE projects between Indian enterprises/ institutions and those abroad, with equitable sharing of results;

vii) facilitating easy mobility of personnel among universities, laboratories, industry (including R&D institutions connected with industry) and the Ministries;

viii) decentralising extramural funding selectively so that institutions and industries can develop productive linkages; and

ix) assigning multi-dimensional responsibility to the existing technical institutions.

8.3 In addition to the actions by the Central Government, industry, universities and the laboratories, the State Governments have a special role to play in encouraging R&DE and in providing linkages at the local levels. Community development in technology extension services through cooperatives, voluntary agencies, agricultural universities and other local institutions will be given special emphasis.

8.4 The above measures will be directed to result in reduced dependence on the Governmental initiative and financing and to move in an accelerated manner towards self-supporting R&DE. These will also help in the achievement of synergy of the strengths existing in the country's academic institutions, national laboratories, industrial units and voluntary organisations.

9. Policy Implementation

It is recognised that a policy spell our directions, even so, a set of measures for its implementation is considered essential to be stated here and the following have been identified for early action:

i) It is necessary that in order to achieve the goals set forth in this Policy Statement an integrated set of measures should be taken. To ensure this, appropriate executive actions or legislative measures will be taken.

ii) Since many of the technology programmes are bound to be multi-disciplinary in character, it is necessary to ensure multi-institutional involvement in the trust areas for timely and successful achievement of the goals. Increased inputs from financial institutions, consultancy organisations, and user agencies are essential. Actual implementation will be done without undue centralisation in government departments and through empowerment of implementing institutions and teams.

iii) Keeping in view the climate of liberalisation, technology development/acquisition and investment must take place in a a competitive environment and for this purpose industrial R&DE must be appropriately reoriented in order to mitigate technological multiplicity. While technology imports can continue, the absorption system would be strengthened in order to minimise repetitive imports.

iv) In evolving specific measures to implement the technology programmes and plans in the socio-economic Ministries, appropriate S&T advisory group and institutional linkages with R&D institutions would be further strengthened so that continuous inputs would become available ensuring their timely and successful implementation.

v) Specific and sizable allocations would be made for technology diffusion for societal benefits.

vi) Recognising the need for specific incentives to meet an intended target, a standing mechanism would be identified which will examine and bring about the required specific and appropriate fiscal incentives for industry from time to time.

vii) R&D institutions including academic institutions would be encouraged to interact with industry and other agencies for contract projects. Income arising out of such initiatives will become additional resources for furthering their infrastructure and other R&DE activities.

viii) To encourage the use of indigenously developed technologies, measures like development contracts would be adopted.

ix) Suitable measures to create a market for domestic technology, like purchase preferences by the Government departments and organisations controlled by government will also be adopted.

x) In order to encourage innovations by individuals and institutions, and their commercialisation, selective support would be extended for patenting and other forms of intellectual property rights.

xi) For successful commercialisation of new technologies by entrepreneurs, a full technology package including design, engineering, finance and servicing of indigenous technologies will be encouraged.

xii) All measures will be taken to accelerate the process of transformation of a laboratory technology to an industrial operation through strengthening and involvement of design, consultancy and project implementation groups. Necessary fiscal measures will be introduced for equipment, accessories and consumables which are essential for proving developed technologies through pilot scale production and marketing of the products.

xiii) In order to protect the interests of consumers, it is intended to enlarge and strengthen systems and mechanisms for testing, calibration, standards, inspection and other quality systems in industries and laboratories.

xiv) Rapid technological advancement brings about widening technology gaps with adverse effects in making many industries less profitable and leading to industrial sickness. Appropriate systems would be established to identify existing technology gaps and provide for essential inputs from advances in technology.

xv) Government will initiate specific goal oriented and time bound technology development and application projects and missions in key areas.

10. Monitoring and Review

Every initiative taken to inject new technologies in the country from outside and from within has to be constantly and continuously monitored and reviewed to achieve sustained results. The approach to detailed technical evaluations on a continuous basis requires a combination of centralised and decentralised mechanisms. Special measures will be brought into being to set up dedicated systems for this purpose. Methodologies will be evolved for a comprehensive watch on the generation of R&DE results and their application in manufacturing and service industries. It will be further ensured that a feedback would be available to Government and corporate sector for taking timely and appropriate corrective measures.

14. HOW A MAJOR PUBLIC POLICY INITIATIVE CREATES IMPACT : The Case of Indian Computer Hardware Industry (1984-1990)

Rajnish Karki
Ahmad Cameron

1. Introduction

Policy initiatives periodically taken by government are instruments to achieve national objectives. They announce new opportunities, at times remove constraints, and ultimately give direction to process of development in the country. New Computer Policy announced in November 1984, is taken as an example of a public policy initiative to catapult the computer hardware industry in India. This policy which had a wide-ranging impact was primarily "implemented" by the private sector enterprises. The experience of computer hardware industry, is a good "looking glass" for future interactions between public policy and activities of the corporate sector in the liberalised Indian economic environment.

The paper examines the interaction between the contents and objectives of New Computer Policy and six variables which capture computer industry scenario. Policy initiative and variables are considered as constituting a system; and systems analysis approach is used to understand the experience. The paper begins with a brief review of relevant streams of literature. The case of computer hardware industry from 1984 to 1990, is analysed to draw conclusions regarding type and process of impact of public policy.

2. Perspective from Literature

Two streams of literature which have addressed the issues related to post-formulation stage of policy are: research on implementation—evaluation aspect of public policy; and research in strategic management of enterprises, which is attempted to be extended to public policy context.

The research on implementation of public policy picked up only in mid-1970s, when several policy initiatives in U.S. and U.K. created very small impact as compared to what was desired or aimed (Hogwood and Gunn, 1984).[1] The "perfect administration" of a public policy as an ideal situation was proposed by Hood (1976).[2] However, perfect administration of a public policy is virtually unattainable in practice, due to one or more of the following conditions remaining unfulfilled: the circumstances external to the implementing agency do not impose crippling constraints; adequate time and sufficient resources are made available to the programme; the required combination of resources is actually available; the policy to be implemented is based upon a valid theory of cause and effect; the relationship between cause and effect is direct and that there are few if any, intervening links; the dependency relationship are minimal; there is understanding of, and agreement on, objectives; the tasks are fully specified in correct sequence; there is perfect communication and co-ordination; and those in authority can demand and obtain perfect compliance (Gunn, 1978).[3] It is often argued that the policy-action relationship should be seen as a process of interaction and negotiation, taking place over time, between those seeking to put policy into effect and those upon whom (individuals or organisations) the action depends (Barrett and Fudge, 1981).[4] Therefore a complex dynamics is likely to ensue, with the implementation of a public policy. With the gradual emergence of changes in environment and inadequacies vis-a-vis "perfect administration" situation, extent and complexity of dynamics also changes with time.

On the other hand monitoring and evaluation mechanisms for a public policy are instruments to oversee effective implementation and to make any mid-course corrections, respectively. Monitoring is the collection of information to find out the extent to which policy objectives are being met, and exercise of power by implementation bodies to correct any deviations. Evaluating the impact of a public policy is a complicated exercise. The starting point in evaluation is the availability of clear-specific goals of public policy. The goals of a public policy are often not clearly stated, for fear of bringing out into open the underlying conflicts among the interest groups and thereby loosing some political support. In addition there can be severe conflicts between goals set by the policy formulators and the goals actually practiced by policy administrators (Weiss, 1972).[5] Similarly there are often difficulties in arriving at an acceptable criteria of success defined in terms of weightages or priorities among (more often than not) multiple objectives; in determining the extent of achievements, which can be taken as success; in identifying side effects—damages or benefits; in determining the kind and amount of information to be collected; in separating the programme impact from other influences; and in assessing the distribution of impacts among target groups. Other critical issue is the utilisation of evaluation results, regarding the political sensitivity and the continuation of support of various interest groups.

Concept of strategy for enterprises evolved in mid-1960s. It emphasised formulation of an explicit strategy, for the success of an enterprise. Strategy formulation was proposed as an analytical exercise involving consideration of internal competencies (strength-weakness) and environment (opportunities-threats) of an enterprise, and aimed at evolving a plan which develops and exploits the "best fit". Implementation of strategy was seen as seperate from formulation. But many empirical research works on strategy formulation-implementation concluded that there are vast differences between the strategy which was formulated and strategy which was actually implemented by the enterprises. Some of the components of formulated strategy were rendered unrealisable due to unrealistic expectations, maladjustments, or changes in the environment. Some new components emerged in the implemented strategy, either because no formulated components exists or because formulated components got displaced along the way (summarised by Minitzberg and Waters, 1985).[6] And in the early 1980s concept of strategic management was proposed. Strategic management conceives that an enterprise has to manage its strategy, like any other activity; and it considers formulation—implementation—evaluation as closely interlinked.

Few researchers have tried to explore the linkage between national policy related to an industry and the corporate strategies of the enterprises. This stream is especially relevant for the case of Indian Computer Hardware industry in which New Computer Policy of November 1984 was essentially implemented through the corporate strategies of the enterprises in the computer industry. The critical elements for success of a national policy are proposed to be complementarity of the national policy with strategic interests of the enterprises; consistency of strategic signals that various national policies send to the enterprises; and continuity in national policies which allow enterprises to develop large time-resource consuming competencies (Leone and Bradley, 1983).[7] Chakravarthy (1985)[8] in his study of American Synthetic fuels industry found several areas in which government can play an important role in strengthening the industry. The role of government is critical in industries having very high technological and commercial risks; and government should focus on neutralisation ofbusiness risks through financial incentive programme and complementarity in technology creation.

3. Systems Approach

Social, economic, political and technological sectors of countries are extremely complex in charateristics. Each one of them comprises of a number of sub-systems interacting with one another within the entire whole. All these sub-systems constitute to make larger and complex super-systems. Certain sectors have a direct link with the global developments e.g. economic, technological etc. Understanding the dynamics of such sectors becomes even more difficult. Thus policy designers and formulators have a very difficult task in front of them before making policy announcements. They have to understand the dynamics of the given sector within the complex mosaic called nation. In recent years a new approach to public-policy decision making, called systems analysis, has been successfully attempted in several countries (Srivastava, 1979).[9]

Systems approach was primarily developed for defence related problems in USA during post Ward War-II period. The technique implies a cycle of the definition of objectives, identifying the boundaries of the sub-systems along with the conflicts occurring between them, exploring the alternate solutions to achieve the objectives etc. Consequently, the policy framer must recognise that each element is one of a number of components that work together to serve a larger purpose.

In case of the computer hardware industry, technology is one of the key sub-system. Further, it is very closely linked with the developments taking place around the world. Foremost in it is the development of the computer architecture, which in turn is based on the developments in the Integrated Circuits (IC) Technology. Growth and innovation within the ICs technology is dependent on the R&D in material science as well as in reducing the size and integrating the number of circuits on the chip. Further, with increasing integration of larger number of circuits on a single chip, there has been a reduction in the cost of the products along with an increase in the speed of processing. The other off shoot of this phenomenon has been the use of computers in newer and diverse fields e.g. engineering analysis, graphics, printing, communications, medicine, manufacturing etc. This has given rise to two parallel activities viz, developments in the direction of integration of computers and communications technology. Second, an entire new area of software development, which is an ocean in itself and having its own variables to direct its growth, has come to the forefront. The software component has grown so large that it may require a study of its own separately and is hence not discussed here.

In India the aspect to be analysed within the technological variable, is the development of newer products on one hand and the progress in the direction of import substitution on the other.

Another variable needing review is the growth of computer hardware industry in comparison with the overall industrial growth. Secondly, the component of investment in the computer and allied industry in comparison with other key industries/sectors.

The next variable which plays a key role in the progress of computer industry is the infrastructure development having direct impact on the industry. On the one hand it refers to the Human Resource development. On the other, it concerns with the launching of computerisation programmes which are going to use the products produced by this industry at large.

It can, therefore, be seen from Fig. 14.1 how different sub-systems within India interact vis-a-vis Indian Computer Hardware Industry. It also shows the Indian system at large interacting with the global system. For formulating any policy for Indian Computer Hardware Industry (ICHI), it will be necessary to analyse the role of each of the sub-system and its contribution to the dynamics of this industry.

4. Case of Indian Computer Hardware Industry:1984-90

The era of computers and computerisation started in India in 1955. At ISI Calcutta a Russian computer was installed in that year. The second system that came up was IBM 1400 at Standard Esso Ltd.—a multinational company. Next to follow were Hindustan Aeronautics Ltd. and TIFR, Bombay.

The period between 1955-77 saw the dominance of IBM as it controlled 70 per cent of the Indian market. This period was also analogous to the one we had witnessed in our automobile sector. M/s. Hindustan Motors or Walchand Group had gone into collaboration for the production of Hindustan/Ambassador or Fiat cars respectively. The policy had been to buy outlived automobile plants from their collaborators who had stopped the production of those models of cars as the domestic market of those cars had gone down in their areas of operations. Similarly in computer hardware industry this phase saw IBM or ICL etc. bringing in those punched-card systems which had become obsolete in the developed countries.

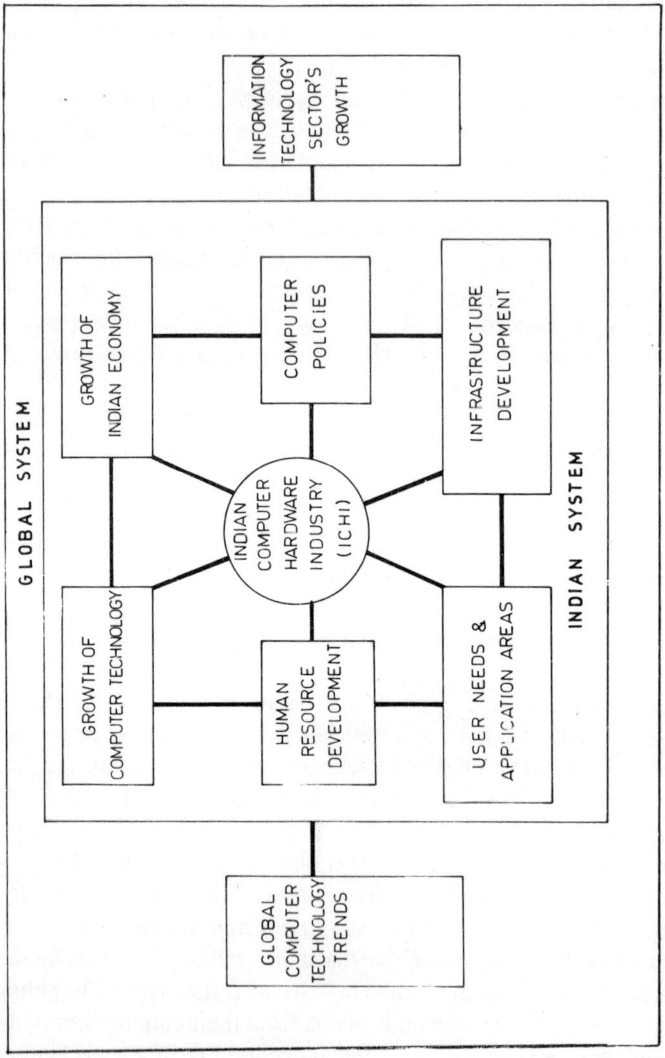

FIG. 14.1: Block Diagram Showing Interactions between Global and Indian Sub-Systems for ICHI.

IBM concentrated on the research and academic institutions of India who were in a look out for computing facilities. It extended a sound maintenance back up. This enabled IBM to dominate the Indian market till 1971 when it ran into an argument over providing computer systems and services in India. This event became a turning point in the evolution of computer industry in India.

A committee under the chairmanship of Prof. M.G.K. Menon was established. Its recommendations gave rise to the establishment of Electronics Commission in 1971, Computer Maintenance Corporation (CMC) Ltd. and Semi-Conductor Complex (SCL) Ltd. in 1976. Further, organisations such as Electronics Corporation of India Ltd. [ECIL] established in 1967, got a boost during this period by entering into Computer Hardware industry. Simultaneously, in terms of allied industry Central Electronics Limited came up under Department of Science and Technology in 1974. By 1977 the government had realised the importance of information technology. It had taken crucial initiatives which finally paved the way for the eventual growth of computer industry in India.[10]

There was one major landmark during this period, which was though not directly related to computer industry, had a lot of bearing on its growth eventually. This was promulgation of Foreign Exchange Regulation Act of 1974 (FERA). By virtue of it, foreign companies operating in India were allowed to hold only 40 per cent equity. This became a catalyst in the process of exit of IBM from India which came into effect in 1977. IBM had during its operations only rented out its machines to various Indian organisations and taken care of their maintenance to date. Now it started the process of transferring these systems to them by taking a final payment.

The exit of IBM created a major vacuum in the field of systems maintenance which was plugged in by CMC Ltd. On the other hand, ECIL started the production of 12-bit systems and subsequently progressed to produce 16 and 32 bit mainframes comparable to French IRIS 55 Systems.

The private sector made its entry into the computer market through calculators. Facit mechanical calculators and hand-held slide rules were the order of the day till then for everyday calculating needs. Private Sector companies such as DCM, Televista, Omron, HCL and even ECIL launched desk-top and pocket size calculators using LEDs. As a result of this there was a perceptible shift from mechanical calculating systems to the calculators amongst all the engineering, science and accounting related professionals.

Towards the end of this phase (1983) government announced a New Electronics Policy. By virtue of this customs and excise duty on electronics industry was reduced by 6 per cent. Private sector witnessed the birth of companies like ORG, PSI, WTIL etc. The Indian computer manufacturing industry started producing proprietary hardware as well as operating systems thereby casting off the dependence on foreign manufactures and suppliers.

4.1 *New Computer Policy 1984*

Untimely death of Mrs. Indira Gandhi brought a young, modern and a dynamic man—Mr. Rajiv Gandhi—at the helm of affairs. New Computer Policy (NCP) was announced in Nov'84. Some of the key issues which NCP addressed were:

(a) Regulation of all clearances through Inter-Ministerial Standing Committee (IMSC);
(b) Reduction in import duty on peripherals;
(c) Liberisation on the import of computers;
(d) Granting permission to foreign equity participation;
(e) Recognising software as a seperate industry and formations of a Software Development Agency for the overall growth of this industry; and
(f) Allowing import of computers by government institutions as well as R&D organisations.

One of the biggest result of this policy was reduction in the prices of the systems by as much as 25 per cent. This policy announcement along with the impetus from the top man in the country to dovetail India into 21st century on high technology areas, is one of the key reasons for the growth of the computer hardware industry as a whole.

4.2 *Infrastructure Development*

This phase also saw the boost given to the process of computerisation by organisations and institutions belonging to the government. National Informatics Centre (NIC) had played a pivotal role during the processing and analysing of Asiad'82 results. During this exercise it had also demonstrated the establishment of a Wide Area Network (WAN) within Delhi using its Cyber 170/730 mainframe system. This period saw the announcement of building up of NICNET (NIC Network) through INTELSAT/INSAT satellite upto the district level. Through this project plans were launched for major computerisation drive at the Central/State/District level government offices.

Amongst other major initiatives were the announcement of the launching of Computerised Railway Reservation System; mooting of INDONET; Computerisation of Passport Offices and last but not the least, organisations such as Indian Airlines, ONGC, SAIL etc. launching schemes of computerising their operations.

With NICNET attaining its target of reaching district level by the end of 1989, the problem of working on computers in regional language became a major issue. Consequently this problem was solved by academicia of IIT, Kanpur by developing Graphics Indian Script Terminal (GIST) card. The initiation of computerisation of Land Records at Morena (MP) and Kanpur (UP) gave another fillip to the process of computerisation in particular and the computer industry at large.

4.3 *Human Resource Development*

Simultaneously to supplement the manpower requirements of this industry, government initiated the CLASS project to cover over 10,000 schools. The objective was to produce the new generation which is "Computer Literate". At universities and engineering college levels, a number of new courses such as Masters of Computer Applications, Diploma in Computer Applications, B.Tech/B.E. in computers etc. were introduced. In Private Sector it started the process of opening up of computer training centres such as NIIT, ICE, ICS, etc.

4.4 *Growth of Computer Technology*

Within developed countries this period saw rapid strides being made in IT industry as a whole—particularly increasing integration of the computer and communications technology. If Apple brought out Mackintosh - a 32 bit Computer, IBM introduced a new PC/XT having a system clock/ calendar etc. Motorola came out with 68020 chip; while its competitor, Intel, soon produced 80386 processor. This marked the beginning of a kind of a race in developing newer processors enabling the development of a new era in microcomputer architecture.

Compaq incorporated 80386 processor to launch its new range of micro computers. It forced IBM to bring out RISC-PC and Motorola to make 68030 processor. Simultaneously problems related to distributed data processing, formation of local area networks (LANs), development of necessary hardware as well as software were addressed to.

Similarly for solving problems of engineering/construction industry, the R&D in computer hardware focussed its attention on developing better resolution monitors capable of dealing with high resolution color graphics. Also, workstations too started appearing in the market and brands such as Tektronix 41XX series started becoming popular. It needs no stressing that in parallel the industry was going ahead with developing newer softwares in DBMS, CAD/CAM, Image Processing etc.

4.5 *Composition of Computer Hardware Industry*

Within India interesting developments started taking place. Items banned on the import list such as Dot Matrix Printers, Floppy Drives, Power Supplies, Monitors, Keyboards etc. became freely available and some domestic production also started. In spite of this the industrial units in Private Sector were found wanting in building a reliable R&D base of their own. They were more eager to develop/produce microprocessor based Supermicros and PC-compatibles. Even for doing this they preferred collaborations with prominent foreign manufacturers. In Public Sector, ECIL tied up with Control Data Corporation (CDC) of USA to produce mainframes and Norsk Data (ND) of Norway for superminis. SCL started producing LSI chips. ET&T was identified to produce low cost high quality electronics products.

In 1984-85 top ten companies accounted for 90 per cent of the industry's turnover. This was reduced to about 60 per cent by 1990-91. There were changes every year with enterprises entering and dropping-out from the list of ten largest enterprises. The competition became increasingly severe due to entry of large number of enterprises and overpowering thrust on growth by incumbents.

4.6 *User Needs*

Initially when computers entered India, they were primarily used by the scientific organisations for their research and development activities. Slowly the computers started finding their utility in the area of Electronic Data Processing (EDP) in organisations which required handling of huge data e.g., NSSO, Census and in payroll area. However, with the entry of PCs in post 1984 period, there was a definite broadening of the scope of computers in an area which till then had not been explored in India - more and more organisations started using computers for wordprocessing activities. This soon graduated into Desk Top Publishing area by 1989-90 on a regular commercial basis. Then came in the use of computers in the area of inventory management, on-line transaction processing etc., which found utility in a number of private/public sector organisations.

.7 Economic Growth

'able 14.1 gives the turn-over of the computer hardware industrial roduction of India during 1983-91. It can be seen from the Tables 14.1 nd Table 14.2, that in comparison with the overall industrial growth,

TABLE 14.1 Growth of Indian Computer Industry 1983-91*

Sl.No.	Year	Industry Turnover (Rs. in Crores)	% Growth
1.	1983-84	125.0	31.58
2.	1984-85	138.0	10.40
3.	1985-86	288.0	108.70
4.	1986-87	413.0	43.40
5.	1987-88	582.0	40.92
6.	1988-89	1010.00	75.54
7.	1989-90	1675.00	65.84
8.	1990-91	2012.00	20.12

TABLE 14.2: Index of Industrial Production **
(Percentage Change Over Previous Year)

1977-78#	4.2
1978-79#	7.6
1979-80#	–1.7
1980-81#	4
1981-82	9.3
1982-83	3.2
1983-84	6.7
1984-85	8.6
1985-86	8.7
1986-87	9.1
1987-88	7.3
1988-89	8.7
1989-90	8.6
1990-91	8.5

Based on old index (1970-71=100) till 1980-81 and new index (1980-81=100) thereafter

R. Bhatnagar (1991): "Evolution of IT Industry in India - A Report", submitted to IIM/A.

Economic Survey 1991-92, Part II Sectoral Developments, Eco. Divn., Min. of Finance, GOI, pp83.

TABLE 14.3: Seventh Plan Outlay for Key Sectors

(Rs. in crores)

S.No.	Department	VI Plan Approved Expenditure Outlay	VII Plan percentage (anticipated)	Outlay	Increase
1.	Deptt. of Electronics	140.28	173.82	471.00	70.2
2.	Deptt. of Steel	4000.0	4807.54	6420.13	37.69
3.	Petrochemicals,	935.00	491.77	307.70	7.81
	Engg. Units, Nat.		+ 706.55		
	Gas etc.@			1014.25	
4.	Deptt. of Fertilizers	2350.0	2045.12	2025.75	-1.6
5.	Deptt. of Agri & Coop.	325.0	594.01	635.0	48.8

@ Figure for Chemicals and Petrochemicals alone

* Handbook of Industrial Statistics 1989, p 34.

the computer hardware industry was growing at a much faster rate. Globally the computer hardware industry was growing during this period at the rate of 12 to 15 per cent (Chopra, 1993).[11] *How a Major Public Policy Initiative creates Impact*. On the contrary the ICHI grew at almost four times the Indian Industrial growth rate.

Table 14.3 gives the Seventh Plan outlay for key sectors. A closer scrutiny of the data shows the outlay for the Department of Electronics has been increased about 2.3 times compared to Sixth Plan outlay — a 70.2 per cent increase. In contrast for Steel, Petro-chemicals, Fertilizers and Agriculture the outlay had increased by 37.69, 7.81, 1.6 and 48.8 per cent respectively (Table 14.3). This establishes the concern of the government to give greater impetus to the electronics sector at large of which ICHI was one component.

5. Conclusions on Impact of New Computer Policy(NCP)

The 1984 to 1990 period saw extraordinary growth in computer hardware industry in India. The growth was a result of fast developments and changes in all the variables of the system. Now the dynamics of interrelation between NCP and each variable is examined for its impact, i.e. on growth and capability improvement of Indian computer hardware industry.

5.1 *Computer Technology Changes*

During the period technology development was one of the fastest in computer industry. The significant developments were emergence of personal computers as powerful office tool, networking of computers of different manufacturers and processing capacities, and workstations for CAD/CAM applications. The technology trend was towards standardisation (from proprietary). The pace of technology was so fast that computers based on a new technology were introduced every three years and product life cycles were less than an year. Barring United States, all the countries acquired the technologies through licensing, collaboration, or by inviting U.S. multinationals. Even in U.S. the technologies were developed by large number of severely competitive enterprises. It was impossible for any country to develop entire range of computer technologies on its own and also keep pace with the developments. There was no single source of all the technologies, and the technology was complex; it was imperative for government to facilitate the access to the technology. NCP provided for freer access to the needed technology and faster clearances. NCP made it possible for Indian enterprises to launch computer products of nearly all types after making some adaptations (some enterprises acquired capabilities), and more importantly almost at the time of their worldwide introduction.

5.2 *Changing Composition of Hardware Industry*

The intensity of competition increased in ICHI over the years. The number of enterprises which accounted for 70 per cent of the industry's turn-over changed from seven to fifteen, and there was frequent re-shuffling of enterprises. This occurred due to the entry of a large number of enterprises, who could import technology in the form of SKD/CKD kits, as a result of NCP's provisions. Increased competition amongst the players culminated in severe price cuts during late 1985 and late 1988. The price cuts further fuelled rapid expansion of the industry.

5.3 *Infrastructure Development*

A direct consequence of NCP was to facilitate institutions, laboratories, and large government organisations to import computers. This became easier and faster through Inter Ministerial Standing Committee. One of the biggest outcome was the establishment of NICNET through NEC-1000 super computers and ND-500 superminis between 1986-89, which facilitated intensive and extensive use of computers in the country.

5.4 *Human Resource Development*

Shortage of technical/skilled manpower was felt in the industry specially after 1987. This was primarily due to the rapid growth in the requirements of the industry as a result of its expansion catalysed by the provisions of NCP. Further, there was a qualitative shift in the composition of manpower—from earlier pure Science (Mathematics, Statistics, Physics etc.) graduates to Engineers, MCAs, DCAs and MBAs.

5.5 *User Application*

NCP acted as a catalyst towards widespread (e.g. CAD, CAM, MIS, Project Mgmt. etc.) application of computers even in organisations which were conventional in their operations (such as engineering construction and manufacturing units). This was due to the availability of a large number of software packages and hardware configurations, along with the approach of computer companies to adopt aggressive marketing techniques.

5.6 *Growth of Indian Economy*

Indian economy grew at a healthy rate of 5.5 per cent and overall industry at 8.5 per cent during 1985-90. Whereas ICHI grew almost at an average rate of four times this rate. This 'disproportionate' high rate of growth of ICHI was possible due to strong thrust by the government for computerisation, reduction in cost of computers, and easier availability of hardware options and software solutions as a consequence of NCP.

New Computer Policy of November 1984 thus had a significant impact on the evolution of ICHI. The impact of NCP was essentially in two ways. First, it made possible for ICHI to be latched with the global computer industry by allowing free access to technology and components. Second, it induced and attracted a large number of enterprises in the ICHI fold which led to competition, resulting in easier availability of computer solutions at lower costs. NCP provided advantages of globalisation to Indian Customers by making it possible for Indian and global computer industry to join hands; and ensuing competition led to the advantages of liberalisation reaching the customers.

REFERENCES

1. B.W. Hogwood and L.A. Gunn (1984); *Policy Analysis for the Real World,* Oxford University Press.
2. C.C. Hood (1976), *The Limits of Implementation,* London: Wiley.
3. L.A. Gunn (1978); "Why is Implementation so Difficult?" *Management Services Government* 33, 169-176.
4. S. Barrett and C.Fudge (1981); *Policy and Action,* London, Methewa.
5. C.H. Weiss (1972): *Evaluation Research: Method of Assessing Program Effectiveness,* Englewood Cliffs, NJ : Prentice-Hall.
6. H. Mintzberg and J.A. Waters (1985); "Of Strategies, Deliberate and Emergent" *Strategic Management Journal,* Vol. 6., pp 257-272.
7. R.A. Leone and S.P. Bradley (1983) "Towards an Effective Industrial Policy", Harvard Business Review on Public Policy and Private Enterprise.
8. B.S. Chakravarthy (1985)," Business Government Partnership in Emerging Industries: Lessons from American Symbols Experience", *Advances in Strategic Management* Vol. 3 Jai Press, Greenwich.
9. S.S.Srivastava (1979): "Systems Analysis", Management in Government, Ed. Mathur, Diesh & Sekharan: Publ. Divn., Min. I&B, GOI, pp 205.
10. Public Enterprises Survey (1988-89), Vol 2, Bureau of Public Enterprises, Min. of Industries, GOI.
11. R.C. Chopra (1993), "Education Training Requirements for Software Industry", Electronics Information & Planning, pp 153.

15. EMERGING LONG-TERM ENERGY POLICY FROM THE BROADER NATIONAL GOALS AND PRIORITIES IN THE S&T POLICY OF INDIA

C. Subhash

1. Introduction

One thing is clear. So long as man could kill his like, but not all his like, he lets the gods worry that the sun should rise each day, the rivers should flow, and the human race should live on. Today, when man has gained powers comparable to those of nature, when he is able to destroy all life on earth, he has found that nothing but his own reason and conscience are responsible for the future of the world. Man and man alone must make sure that rivers flow and flowers bloom, and that there should be people to admire the sun rise. Man is now the Atlas bearing the universe on his own shoulders. No one but other men can aid him and share his responsibility for the future. But this dramatic situation breeds hope. As this sense of responsibility sinks deeper it shapes a solidarity of one and all. People are brought together by the idea that life on earth and the opportunities for its further advancement are the greatest values of all, and the interests of society are supreme and the answer lies in brotherhood of man (Streltsova, 1987).

There is no dearth of arguments that science has a great impact on societies and that it is the basis of much material progress. But the blessings of science are not undisputed. The same area of research which has released seemingly unlimited sources of energy has also unleashed forces of unimanginable destruction.

Accordingly, it is extremely essential to consider the long-term energy policy of any nation in particular and global community in general, with the clear-cut linkages to environmental aspects, and the Science and Technology (S&T) Policies.

In the Indian context the S&T policy is enshrined in the constitution of India (1950) which states: "It shall be the duty of every citizen of India to develop scientific temper, humanism and spirit of inquiry and reform". It is quite a general statement. However, The Scientific Policy Resolution (SPR) of 1958 and The Technology Policy Statement of 1983 are more specific. To quote from SRR, "The key to national prosperity apart from the spirit of the people, lies in the modern age, in the effective combination of three factors, technology, raw materials and capital of which the first is perhaps the most important; since the creation and adoption of new scientific techniques can, in fact, make up for deficiency in natural resources, and reduce the demands on capital. But technology can grow out of the study of science and its applications". Whereas SPR is applicable to all sectors of economy, its relevance to the Energy Sector is quite important (Lavakare, 1990).

2. Developments in the Energy Sector

Energy sector is very vast and can be described in several ways:

* primary sources;
* secondary fuels;
* end-use technology characteristics;
* imports;
* supply and demand of energy; and
* rural and urban issues.

Although all along there has been a Ministry of Energy which has been planning, implementing and controlling the activities of this sector through the various departments e.g. Coal, Petroleum, Central Electricity Authority, Oil etc. on one hand and BHEL, NTPC, NHPC, State Electricity Boards on the other, it is quite clear that this sector has mainly been in the domain of Centre and States and the Public Sector without much participation of the private sector.

If one looks at the energy sector in terms of an energy vector, one can notice that wood was a vector in earlier days, then coal and oil and presently electricity is the energy vector of not only India but the whole of the mankind. In order to plan and undertake suitable R&D activities along with necessary science and technology it is important to know what is going to be the energy vector of tomorrow i.e. HYDROGEN.

A policy maker or planner confronting any system as complex and diverse as the national energy system must assimilate and analyze a vast array of information about technology, existing policies, regulations, economics and political forces; and anticipate the reaction of constituent groups to any future action (Subhash, 1988).

3. Historical Perspective

A Working Group on Energy Policy (WEP) had been set up in 1977. The Group submitted its final report which includes some perspectives on the energy sector upto A.D. 2000. It used simple methods such as trend extrapolation of GDP elasticity method for obtaining reference level projections to determine policy guidelines (GOI, 1979). Another important study has been done by Parikh (1981): "Modelling Energy Demand for Policy Analysis". According to this study, the formulation of any model goes through the following steps:

* analysis of the past and present data;
* decisions concerning the structure of the problem;
* identification of factors: which are going to change in future e.g. prices, efficiencies, technical changes; or those factors which are controllable through policy, and socio-economic changes (e.g. urbanization);
* formulation of the mathematical model of the above mentioned identified factors;
* verification of the model;
* judgment concerning numerical inputs i.e. scenario variables; and
* running the model for various scenarios, examination of results and interpretations in terms of policy.

Another important national study has been conducted by the Advisory Board on Energy titled "Towards a Perspective on Energy Demand and Supply in India in 2004/05", in May 1985. One of the major conclusions of the report is: The requirement for electricity in 2004/05, in terms of installed capacity varies between 1,39,000 MW and 1,88,000 MW. for a PLF of 58 per cent and GDP growth of 5 per cent, capacity requirement would be about 1,64,000 MW. Another conclusion states: assuming an oil price of $ 45/barrel (1984-85 dollars) in 2004/05, our oil imports could be valued at $ 8500 million. Lastly it states that total investment required would be around Rs. 4,50,000 Crore at 1984/85 prices (GOI, 1985).

4. Policy Options in the Energy Sector

Some of the major policy decision require energy demand management. On the one hand we want the economy to grow fast. This requires high investment as well as high energy demand. But the supply of energy is constrained and has so far been lagging behind the growth in energy demand. The policy options for demand management are energy conservation and smoothing the peak load demand. The policy options for energy supply management are : (i) develop alternate energy sources, and (ii) improve the efficiency of existing devices.

Government policy for demand side management has two options. viz., regulation and promotion. Under regulation we have:

* licensing;
* mandatory energy reporting; and
* enforcing energy conservation norms.

On the promotional side of energy demand management there are four policy options:

* energy pricing policy;
* incentives to energy efficient technology;
* funding training and awareness programmes; and
* research and development support.

Similarly Government Policy options for the supply side management of energy can be divided into long-term and short-term options as follows;

Long- Term

* Technology R&D
* Exploration
* Infrastructure Development

Short-Term

* Controlling Time/Cost overrun of ongoing project
* Improving device efficiency e.g. Plant Load Factors and Transmission and Distribution Losses.

It is quite evident that energy conservation as a policy can have a significant effect on the energy demand and supply balance. This policy need not be the course only of Government, but at the level of the firm or company (both energy producing and energy consuming) too it can have profound effects. For any energy consuming industry the strategic (long-term) and operational (short-term) options are as follows:

Long-Term (Strategic)
Hardware:

* Technology Selection
* Capacity Selection
* Extent of Automation
* Energy Metering Devices

Software:

* Corporate Goals
* Organisation Structure
* Energy Information System
* Training
* Awareness.

Short-Term (Operational)
Hardware:

* Retrofitting
* Insulation

Software:

* Maintenance
* Energy Audit
* Work Method Improvement.

Management of energy conservation requires suitable training programmes at different levels of management emphasising relevant aspects:

Top Management — Energy strategy formulation, technology selection, organisation etc.
Senior Management — energy policy implementation, operational

		planning, technology upgradation, design energy audit and information system.
Middle Management	—	Maintenance programme, energy audit procedures, energy report, information on alternative energy consuming and saving devices, establishing potential area of energy conservation etc.
Junior Executives and Supervisors	—	Carrying out energy audits, collecting energy information, maintenance procedures and daily schedules, detecting areas of energy losses etc.

5. Policy of Substitution and Augmentation of Energy Sources

Substitution means interfuel substitution. For example, if we take the end-use of cooking in rural areas, where traditionally fire wood has been used as a fuel, substitution could offer several possibilities:

* use of biogas;
* use of solar cookers;
* use of LPG; and
* use of Crop-residue briquettes.

Thus through the policy of substitution we can shift the consumption pattern of any particular fuel by more suitable fuels. The criteria for suitability could emerge from ecological or environmental or economic factors. Another example of substitution could include a shift from petrol driven vehicles which generate lots of lead pollution to those driven by CNG (Compressed Natural Gas).

The policy of augmentation means augmenting new energy sources to improve the balance of payments or to meet the growing needs of the agricultural and household sectors. The real option to meet of energy needs in different sectors both in rural and urban areas lies in new and renewable energy sources. One must consider seriously the decentralised energy systems where local population will have control of production and management of their own energy requirements. It is here that one must emphasise the role of national policy. Several steps have been taken in the past by the GOI in various spheres for formulation and implementation of appropriate policies and incentives so that new and renewable energy options can start contributing adequately.

The governmental efforts towards the policy of augmentation started in early eighties with the Commission for Additional Sources of Energy (CASE) within the Deptt. of Science and Technology.

In 1982, GOI created a new organisation called the Department of Non-Conventional Energy Sources (DNES) under the Ministry of Energy. In 1987 another independent organ Indian Renewable Energy Development Agency (IREDA) was set up as a public limited company under the Companies Act. The main objective of this company is to promote technologies relating to new and renewable sources of energy by extending financial assistance on soft term basis both to the industry and the user.

According to the Annual Report 1991-92 of DNES, the potential of different New and Renewable Sources of Energy are as below (GOI, DNES 1991-92):

Source/Technology	Approx.	Potential
Biogas Plants	40	Million
Boimass	17000	MW
Improved Chulha	120	Million
Solar Energy	5×10^{15}	KW hr/Yr.
Mini-Micro Hydro	5000	MW
Wind Energy	20000	MW

Different programmes undertaken by DNES, since its conception in 1982 include the following:

1. Biogas Programme.
2. National Programme on Improved *Chulha*.
3. Solar Thermal Energy.
4. Solar Photovoltaics.
5. Wind Energy Programme.
6. Micro-Mini Hydro Programme.
7. Urjagram Programme.
8. Biomass Programme.
9. Energy from Waste Recycling.
10. Magneto Hydro Dynamics Programme.
11. Hydrogen Energy Programme.
12. Chemical Sources of Energy.
13. Ocean and Other Energy Sources Programmes.
14. Alternate Fuels for Transport.
15. Human and Animal Energy Programme.

Recently, the DNES has been upgraded and converted into an independent ministry called Ministry of Non-Convertional Energy Sources (MNES).

6. Conclusions

It is evident from the above how a commission which nucleated under the Deptt. of S&T (CASE) has emerged as a Ministry dictating the Long-term Energy Policy of our country. In this process of development all the three aspects of Energy Policy viz. Conservation, Substitution and Augmentation have been well taken care of through various programmes of New and Renewable Sources of Energy. It can be safely predicted that name of the MNES would be suitably changed to Ministry of New and Renewable Sources of Energy and it would be this ministry alone which would usher India into the new energy vector of the next century namely Hydrogen. The author, however, is not satisfied with the present level of research in this area in India. The main reason is the lack of easy access to available technology from the developed countries. Recently, with the refusal of Russia to provide Cryogenic Rocket Engines to India, has surely provided a new direction and dimension to the Indian scientists and political executive.

The declaration of Prime Minister of India that India will press ahead with its missile and space programmes and the confidence he has shown in the capability of Indian scientists to develop Cryogenic Technology is a healthy sign. This would surely bring India closer to realising Hydrogen as energy vector although indirectly. But that is the way things are in the field of Science and Technology. The developments in the Space and Missile Programme would affect the lives of common people in about another 25-30 years. By 2025 a family might be cooking its meals not by LPG or electricity but by burning hydrogen and driving their scooter/car not by the power of petrol or diesel but by burning hydrogen gas and in turn producing water vapours instead of environment degrading smoke.

REFERENCES

GOI, (1979) *Report of the Working Group on Energy Policy,* New Delhi: Planning Commission.

GOI, Advisory Board on Energy (1985) *Towards a Perspective on Energy Demand and Supply in India in 2004/05,* New Delhi: S.K. Verma & Co.

GOI, DNES (1991-92) *Annual Report,* New Delhi: Min. of Power and Non Conventional

Energy Source.

Lavakare, P.J. et al (1990) *Science Policies in International Perspective,* New Delhi: Wiley Eastern.

Parikh, J.K. (1981) *Modelling Energy Demand for Policy Analysis,* New Delhi: Planning Commission.

Streltsova, Nines, (1987) *Looking into the Future,* Moscow: Progress Publishers.

Subhash, C. (1988) *Ph.D. Thesis: Planning and Management of Rural Energy Systems,* New Delhi: I.I.T. Delhi.

16. SOME EMERGING TECHNOLOGIES INCLUDING SUPERCONDUCTIVITY: An International Competitiveness and Support Scenario

V.K. Misra

In these days of instant global communications and fast transportation and in the post liberalisation policies framework, the national economies are getting more interactive through expanded exchanges in trade, commerce, industry, culture etc. The roles that individual Governments play singly or collectively in improving the international trade performance and in sustaining socio-economic developments in their nations, to a large extent also depend on the technological and industrial strengths. These are reflected in production of higher value added quality products with competitive cost performance. Apart from industrial infrastructure this is related to availability of innovative/inventive manpower and the skill/knowledge base and the scientific and productive capabilities of population at large. The education, science, technology and industrial policies of various countries either proclaimed and practiced or actually practised at ground levels largely are for improving the knowledge/skill and science support and practice base, making R&D more productive and contributive to the socio-economic growth and making technology and industrial base dynamically leading and competitive. In developing countries while these policies aim at basic sustenance, the same contribute to improvement of quality of life in the developed world while security remains a common concern.

This trend is also reflected in the overall role of the Federal Governments in promoting science, technology and industry. In developed competitive economies, the Governments generally fund long-lead-time high-risk and generic science and technology or industrial development programmes requiring high finances; and many emerging/critical technologies do come in that category. In developed countries wider spectrum of scientific/technological/industrial developments, mainly for meeting local needs and exports and for familiarisation with technologies, are promoted and in some cases even basic research and academic research gets high priority, like in India. However, as the international trade barriers are in process of getting eased out and with enhanced emphasis on IPR etc., technology and technology applications like science have also become international in nature, and are making demands on domestic support base to be internationally competitive.

Certain technologies, mostly science based, have come to be recognised as candidates for long-term support due to their high potential for growth, correlating contributions and security considerations etc. These are called by various names such as emerging technologies, critical technologies, futuristic core technologies etc. and are being promoted by Federal Governments all-over.

In Table 16.1 and Figs 16.1 to 16.4 as the end some data/examples are given for—

(i) Growth indication in US, Europe and Japan for some Emerging/ Critical Technologies;
(ii) Government support/funding pattern of one of Emerging/Critical Technologies (Superconductivity) in USA, Japan and India; and
(iii) Growth/Competitiveness pattern of superconductivity.

Order of funding in superconductivity and many of the Emerging Technologies/Critical Technologies by the US and Japanese Governments are similar but the contributions and focus of the large companies/ industries differs. Very interesting and some times confusing situation is seen in many emerging technology areas in R&D and production where very often USA and Japan lead in R&D and production efforts/capacities potentials respectively. The US and Japanese laboratories and industries including academia also have multistream cooperations encouraging these trends. Illustrative areas are superconductivity, SQUID based medical devices, SOR, MRI/MRS, Genetic Engineering etc. The long-term leadership will be determined by industrial innovations, production and marketing performances and their active involvement in long-term commitment to research and technological growth and their applications. In superconductivity some special growth areas appear to be:

USA : Sensors, space and Strategic Applications, Defence, Nuclear/Atomic Science and Engineering, NDT, medical Diagnostics, Communications and computing etc., materials processing.

Japan: Power and transportation Sectors, SOR, Medical and NDT uses, Material processing, Communications and computing etc.

Europe: Communications and computing, Material processing, Nuclear applications, SOR.

The efforts and performances of major corporations like IBM, AT&T, GEC, HUGHES, ROCKWELL, US Steel, Dupont etc. in USA; Nippon & Kobe Steel, Sanyo, Fujitsu, Mitsubishi, Hitachi, NEC, Toshiba, Toray, Asahi, Sumitomo & JNR etc. in Japan; and Siemens, Philips, CSF etc. in Europe will be interesting to watch in many emerging/critical Technological areas including superconductivity. Many of the Indian companies (e.g. BHEL, IPE etc.) and research establishments, specially those of DAE, ISRO etc., shall also contribute to the growth of superconductivity and some sectors of emerging technologies and their applications in India. However in India as the industry at large is not yet ready to contribute in a significant manner in Emerging/Critical Technologies development and the Government sector contribution in many cases is two orders or more lower than of its counterparts in West. This situation, coupled with high, degree of correlation in complementarity/ cogrowth of many Emerging Technologies, makes the Indian situation special needing newer and innovative approaches to forge bilateral and international alliances and networks based on utilisation of mutual strengths and resources to supplement the purely indigenous/self-reliant efforts.

Some promising illustrative areas in Indian context where traditional eastern wisdom and knowledge, craftsmanship innovativeness and proven initiatives, indigenous resources base can be combined with emerging frontier science and technology tools and information to have the competitive edge, are suggested below:

— Special materials and materials processing;
— Diamonds, Gems and Jewellery;
— Low cost and holistic approaches of Ayurvedic/ Homeopathic Systems of medicines;
— Medicinal plants;
— Software and Brainware;
— Fuzzy theory and applications of parallel/neural computing;

— Massively replicable health/diagnostic tools and techniques;
— Novel SC Devices and ASICS;
— Chemicals and pharmaceuticals; and
— Wide bond digital ISDN and low cost satellite based massaging/ communication systems etc.

TABLE 16.1: Some Emerging/ Critical Technologies-US, EEC and Japan

	USA		EEC		JAPAN	
	R	P	R	P	R	P
Advance Materials	B	C	B	C	B	A
Intelligent Materials and Processing	A	C	B	C	B	B
Advanced Semiconducting Devices	B	C	B	C	B	B
Super Conducting Devices	A	B	B	B	B	B
Biotecnology	B	B	B	B	B	A
Bio-Electronics	A	B	B	B	A	A
Sensors	A	A	A	B	B	B
Super Conductors and Systems	A	A	A	B	A	A
Digital Imaging Technology	B	A	A	B	B	A
High Density Data Storage	A	B	B	B	A	A
Parallel Computing and SMA	B	A	B	C	C	
High Performance Computing	A	A	B	B	B	A
Medical Devices and Diagnostics	B	B	B	A	B	A
Optoelectronics and Photonics	A	A	A	A	A	A
Fuzzy Logic and Neural Computing	A	C	B	C	A	A
Genetic Engg and Products	A	A	A	B	B	A
Weather Forecasting						
Now-Casting	A	A	A	B	B	A
Medium Range	B	A	A	A	B	B
Long Range	B	B	B	B	B	B

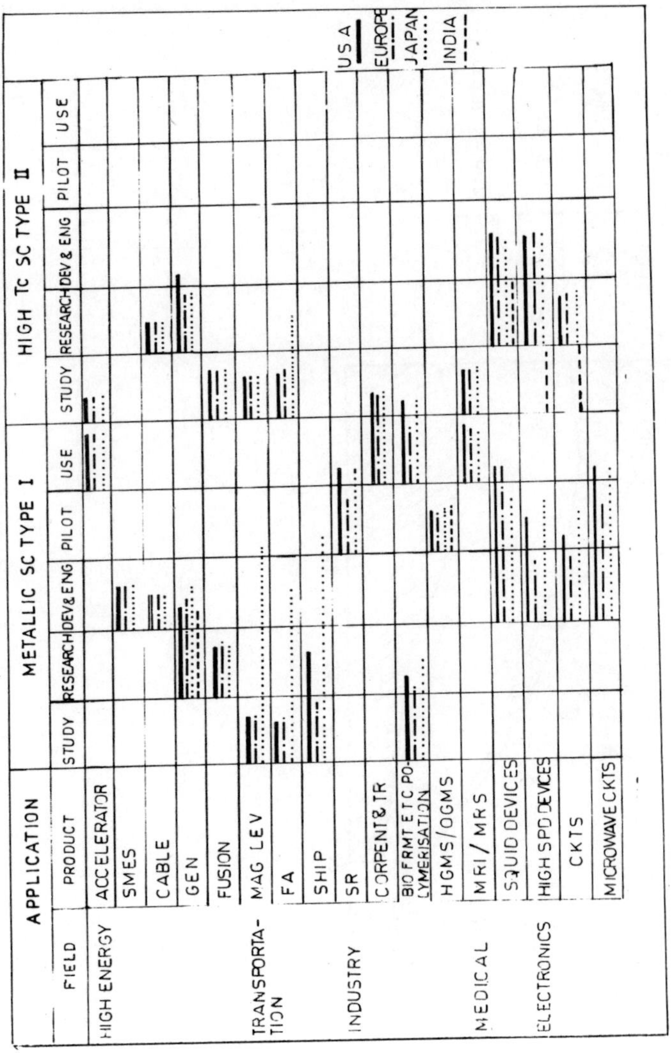

FIG.: 16.1: A Broad Status of Superconductivity.

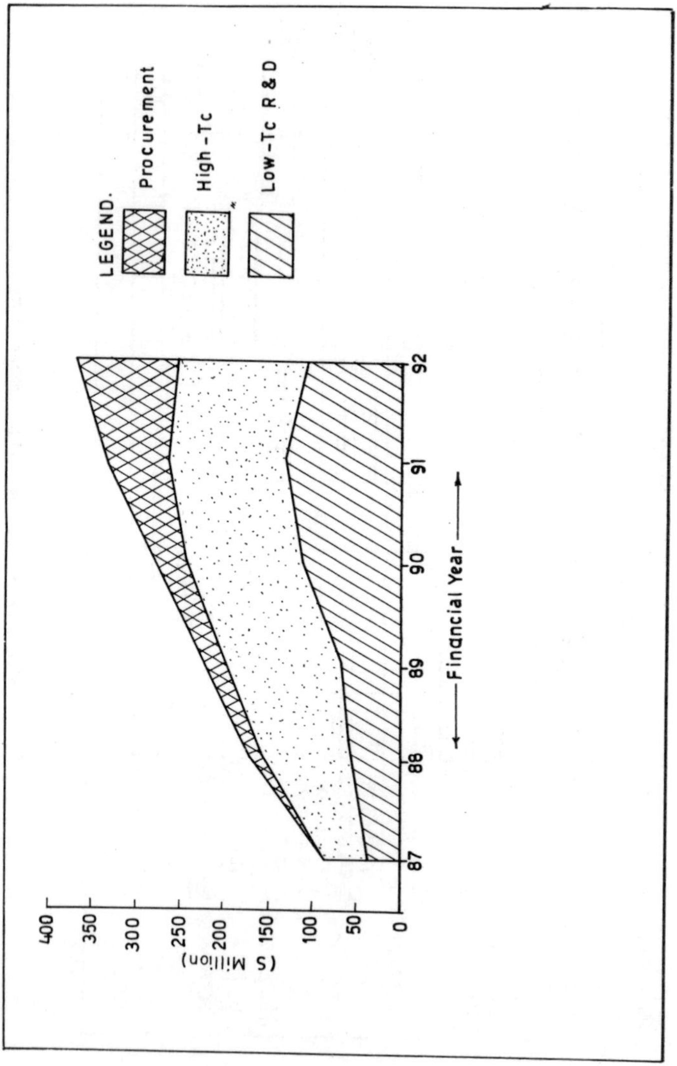

FIG.: 16.2: U.S.A. Federal Spending on Superconductivity

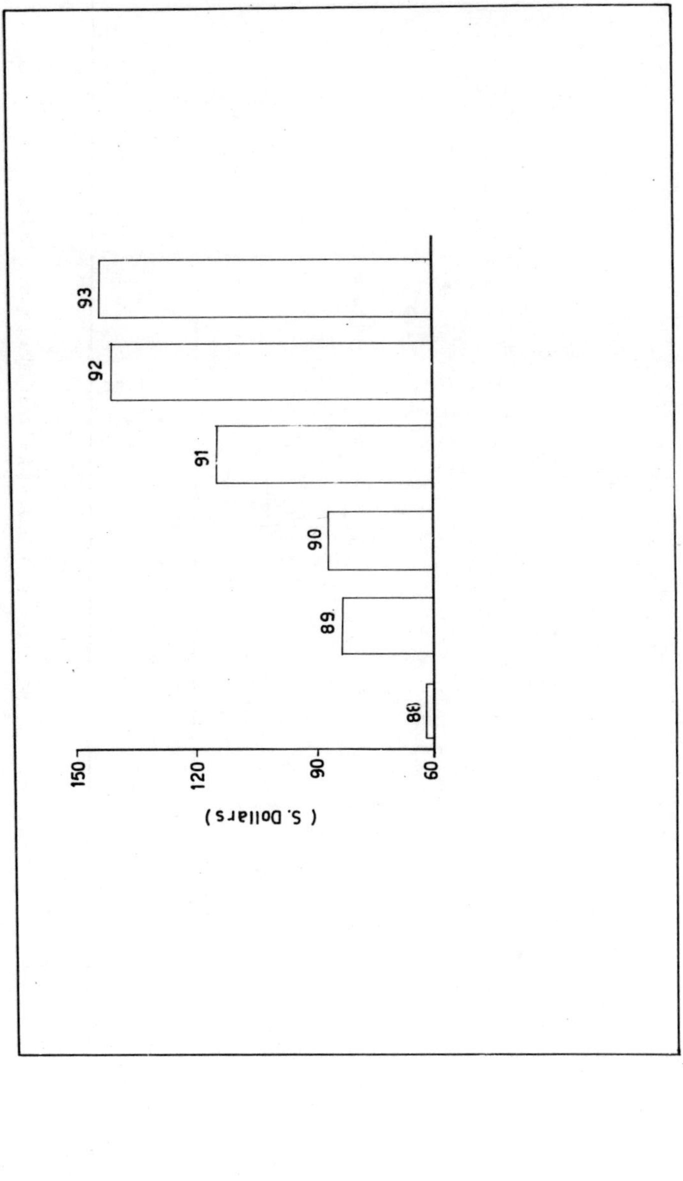

FIG.: 16.3: Trends of Superconductivity Funding by Japanese Government

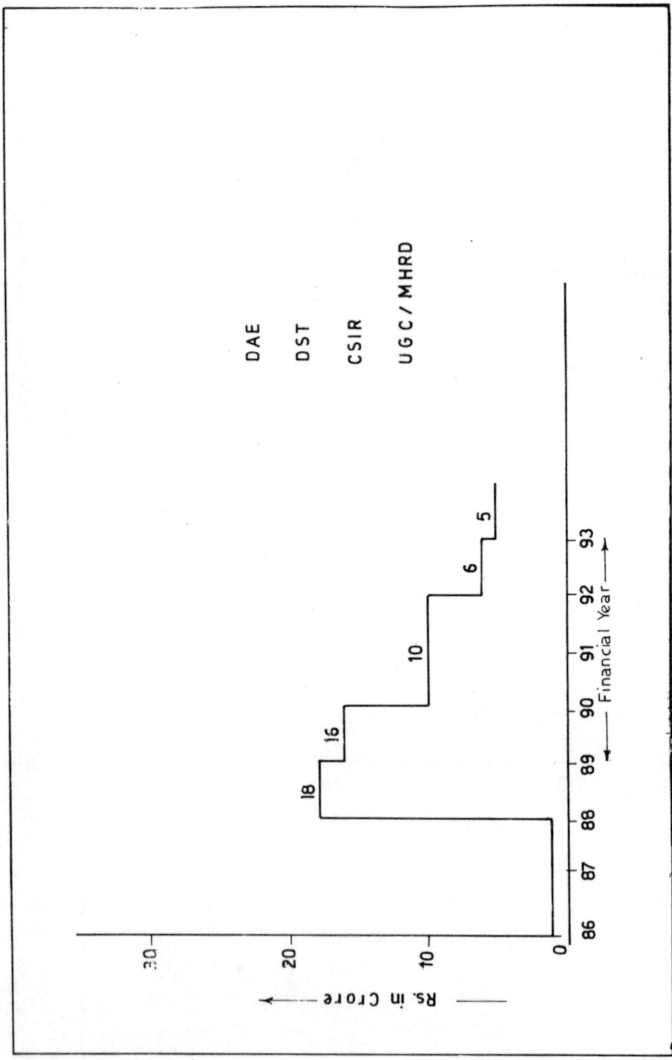

FIG.: 16.4: Govt. SC. (R & D & E) Funds Allocation in India. (Approx. Order)

PART-II

METHODOLOGIES

17. INTEGRATED DESCRIPTIVE AND NORMATIVE INDUSTRIAL POLICY FOR INDIA: A Hierarchical Structuring

S.K. Gaur
D.S. Mishra
P.S. Satsangi

Introduction

The importance of manufacturing and its effect on the general standards of living cannot be over-looked. Manufacturing industries generate a substantial proportion of wealth of most developed countries and employ a larger part of train working population (Mare, 1982). The manufacturing sector permeates the very fiber of most industrial societies of the world, providing the major outlets for their raw material, are energy industries, constituting the basis of their transport and distribution industries and supplying the products for their agricultural, textiles, small scale and large scale industries. The manufacturing sectors of many countries also play a key role in international trade because manufactured exports provide a major source of international currency to purchase food and raw materials from countries better endowed with natural resources. Exports also provide the means of affording the luxury products and technologies developed by other nations. These are the major factors that play an ever-increasing part in motivating less developed countries to expand their own manufacturing capabilities.

Since industrialisation accelerates economic growth and increases national income, it assumes much importance in the context of economic development of particularly the underdeveloped or developing countries.

Although India still remains an agrarian economy, the industrial base and the structures erected on it have become strong and considerably diversified.

The process of rapid industrialisation in India on scientific lines began since the inception of Five Year Plans; expansion and diversification of the industrial structure have been achieved with the establishment of new units in the existing fields as well as setting up of new enterprises (Sahy *et. al.* 1992). According to World Bank figures India stood 15th on the basis of net industrial output in 1980 (Table 17.1).

TABLE 17.1: Net Industrial Output, the Output of Selected Industries and Vehicle Stocks in India and in Major Industrial Countries, 1980

Sl. No.	Countries	Total value Added at 1975 price (US $ (billions)	OUTPUT (000 metric tonnes)					STOCK (000)		
			Sugar	Nitrogenous Fertilizers	Plastics	Steel	Aluminuim	Cars	Commercial Vehicles	Tractors
1.	USA	437	5313	11788	12418	101456	6123	118459	33411	4775
2.	Japan	234	812	1202	6420	111395	1896	23559	13193	1096
3.	West Germany	185	2935	1436	6710	43838	768	23192	1571	1463
4.	France	108	3913	1640	2820	23176	602	18400	2686	1504
5.	U.K.	57	1347	1157	2162	11277	537	—	—	512
6.	Brazil	44	8270	25	638	10232	314	—	—	330
7.	Italy	—	1892	1388	2464	26501	537	17686	1688	1072
8.	Canada	36	92	1755	942	15901	1075	10256	2955	675
9.	Spain	33	1081	960	1145	12533	—	7557	1381	529
10.	Mexico	29	2642	753	332	7003	43	4255	1573	120
11.	Australia	25	3415	223	709	7895	314	—	—	332
12.	Netherlands	24	951	1624	1975	4959	312	—	—	178
13.	Belgium	20	874	743	—	12323	1	3159	319	116
14.	Sweden	19	333	180	—	4237	121	—	—	181
15.	India	16	4528	2164	138	9327	185	925	809	418

There are three factors of production, namely land, labour and capital. In a country of India's geographical and demographic dimensions, there is no shortage of the first two factors of production, that is land and labour. Capital had been scarce in the past and it continues to be scarce even today.

In a country where more than 30 per cent of the population is below the poverty line, the propensity to save and form capital is much lower. Nevertheless there are capital-intensive industries where the large scale sector is the only remedy. However, the large scale sector and the small scale sector have to coexist for the balanced development of the economy of any country.

The Seventh Five Year Plan envisaged an annual average rate of growth of 8 per cent in industrial production. Apart from the public sector programmes, considerable expansion in capacities and output is envisaged in the private sector particularly in industries such as cement, fertilisers, industrial machines, automobiles, consumer durables and electronic goods. A statement indicating the capacity and production targets for selected industries for 1989-90 is given in Table 17.2).

In spite of all the above facts, the small scale sector has continued to perform well. According to estimates provided by the Development

TABLE 17.2: Capacities and Production Targets for Selected Indian Industries for 1989-90

Sl. No.	Industries	Target	Production
1.	Mining		
	(a) Coal (million tonnes)	—	226
	(b) Crude Oil (-do-)	—	34.53
2.	Basic Metals		
	(a) Hot metal (Integrated steel Plant)	15.26	13.07
	(b) Capper (Refined)	47.5	42.75
	(c) Aluminum	580	499
3.	Metal Products		
	(a) Steel Castings (million tonnes)	230	120
	(b) Steel Forgings (m.t.)	375	240
4.	Non-metallic Mineral Products		
	(a) Cement (million tonnes)	60	49
	(b) Petroleum Products	—	45.47
5.	Basic Chemicals		
	(a) Caustic Soda (m.t.)	1200	950
	(b) Soda Ash (m.t.)	1330	1140
6.	Agricultural Chemicals		
	(a) Nitrogenous Fertilizers (000 tonnes)	9253	6560
	(b) Phoshatic Fertilizer (000 tonnes)	2891	2190
7.	Thermoplastics PVS (000 tonnes)	288.0	233

Commissioner, Small Scale Industries, the number of small scale units increased from 14.76 lakhs in 1986-87 to 15.92 lakhs in 1987-88. These units provided goods and services worth Rs. 85,700 crores valued at current prices in 1987-88, showing an increase of above 18.6 per cent in nominal terms. Employment in this sector increased from 101.40 lakh persons to 107.0 lakh persons in 1987-88 marking an increase of 5.5 per cent. Exports from the small scale sector during the year 1986-87 amounted to Rs. 3648 crores and accounted for a share of 29 per cent in the total diverse export from the country curing the year (Thakur *et al.*, 1991).

Background

A common characteristic of a complex system is that it has a structure associated with it. This structure may be obvious and properly oriented or may be less obvious.

Effective policy-making will be easier if the knowledge of contextual mapping among various pertinent elements in designing a policy is available.

The term 'Interpretive Structural Modelling' (ISM) is used to refer to the systematic applications of some elementary notions of graph theory in such a way that theoretical, conceptual and computational leverage is exploited to efficiently construct a directed graph or network representation of the complex pattern of a contextual relationship among a set of elements (Malone, 1977). Further, ISM can also be visualised as a method which converts the mental model of the system into a structure through a matrix model on the basis of information supplied by the domain experts (Satsangi, *et al.*, 1991). However, it is very important to clearly identify and rank in order the relevant elements whose structure is to be interpreted. This can be done with the help of the Nominal Group Technique (NGT) which involves asking the experts to identify a few objectives which according to them are the most important.

Interpretive Structural Modelling Methodology

This paper reports research investigations carried out in a series of workshop sessions for developing an ISM each for the two compiled lists of integrated descriptive and normative national industrial policy objectives for the growth of the Indian Industrial environment and rank ordering these objectives. The exercise was carried out in a phased manner in which about 10 to 12 domain experts were involved including the authors.

A working paper circulated to the resource persons before the Workshop contained separate lists of elements of general policy objectives, elements of national industrial policy objectives and elements of small scale industrial policy objectives. The list of general policy objectives particularly incorporated such objectives that were relevant to the industrial environment in India. These lists were based mainly on the VII Plan document and the annual report of the Small Industries Development Organisation 1989-90, Government of India.

During stage one, these lists were discussed, clarified and edited with the help of resource persons and an agreed list of integrated descriptive policy elements for the Indian industrial environment was generated. Further, seven-important aspects from the point of view of industrial development, namely, Production (P), Marketing (M), Raw Materials (RM), Administration and Organisation (AO), Socio Economic (SE) perspective, Credit, Savings and Finance (CSF) and Cultural Heritage (CH) were preliminarily identified and agreed upon by the resource persons. The resource persons were then requested to classify each element of the integrated list of descriptive policy objectives under the above categories.

During the next stage of the exercise, the resource persons were called upon to rank the policy objectives using the Nominal Group Technique. To facilitate quick understanding, each of the elements were designated by a key-word and were also codified. The use of NCT incorporated asking resource persons to identify at least three objectives that they considered most important for each identified category from among the three lists of industrial policy objectives, national policy objectives and policy objectives of small scale industries in an integrated way.

For this purpose the following trigerring question was posed to them:

> "Which of the policy objectives according to you has the greatest potential for positive or negative impact on Indian Industries as a whole? Give a list of three of each type ranked in order of intensity of their potential impact."

The positive or negative impact so recorded by each resource person was tabulated and totalled up ignoring the sign. Those elements which polled no vote or only one vote to their credit were disregarded. The list of final elements was thus obtained and is given in Annexure I of this paper. This reduced the policy elements from 116 to 46. For developing an integrated list of normative policy elements, the idea engineering approach was used. A preliminary statement of need was put before the resource persons and they were requested to give three ideas each for achieving the aim, identifying hindrances or constraints and suggesting solutions to the possible constraints. The statement of these ideas and the number of votes that each idea polled formed the integrated list of normative policy elements for the Indian industries. This list is given in Annexure-II.

Creation of SSIM

The resource persons after agreeing upon the final list of descriptive integrated policy elements were asked to develop a Structural Self-Interaction Matrix (SSIM) on the basis of the chosen contextual relation "affects". Each element of the descriptive ranked list was compared with another element under the relation "affects" and the group responses were symbolically put in the form of *V*, *X* or *O* in SSIM according to the following rules:

Consider whether element X_i affects X_j or *vice-versa* or both ways or neither.

- (i) In the relation holds from element X_i to X_j and not in both direction put *V* as symbolic of direction from upper element i to lower element *j*.
- (ii) If the relating holds from X_j to X_i but not in both directions put *A* as symbolic of direction from the lower *j* to the upper *i*.
- (iii) If the relation perceived by the group holds in both directions put *X* as symbolic of both directions in the appropriate cell of SSIM.
- (iv) If the relation does not appear to be valid in either direction put *O*

Reachability Matrix

The transformation of SSIM format to reachability matrix was accompanied by transforming each entry of SSIM in 1^s and O^s in the *(i, j)* and *(j, i)* entry of the reachability matrix (Satsangi *et. al.* 1991). If the *(i, j)* entry of the SSIM is *(O)* then both *(i, j)* and *(j, i)* entries of reachability matrix become *(O)*. If the *(i, j)* entry of SSIM is *X* then both *(i, j)* and *(j, i)* entry of reachability matrix become *1*. If the *(i, j)* entry of (SSIM) is a *V*, then *(i, j)* entry of reachability matrix becomes *1* and *(j, i)* entry becomes *(O)*, Likewise, if *(i, j)* entry in the SSIM is an *A*, then *(i, j)* entry in the reachability matrix becomes *(O)* and *(j, i)* entry becomes *1*.

Partitions on the Reachability Matrix

Once the reachability matrix has been created it is processed to extract the digraph and the associated structural model by the use of a series of partitions induced by the reachability matrix on the set and subsets of the elements of the compiled integrated list given by $Q = (Q_i)$ as per procedure given by Warfield (Satsangi, *et al* 1991).

The Level Partition

For every element q_f, the reachability set $R\ (q_f)$ is the set of elements reachable from q_f. It is determined by inspection the row corresponding to q_f. Similarly, for every element q_j an antecedent set $A\ (q_j)$ is the set of elements which reach q_f. This is determined by inspecting the column corresponding to q_f.

The elements in the top level of hierarchy do not reach any element above their own level, hence the intersection of the reachability set and the antecedent set will be the same as the reachability set, if q_j is in the top level.

Mathematically,

$$R(q_f) = R\ (q_f)\ \Omega\ A(q_i) \quad \text{——————} \quad (i)$$

After Identifying the top level element in this manner, we may remove them from consideration and find the next set of top level elements using the remaining subgraph.

If we define the *Oth* level as the empty set

$$L_o = (\phi),$$

Then

$$L_j = (q_i\ \Sigma\ Q\text{-}L_o - L_1 \ldots\ldots L_{j-1}$$

$$R_{j-1}\ (q_i) = R_{j-1}\ (q_i)\ \Omega\ A_{j-1}\ (q_i) \quad \text{————} \quad (ii)$$

In the present problem, Domestic Competition, Life Quality Improvement and Growth with Social Justice are the three topmost level mission objectives.

Basic needs and women's labour are at the next level of hierarchy.

Supply of Wage Goods, Economic betterment, Occupational Profile and Employment are in the next level of hierarchy.

Labour Welfare is at the fourth level from the top.

For finding out the overall structural model bottom level sets and

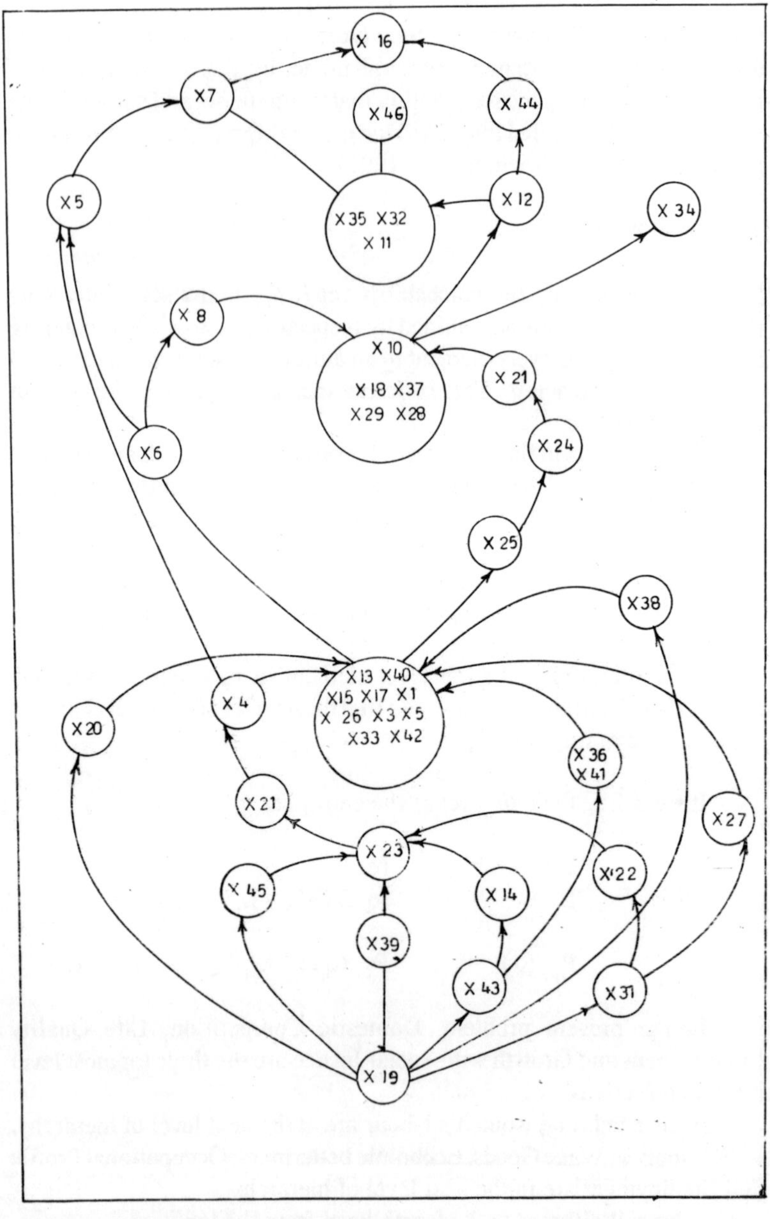

FIG. 17.1: Interpretive Structural Model for Integrated Descriptive Policy Elements for Industrial Development

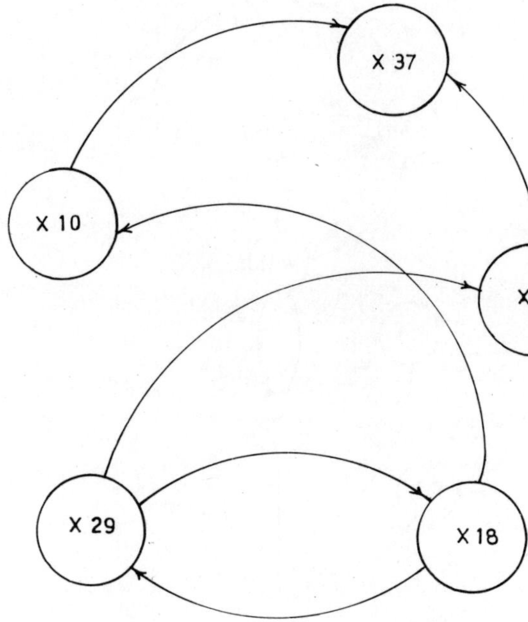

FIG. 17.2: Cycle in the I.S.M. of Integrated Descriptive Policy Elements for Industrial Development.

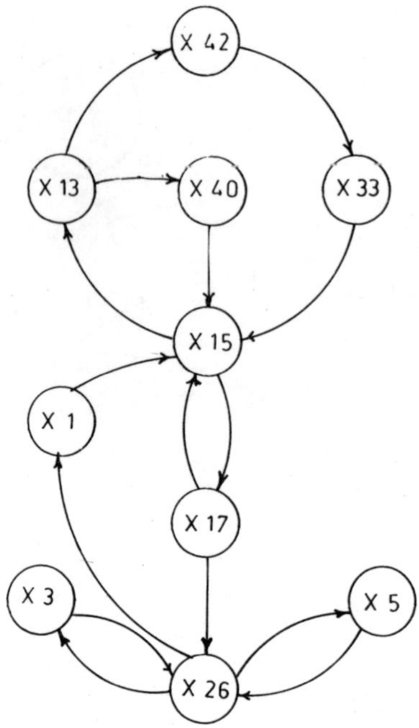

FIG. 17.3: Cycle in the ISM of Integrated Descriptive Policy Elements for Industrial Development

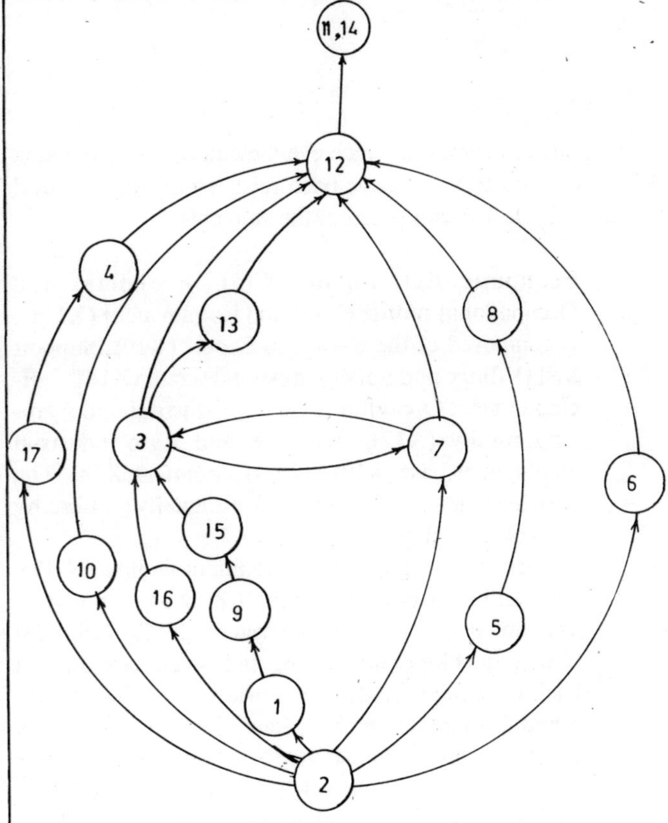

1. TRAINING
2. DELAY
3. QUALITY RAW MATERIAL
4. MARKET SUPPORT
5. CONSULTANCY SERVICES
6. EMPLOYMENT
7. TECHNOLOGY
8. ANCILLARISATION
9. RESTRICTED ZONES
10. DYSFUNCTION
11. BASIC NEED
12. ECONOMIC IMPROVEMENT
13. CAPACITY UTILISATION
14. GROWTH WITH SOCIAL JUSTICE
15. FLEXIBLE FINANCING
16. QUALITY ASSURANCE
17. INFRASTRUCTURE

FIG. 17.4: I.S.M. for Integrated Normative Policy Elements.

disjoint and strongly connected subset partitions were also found out.

The overall ISM so obtained is depicted in Fig. 17.1. Similarly an ISM for normative elements was also obtained which is depicted in Fig. 17.4.

Cycles

The following significant cycles in which every element is connected to all other elements in the cycle set have been revealed during the level partition exercise. Cycle 1 is composed of the elements:

Cycle 1 Economic Betterment (X35), Economic and Occupational profile (X32) and Employment (X11),

Cycle 2 is composed of the elements, Export (X10), Support VSI (Village and Small Industries) sector (X18), Self-employment Opportunity (X37), Industrial and Agro-Opportunity (X37), Industrial and Agro-industrial employment base (X29) and Service outlets (X28). The way these elements of the cycle are mutually reinforcing each other is depicted in Fig. 17.2.

Cycle 3 consists of Design and Development facility (X-13), Balanced environment (X15), R & D activity (X17), Technology acceptable to farmers (X26), Balanced Urban development (X33), Industrial opening in backward areas (X42), Appropriate technology (X40) S and T upgradation (X1), Raw Material Availability (X3) and Power Availability (X5). The connectedness of these elements in a cycle is shown in Figure 17.3.

Cycle 4 Comprises of only two elements. Wage policy (X36) and Labour legislation (X41).

Conclusion

The interpretive structural model for the descriptive integrated industrial policy for India shows an ordered approach to the exploration of the Contextual relation defined as 'affects'. In the present problem the three top level elements, namely Domestic Competition, Life Quality Improvement and Growth with Social Justice are the mission objectives. The element Delays (X19) surprisingly is the single bottom-most element of the present ISM and is, therefor, affecting all the other 45 elements of the policy objectives. Hence, this becomes the critical grass-root objective which has to be tackled in order to achieve the goals. X 20 Create stock of scarce raw material, X4 Marketing support, X 21 marketing strategy, X23 Fiscal policy, X27 Training, X45 Partial disinvestments, X39 Resource to finance, X14 Financial support, X43 Exemption for sick units X38 Industrial Licensing, X31 Create data base, X36 Wage policy and X14 Labour legislation can be considered as the action objectives and require decisions to be taken in order to achieve the mission objectives. Further, the ISM so obtained can be helpful for designing policy alternatives. This exercise has also been attempted by the authors and has been reported in another paper. Besides, as revealed by Fig. 17.4, the ISM for normative policy objectives gives Basic needs and Social justice as the two mutually supporting top level elements followed by Economic improvement and Employment. Delay is once again, the single bottom level element for the normative policy as well and affects all the eighteen elements of it.

Thus, the ISMs obtained give a clear insight into the structures of the policy elements and pave the way for designing policy alternative.

REFERENCES

Desai, A. V., (1988) *Technology Absorption in Indian Industry,* Wiley Eastern United, New Delhi, 1-4 pp.

Melone, D.W., (1977) 'Systems Engineering: Methodology and Applications'. In: Andrew P, Sage (Ed.), *Selected Reprint Series,* IEEE Press, New York, 70 pp.

More de la, R.F., (1982) *Manufacturing Systems Economics,* Holt, Rinechart and Winston Limited, Sussex, 3pp.

Sahu, P.K. and Mishra, D.P. (1992) *The Critical Appriasal of Industrial Sickness.* Kanishka Publishing House, New Delhi, 22p.

Satsangi, P.S., Swani, N.M., Mathul, M.C. and Agnihotri, V.K., (1991) *Handloom Policy Analysis—An Interpretive Structural Modelling Approach,* Vol. I, A Report, Indian Institute of Technology, New Delhi.

Thakur, Devendra and Jha, K., (1991) 'Small Industry Development in India'. In: V.S.P. Rao and D. Nagaiya (Eds.). Discovery Publishing House, New Delhi, 26 p.

ANNEXURE I

RANK-ORDERED LIST OF INTEGRATED POLICY ELEMENTS (DESCRIPTIVE)

Code	Sl. No.	Elements	No. of Votes (+)
X1	01	To improve productivity and restructure product-mix through upgradation/ promotion of science and technology and modernisation (PRODUCTIVITY IMPROVEMENT AND S & T UPGRADATION)	11
X2	02	To preserve and promote craftsmanship and art heritage of the country (RESERVE HERITAGE)	11
X3	03	To ensure supply of good quality raw material at reasonable cost (RAW MATERIAL AVAILABILITY)	10
X4	04	To provide marketing support (MARKETING SOPPORT)	08
X5	05	To ensure adequate and regular availability of power to industry. (POWER AVAILABILITY)	06
X6	06	To improve capacity utilisation of man and machine (CAPACITY UTILISATION)	06
X7	07	To meet the basic needs of people (BASIC NEED)	06

Code	Sl. No.	Elements	No. of Votes (+)
X8	08	To promote ancillarisation (ANCILLARISATION)	06
X9	09	To promote adequate supply of wage goods and consumer articles of mass-consumption at reasonable price and acceptable quality. (SUPPLY OF WAGE-GOODS)	06
X10	10	To promote export (EXPORT)	05
X11	11	To generate employment (EMPLOYMENT)	04
X12	12	To make provision for welfare and better working and living conditions of unorganised labour (WELFARE OF UNORGANISED LABOUR)	04
X13	13	To provide product design and development facilities to a cluster of units. (DESIGN AND DEVELOPMENT FACILITY)	04
X14	14	To rehabilitate through financial support from State Government (FINANCIAL SUPPORT)	04
X15	15	To ensure balance eco-systems and environment (BALANCED ENVIRONMENT)	04
X16	16	To improve the quality of life of people in terms of health, education and family welfare (IMPROVE LIFE QUALITY)	04

Code	Sl. No.	Elements	No. of Votes (+)
X17	17	To enhance R&D activity and ensure its proper transfer to field areas. (R&D ACTIVITY)	04
X18	18	To promote and support VSI Sector (SUPPORT VSI SECTOR)	03
X19	19	To eliminate procedural delays (DELAYS)	03
X20.	20	To create buffer stock of essential and scarce raw material (CREATE STOCK OF SCARCE RAW MATERIAL)	03
X21	21	To reorient marketing strategy (MARKETING STRATEGY)	03
X22	22	To rationalise subsides (SUBSIDIES)	03
X23	23	To attain international competitiveness (INTERNATIONAL COMPETITIVENESS)	03
X24	24	To rationalise fiscal policy to ensure rapid growth(FISCAL POLICY)	03
X25	25	To promote specialisation in production and export oriented industries (SPECIALISATION)	03
X26	26	To evolve technology acceptable to farmers in low land areas to increase agricultural production. (TECHNOLOGY ACCEPTABLE TO FARMERS)	03

Code	Sl. No.	Elements	No. of Votes (+)
X27	27	To make suitable arrangements for education, training, re-training and re-orientation of workers and entrepreneurs(TRAINING)	03
X28	28	To establish service outlets in centres of industrial activity (SERVICE OUTLETS)	03
X29	29	To promote industrial and agro-industrial employment base. (INDUSTRIAL & AGRO-IND. EMPLOYMENT BASE)	
X30	30	To require that large industries settle bills to smaller units in time (SETTLEMENT OF BILLS)	
X31	31	To create realistic data-base and improve data flow from VSI sector for planning and policy making purposes. (CREATE DATA-BASE)	03
X32	32	To improve economic and occupational profile of rural, semi-urban and weaker sections of society (ECONOMIC & OCCUPATIONAL PROFILE)	02
X33	33	To promote balanced urban development (BALANCED URBAN DEVELOPMENT)	02
X34	34	To promote competition in domestic market (DOMESTIC COMPETITION)	02
X35	35	To ensure economic betterment of poorer sections (ECONOMIC BETTERMENT)	02

Code	Sl. No.	Elements	No. of Votes (+)
X36	36	To formulate appropriate wage policy (WAGE POLICY)	02
X37	37	To increase opportunity for self employment (SELF-EMPLOYMENT OPPORTUNITY)	02
X38	38	To liberalise industrial licensing (INDUSTRIAL LICENSING)	02
X39	39	To raise resource for financing development (RESOURCE TO FINANCE)	02
X40	40	To develop and disseminate appropriate technology (APPROPRIATE TECHNOLOGY)	02
X41	41	To revise labour legislation (LABOUR LEGISLATION)	02
X42	42	To attract industrial openings in backward areas (INDUSTRIAL OPENINGS IN BACKWARD AREAS)	02
X43	43	To exempt sick units from payment of minimum bonus for a limited period of time. (EXEMPT SICK UNITS)	02
X44	44	To give special recognition and to promote facilities for women's labour. (WOMEN'S LABOUR)	02
X45	45	To encourage partial disinvestments of Government's share in public sectors. (PARTIAL DISINVESMENT)	02
X46	46	To achieve growth with social justice for all including child and bonded labour. (GROWTH WITH SOCIAL JUSTICE).	1+

ANNEXURE-II

RANK ORDERED LIST OF POLICY ELEMENTS (NORMATIVE)

S.No.	Code	Elements	Votes
1.	N1	To arrange training/awareness/ motivational programme in entre-preneurship and related areas and also in regard to new technological developments for entrepreneurs and workers (TRAINING)	11
2.	N2	To minimise procedural delays, red-tapism and corrupt practices (DELAYS)	7
3.	N3	To ensure supply of good quality raw material at reasonable cost (RAW MATERIAL SUPPLY)	6
4.	N4	To provide marketing support and promote competitiveness in market for small scale industries and its products (MARKETING SUPPORT)	6
5.	N5	To reorient government departments dealing with SSI to offer consultancy and help in matters of finances accounting and other areas of technological importance (CONSULTANCY SERVICE)	6
6.	N6	To create employment opportunity (EMPLOYMENT)	5
7.	N7	To upgrade technology while developing and disseminating appropriate technology (UPGRADATION OF TECHNOLOGY)	5
8.	N8	To promote ancillarisation (ANCILLART-SATION)	3

S.No.	Code	Elements	Votes
9.	N9	To identify restricted zones with pollution free environment and promote establishing non-hozardous industries by providing proper support and facilities in terms of marketing, finance and other requirement (RESTRICTED ZONES)	3
10.	N10	To diagnose industrial dysfunction and suggest means of rehabilitation of sick units (DIAGNOSING DYSFUNCTION)	2
11.	N11	To meet basic needs of people (BASIC NEED)	1
12.	N12	To improve economic and occupational profile of rural, semi-urban and weaker sections of society (ECONOMIC IMPROVEMENT)	1
13	N13	To increase capacity utilisation of man and machinery (CAPACITY UTILISATION)	1
14.	N14	To achieve growth with social objectives (GROWTH WITH SOCIAL OBJECTIVES)	1
15.	N15	To provide for easy and flexible financing for VS1 sector (FLEXIBLE FINANCING)	1
16.	N16	To develop consumer cooperative society for quality assurance (QUALITY ASSURANCE)	1
17.	N17	To provide transport and other infra-structural facilities for marketing (INFRASTRUCTURAL FACILITY)	1

18. ALTERNATIVE INTEGRATED POLICY DESIGNS FOR INDIAN INDUSTRIES

S.K. Gaur
D.S. Mishra
P.S. Satsangi

Introduction

In this age of planned economic development, rapid industrialisation is considered necessary to make thc economy strong the beneficial. In this context, industrialization becomes the driving force that accelerates economic growth, brings about structural change in the economy, by way of increasing the level of resource utilisation, income generation, foreign trade, and thereby induces social change. Industrialisation assumes much more importance as it acts as a catalytic agent in the process of economic development of particularly the underdeveloped or developing countries. In India, industrialisation began right from the introduction of Five Year Plans in 1951. In the First Plan period, industries and mining received an investment of Rs. 398 crores while the figure for the Sixth Five Year Plan period stood at Rs. 28,700 crores. Till the end of the Sixth Plan period an aggregate amount of Rs. 54,239 crores have been invested in industrial development wherein the share of public and private sector was 52 per cent and 48 per cent respectively. The industrial growth rates during different plan periods have been 7.3 per cent in First Plan, 6.5 per cent in the Second Plan, 9.0 per cent in the Third Plan, 4.7 per cent in the Fourth Plan, 5.9 per cent in the Fifth Plan and 5.5 per cent in the Sixth Plan (Sahu, *et al.*, 1992).

The industrial growth rate for the first three plan periods was quite encouraging while subsequent plan periods showed a slow growth rate for the industrial sector. This fall can be attributed to various factors. Some of these are under-utilisation of capacity, regional imbalance in industrial development, poor performance, inadequate ancillarisation etc.

The above factors lead to industrial malfunction, and further deterioration might set in if remedial action is not considered in its proper perspective. One of the important considerations will be reorientation of prevalent industrial policies in thc above context through a systematic and logical approach to policy design. This paper attempts to focus on a complete exercise of developing alternative policy designs for descriptive integrated national policy objectives of the Indian Industrial environment using interpretive structural modelling, options field methodology and fuzzy-set evaluation technique.

Background

Ordinarily imprecision and indeterminancy are considered to be statistical. In the real situation a frequent source of imprecision is not only the presence of random variables but the impossibility in principle of operating with exact data as a result of complexity of the system.

At the same time, classes of objects appear in the problems that do not have clear boundaries; the imprecision of such classes is expressed in the possibility than an element does not only belong or not belong to a certain class, but intermediate grades of membership are also possible (Kandel, 1980). Such situations, where transition from membership to non-membership is not sharply defined, are called fuzzy in nature and require qualitative data to be handled.

Designing policy is a difficult and complex exercise as it is a combination of complex dynamic inter-relationships between many sub-policies, decisions and sub-decisions, each of which is a composite of hierarchial process and at the same time is fuzzy.

Project Schedule and Procedures

A working paper was circulated among the participants (resource persons) well in advance to explain the background of the project and provide a brief description of the proposed methodologies.

Interpretive Structural Modelling (ISM)

A common characteristic of complex systems is that each has a structure associated with it, however ill-defined it may be (Sage, 1977). Interpretive Structural Modelling enables groups to structure information with computer assistance, while simultaneously clarifying the component ideas or elements of the issue under consideration (Warfield, 1976). The common methods for identifying the elements are Idea Engineering Approach and Content analysis of selected documents carried out with the assistance of domain experts or resource persons. The contextual relation chosen should be transitive. A mental model is converted into an interpretive structural model by using a series of model exchange isomorphisms. The ISM software (developed by the Tata Consultancy Services) first constructs a matrix model of the structure of information supplied by the resource persons (as group responses to the contextual questions posed). A matrix model is transformed into a basic structural model which is a minimum edge multi-level digraph. Finally, an interpretive structural model is created by inserting suitable descriptions for the elements and the contextual relation.

Methodology

The exercise for designing alternative national industrial policies in the Indian context has been carried out in a phased manner in which 12 domain experts including the authors were involved. The first phase of the exercise addressed itself to the development of an interpretive structural model of 46 descriptive integrated national policy elements under the contextual relation 'affects' as has been reported in our earlier paper (Gaur *et al.*, 1992). A list of the above mentioned 46 policy elements as given in Annexure-I was finalised as a consensus after the due process of editing, amendment, deletion and addition had been applied to the originally circulated list of 116 elements (arrived at through the content analysis of relevant documents by the authors).

(a) *Arranging Policy Options into Categories, Dimensions and Clusters*

During the next stage the resource persons worked on the following aspects:

(i) PLACING OPTIONS INTO CATEGORIES

For placing options (policy elements) into categories the resource persons responded to the following relational question: "Is option A in the same category as option B?"

Seven categories were thus identified.

(ii) NAMING THE CATEGORIES

The seven categories were named as:

1. Production (P)
2. Basic Inputs (BI)
3. Marketing (M)
4. Social-Economic Aspects (SE)
5. Administration and Organisation (AC)
6. Credit, Savings and Finance (CSF)
7. Labour Resource Development (LRD)

(iii) IDENTIFYING DESIGN DIMENSIONS

The resource persons were of the opinion that all the seven categories were also the essential dimensions of the issue under consideration namely designing industrial policy for better improved growth and development of the country. The final list of design dimensions with serial numbers of policy elements (option) contained in each of them is given in Table 18.1.

TABLE 18.1: Policy Design Dimensions and their Relevant Options

Sl. No.	Design Dimensions	Policy Options
1.	Production (P)	X1, X6, X26
2.	Basic Inputs (BI)	X3, X5, X20
3.	Marketing (M)	X4, X9, X10, X21, X24, X34
4.	Socio Economic Aspects (SE)	X2, X15, X16, X32, X35, X46
5.	Administration and Organisation (AO)	X8, X13, X17, X18, X19, X25 X28, X31, X33, X38, X40, X42, X43
6.	Credit, Savings and Finance (CSF)	X14, X22, X23, X30, X37, X72
7.	Labour, Resource, Development (LRD)	X11, X12, X27, X29, X36, X37 X41, X44

(iv) DISCOVERING CLUSTERS

For effective policy design it is important to identify dependencies among design dimensions. Two dimensions are said to be dependent if the choice of option in one of them restricts or limits the choice of options in the other dimensions. In case of such dependent dimensions or clusters, it is desirable to make choices of options in the light of the inter-dependency within the clusters.

For identifying the clusters (dependent dimensions), the resource persons used the following relational question:

"Is dimension I independent of dimension J?"

Using a modified version of ISM (Interpretive Structural Model) a structural self-interaction matrix was obtained which is given in Figure 18.1. Two clusters and one independent dimension were obtained from the modified SSIM. Cluster 1 consisted of Basic Inputs and Production whereas the other Cluster included Marketing, Labour Resource Development, Socio-Economic Aspects and Administration and Organisation. Credit, Savings and Finance came out to be an independent dimension.

FIGURE 18.1: Modified Structural Self Interaction Matrix (SSIM)

Prod.	2	3	4	5	6	7
BI	N	Y	Y	Y	Y	Y
	M	Y	Y	Y	Y	Y
		SE	N	N	Y	Y
			AO	N	Y	N
				CSF	Y	N
					LRD	Y

Relational Question: Is Dimension I independent of dimension *J* ?

Rule : If the answer to the above question is Yes put *'Y'* if No write *'N'*

(v) SEQUENCING CLUSTERS AND DIMENSIONS

An important requirement of an adequate policy design is that clusters and dimensions must be arranged in order of priority. This objective was achieved through a two-step exercise taken up by the resource persons.

The resource persons used the following relational question:

"Should Cluster/independent dimension *I* be considered before Cluster/independent dimension *J* in making choices of options?"

The following sequence was generated:

CSF, Cluster 1, Cluster 2.

(vi) SEQUENCING DIMENSIONS WITHIN CLUSTERS

Using the following relational question, the dimensions within Clusters were sequenced.

"Should dimension *A* be considered before dimension *B* in making choices of options?"

As a result of this exercise, the following sequence of dimensions within the clusters emerged:

Cluster 1	- Basic Inputs (BI), Production (P)
Cluster 2	- Marketing (M), Socio-Economic aspects (SE), Administration and Organisation (AO), Labour Resource Development (LRD).

(b) *Generating Alternative Policy Designs*

The options profile methodology (Warfield, 1990) is used to generate a design alternative, consisting of a set of options, with a least one option selected from each dimension in the Options Field. The choice of options from dimensions within a Cluster is made simultaneously in view of the inter-dependency among those dimensions. Options chosen from a given dimension may be single or compound (A compound option is a set of individual options-chosen together from a given dimension). This choice of options is made from the clusters and dimensions in the order in which they have already been sequenced following Options Field Methodology (OFM). In practice, it is common to construct several options Profiles (Design Alternatives) from a given Options Field.

The resource persons decided to generate seven alternative policy designs each with a definite character as follows:

Alternative One : One which has the achievement of domestic competition for the industrial sector in the Indian Context as the only mission level objective.

Alternative Two : One which has growth with social justice for the Indian Industrial policy as the only mission level objective.

Alternative Three : One with the Life Quality Improvement as the only mission level objective.

Alternative Four : One which is the combination of the mission objectives of alternative one and alternative two as its mission level objective.

Alternative Five : One which is the combination of the mission objectives of alternative one and alternative three as its mission level objective.

Alternative Six : One which is the combination of the mission objective of alternative two and alternative three as its mission level objective.

Alternative Seven : One which is the combination of the mission objectives of alternative one, two and three as its mission level objective.

The resource persons were advised to generate a total set of about 18 to 20 options for each alternative and were also advised that, as far as possible, the set of options chosen from a particular dimension should be different for each alternative policy design. The resulting alternative policy designs are given in Annexures II, III, IV, V, VI, VII and VIII.

The alternative option profiles (policy designs) were checked against the ISM of the descriptive integrated national policy elements to confirm their reachability for the relevant design specification of mission level objectives. The positive confirmation of the realisation (reachability) so obtained of the design specifications (relevant mission level objectives) for each policy alternative serves as verification and validation of the design process of the Options Field methodology and the Options Profile Methodology against the yardstick of the ISM.

Fuzzy-Set Evaluation of Policy Alternatives

It has become increasingly apparent that a need exists for a general decision-making test which can accommodate non-quantitative (intangible) factors and also reflect the view point of various stockholders. (Alley *et al.*, 1979; Satsangi *et al.*, 1991). The fuzzy-set evaluation methodology seems to fit the bill as it not only meets the above need but also combines the quantitative as well as non-quantitative evaluation in a single methodology.

Accordingly, a fuzzy-set evaluation exercise was carried out in order to decide the rank-ordering of the seven alternative industrial policy designs generated by the resource persons. For this purpose, a set of seven opinion poll matrices were developed, one each for the seven dimensions of the policy options were the respective sets of options for the concerned dimensions were listed as columns of the matrix and a judiciously chosen set of 12 features were listed as rows against which the alternatives were to be evaluated for their degree of membership in the feature fuzzy-sets. The set of 12 features identified on the basis of the goal dimensions of the ISM for the descriptive and normative policy elements is given in Table 18.2 together with the corresponding 'fuzzy' membership characteristics.

Each of the eight resource persons was given this set of seven response sheets (one each for the seven dimensions) to record their qualitative assessment regarding the degree of membership of each policy alternative and its constituent options for the concerned dimension in the 12 fuzzy-sets represented by the identified features on the basis of a five

TABLE 18.2: Use of Features for Evaluating Alternatives Industrial Policy Designs

Sl. No.	Features	Fuzzy Characteristics
1.	Environment	Option will reduce environmental hazards
2.	Employment	Option will generate better employment opportunity
3.	Export	Option will promote more export
4.	Generation of Income	Option will increase income generation of people
5.	Standard of Living	Option will increase living standards of people
6.	Social Justice	Option will promote better Social Justice
7.	Rural Development	Option will promote better development of rural areas
8.	Urban Development	Option will provide a balanced urban growth
9.	Quality Assurance	Option will ensure better quality product to the satisfaction of consumers
10.	Welfare	Option will cater to the need of well being of people.
11.	Industrial Health	Option will prevent industrial sickness
12.	Implementation Cost	Option will minimal cost

point scale of linguistic variables namely very good, good, average, poor and very poor. Notice that, as it is very difficult to evaluate the various alternatives keeping in mind all the seven dimensions under consideration, it was decided to generate seven position matrices, one each for the seven dimensions for a consistent and meaningful evaluation.

Analysis of Evaluation and Policy Recommendations

The linguistic variables were quantified for the grade of membership chosen as per the following correspondence:

Very good = 1.0, Good = 0.8, Average = 0.6
Poor = 0.4, Very poor = 0.2

Each set of seven opinion poll matrices was then averaged to given eight position matrices for the eight resource persons. These were further averaged to obtain the overall mean aggregate position matrix as given in Table 18.3. Also, the pessimistic aggregate position matrix was obtained by taking the minimum values of all the *(ij)* entry among the eight position matrices of resource persons.

A modified mean aggregate position matrix was obtained by taking

TABLE 18.3: Mean Aggregate Position Matrix for Dominant Policy Alternative

Features	POLICY ALTERNATIVES						
	Alter- native 1	Alter- native 2	Alter native 3	Alter- native 4	Alter- native 5	Alter- native 6	Alter- native 7
Environment	.606	.706	.614	.651	.556	.587	.666
Employment	.740	.762	.784	.679	.674	.686	.711
Export	.75	.806	.666	.725	.764	.731	.784
Generation of Income	.755	.727	.751	.779	.765	.784	.821
Standard of Living	.712	.761	.737	.761	.776	.775	.805
Social Justice	.679	.712	.776	.761	.725	.771	.750
Rural Development	.731	.755	.734	.785	.767	.785	.779
Urban Development	.710	.822	.725	.726	.792	.760	.795
Quality Assurance	.668	.820	.655	.694	.768	.766	.771
Welfare	.684	.622	.710	.733	.733	.755	.726
Industrial Health (Prevention for Sickness)	.724	.755	.688	.74	.743	.743	.761
Implementation Cost	.581	.514	.588	.555	.552	.553	.540

the average of the mean aggregate position matrix and the pessimistic aggregate position matrix as shown in Table 18.4.

Ranking Procedure

The basis for deciding the superiority of an alternative over another is the construction of a dominance matrix. An alternative is said to dominate another alternative for a given feature if its aggregate membership value for that feature is greater than that of the other alternative.

An alternative is said to be superior to another if it dominates the latter in more number of features than the number of features in which the latter dominants the former.

Dominance Matrix

In order to display the dominance between all possible pairs of alternatives

TABLE 18.4: Fuzzy Modified Mean Aggregate Position Matrix for Dominant Policy Alternative

Features	POLICY ALTERNATIVES						
	Alter-native 1	Alter-native 2	Alter native 3	Alter-native 4	Alter-native 5	Alter-native 6	Alter-native 7
Environment	0.543	0.673	0.507	0.585	0.528	0.578	0.613
Employment	0.71	0.716	0.752	0.704	0.687	0.678	0.720
Export	0.675	0.753	0.613	0.642	0.682	0.665	0.732
Generation of Income	0.677	0.728	0.675	0.709	0.732	0.742	0.790
Standard of Living	0.636	0.740	0.708	0.720	0.738	0.737	0.752
Social Justice	0.579	0.636	0.72	0.730	0.662	0.720	0.720
Rural Development	0.665	0.717	0.732	0.727	0.718	0.742	0.704
Urban Development	0.655	0.746	0.662	0.678	0.711	0.715	0.732
Quality Assurance	0.734	0.775	0.627	0.662	0.719	0.698	0.685
Welfare	0.602	0.631	0.655	0.666	0.666	0.712	0.613
Industrial Health (Prevention for Sickness)	0.642	0.712	0.619	0.67	0.696	0.686	0.730
Implementation Cost	0.525	0.457	0.494	0.492	0.476	0.491	.43

a square matrix orders n (where n is the number of alternatives) is obtained. The element d_{ij} of this matrix gives the number of features for which the membership value of alternative *j* dominates or is greater than that of alternative *i*. The dominance matrix for pessimistic aggregate and modified mean aggregate matrices are given in Tables 18.5 and 18.6 respectively.

Because of the uncertainty or fuzziness of the information contained in the aggregate position matrices, a tolerance limit is established.

A dominance is considered only when the difference between the membership values of two alternatives is more than this tolerance limit otherwise the alternatives can be considered equivalent for the concerned features. In the present case this limit was normalised as + 01 pessimistic aggregation and +.003 for modified aggregation.

The ranking of design policy alternatives by fuzzy-set evaluation methodology is given in Table 18.7.

TABLE 18.5: Fuzzy Dominance Matrix for Pessimistic Aggregation

Alternatives	I	II	III	IV	V	VI	VII
I	X	1	4	2	1	1	1
II	10	X	8	8	7	6	7
III	5	3	X	1	2	2	2
IV	10	3	7	X	4	2	2
V	10	2	6	5	X	2	2
VI	9	4	8	7	6	X	3
VII	11	4	8	6	6	6	X

TABLE 18.6: Fuzzy Dominance Matrix for Modified Mean Aggregation

Alternatives	I	II	III	IV	V	VI	VII
I	0	1	5	3	3	3	1
II	11	0	7	8	7	6	7
III	5	5	0	3	4	1	4
IV	9	4	9	0	5	3	4
V	9	5	8	7	0	4	4
VI	9	5	9	8	7	0	5
VII	11	5	7	8	8	6	0

TABLE 18.7: Ranking of Design Policy Alternatives

Sl. No.	Policy Alternatives	Ranking Pessimistic	Ranking Modified Mean
1	1	VII	VII
2	2	I	I
3	3	VI	VI
4	4	V	V
5	5	IV	IV
6	6	III	III
7	7	II	II

Conclusion

It can be concluded that the policy alternative two which emphasizes achievement of growth with social justice is the most preferred alternative. Policy alternative seven which emphasises all the three mission goals of domestic competition, growth with social justice and life quality improvement is the next in order of preference.

It may be remarked that the results of the policy study presented here give fairly good prototype which should assist policy makers in decision making. The most preferred policy alternative two has 18 policy options taken from all the seven policy dimensions which may enable the designers to achieve the concerned mission objectives. The fuzzy-set evaluation of alternative policy designs is indeed very robust in the case study in the sense that both the aggregation techniques lead to the same conclusions.

Acknowledgments

The authors acknowledge the financial support given by Department of Science and Technology, Government of India for this work.

REFERENCES

Alley, H., Bacinello, C.F. and Hipel K.W., (1979) *Fuzzy-set Approaches to Planning in the Grand River Basin,* University of Waterloo, Ontario, Canada.

Satsangi, P.S., (1992) *A Structure for Integrated and Descriptive Policy Elements for Indian Industries,* SYDSIM-92, INDIA.

Kandel, A., (1980) 'Fuzzy Statistics and Policy Analysis', in : Paul F. Wang and S.K. Chang (Eds.), *Proceedings of the Symposium on Policy Analysis and Information System,* Duke University, Durham, North Carolina.

Sage, A.P., (1977) *Methodologies for Large Scale Systems,* McGraw Hill Book Company, New York.

Sahu, P.K. and Mishra, D.P.,(1992) *The Critical Appraisal of Industrial Sickness,* Kanishka Publishing House, New Delhi, pp 14.

Satsangi, P.S., Swani, N.M. and Agnihotri, V.K., (1991) *Handloom Policy Analysis,* III Phase, Indian Institute of Technology, New Delhi.

Warfield, J.N.,(1976) *Societal Systems: Planning, Policy and Complexity,* John Wiley, New York.

Warfield, J.N., (1990) *A Science of Generic Design-Managing Complexity through System Design,* Intersystems Publications, Salinas, California, USA.

ANNEXURE I

RANK ORDERED LIST OF INTEGRATED POLICY ELEMENTS (DESCRIPTIVE)

Code	Sl. No.	Elements	No. of Votes
X1	01	To improve productivity and restructure product-mix through upgradation/promotion of science and technology and modernisation (PRODUCTIVITY IMPROVEMENT AND S & T UPGRADATION)	11^{+}
X2	02	To preserve and promote crafts-manship and art heritage of the country (PRESERVE HERITAGE)	11
X3	03	To ensure supply of good quality raw material reasonable - Cost (RAW MATERIAL AVAILABILITY)	10
X4	04	To provide marketing support (MARKETING SUPPORT)	08
X5	05	To ensure adequate and regular availability of power to industry. (POWER AVAILABILITY)	06
X6	06	To improve capacity utilisation of man and machine (CAPACITY UTILISATION)	06
X7	07	To meet the basic needs of people (BASIC NEED)	06
X8	08	To promote ancillarisation (ANCILLARISATION)	06
X9	09	To promote adequate supply of wage goods and consumer articles of mass-consumption at reasonable price and acceptable quality. (SUPPLY OF WAGE-GOODS)	06
X10	10	To promote exports (EXPORT)	05
X11	11	To generate employment (EMPLOYMENT)	04
X12	12	To make provision for welfare and better working and living conditions of unorganised labour (WELFARE OF UNORGANISED LABOUR)	04

Code	Sl. No.	Elements	No. of Votes
X13	13	To provide product design and development facilities to a cluster of units. (DESIGN AND DEVELOPMENT FACILITY)	04
X14	14	To rehabilitate through financial support from State Government (FINANCIAL SUPPORT)	04
X15	15	To ensure balanced eco-system and environment (BALANCED ENVIRONMENT)	04
X16	16	To improve the quality of life of people in terms of health, education and family welfare (IMPROVE LIFE QUALITY)	04
X17	17	To enhance R & D activity and ensure its proper transfer to field areas. (R & D ACTIVITY)	04
X18	18	To promote and support VSI Sector (SUPPORT VSI SECTOR)	03
X19	19	To eliminate procedural delays (DELAYS)	03
X20	20	To create buffer stock of essential and scarce raw material (CREATE STOCK OF SCARCE RAW MATERIAL)	03
X21	21	To re-orient marketing strategy (MARKETING STRATEGY)	03
X22	22	To rationalise subsides (SUBSIDIES)	03
X23	23	To attain international Compe- titiveness (INTERNATIONAL COMPETITIVENESS)	03
X24	24	To rationalise fiscal policy to ensure rapid growth (FISCAL POLICY)	03
X25	25	To promote specialisation in production and export oriented industries (SPECIALISATION)	03
X26	26	To evolve technology acceptable to farmers in low land areas to increase agricultural production (TECHNOLOGY ACCEPTABLE TO FARMERS)	03
X27	27	To make suitable arrangements for	03

Code	Sl. No.	Elements	No. of Votes
		education, training, re-training and re-orientation of workers and entrepreneurs (TRAINING)	
X28	28	To establish service outlets in centres of industrial activity (SERVICE OUTLETS)	03
X29	29	To promote industrial and agro-industrial employment base. (INDUSTRIAL & AGRO-IND. EMPLOYMENT BASE)	
X30	30	To require that large industries settle bills to smaller units in time (SETTLEMENT OF BILLS)	
X31	31	To create realistic data-base and improve data flow from VSI sector for planning and policy making purposes (CREATE DATA-BASE)	03
X32	32	To improve economic and occupational profile of rural, semi-urban and weaker sections of society (ECONOMIC & OCCUPATIONAL PROFILE)	02
X33	33	To promote balanced urban development (BALANCED URBAN DEVELOPMENT)	02
X34	34	To promote competition in domestic market (DOMESTIC COMPETITION)	02
X35	35	To ensure economic betterment of poorer sections (ECONOMIC BETTERMENT)	02
X36	36	To formulate appropriate wage policy (WAGE POLICY)	02
X37	37	To increase opportunity for self employment (SELF-EMPLOYMENT OPPORTUNITY)	02
X38	38	To liberalise industrial licensing (INDUSTRIAL LICENSING)	02
X39	39	To raise resource for financing development (RESOURCE TO FINANCE)	02
X40	40	To develop and disseminate	02

Code	Sl. No.	Elements	No. of Votes
		appropriate technology (APPROPRIATE TECHNOLOGY)	
X41	41	To revise labour legislation (LABOUR LEGISLATION)	02
X42	42	To attract industrial openings in backward areas (INDUSTRIAL OPENINGS IN BACKWARD AREAS)	02
X43	43	To exempt sick units from payment of minimum bonus for a limited period of time. (EXEMPT SICK UNITS)	02
X44	44	To give special recognition and to promote facilities for women labour (WOMEN LABOUR)	02
X45	45	To encourage partial disinvestment of Government's share in public sectors (PARTIAL DISINVESTMENT)	02
X46	46	To achieve growth with social justice for all including child and bonded labour (GROWTH WITH JUSTICE)	1+

ANNEXURE II

DIMENSIONWISE ELEMENTS OF POLICY ALTERNATIVE 1 AND ITS ISM

Mission Objective	:	Domestic Competition
Basic Inputs	:	Raw Material Avalability (X3) Power Availability (X5)
Production	:	Capacity Utilisation (X6)
Marketing	:	Marketing Strategy (X21) Marketing Support (X4) Domestic Competition (X34)
LRD	:	Training (X27) Wage Policy (X36)
SE	:	Conserve Heritage (X2)
AO	:	Service Outlets (X28)
	:	Specialisation (X25) R & D Facility (X17) Create Database (X31) Appropriate Tech. (X40) Eliminate Delay (X19)
CSF	:	Fiscal Policy (X23) Financial Support (X14)

ANNEXURE III

DIMENSIONWISE ELEMENTS OF POLICY ALTERNATIVE 2 AND ITS ISM

Mission Objective	:	Life Quality Improvement
Basic Inputs	:	Raw Material Avalability (X3) Power Availability (X5)
Production	:	S&T Upgradation
Marketing	:	Supply of Wage Goods (X5) Export (X10) International Competition (X24)
LRD	:	Training (X27) Wage Policy (X36) Self-Employment Opportunity (X37)
SE	:	Economic Betterment (X35) Balanced Environment (X15) Life Quality Improvement (X16)
AO	:	D&D Facility (X13) R&D Facility (X17) Support VSI Sector (X18) Balanced Urban Development (X33) Eliminates Delay (X19)
CSF	:	Fiscal to Finance (X35)

ANNEXURE IV

DIMENSIONWISE ELEMENTS OF POLICY ALTERNATIVE 3 AND ITS ISM

Mission Objective	:	Growth with Social Justice
Basic Inputs	:	Raw Material Avalability (X3) Power Availability (X5)
Production	:	Tech. Acceptable to Farmers (X26)
Marketing	:	Marketing Support (X4) Marketing Strategy (X21)
LRD	:	Employment (X11) Labour Welfare (X12) Ind. and Agro-Ind Employment Base (X25) Labour Legislation (X41)
SE	:	Conserve Heritage (X2) Occupational Profile (X32) Growth with Social Justice (X46)
AO	:	Support VSI Sector (X18) Ind. Opening in Backward Areas (X42) Eliminate Delays (X19)
CSF	:	Subsidies (X22) Settlement of Bills (X30) Partial Disinvestment (X45)

ANNEXURE V

DIMENSIONWISE ELEMENTS OF POLICY ALTERNATIVE 4 AND ITS ISM

Mission Objective	:	Domestic Competition and Growth with Social Justice
Basic Inputs	:	Raw Material Avalability (X3) Power Availability (X5)
Production	:	Capacity Utilisation (X6) Technology Acceptable to Farmers (X26)
Marketing	:	Marketing Support (X4) Domestic Competition (X34) Marketing Strategy (X21)
LRD	:	Employment (X11) Training (X27) Labour Legislation (X41) Conserve Heritage (X2)
SE	:	Growth with Social Justice (X46)
AO	:	Support VSI Sector (X18) Eliminate Delays (X15) Create Data Base (X31) Appropriate Tech. (X40)
CSF	:	Subsidies (X22) Fiscal Policy (X23)

ANNEXURE VI

DIMENSIONWISE ELEMENTS OF ALTERNATIVE 5

Mission Level Objective	:	Domestic Competition and Life Quality Improvement
Production	:	S&T Upgradation (X1) Capacity Utilisation (X6)
Marketing	:	Domestic Competition (X34) International Competitions (X24) Supply of Wage Goods (X9)
LRD	:	Training (X27) Wage Policy (X36)
SE	:	Economic Betterment (X35) Life Quality Improvement (X16)
AO	:	R & D Facility (X17) Support VSI Sector (X18) Delays (Eliminate) (X19) Service Outlet (X28 Create Database (X31)
CSF	:	Fiscal Policy (X23) Resource to Finance (X39)

ANNEXURE VII

DIMENSIONWISE ELEMENTS OF POLICY ALTERNATIVE 6

Mission Objective	:	Life Quality Improvement and Growth with Social Justice
Basic Inputs	:	Raw Material Avalability (X3) Power Availability (X5)
Production	:	S&T Upgradation (X5) Technology Acceptable to Farmers (X26)
Marketing	:	Supply of Wage Goods (X5) Export (X10)
LRD	:	Employment (X11) Labour Welfare (X12) Training (X27)
SE	:	Life Quality Improvement (X16) Growth with Social Justice (X46)
AO	:	Economic Betterment (X35) D&D Facility (X13) Support VSI Sector (X18) Eliminate Delays (X19) Industrial Openings in Backward Areas (X42)
CSF	:	Subsidies (X22) Fiscal Policy (X23)

ANNEXURE - VIII

DIMENSIONWISE ELEMENTS OF POLICY ALTERNATIVE

Mission Objective	:	Domestic Competition + Life Quality Improvement + Growth with Social Justice
Basic Inputs	:	Raw Material Avalability (X3) Power Availability (X5)
Production	:	S&T Upgradation (X1) Capacity Utilisation (X6)
Marketing	:	Supply of Wage Goods (X9) Marketing Support (X4) International Competition (X24)
LRD	:	Training (X27) Wage Policy (X36) Employment (X11)
SE	:	Economic Betterment (X55) Growth with Social Justice (46)
AO	:	R&D Facility (X17) Support VSI Sector (X18) Eliminate Delays (X19)
CSF	:	Subsidies (X22) Fiscal Policy (X23) Resource to Finance (X39)

19. SYSTEM DYNAMICS MODELLING FOR PUBLIC POLICY ANALYSIS

Pratap K. J. Mohapatra

Right from the early days of its development, system dynamics was used in the area of policy analysis and design in industrial systems. The first application of system dynamics to policy analysis in public system was the urban dynamics study of Forrester (1969). Forrester (1971a) again used the system dynamics approach to study the world problems. These two pioneering works had opened up the possibility of analyzing and designing public policies with the help of system dynamics models.

Forrester spent the last sixteen years of his professional life working on a system dynamics model of the US economy. The model endogenously generates the major observed modes of economic behaviour: business cycles, inflation, unemployment, stagflation, the economic long wave, and growth (Forrester, 1981, 1989). The model differs substantially from more familiar econometric models. It is built up from the operating structure within corporations, rather than macro-economic theory. It is derived from management policies as observed in the detailed, practical, working world, rather than from statistical correlations among time series representing economic behaviour. The modelling philosophy of the National Model that Forrester creates is that macrobehaviour is generated from a combination of micro-structure.

During the last two decades, system dynamics approach has been used to understand the origin of problems and to analyze and design policies to mitigate these problems in public systems that range from environment and energy to health, education, and criminal justice.

Public systems are far more complex than technological systems. Therefore, if it is normal for a company to make a prototype and conduct a laboratory test before embarking upon full-scale production, then it is desirable that laboratory models are made and experiments are carried out on them before new laws are promulgated and new government programmes are launched.

Questions are often raised on the validity of a model. But the point remains that in the absence of a formal model, the government still passes laws and launches social programmes, presumably on the basis of mental images (or mental models).

Mental models had been the main anchor of public policy making in the past. Mental images are supported by large information base that also includes information which is of psychological nature and which is based on personal observation and experience.

Unfortunately, mental models are fuzzy, incomplete, difficult to communicate, and change with time, and fundamental assumptions are hidden, and goals are not clear. Most importantly, even though the structure and the assumptions of a mental model are correct, the conclusions drawn from a mental model are not. Human mind is a poor assessor of dynamic consequences.

System dynamics builds upon the large information base of the mental model, and makes use of the principles of cybernetics to develop the structure of a mathematical model that is strikingly similar to the real-world and to the mental framework of a policy-maker, and uses the technique of computer simulation to generate dynamic behaviour of the systems.

Neither mathematical models nor computer simulation is new to public systems analysis. System dynamics models are, however, different in many ways from these traditional mathematical models. A system dynamics model is not derived from time series data. Two misconceptions that prevail in the bulk of the literature on public policy are that data are insufficient and that once data are available, their interpretation is straightforward. The proponents of system dynamics think otherwise. They recognize the vast real-world perception and information that every actor in a system has in his mind. Therefore they see a data-rich situation, though the data always remain in non-qunantitative forms. The causality viewpoint, the feedback loop scheme, the stock-flow mechanism, and the endogeneity concept help the system dynamicist to structure his assumptions in a model form.

Such a model attempts to capture the behavioural aspects of the public system that it depicts. It has the capability of representing the dynamics and the nonlinearitites of the real world. It explicitly considers the real world causalities and models them as components in closed feedback systems. It follow a systems approach to problem solving and attempts to understand and explain a problem situation before forwarding recommendations. finally, it takes a view that policy makers should learn more about their organizations in order to sharpen their intuition and achieve success.

Forrester (1971b) has highlighted three characteristics of public systems:

1. Social systems are inherently insensitive to most policy changes that people select in an effort to alter the behaviour of the system.
2. They seem to have a few sensitive influence points through which the behaviour of the system can be changed. These influence points are not in the location most people expect.
3. There is usually a fundamental conflict between the short-term and the long-term consequences of a policy change.

Forrester has also stressed the nature of counterintuitive behaviour of social systems. Many policies, programmes, laws, and legislations that area passed with great promise and hope prove to be ineffective. At times, they only accentuate the problem rather than solve them. The highly complex, non-linear, multi-loop nature of the social system is responsible for such counterintuitive behaviour. The key to reverse this change lies in understanding this nature of real-world. A help in this direction is provided by system dynamics.

This paper now presents two experiences of the author in using system dynamics models to public systems. The first is the case which makes use of Delphi results to define the problems of the Indian tea industry, forecast the likely occurrence of events that would have profound effect on the performance of the industry, and list the policies which can mitigate both the current and the future problems. With the system dynamics model it is shown that the suggested policies are producing results counter to expectations in the event of changed environmental conditions. The second case makes use of the approach of system dynamics modelling to generate alternative scenarios for projecting energy requirement in the Indian transport sector. The scenarios reflect the effect of various systemic and environmental changes that are likely to take place in the context of the Indian transport sector and the policies that are likely to be followed in response to these changes.

Counterintuitive Behaviour of Delphi Results

A study on Indian tea industry was carried out way back in 1981. The study made use of Delphi method to get consensus opinion of informed individuals in the tea industry and those connected with industry on problems afflicting the industry, likely future developments that will have profound influence on the tea industry performance, and on the policies with which the problems can be surmounted.

The view of the Delphi panelists with regard to the likely future developments are summarized below:

1. A breakthrough in the development of high yielding clone with a reduced dormant period at the start, adoption of technological innovations, and complete understanding of the chemistry of plants will considerably increase the yield of tea plants in the nineties and thereafter.
2. Change in beverage drinking habits, and breakthrough that would considerably reduce the production cost of coffee will lower the world demand for tea even before the beginning of the nineties.
3. China entering the world tea market in the nineties will adversely affect the Indian export in the nineties and thereafter.
4. Better quality of Indian tea and a breakthrough of convenience tea would lead to a higher world market share for Indian tea in the nineties and thereafter.

Of the very important policies suggested by the panelists, the following four policies were selected based on ease of implementation. The ways in which the policies will be implemented are also discussed below:

1. More fund be made available for research on tea. It is assumed that the present contribution of one paisa per kg. of tea production towards research is raised to one and half paise per kg, and that the Government will contribute an equal amount.
2. Tax rate be reduced. It is assumed that the tax rate on profit be reduced to 45 per cent from its present value of 50 per cent.
3. More subsidy be given for replantation. The amount of Government subsidy for replantation is taken as Rs. 5,000 per hectare instead of the present value of Rs. 3,500 per hectare.
4. Quality of tea would be improved through R & D. It is assumed that the quality of tea produced would improve as a result of the contribution or R&D activities.

The Delphi policies have been tested in the framework of a system dynamics model. The details of the model are discussed by Bora (1981) and reported in Bora *et al.* (1990). The model consists of four major sectors: production, domestic marketing, export, and research and development. Production is the largest sector and consists of nine subsectors: cultivation, manufacturing and dispatch, quality, extension, long-term debt, short-term loan, cash flow, profit and loss, and balance sheet.

The problem areas delineated by the Delphi panelists helped in deciding the model boundary. A few examples are:

1. The R & D sector was incorporated into the model because of the heavy emphasis given to it by the panelists.
2. The concern expressed by the panelists about the high level of taxes; the restriction of exports, etc., imposed by the government; the inadequate level of working capital; and the difficulty in obtaining loan, etc., forced the authors to model the financial aspect very elaborately.
3. Dominant factors affecting export sales were recognized to be quality, price, and availability of tea.

For the purpose of model validation, the model was simulated from 1965 to 1975 and the generated model behaviour in respect of many important variables was compared with the actual data.

Certain noteworthy features of the model are:

1. Government decisions regarding export rate and export duty are modelled.
2. Certain qualitative aspects are also modelled. For example, the following are modelled explicitly:

    a. the desire of a welfare-oriented democratic government to make tea available at a cheap rate in the domestic market;
    b. the enthusiasm of the producers to step up shipment of quality tea to the export market in order to increase profitability; and
    c. the sharp reaction of wholesalers to changes in the auction price of tea.

3. The model provides a financial statement for the industry, which is used not only for the purpose of accounting but also for computing financial ratios.
4. The model attempts to simultaneously depict micro- and micro-phenomena corresponding to short-term price fluctuation and long-term growth.

The Delphi policies have been tested in two future environmental conditions (Mohapatra *et al.*, 1984). The first condition (Future Environment I) assumes the persistence of present environmental forces into the future, while the second condition (Future Environment II) assumes the occurrence of likely developments that are expected by the Delphi panelists.

Delphi Policies in Future Environment I

Figure 19.1 shows the behaviour of a few important variables for this case. Compared with the standard policies, the Delphi policies yield more are under cultivation, higher average sales of tea abroad, better average profit after tax, and higher values of retained earning and return on total assets.

The better performance of the industry with Delphi policies could be ascribed to a more favourable financial environment. A higher gearing ratio increases the potential of the industry to borrow long-term debt. Also, low taxation increases profit after taxes. Increased funding for R & D, obtained both from the industry and the government, helps to increase the quality of tea in the long run, and this increases the average sale of tea abroad. The resulting higher retained earnings, availability of increased long-term debt, and higher subsidy for replantation help in extension of the area under cultivation. More areas under tea plantation with higher yield increases production greatly and matches the increasing demand of tea in India and abroad.

Thus, it is clear that Delphi policies result in superior future performance of the industry compared with the present policies, provided that the present environmental forces continue to dominate in the future.

Delphi Policies in Future Environment II

Figure 19.2 gives the behaviour of some important variables until 2000 for this case. It indicates a complete disaster for the industry, with the average profit after taxes dwindling to negative values and return on total assets a meager 0.12 per cent. The reasons for such unwanted industry performance are:

1. ambitious extension plans as a consequence of almost no financial stringency, and
2. occurrence of unforeseen developments, as viewed by the panelists.

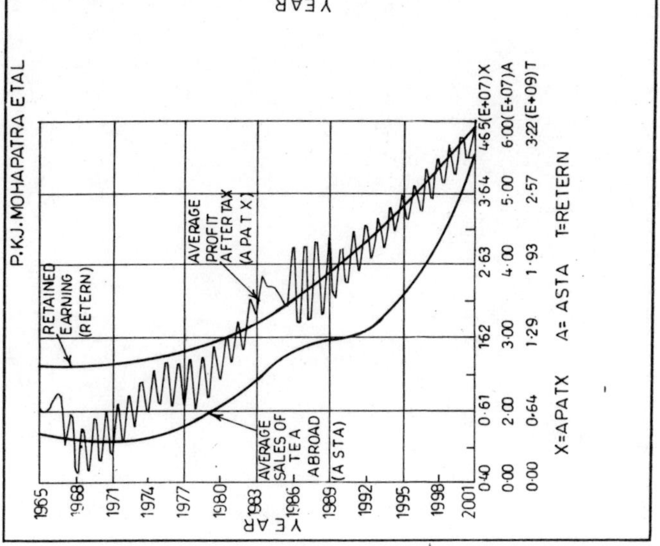

FIG. 19.1 : Delphi Policies in the Present Environment

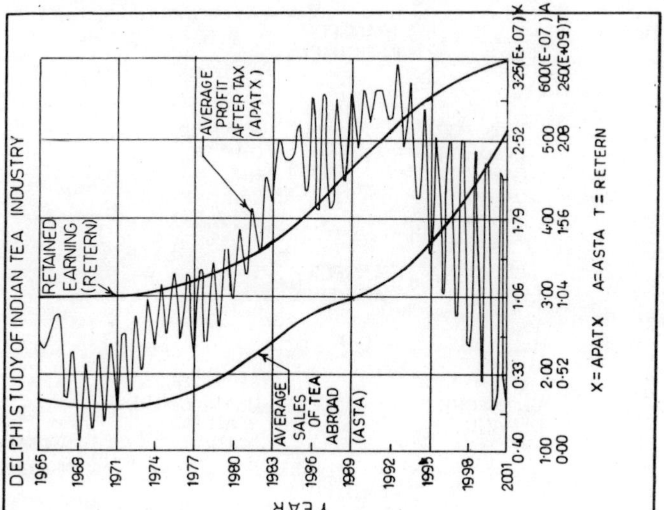

FIG. 19.2 : Delphi Policies with Unforeseen Developments

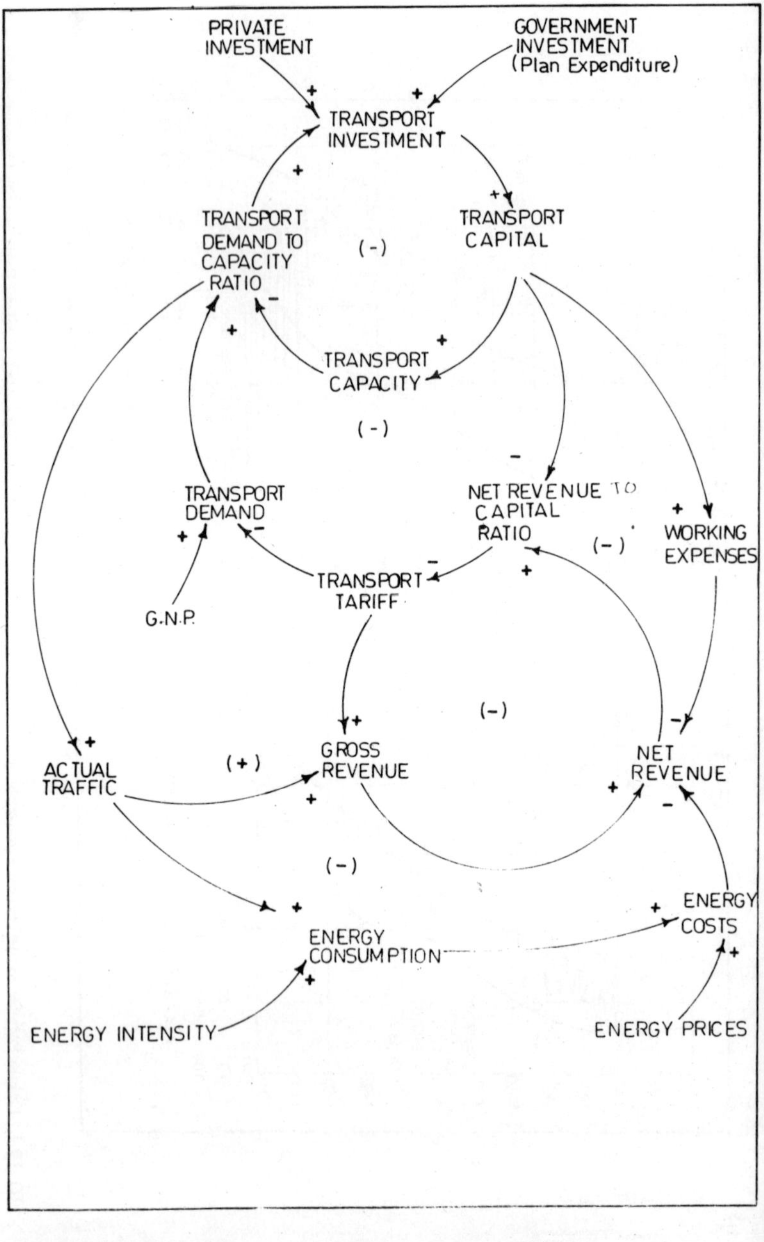

FIG. 19.3 : Causal Structure of Transport Energy Demand Model.

Higher yield from Indian tea gardens coupled with high extension programmes increase total production tremendously, thereby reducing the auction price of tea. Although the exportable surplus is plenty, the low world demand due to a change in beverage drinking habits and the increased supply to the world market greatly reduce the sales potential of Indian tea despite its high quality.

Thus it is seen that Delphi policies, when pursued in a changed future environment, may be unexpectedly counterproductive.

We thus infer that expert opinion survey can be very useful for delineating problem areas, forecasting environmental events, and listing policy alternatives. But it may not be adequate in estimating the dynamic consequences of following any specific policy. The complexity within a public system is so great that its proper comprehension is impossible without resorting to experimenting on a model.

Energy Demand Scenarios for Indian Transport Sector

A study on energy demand scenarios for Indian Transport sector has been recently completed at IIT, Kharagpur (Dutta, 1993). The study used a system dynamics approach to (a) project energy demand up to the year 2011 for different transport modes and types of loads and by different energy forms, (b) generate energy demand scenarios for plausible systemic and environmental changes, and for viable policy alternatives in the individual modes of transport as well as in the integrated transport sector, and (c) evaluate policy alternatives and suggest policy measures that reduce energy requirement in the transport sector.

The inputs to the model are the passenger transport demand, the goods transport demand, the private and government investments in transport, and energy prices. The output of the model is the energy demand by various energy forms. The model considers four modes of transport: rail, road, water, and air. Rail and road are further desegregated into different submodes: types of tractions for railways, and types of vehicles for the road passenger sector.

Each subsectoral model is developed, calibrated, and validated. Later they are integrated into one model.

The basic causal structures of the individual models of the different transport modes are almost identical. Also identical are the causal structures for the passenger and the goods traffic within any individual subsectoral model. This generic structure is shown in Figure 19.3.

Scenarios are generated in the integrated model both for testing the sensitivity of the model and for visualizing the future developments in the transport sector and in its energy requirement. The scenarios are defined as under:

1. Scenario One — *The Base Run* : Continuance of present trends in the transport system and the national economic environment.
2. Scenario Two — *Energy Efficient Technology* : Electrification of railways on a larger scale; use of high capacity, energy efficient electric locomotives; use of fuel efficient, pollution free road vehicles; higher government investment in railways, electric locomotives, and in water transport.
3. Scenario Three — *Energy Intensive Technology* : Electrification and dieselization of railways with high capacity, energy efficient diesel and electric locomotives; higher government investment in road and air transport sectors.
4. Scenario Four — *Energy Efficient Technology with Oil Price Rise* : Assumption for Scenario Two and the assumption of price rise of petroleum products; induction of low capacity, energy efficient, light commercial vehicles in road transport.
5. Scenario Five — *Energy Intensive Technology with Oil Price Rise* : Assumption for Scenario Three and the assumption of price rise of petroleum products; induction of low capacity, energy efficient, light commercial vehicles in road transport.
6. Scenario Six — *High Economic Growth* : High GDP growth with consequent increase in per capita income, transport investment, and in aggregate passenger and goods transport demand.
7. Scenario Seven — *Regional Development and Communication Technology* : Twenty-five per cent reduction in aggregate passenger and goods transport demand because of balanced, decentralized regional development and widespread use of telecommunication facilities.
8. Scenario Eight — *Shortage of Oil Supply* : Very high prices of petroleum products; idle transport capacity because of oil shortage; fifty per cent utilization of oil driven transport services.
9. Scenario Nine — *Alternative Exogenous Inputs* : Second order polynomial fitting to the three time-varying exogenous inputs: transport investment, aggregate passenger transport demand, and aggregate goods transport demand.
10. Scenario Ten — *Optimal Modal investment with Energy Efficient Technology* : Modal investment fractions from the LGP optimization model (Mohapatra and Dutta, 1990) along with the assumptions for Scenarios Two and Four.

The Scenario results are compared with those made by WGEP (1965), NTPC (1980), and Parikh (1981) for the year 2000-2001 and by ABE (1985) for the projection year 2004-2005 and by Somasekhara *et al.* (1992) for the projection years 2000 and 2010 with projections made by this study for the years 2001 and 2011. The other studies are not as comprehensive as the present study; thus, comparison in respect of all variables was not possible. Most studies did not consider air and water modes of transport. They also projected very high values of traffic and energy variables compared to the present study, probably due to an ambitious plan target growth rate assumed for GDP.

From an analysis of scenario results it is seen that the actual traffic and energy demand in transport sector is highly sensitive to aggregate transport demand, moderately sensitive to intermodal investment and per capita income and virtually insensitive to fuel prices and vehicle capacity.

The policy analysis through scenario generation suggests that the best policy to be pursued in the transport sector, with a view to reducing energy demand, and its dependence on petroleum products, would be a combination of actions to be undertaken at different hierarchical levels in the transport sector and in its operating environment.

The modal investment for energy efficient railways and water transport systems should be enhanced with commensurate decrease in energy intensive modes like air and road transports. Even in the railways, considerable saving in aggregate energy consumption may be achieved through technology upgrading with large scale electrification of the railways.

The highest saving in energy consumption may only be effected through the combined policies of induction of high capacity energy efficient locomotives in the railways and fuel-efficient pollution free vehicles in the road sector with optimal intermodal investment in transport sector; restricting the investments in air transport sector to a minimum possible level and augmenting those in railways, inland water transport and coastal shipping.

Linear, log-linear, and second-order polynomial curves were fitted to the median values of all eleven scenarios at different time points. The second-order polynomial curve gave the best fit in all cases. For the traffic related variables and for most of the energy-related variables, the log-linear curve gave better fit than the linear curve (measured in terms of the R^2 values).

Log-linear curves helped in estimating the doubling time for various variables. The doubling time for the railway passenger traffic is nearly 17 years; it is maximum at 32 years for the water transport oil demand and minimum at 10 years for the rail electricity demand. For the crucial total transport oil demand, it is about 13 years, and for the total transport energy demand it is about 16 years.

The most viable policies that appear to hold high leverage in arresting the accelerating growth of energy requirement in the transport sector are given below:

1. At the plan allocation level, the government investment in the railways and in the water transport sector are to be increased disproportionately at the cost of road and air transport sectors.
2. Rigorous efforts should be made, also at the government level, for balanced and decentralized regional development, and for widespread use of telecommunication facilities, that will reduce the aggregate traffic demand and, hence, the transport oil and energy demand.
3. In the railway sector, technology upgrading should be pursued vigorously with higher electrification of the railway routes, induction of high-capacity, energy-efficient, electric locomotives and related conservation measures.
4. In the road sector, efforts should be made to induct more and more light commercial vehicles that would reduce unit fuel consumption, and yet increase the aggregate transport capacity. This can be made possible by motivating the potential transport operators to buy these vehicles through price discounting and tax concessions.
5. Air transport is the most energy intensive mode. To reduce its energy requirement, investment in air transport sector is to be kept to the minimum possible level so as to provide the basic minimum service level. Such a policy, however, is difficult to implement in the face of rising standard of living and rising pressure for air travel. The present policy of the government to maintain a very high air fare compared to the fares in the other modes appears to be a good policy to contain the pressure for air transport.
6. Modernization of inland water transport and coastal shipping services and provision of the required infrastructural facilities should be undertaken in a big way to increase their popularity and their share of aggregate traffic.
7. The present policy of the Government to raise oil prices from time to time has to be continued to restrict the oil consumption.

Final Remarks

This paper highlights the early works of Forrester involving the use of system dynamics modelling to the problems of public systems. The paper then presents two cases, one pertaining to the Indian tea industry and the other to the Indian transport sector, depicting the author's experience in applying system dynamics modelling to the problems of public systems. In the first case it is shown that the mental models do not correctly estimate the dynamic consequences of policies; in the second case the use of system dynamics modelling in scenario generation and policy analysis is presented.

The cases presented here do not portray the full power of the system dynamics modelling, nor do they present the complexity of a public system. Given the support and the time, and the motivation, it is possible to use this powerful method to carry out in-depth policy analysis and design for any complex public system.

REFERENCES

ABE (1985) *Towards a Perspective of Energy Demand and Supply in India in 2004/2005,* Advisory Board on Energy, Government of India, New Delhi.

Bora, M.C. (1981) *A System Dynamics Study on Policy Design for Prices Stabilization and Long-Term Growth of Indian Tea Industry,* Unpublished Ph.D. Dissertation, IIT, Kharagpur.

Bora, M. C., P.K.J. Mohapatra, and K.C. Sahu (1990) 'Designing Price Stabilization and Growth Policies in Indian Tea Industry', *System Dynamics: An Int. J. of Policy Modelling,* pp. 101-134.

Dutta, R.K. (1993) Energy Demand Scenarios for Indian Transport Sector, Ph.D. Thesis Submitted to IIT, Kharagpur.

Forrester, J.W. (1969) *Urban Dynamics,* MA: Productivity Press, Cambridge.

Forrester, J.W. (1971a) *World Dynamics,* The MIT Press, Mass, Cambridge.

Forrester, J.W. (1971b) 'Counterintuitive Behaviour of Social Systems', *Technology Review,* pp. 53-68.

Forrester, J.W. (1981) 'Inflation and Unemployment', in B.E. Paulre (ed) *System Dynamics and Analysis of Change,* North-Holland, Amsterdam, pp. 111-135.

Forrester, J.W. (1989) 'The System Dynamics National Model: Macrobehaviour from Microstructure', in Milling P.M. and E. Zahn (eds) *Computer-Based Management of Complex Systems,* Springer-Verlag, Berlin, pp. 3-12.

Mohapatra, P.K.J., M.C. Bora, and K.C. Sahu (1984) 'Incorporating Delphi Results in System Dynamics Models: A Case of India Tea Industry', *Tech. Fore & Soc. Change,* vol. 25, pp.159-177.

NTPC (1980) *Report of National Transport Policy Committee,* Planning Commission,

Government of India, New Delhi.

Parikh, J.K. (1981) *Modelling Energy Demand for Policy Analysis,* Planning Commission, Government of India, New Delhi.

Somasekhara, N., T.R. Krishna Mohan, K. Rajaram, and K.S. Yajnik (1992) 'Modelling the Transport Sector in India', *Journal of Scientific and Industrial Research,* vol. 51, pp. 696-708.

WGEP (1965) *Report of the Working Group on Energy Policy,* Planning Commission, Government of India, New Delhi.

20. ENVIRONMENTAL POLICY ANALYSIS: System Dynamics Approach

K. Vizayakumar

1. Introduction

There is world wide concern for the degradation of environment being caused by the phenomenal growth in technology (Agarwal, 1984; Berreman, 1981; and Randers and Meadows, 1973). Technology, no doubt, has been accepted the world over as the most fundamental force for the economic and social progress of man but it is also seen with suspicion owing to its many negative, often disastrous, side effects. One of the most visible negative side effects is its undesirable impact on bio-geo-physical environment.

The awareness and these negative effects came as early as the sixties. Developed countries like U.S.A. passed legislation to protect environment in late sixties and early seventies. Since then, several scientists, all over the world, are studying the environment, its status, the degrading trends, the sources of degradation, remedial measures and the policy alternatives.

Several authors such as Leopold *et al.* (1971), Heer and Hagerty (1977), have developed some specific methods to study the environmental impacts such as checklists, matrices, numerical methods, overlays, etc. However, these methods are useful to identify the impacts and their interactions. Though some of these are used to evaluate alternatives, they do not consider the inter-relationships among the factors and the resultant changes, as these methods are subjective in nature and static in time frame.

The analysis thus made leads to a trial and error method in implementing policy alternatives. That is to implement a policy which is thought as the best one, see the results and if necessary change the policy. This becomes a costly exercise as the delays involved in environmental systems are pretty large. Any effect may only be realized after a few years. Realising this trauma, Sondheim (1978) said that there is the technique of dynamic systems modelling, by far the most sophisticated and potentially worthwhile but at this point of time, it is still in an embryonic stage as applied to environmental impact. In fact, system dynamics developed by Jay. W. Forrester at MIT in 1968, was used for the modelling and analysis of environmental systems in early seventies itself (Meadows and Meadows, 1973).

2. System Dynamics

System Dynamics, a modelling and simulation methodology, permits an analyst to represent graphically and mathematically the interactions governing the dynamic behaviour of complex socio-economic systems. The method is useful both in understanding the causes of present problems and in testing the effectiveness of alternative policies. Various diagrammatic tools, like sectoral overview diagram, causal loop diagram, policy structure diagram, and flow diagram are used to conceptualise and formulate the model. Simple difference equations (Euler's Approximation) are used to express the relationships mathematically. The model is simulated using DYNAMO, DYSMAP, or DYMOSIM. Certain important features of system dynamics (Vizayakumar, 1990) are its ability to

(i) dynamically model complex relationships of a large number of variables,
(ii) model a wide variety of real world situations,
(iii) incorporate features of both exploratory and normative approaches,
(iv) consider many related aspects of a problem resulting in a holistic approach,
(v) explicitly model qualitative factors,
(vi) experiment with policy alternatives, and
(vii) generate future scenarios.

2.1 *Modelling of Environmental Systems with System Dynamics*

System dynamics modelling of environmental systems facilitates both the understanding of environmental problems and the testing of alternative policies for the survival and maintenance of the system through simulation.

System dynamics models do not, of course, permit one to predict the future. Rather, the objective is experimental. It is to assemble the diverse bits of quantitative and qualitative information already available and evaluate which data are most important in understanding the system as a whole. The primary use of system dynamics is thus in making the best possible estimate of the impact of the impact of a given policy using only the information currently available about the system.

System dynamics has another use as well. Much environmental research to day is directed toward refining the estimates of factors that are already known well enough to permit improved policy. One should instead strive to focus the limited research resources on those areas of ignorance that are still great enough to make it impossible to identify the better of two alternative policies. System Dynamics tools are extremely useful for identifying more efficiently those parameters and structural relationships whose precise values are of critical importance to decision makers (Randers and Meadows, 1973).

A basic dilemma confronting the society as it attempts to address environmental problems is that political institutions and other social organizations are specifically adapted to develop and implement solutions to short term problems only. However, many basic environmental problems must be foreseen far in advance and approached in a consistent fashion over a period of fifty years or more if they are to be solved. It is important to obtain additional data on the causes and consequences of environmental deterioration, but it is also necessary to impart longer time horizons to the institutions involved in environmental policy formulation.

Improved long-term policies can be designed in the absence of precise data as long as the underlying structure of the environmental system is understood. It is the basic structure of the causal relationships that determines the system's possible behaviour modes, not the exact numerical values of its components. While individual coefficients will change over time, the underlying structure typically does not. Effective environmental policies are those that produce the desired behaviour mode in the system. Thus policy design can proceed, on the basis of an understanding of system structure, to identify those policies that are robust under a variety of parameter values.

3. Examples

To illustrate the use of system dynamics for environmental policy analysis, two examples are presented here. The first case model a real world situation of technology use and environmental degradation, uses hypothetical or relative parameter values and analyses the system for various policy instruments. This is a macro level analysis dealing with national level policy making.

The second case is a micro level analysis of environmental aspects of a coal mining area. It studies a specific area in Bihar state consisting of 20 coal pits, 4 being open cast mines. It models the various pollutants emitted due to mining, the social impacts, and tests the alternatives available for pollution abatement.

4. National Environmental Policy Analysis

The objectives of the model are:

(i) to depict the consequences of an unabated growth of a pollution generating technology in a traditional society with developing economy which is non-responsive to environmental deterioration, and

(ii) to test various alternate policies and assess their impacts.

The stated objectives of the model make technology and pollution generated by it as the obvious factors to be included in the model. The technology is expressed in terms of the net block of the industry using this technology. The quality of environment is measured by means of a quality of environment index after a similar proposition by Thomas (1972). The index is represented by the ratio of a set norm (standard) for pollution level to its actual value. Pollution is considered as an aggregate factor representing all types of pollution emanating from this technology. In the third world countries, the influence of industrialists is quite strong. Therefore, though anti-pollution laws are in existence, hardly any law is effectively put into practice (Agarwal and D' Monte, 1985). Technology provides benefits to the society in the form of material goods and employment. However, pollution generating technology also creates health hazards. Therefore, the model also considers such factors as quality of life, social benefit index, and affected population. Several studies and reports (Baumol and Oates, 1979; O'Riordan, 1976; Newstime, 1986; Bhattacharya *et al.*, 1987; Raghu, 1989) indicate the necessity and existence of pressure groups among the citizens to build up pressure on the government to ensure control of pollution. However, the industry also may bring counter pressure on the government. In consideration of the importance of such pressure groups, the model includes such factors as social pressure and counter pressure. Figures 20.1 and 20.2 show the causal loop diagram of the basic model and the simplified flow diagram respectively.

Though the awareness about environment among the people in the third world countries is very low, there are signs of building up such awareness and social pressure. Therefore it is presumed that the government acts only when there is substantial level of social pressure. When the government responds to social pressure, it is expected to choose one of the

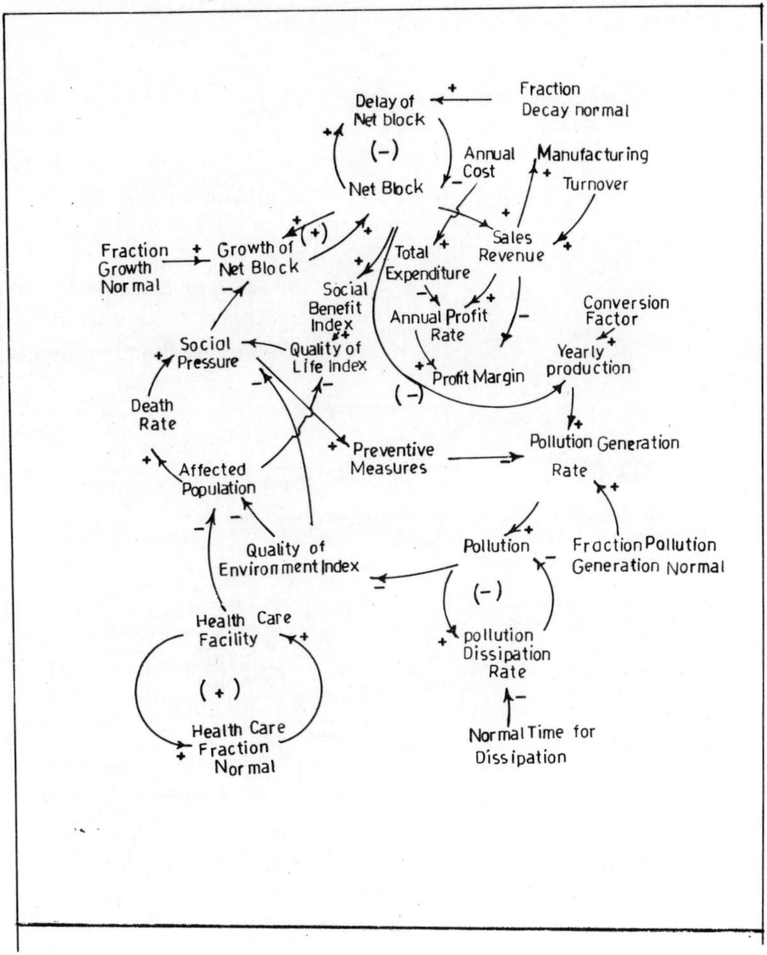

FIG. 20.1: Causal Loop Diagram of Basic Model

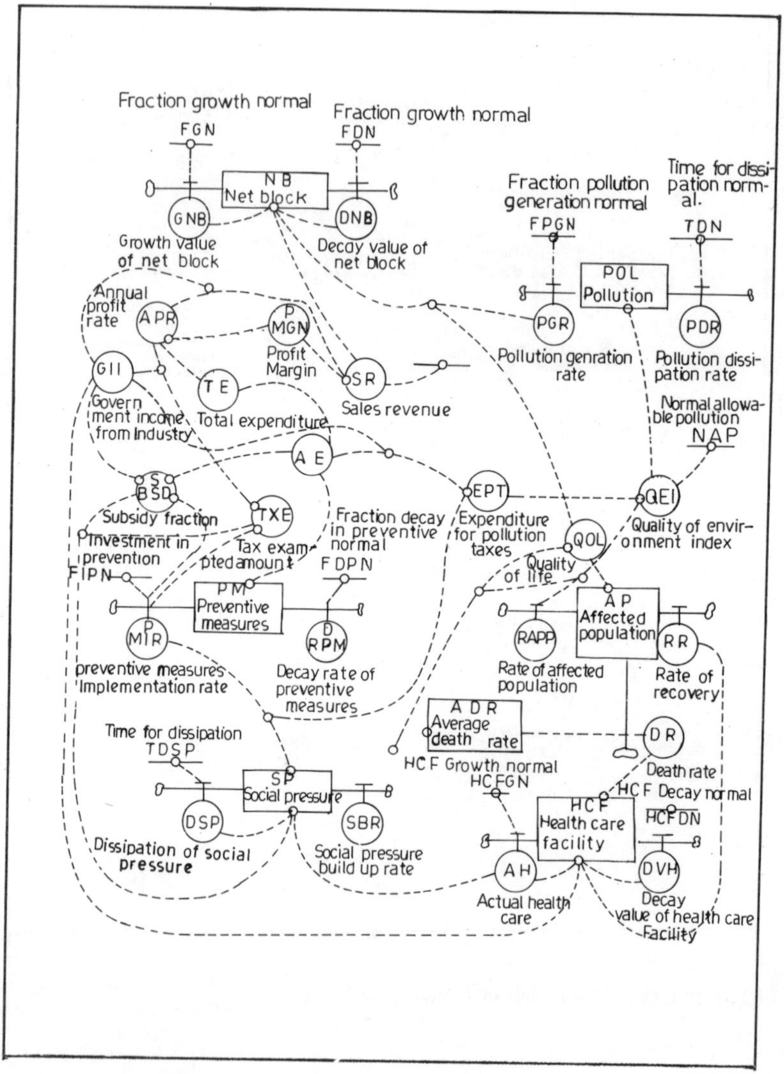

FIG. 20.2: Simplifide Flow Diagram.

following alternatives or any combination of some or all of these alternatives.

(i) *Government Investment on Health Care*

Improve healthcare facility : In the event of health hazards caused by environmental pollution from the industry and the resulting social pressure, the government may increase health care budget, improve health care facility, and fight health hazards.

(ii) *Direct Control Through Legislation*

Enact anti-pollution laws: The government makes laws against polluting the environment. But due to the existing socio-political culture which overemphasizes industrial development, the power lobby and the industrialists carry with the political leaders and has its effect on all levels of administration, pollution control by direct regulation has become virtually ineffective in many countries including India.

(iii) *Market Processes*

(a) *Provide subsidy:* The government may provide subsidy to the industry for implementing pollution control measures in terms of percentage of the amount invested in pollution control.
(b) *Tax exemption:* The government may exempt the amount spent by the industry on pollution control from taxes.
(c) *Impose pollution tax:* Special tax on the industry for emitting pollutants may be levied depending on the quantity and type of emissions.

The policies are evaluated generating the behaviour of the model with each policy using simulation. The variables selected for evaluation are

(i) Profit margin for the industry (PMGN), which is a ratio of annual profit to the sales revenue.
(ii) Quality of environment index (QEI).
(iii) Quality of Life index (QOL), which is an aggregate measure of benefits as well as hazards.
(iv) Government's Income from this Industry (GII), which is revenue from taxes, less the expenditure due to policy measures, i.e., additional expenditure on healthcare, subsidy and tax exemption.

Figure 20.3 depicts the behaviour of these chosen variables for the basic model, i.e, with negligible social pressure.

The experiments on various policy alternatives bring forth three policies as viable: (i) subsidy, (ii) tax exemption, and (iii) pollution taxes. However, many a time, a combination of options are implemented as they yield results which are better than the original results (Renders and Meadows, 1973). The model is tested here with the following combinations:

(i) subsidy and tax exemption policy
(ii) subsidy and pollution tax policy
(iii) tax exemption and pollution tax policy
(iv) subsidy, tax exemption and pollution tax policy.

The behaviour of the selected variables are generated for the above four policies. They are then compared with the behaviour of the individual policies of subsidy, tax exemption, and pollution tax. Figure 20.4 presents the behaviour of the variables with these seven policies. The numbers given to the policies in the figure represent the following:

1 - 50 per cent subsidy
2 - 100 per cent tax exemption
3 - 20 per cent pollution tax
4 - 50 per cent subsidy and 100 per cent tax exemption
5 - 50 per cent subsidy and 20 per cent pollution tax
6 - 100 per cent tax exemption and 20 per cent pollution tax
7 - 50 per cent subsidy, 100 per cent tax exemption and 20 per cent pollution tax.

These results indicate that subsidy and tax exemption are very effective instruments for initiating pollution control measures but their demand on the public exchequer is very heavy. The former is an actual financial loss while the latter is an opportunity loss. Provided that these losses are not considered important, vis-a-vis the loss in quality of environment and human life, policies 4 and 7 are the best. But otherwise a good compromise appears to be offered by policy 6. It emphasizes the practice of exempting taxes on investment in pollution control and of levying taxes based on pollution caused by the industry.

5. Environmental Impact Analysis of a Coalfield

A system dynamics model is built to capture the interactions among the

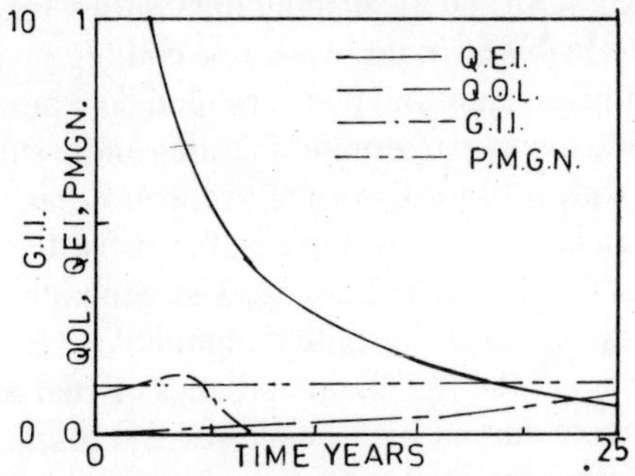

FIG. 20.3: The Basic Model Behaviour

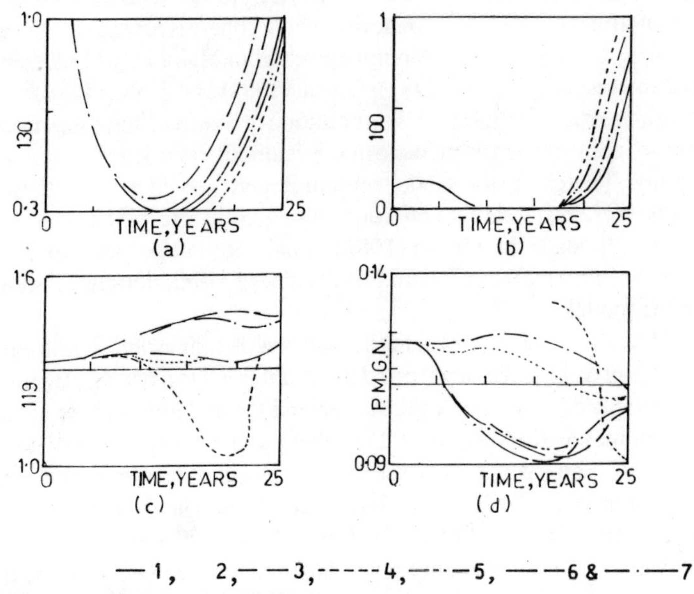

FIG. 20.4: Behaviour of Variables with Policies Chosen for Comparison

activities and impacts of coal mining and to test the viability of alternative pollution control policies. This study has been conducted in an area which includes a semi-urban town and its surroundings, with a total population of more than 50,000. In this area, there are nine collieries with four open cast mines and twenty underground pits. The total coal production from this area is about 2000 tonnes per annum. The area under study covers all the collieries lying within 10 km radius of the semi-urban town.

The causal structure shown in Figure 20.5 is used as the basis to develop the model. The model is later used to generate the dynamic behaviour and to test the effect of policy alternatives. Extraction and transportation of coal are the two main activities of coal mining. Both these activities generate dust in high quantities and discharge it to the atmosphere, thus deteriorating the quality of surrounding air. Water quality is also adversely affected by mine drainage. The pollution, thus created, poses hazards to human health, reduces crop yield, and deteriorates cattle health.

Another source of air pollution is the combustion of coal as a domestic fuel. The combustion of coal releases pollutants in the form of particulate matter, sulphur dioxide, nitrogen oxides, carbon monoxide, and hydrocarbons. Carbon monoxide is generated during the incomplete combustion of both coal and fuel oil. Butler (1979) reports that the concentration of the carbon monoxide in the troposphere is not considerable and remains sensibly constant though emission rates are very high even from natural resources. Bose (1982), Ghosh (1983) and Sinha (1987), in extensive and experimental studies on pollution in coalfield, have reported the presence of suspended particulate matter, sulphur dioxide and nitrogen oxides only. Therefore, the model presented here considers only these three emissions. The weather conditions also greatly affect the pollution levels in the atmosphere. Ghosh (1983) found correlations between the weather conditions and the pollutant levels. These correlations have been used in the model.

Production of coal produces high quantities of drain water. The drain water is pumped out to the surface and most of it is led to a nearby stream. The inhabitants of the area use the stream and the underground wells as the main sources of drinking water. Both these sources are polluted by the mine drainage. Some people even use the drained out water directly before it reaches a stream. This is very hazardous to human health as this untreated water contains suspended solids and dissolved solids, and is of high ph value. The water quality is modelled here as an index that is a function of ph, bio-chemical oxygen demand (BOD), chemical oxygen demand (COD), levels of dissolved oxygen (DO) and dissolved solids

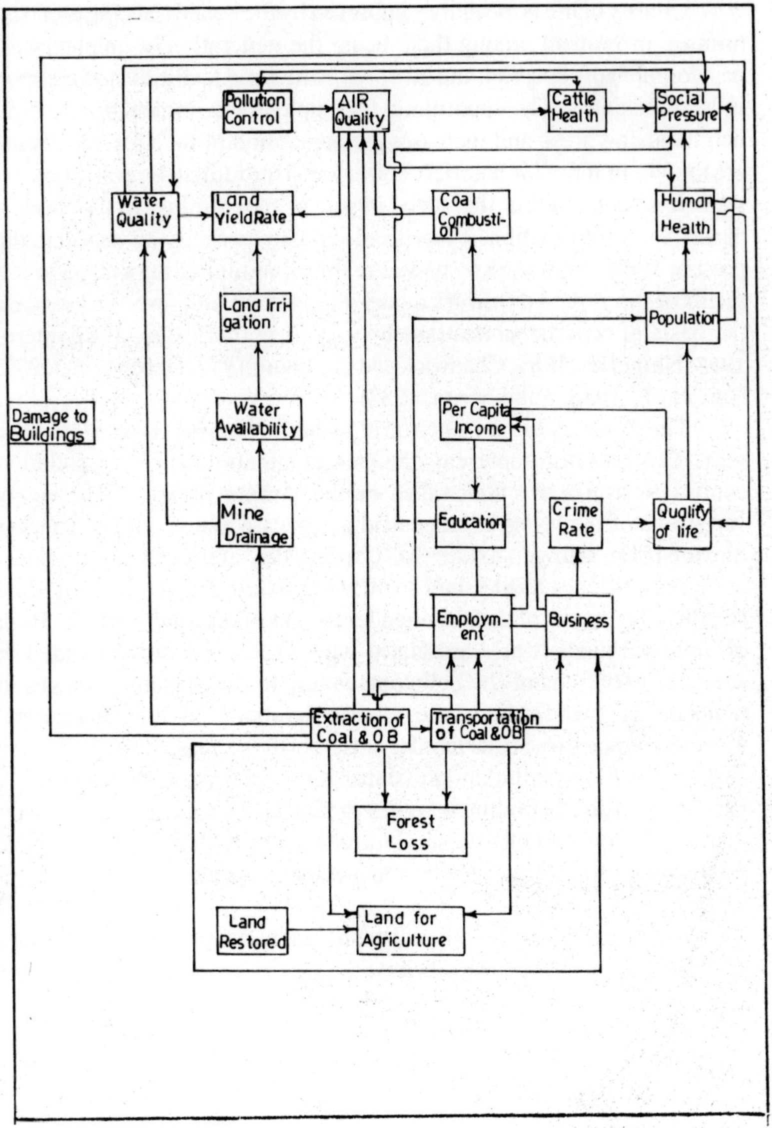

FIG. 20.5: Interpretive Structural Model of a Coalfield

(DS). The air and water pollution cause health hazards reducing the quality of life.

Quality of life is, of course, improved by the beneficial effects of coal mining, prominent among them being the generation of employment, development of education and other infrastructural facilities, and increase in local business. The opportunity for employment attracts people from neighbouring areas and increases the population of the area. Coalfields are known in India for notoriety and crime. Unfortunately, no systematic study has been made of this social impact of coal mining. In the absence of sufficient information, it was decided not to consider this aspect in the present study. Figure 20.6 shows the flow diagram of the air pollution sector of the system dynamics model. Parameter values were selected on the basis of reports/publications by various authors (Jha, 1987; Stern, 1968; Nair *et al.*, 1987; Chadwick and Lindman, 1982; Ghosh *et al.*, 1987; Nair *et al.*, 1988: ; and Misra, 1982).

The model is run for a period of twenty years with 1982 as the base year. This base run represents the present situation where no pollution control measures are undertaken by the mining industry. The yearly variations of the levels of suspended particulate matter (SPM), sulphur dioxide (SD), nitrogen oxides (NO), and quality of life (QOL) are shown in Figures 20.7, 20.8, 20.9, and 20.10 respectively. These figures indicate seasonal variations of the pollution levels and of the quality of life. Each of these variables is also associated with a secular positive trend. The seasonal variations of the pollutants is due to the seasonal changes in temperature, wind speed, and relative humidity in the atmosphere, whereas the positive secular trend results from the increased coal production and the resultant pollutant emissions. Since quality of life is inversely proportional to the pollutant values are high and vice-versa. However, instead of showing negative secular trend, QOL is also showing positive trend. Such a trend has resulted from the benefits of coal mining discussed earlier.

The model is tested with six pure policies and with six combinations of these policies as indicated below:

1. The base run,
2. Spray the face with water before drilling,
3. Use dust arrestor during drilling,
4. Use water-ampoule stemming,
5. Spray the face with water-wetting agent mixture,
6. Spray water during loading and transportation,
7. Use soft coke instead of raw coal as domestic fuel,

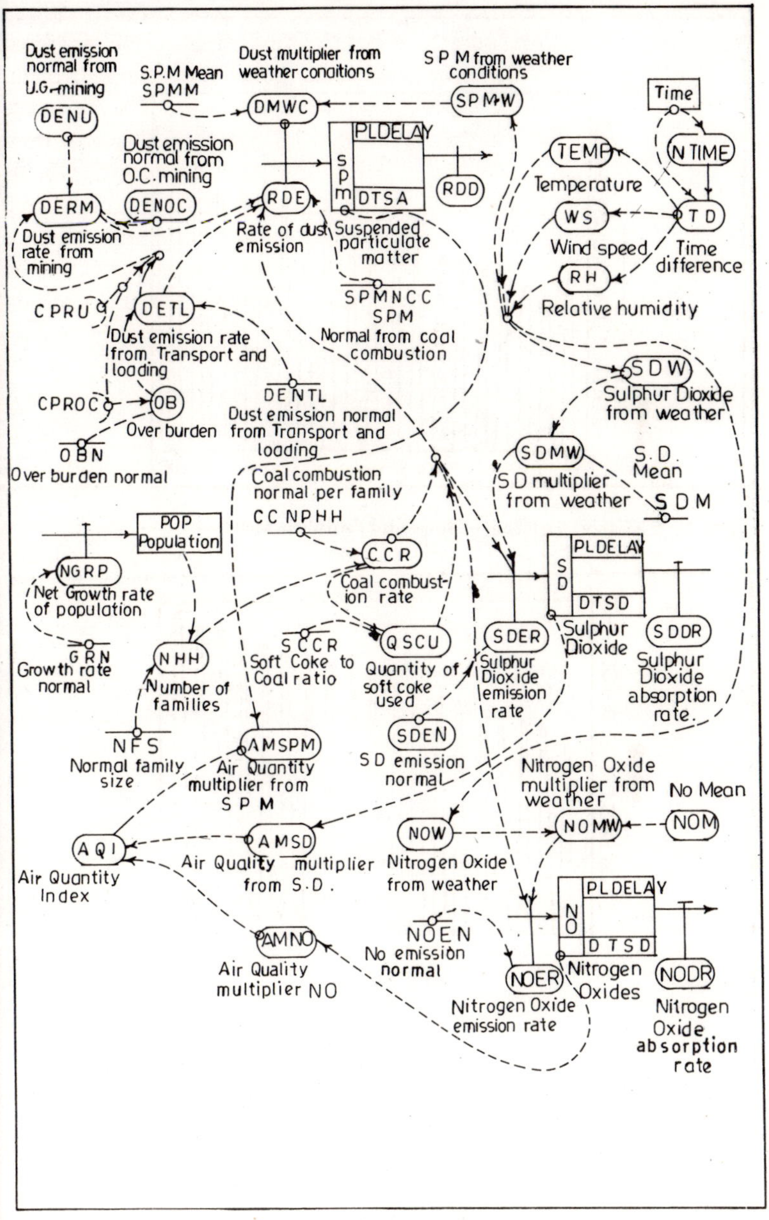

FIG. 20.6: Air Pollution in Coal Mining

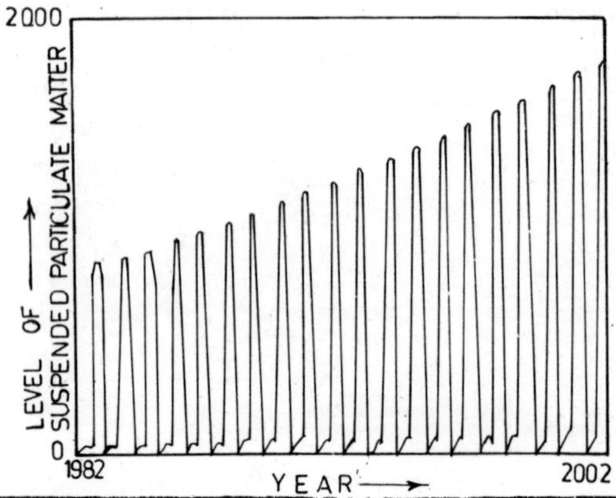

FIG. 20.7: Seasonal Variations of Suspended Particulate Matter.

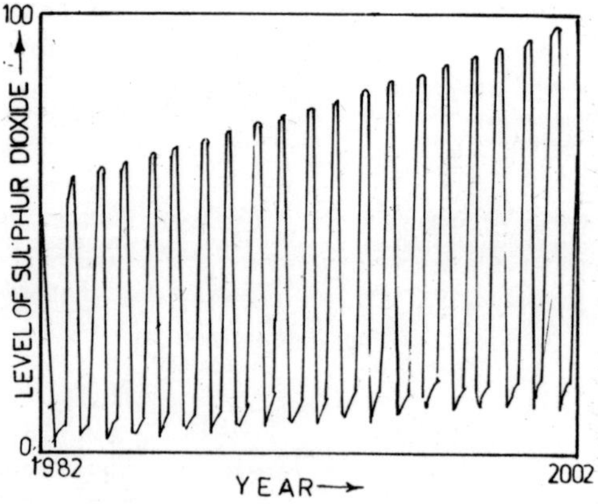

FIG. 20.8 : Seasonal Variations of Sulphur Dioxide.

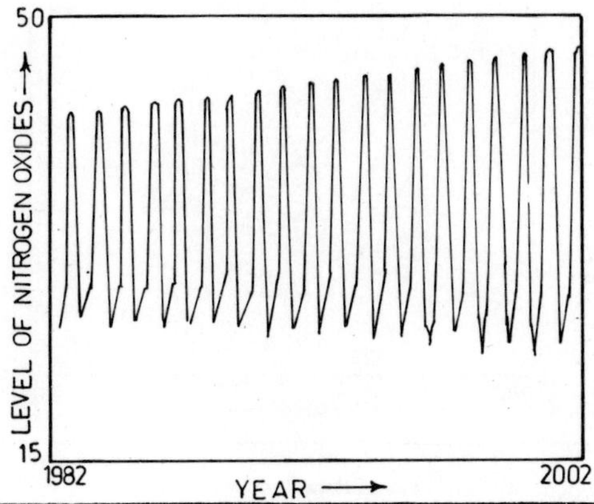

FIG. 20.9: Seasonal Variations of Nitrogen Oxides.

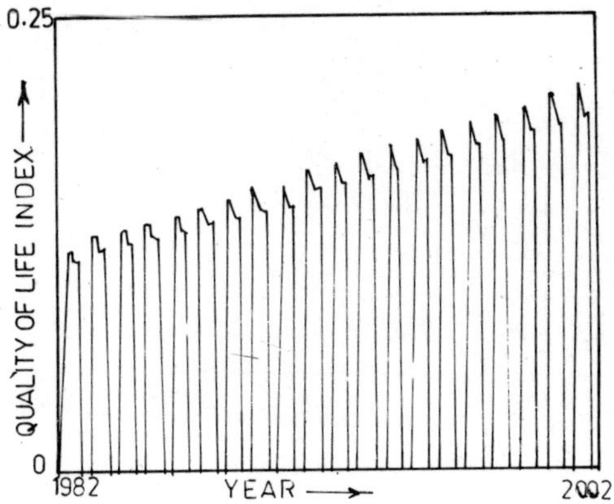

FIGURE-20·10 SEASONAL VARIATIONS IN QUALITY LIFE.

FIG. 20.10 : Seasonal Variations in Quality Life.

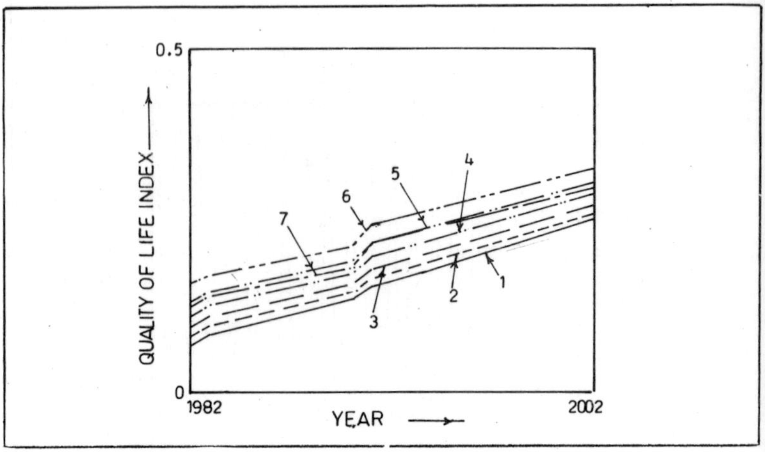

FIG. 20.11: Behaviour of Base Run and Pure Policies.

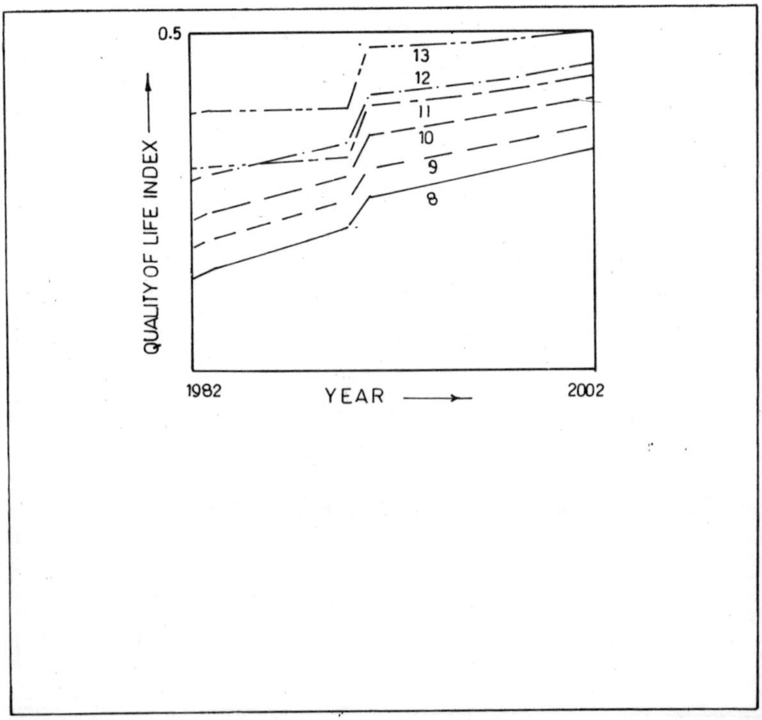

FIG. 20.12 : Behaviour of Policies in Various Combinations.

8. Spray the face with water before drilling and use dust arrestor during drilling,
9. Use water-ampoule stemming and dust arrestor during drilling,
10. Spray the face with water before drilling, use dust arrestor during drilling and use water-ampoule stemming,
11. Spray the face with water-wetting agent mixture before drilling, use dust arrestor and water ampoule stemming,
12. Spray the face with water before drilling, use dust arrestor, use water-ampoule stemming, spray water during loading and transportation, use soft coke instead of raw coal as domestic fuel, and treat mine drainage water, and
13. Spray the face with water-wetting agent mixture, use dust arrestor, use water-ampoule stemming, spray water during loading and transportation, use soft coke instead of raw coal and treat mine drainage water.

The model behaviour for these policies also varies seasonally. For the sake of comparison, however, only the peak values of QOL are plotted as shown in Figures 20.11 and 20.12. the numbers in figures correspond to the numbers of the policies listed above.

This case study shows that system dynamics modelling is an effective means of synthesizing knowledge in various fields in environmental impact analysis and of designing viable policies for effective pollution control.

6. Conclusions

This paper proposes system dynamics as a method for environmental policy analysis. In order to explicate the use of system dynamics in environmental policy analysis, a model of a real world problem with assumed relative data and a case study of environmental impacts of a coalfield are modelled and analysed for various policy alternatives. With greater participation from the policy makers and administrators, it can be used more fruitfully and effectively.

REFERENCES

Agarwal, A. (1984), "The Poorman's Problem", *Herald Review,* 1(3), 43-44.

Agarwal, A. and D. D'Monte 1985), "Industrialization: The Darker Side", *Indian Express,* 3rd

February, p.6.

Bandyopadhyay, J. and V. Shiva (1985), "The Conflict over Limestone Quarrying in Doon Valley", *Environmental Conservation,* 12 (2), 133-142.

Baumol, W.J., and W.E. Qates (1979), *Economics, Environmental Policy, and Quality of LIfe,* Prentice Hall inc. NJ.

Berreman, G.D. (1981), "Progress Stratification and quality of Life: A view from Anthropology", in G.E. Lasker (ed), *Applied Systems and Cybernetics,* Vol. 1: The Quality of Life-Systems Approaches, Pergamon Press, NY

Bhattacharya, J.P. Singh, P. De, and D. Dutt (1987), "Adoption of Environmental Strategies in the Planning and Operational Phase of Mine Development", in S.C. Ray, G.B. Misra, S.D. Barve, M.N. Biswas, and N. Mukherjee (Eds.),*Proceedings of the National Seminar on Environmental Pollution and Control in Mining, Coal and Mineral Based Industries,* IIT, Kharagpur.

Bose, S.K. (1982), *Air Quality Study in Jharia Coalfield,* Ph. D. Thesis, Indian School of Mines, Dhanbad.

Butler, J.D. (1979), *Air Pollution Chemistry,* Academic Press, London.

Chadwick, M.K., and N. Lindman (1982), *Environmental Implications of Expanded Coal Utilization,* Pergamon Press, oxford.

Ghosh, S. K. (1983), A Study of Air Pollution including Toxic Trace Elements in an Indian Coalfield and its likely Impact on incidence of deseases, Ph. D. thesis, Indian School of Mines, Dhanbad.

Ghosh, S.K., T.P.M. Singh, R.K. Tewari, and — Singh (1987), Improvement of Mine water quality for community consumption in mining areas, in S.P. Banerjee (ed.), *Proceedings of the Colloquium on Water Pollution and Land Reclamation in Mining areas with special reference to Jharia coalfields,* Indian School of Mines, Dhanbad.

Heer, J. Jr., and J. Hagerty (1977), *Environmental Assessments and Procedures,* Von Nostrand Reinhold Company, NY.

Jha, M. (1987), "Environmental Management of Mining Operations in Singrauli Coalfields", in B.B. Dhar (ed), *National Workshop on Environmental Management of Mining Operations in India - A Status Paper,* B. H.U., Varanasi.

Leopold, L.B., F. E. Clarke, B.B. Hansaw, and J.R. Balsey (1971), A Procedure for Evaluating Environmental Impact, *Geological Survey Circular 645,* Government Printing Office, Washington.

Meadows, D.L., and D.H. Meadows (1974), *Dynamics of Growth in a Finite World,* Wright Allen Press Inc., Cambridge, MA.

Misra, G. (1982), *Some Social Problems of Industrial Health in a Coalfield Setting,* Ph.D. Thesis, Banaras Hindu University, Varanasi.

Nair, P.K., J.K. Sinha, A.K. Bose, and B. Singh (1987), "Particulate Emissions from Underground Coal Mines and its Impact on General Environment of a coal mining area - A Case Study", *Indian Journal of Environmental Protection,* 7 (1), 330-333.

Nair, P.K., A. Rashidi, and J.K. Sinha (1988), "Dust Problem during Coal Transportation by High Speed Multi-stage Conveyer Belts", *Indian Journal of Environmental Protection,* 8 (3), 179-183.

News Time (1986), "The Chemical Slaughter", July 28, p.5.

O'Riordan, T, (1976), *Environmentalism,* Pion Ltd., London.

Raghu, A. (1976), "Patancheru Environment with Poisonous Gases", (in Telugu), *Nalupu,* 1 (7), 5-8.

Randers, J. and D.L. Meadows (1973), "The Dynamics of Solid Waste Generation", in Meadows, D.L., (ed.), *Toward Global Equilibrium: Collected Papers,* M.I.T. Press, Cambridge, MA.

Randers, J. and D.H. Meadows (1973), "The Carrying Capacity of our global Environment: A look at the Ethical Alternatives", in Meadows, D.L., (ed.), *Toward Global Equilibrium: Collected Papers,* M.I.T. Press, Cambridge, MA.

Shiva, V. and J.Bandyopadhyay (1986), "The Evolution, Structure, and Impact of the Chipko Movement", *Mountain Research and Development Journal,* 6(2), 131-139.

Sinha, J.K. (1987), "Dust Control Techniques for Indian Coal Mines", in S.C. Ray, G.B. Misra, S.D. Barve, M.N. Biswas, and N. Mukherjee (eds.), *Proceedings of the National Seminar on Environmental Pollution and Control in Mining, Coal and Mineral Based Industries,* Indian Institute of Technology, Kharagpur

Sondhiem, M.W. (1978), "A Comprehensive Methodology for Assessing Environmental Impact", *Journal of Environmental Management,* 6, 27-42.

Stern, A.C. (1968), *Air Pollution,* Academic Press, NY.

Thomas, W.A. (1972), "Indicators of Environmental Quality - An Overview", in W.A. Thomas, (ed.), *Indicators of Environmental Quality,* Plenum Press, NY.

Vizayakumar, K. (1990), *A Study on Some Aspects of Environmental Impact Analysis,* Ph. D. Thesis, Indian Institute of Technology, Kharagpur.

21. POLICY ANALYSIS AND DESIGN USING FLEXIBLE SYSTEMS METHODOLOGY

Sushil

1. Introduction

Formulation of public policy involves a wide cross section of people and is having very far reaching consequences. It requires a sound and thorough analysis and design before it can be implemented. It is also helpful to obtain an intermediate feedback about the efficacy of policies contemplated.

A significant consideration in the provision of formal management support for policy formulation is the assessment of impact of policies. More effective policies result through the feedback about their impact on the performance of the systems. Conventionally the understanding of a system in terms of mental models is used for policy making through debate and then "implementing" in the real life. The feedback about the efficacy of policies is received from their impact on the real life systems, which is very costly and time consuming as shown in Fig. 21.1. Since policies govern the decision on a longer time frame and encompass a wider scope, the costs of a wrong policy may be very high.

Real life experimentation with the policies and obtaining feedback about their efficacy from the real life is an inefficient and ineffective way of policy making. If it is possible to obtain an intermediate feedback about the possible impact of policies on the real systems before their implementation it will help a great deal in improving the policies. It will reveal the weaknesses of policies and guide the points of intervention for possible improvement. The creation of a simulation model of the real system and its policy structure will provide effective management support for policy experimentation and improvement. It will involve little resources as compared to real life experimentation in terms of time, money, and opportunities.

Since different public policies deal with issues which are at different levels of complexity, the perspectives associated may be narrow, wide, or even conflicting; the data requirements and availability are different; and

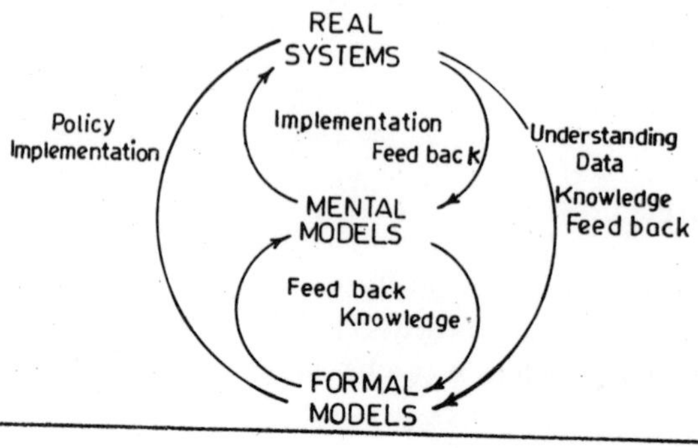

FIG. 21.1: Feedbacks in Policy Modelling and Implementation.

the policy issues range from unstructured to well structured; it is not possible to handle all of them with a single modelling approach.

Systems concepts and methodologies are developed as a response to the ever-increasing complexity of the socio-technical and managerial systems. Many techniques and approaches based on systems philosophy have been developed which help in analyzing various problem situations in multiple ways. In the past, attempts have been made to judge the supremacy of one technique or approach over the others, but all such debates have not been able to lead to conclusions which are universal in nature. Different approaches have found favour in different situations, and have their own strengths and limitations. The task of designing or selecting methodology for a particular problem situation is becoming more difficult with ever increasing choice of techniques.

It has been a constant endeavour in systems thinking to relate the developments in systems based techniques and approaches to project the trends and develop conceptual frameworks. Bertalanffy (1972) has reported extensive developments in the field of General Systems Theory and discussed the trends in Systems Science : Mathematical Systems Theory; Systems Technology; and Systems Philosophy. General Systems Theory worked to structure sciences and systems (Boulding, 1956) and tried to provide answers to a variety of systems such as material systems, informational systems, and conceptual systems. It worked more as an umbrella under which the philosophical as well as mathematical systems concepts developed.

The systems movement has been reviewed by Checkland (1981a,b) giving developments on different fronts and finally concluding the earlier development to be on the hard systems thinking and the later developments to be more on soft systems thinking with a "learning" paradigm. Though it tries to rethink the total systems approach it rather resulted in systems thinking at the ends of the systems continuum.

In order to use the available techniques more systematically there is an increasing trend to develop schemes that relate these techniques in a meaningful manner. A thought provoking review by Troncale (1988) puts the developments in systems sciences together. It defines the domains of systems science as General Theory of Systems, Systems Theory, Systems Analysis, and Systems Applications. It provides a morphology of different fields of knowledge related with systems science, and also linkage propositions between systems concepts (isomorphies). Further, it outlines various systems techniques or methods including both 'hard' and 'soft' types. It discusses the unified spectrum of systems approaches and the opportunities that could be derived from information transfer between operational research and systems science such as: (i) a rigorous taxonomy of systems; (ii) a rigorous taxonomy of isomorphies; (iii) a rigorous taxonomy of general systems functions; and so on. This paper derives inspiration from such a relational approach and goes further to propose a cohesive methodological framework that captures the essence of spectral and relational thinking and provides a flexible approach for using the isomorphies and systems techniques and methods.

A set of consensus methodologies has been suggested by Warfield (1990) while presenting a science of generic design. The set of consensus methodologies is composed of primarily the qualitative techniques. The concept is expanded here to involve the whole range of techniques from quantitative to qualitative. Another recent development is the concept of "Total System Intervention" as proposed by Flood and Jackson (1991). The concept of "Total System Intervention" talks of six clusters of systems based techniques depending on whether the systems are simple or complex and the people are unitary, pluralistic or coercive in different problem situations. It finally leads to the selection of a particular technique for the problem situation in a creative manner. Here the concept is further generalized to enmesh the clusters so as to form a continuum of systems based techniques which can be used flexibly by suitably interfacing these techniques as per the requirements of the problem situations.

The use of relating various systems modeling approaches can be effectively seen in the area of Decision Support Systems (DSS) and Artificial Intelligence (AI), which present quantiative as well as qualitative approaches in cohesive and symbiotic frameworks. These have been called by different names like expert support systems, intelligent decision support systems, knowledge based decision support systems, etc.

Thus, it can be seen that the philosophy of integration of quantitative and qualitative tools is emerging very rapidly to cater to the diverse requirements of the decision making and managerial processes. Deriving inspiration from the developments in systems methodology in terms of schemes of systems techniques, and a wide applicability of integrated systems in computer based management, the philosophy of integration of techniques is generalized over the whole spectrum of system techniques. It is presented in the form of an evolving methodology, in subsequent sections, which can take care of the varied requirements of problem situations in a flexible manner.

The application of flexible systems methodology (Sushil, 1993) is illustrated by two case studies which represent two different kinds of integration of systems based techniques. One case study pertains to agricultural waste management which represents a sequential integration of techniques, whereas the other deals with the energy policy analysis, which represents the submerging of one technique into the other.

2. Flexible Systems Methodology: An Overview

An overview of the proposed flexible systems methodology is provided in terms of its purpose, philosophy and paradigm.

2.1 *Purpose*

To formulate a problem solving approach based on systems philosophy and using systems techniques flexibly for problem situations lying on the whole continuum, e.g. ranging from unstructured to well structured.

2.2 *Philosophy*

There are two possible extreme philosophies to handle problems by conceptual frameworks, e.g. isolationist and contingency.

According to isolationist philosophy a best approach is to be developed which will be useful in all possible problem situations. Traditionally, a lot of work in this direction has been done in different disciplines. For example, in management spheres attempts have been made to develop a management style which is the best. In systems literature work on development of frameworks was done to suit all classes of problems, e.g. General Systems Theory (GST) (Klir, 1969).

On the other hand the contigency philosophy believes in developing a unique approach for each problem situation. It is built on the belief that every problem situation is unique in its own right, and thus, needs a unique way of handling it. For example, situational management, and developing heuristics to solve typical problems.

Both these philosophies have worked but have encountered failures also. The isolationatist view is bogged down with the development of a grand paradigm, which is an ideal but difficult to achieve. To encompass every possible variation in a single approach is almost self-defeating. Moreover, a lot of debate takes place to judge the supremacy of the approach, and the practical aspects are ignored. Similarly, developing a unique approach for each problem situation is very time and resource consuming, and thus, is not a practical proposition.

The philosophy which lies in between these two extremes is of "flexibility", and is the basis of the proposed methodology. According to it there are multiple ways of reaching the same end, and the suitability of the way or a combination of ways will depend upon the nature and attributes of the problem situation at hand. It does not advocate inventing a new approach for each problem situation, rather selecting an approach out of the existing well researched ones, or a suitable combination of them so as to match the requirements of the problem situation. It thus integrates all systems approaches and techniques into a family in which every one either individually or collectively contributes meaningfully. A similar spirit underlies other disciplines also, e.g. contingency theory of management (Luthans and Steward, 1977).

2.3 *Paradigm*

The Flexible Systems Methodology is built on a "spectral and integrative" paradigm. It tries to resolve the end of continuum paradoxes as it is based on the spectral paradigm, treating all the systems based methodologies and techniques as lying on a continuum ranging from hard to soft; and all the problem situations also on a continuum ranging from well structured to unstructured, as shown in Fig. 21.2.

As can be seen by the basic nature of various systems based methodologies and techniques, they may be at different points on the continuum from hard to soft. There is a heavy clustering of methodologies and techniques towards the ends of the continuum, leaving a gap in

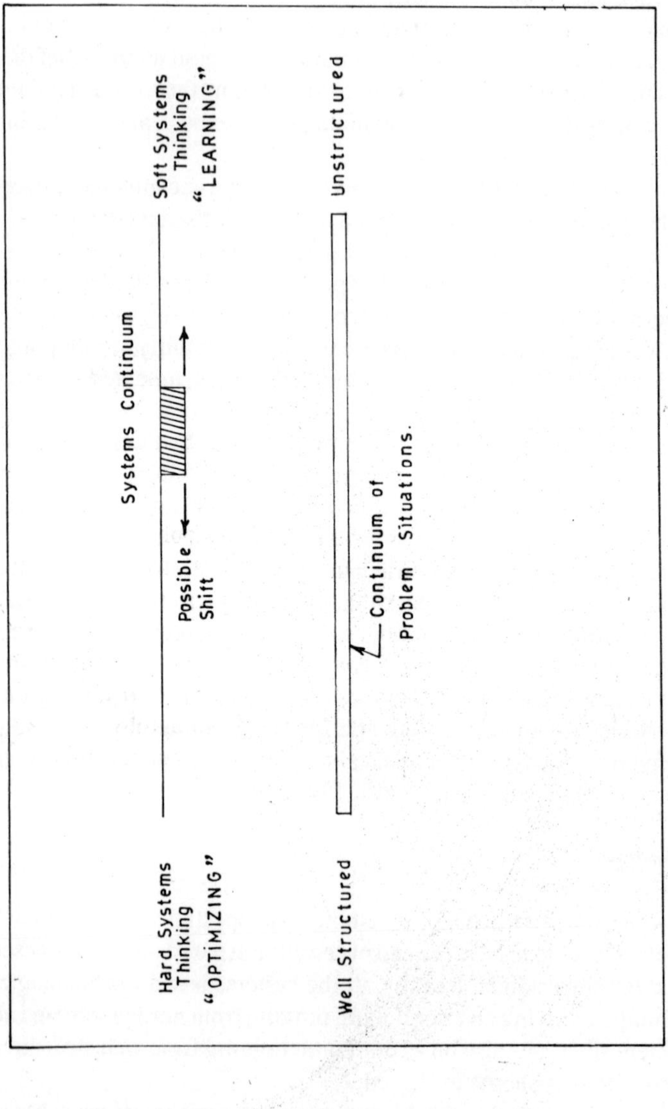

FIG. 21.2: Systems Continuum : A Spectral Paradigm.

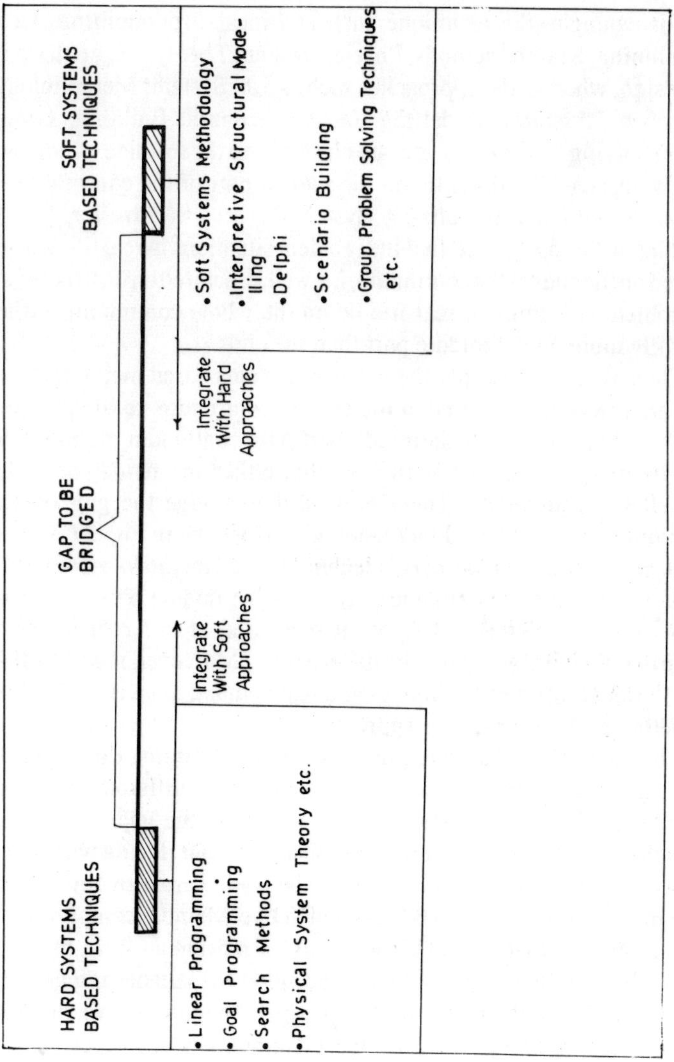

FIG. 21.3: Bridging the Gap on Systems Continuum.

between as shown in Fig. 21.3; as the two governing paradigms had been "optimizing" or hard systems thinking and "learning" or soft systems thinking.

For example, the technique such as Linear Programming, Goal Programming, Search Methods, Physical System Theory, etc. are hard in their design, whereas the approaches such as Soft Systems Methodology, Interpretive Structural Modelling, Delphi, Scenario Building, Group Problem Solving Techniques, etc. are clustered on the soft side. There are very few approaches which lie on the middle part of the continuum in between the hard and the soft, e.g. System Dynamics (Forrester, 1961).

It has to be appreciated that the problem situations in real life are not clustered on the ends of the continuum, i.e. well structured on unstructured. The problem situations in real life lie on the whole continuum; rather practically more on the middle part than the ends.

Thus, in order to apply the existing systems based methodologies which are primarily clustered at the ends of continuum, to the problem situations which lie more on the middle part of the continuum, assumptions are to be made to match the two, so that either the harder or softer approaches are adopted. There is a need to bridge the gap on the continuum of systems based methodologies as shown in Fig. 21.3. This gap can be bridged by creating new techniques and methodologies which can cater to the problem situations lying in the middle part, i.e. some portions well structured and some ill structured at different levels of structuring; which is going to take its own time. Moreover, it will further add to the existing set of techniques and will demand more from the user in selection of the appropriate approach.

The alternate and a more pragmatic way of bridging this gap is to follow an "integrative" paradigm, i.e. integrate different existing techniques and methodologies suitably to bridge the gap. The hard approaches are to be made comparatively softer by interfacing with softer approaches, and softer approaches are to be made harder by interfacing with harder approaches to make them effectively handle comparatively harder problem situations. This will make a movement from the ends towards the middle and the gap will be filled by suitable integration. However, ample care should be taken while integrating two or more systems based techniques so that the integration is not superficial; it should be done by matching the philosophical and theoretical foundations of the techniques to be integrated so that deep linkages can be established.

The integration can be of different types e.g., one way integration; both ways integration; submerging of one into another with identity; and full mixing of two techniques, as shown in Fig. 21.4. The Flexible Systems

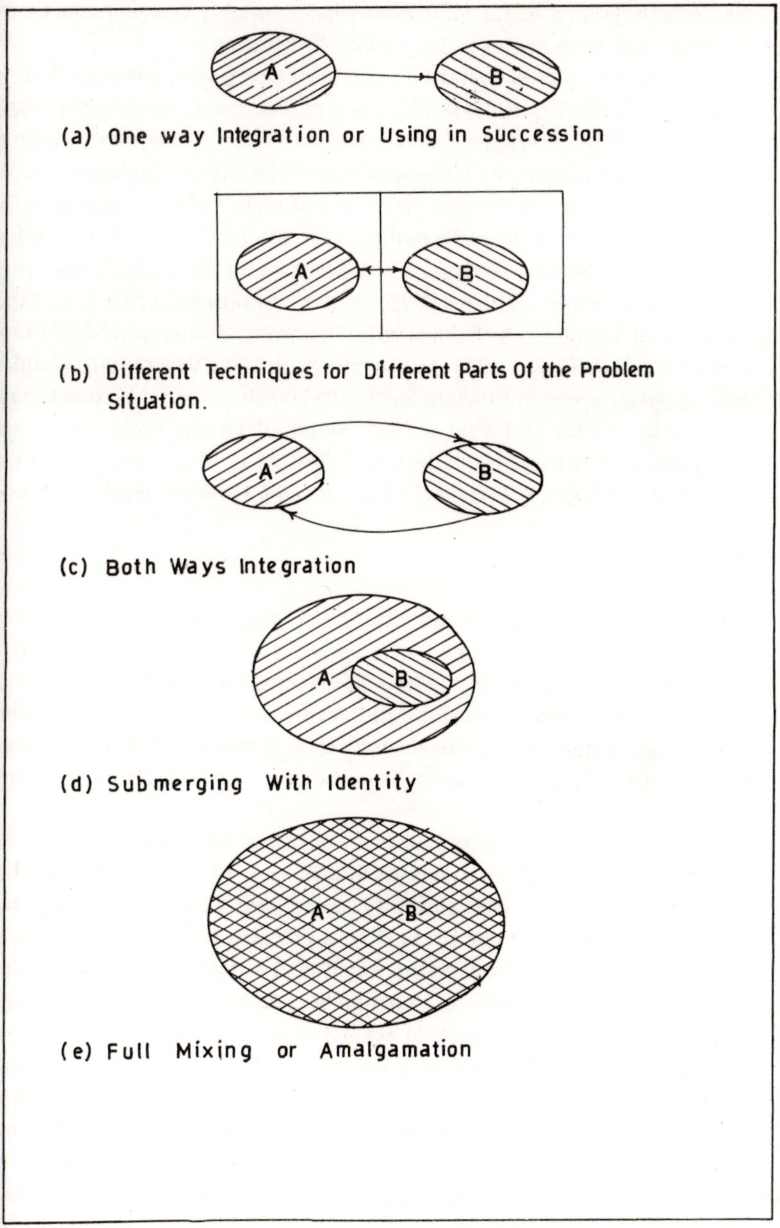

FIG. 21.4: Possible Schemes of Integration of Techniques

Methodology proposes to work with different types of integration of well researched systems based methodologies to suitably complement their strengths and weaknesses as the situations warrant.

Some examples of well tried integrations are physical system theory (Koenig *et al.*, 1967) with System Dynamics (Forrester, 1961) by Vij, Vrat and Sushil (1988), and Kumar and Satsangi (1993); Linear programming and Goal Programming with Physical System Theory by Singh and Sushil (1990); System Dynamics with Fuzzy sets (Zadeh, 1961) by Pankaj, Seth and Sushil (1992); System Dynamics with Monte Carlo Simulation by Pankaj (1992); System Dynamics with Interpretive Structural Modelling (Warfield, 1990) by Pankaj (1992), and Vizayakumar, (1990); Delphi with System Dynamics by Bora (1981); Interpretive Structural Modelling with MICMAC (Godet, 1987) by Saxena, Sushil and Vrat (1990); Delphi and Analytic Hierarchy Process (Saaty, 1984) with Fuzzy Set Methodology by Saxena, Sushil and Vrat (1990); Nominal Group Technique with Interpretive Structural Modelling by Warfield (1990); Expert systems with Decision Support Systems by Luconi *et. al.* (1986) and many others.

2.4 *Steps*

The steps in the implementation of the proposed flexible systems methodology are as follows:

2.4.1 *Conceptualization:* The problem situation is to be conceptualized in terms of the nature of systems and people involved, and its attributes of structure, nature of outcome desired, level in the organization, clarity, uncertainty, data availability, functional area, situation specific characteristics, etc.

2.4.2 *Fuzzy Clustering:* In terms of nature of systems and people involved in the problem situations and in view of their attributes, the problem situations as well as the systems based techniques need to be clustered in a fuzzy manner. That is, a problem situation as well as a technique will have a membership function in different possible clusters. Different alternative clustering approaches can be used. One useful way available with the literature is of Total Systems Intervention (Flood and Jackson, 1991). This can be converted into "Fuzzy Total Systems Intervention" as in the real life it is difficult to say whether a problem situation involves systems which are either simple or complex, and the people are unitary on pluralistic. These can be treated as fuzzy sets and the fuzzy clustering of problem situations and techniques can be done. By identifying the characteristics of the problem situation the possibility of the usefulness of a set of techniques can be assessed. An expert system for this can be prepared or this can be done in a more creative manner.

2.4.3 *Matching Attributes:* The specific attributes of the problem situation in terms of structure, clarity, uncertainty, etc. can be matched with those of the systems based techniques which have been identified with comparatively high possibility.

2.4.4 *Selection:* Based on the matching of the attributes either one or a set of systems based techniques can be selected for analyzing the problem situation that can be used either in succession or in combination for different components of the problem situation. The selection can be facilitated through the use of Expert Systems, or can be practised in a creative environment.

2.4.5 *Integration:* Different schemes of integration of techniques can be adopted. some possible ones are as shown in Fig. 21.4.

- — Using techniques in succession.
- — Using different techniques for different components in the problem situation.
- — Using a both way integration of techniques.
- — Using submerging of one technique into another.
- — Using an amalgamation of techniques leading to a new technique.

2.4.6 *Implementation:* Once a suitable approach is designed in terms of proper selection and/or integration of the systems based techniques this should be implemented to model and analyze the problem situation at hand. The nature of implementation will depend upon the type of techniques finally selected.

2.4.7 *Dynamic Shift:* As the problem situations are analyzed using a particular set of systems based techniques and interventions are made, their takes place a dynamic shift in the attributes of the problem situation and so in the use of techniques required for analysis. The application of the proposed methodology can be done flexibly on the continuum of fully creative to fully computer assisted, depending upon the nature of problem situation, cognitive burden, and expertise available. The above-mentioned steps are only suggestive guidelines to design an appropriate approach. The process of selection and integration of techniques is to be adopted flexibly in the practical situations.

2.5 Strengths and Limitations

The major strengths and limitations of the proposed flexible systems methodology are as follows:

2.5.1 *Strengths*

(i) It puts together all the systems based techniques in a cohesive framework;
(ii) It complements the strengths and weaknesses of different techniques so as to use them effectively in a problem situation;
(iii) It provides a conceptual framework for the selection of appropriate methodology to analyze a problem situation in its totality;
(iv) It bridges the gap between qualitative and quantitative techniques by their suitable integration;
(v) The methodology designed to analyze a problem situation is more realistic and the assumptions in modelling are minimized;
(vi) It is flexible and can be adapted to suit any problem situation according to its requirements;
(vii) It facilitates more learning of the user about the nature of the problem situation and its conceptualization;
(viii) It resolves the paradoxes in literature about "hard versus soft systems thinking", "quantitative versus qualitative analysis", etc.;
(ix) It inbuilds more creativity in the analysis of problem situations; and
(x) It brings different schools of thought closer to each other.

2.5.2 *Limitations*

(i) It requires for the user to have the knowledge of the whole spectrum of systems based techniques, thus calling for higher level of expertise;
(ii) It demands time and resources for the selection of appropriate techniques and design of the methodology;
(iii) It needs more research to be conducted to suitably interface different modelling methodologies; and
(iv) It requires more software resources to practise complementary methodologies.

The above limitations, to a great extent, can be overcome by developing a suitable "Expert System" for this purpose. A research project in this area is in progress under the supervision of the author.

3. Case Study I—Agricultural Waste Management

The flexible systems methodology is used to carry out a policy design exercise in a multilevel framework for the management of system waste in the Indian context by Sharma (1992). An overview of a national level study of management of system waste using flexible systems methodology has been presented by Sharma, Gupta, and Sushil (1993). Here a component of this study for the policy design for the management of system waste is overviewed to illustrate the flexible systems methodology. This application represents a sequential integration of systems based techniques to cater to different requirements of the policy design study.

In this section a consensus mythological study is overviewed, in which modified ideawriting was used to create a good list of simple utilization and disposal options with respect to the agricultural waste. The list was converted into a conceptual design for the utilization and disposal of agricultural waste. Options Field/Profile Methodology (Warfield, 1990) was largely used as a basis for this purpose. Finally the alternative options profiles developed were got ranked using Analytic Hierarchy Process (Saaty, 1980) and Fuzzy Set Methodology (Zadeh, 1965).

3.1 *Study Design*

The study was conducted in the following steps:

(i) Generation of a list of options for the utilization and disposal of agricultural waste.
(ii) Structuring the list into an options field.
(iii) Development of option profiles.
(iv) Weighing and ranking of alternative options profiles.

The methodologies employed in various steps are sequentially integrated as shown in Fig. 21.5.

3.2 *Generation of Options*

An open-ended questionnaire with no suggestive uses or restrictions was sent to the group so as to tap the group's creativity, infinitive knowledge and experience to the fullest extent. Sixty-five persons who had deep knowledge and long working experience in agricultural field were requested to participate in the study. Twenty persons responded, which include administrators, agricultural scientists and engineers, researchers,

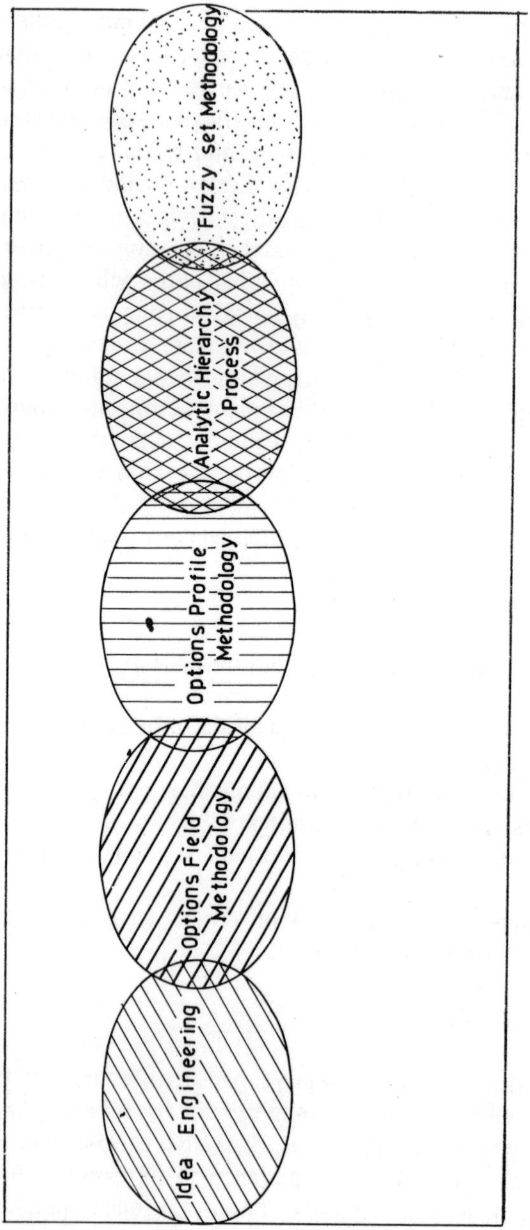

FIG. 21.5: Integration of Techniques for Case Study on Agricultural Waste Management.

farmers, etc.

A total of 286 simple uses of agricultural waste were received from the respondents. The list was collated and edited to short list exclusive uses to the extent possible, and a list of 61 almost distinct and identifiable options was compiled.

3.3 *Creation of Options Field and Profiles*

In this study the edited list of 61 simple options was manually sorted into 12 dimensions which have been named on the basis of end use. Nomenclature of dimensions provides more useful information regarding utilization and disposal.

Three generic options profiles were chosen as follows:

(i) Labour intensive, environment friendly, non-industrial use options profile;
(ii) Rural small capital, labour intensive, industrial use options profile; and
(iii) Capital intensive, labour saving, industrial use options profile.

The three options profiles are shown in Fig. 21.6.

3.4 *Ranking of Options Profiles*

The following criteria were used to evaluate the options profiles:

(i) To generate rural employment;
(ii) To protect environment;
(iii) To save energy;
(iv) To ensure health and hygiene for all;
(v) To minimize waste generation;
(vi) To replace chemical fertilizers; and
(vii) To help achieve rural industrialization.

Paired comparison of the above by Analytic Hierarchy Process (AHP) was got done by respondents to decide relative weights which should be given to each of the above criteria in any agricultural waste utilization options profile.

The options profiles were ranked using the fuzzy outranking methodology, and the position and dominance matrices were developed using optimistic, pessimistic and average aggregation. Table 21.1 gives

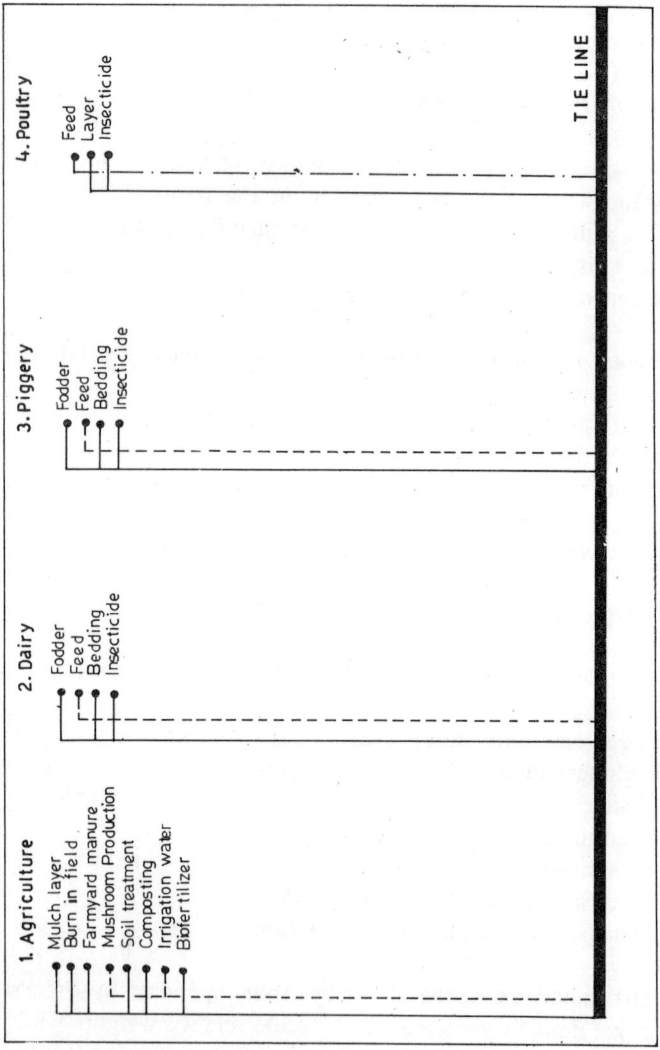

FIG. 21.6: The Three Options Profiles

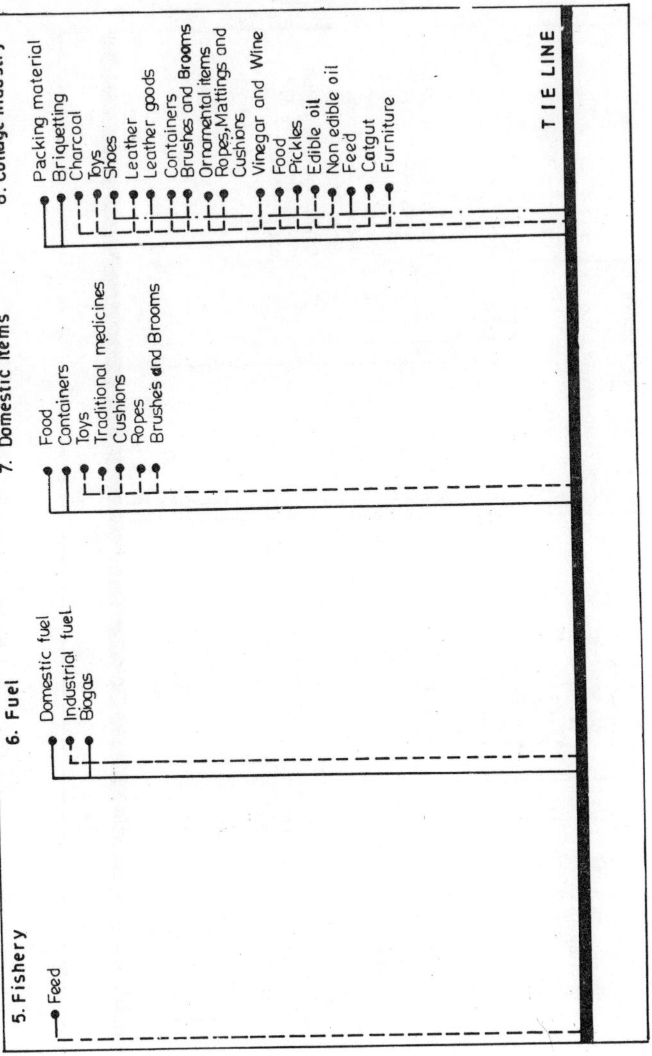

FIG. 21.6: The Three Options Profiles (Continued)

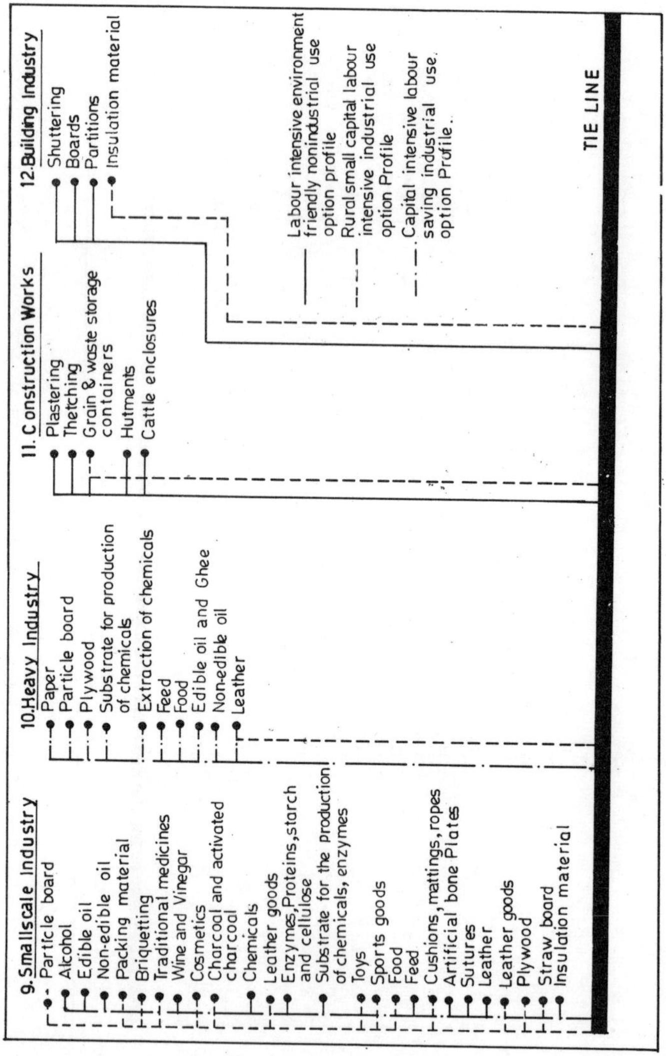

FIG. 21.6: The Three Options Profiles (Concluded)

TABLE 21.1: Ranks of Options Profiles

Profile	Scheme					
	100% Optimistic	80% Optimistic	50% Optimistic	20% Optimistic	100% Optimistic	Average Optimistic
I Labour intensive environment friendly non industrial use	1	1	1	1	2	2
II Small capital labour intensive rural industrial use	3	3	2	2	1	2
III Capital intensive heavy industrial use	2	2	3	3	3	3

the outcome of the ranking process. The ranking evolved do not change much but they show changes under pessimistic scenario which is quite true in a practical sense.

Labour intensive environment friendly non-industrial uses are judged the best in almost all alternative schemes of optimism and pessimism since it is relegated to the second rank only in completely pessimistic scheme. It is, therefore, recommended by the conceptual design that in dealing with agricultural wastes in totality the guiding principle should be to use and dispose of the waste as and where it occurs in an environmental friendly way without recourse to industrial options.

4. Case Study II — Energy Policy Analysis

A significant application of physical system theory and system dynamics has been made by Vij (1990) in the flexible systems methodological framework for energy policy analysis. An overview of the integrated implementation is presentated here.

4.1 *Model Overview*

The inherently complex and multifaceted nature of energy issues clearly implies that no single modelling methodology can describe and inter-relate all the variables of interest in the energy policy area. In this study an attempt has been made to develop a multi-level hierarchial system dynamics model by using a sectorial approach for demand management and energy conservation, and a macro-level approach for energy-economy interaction and transition dynamics.

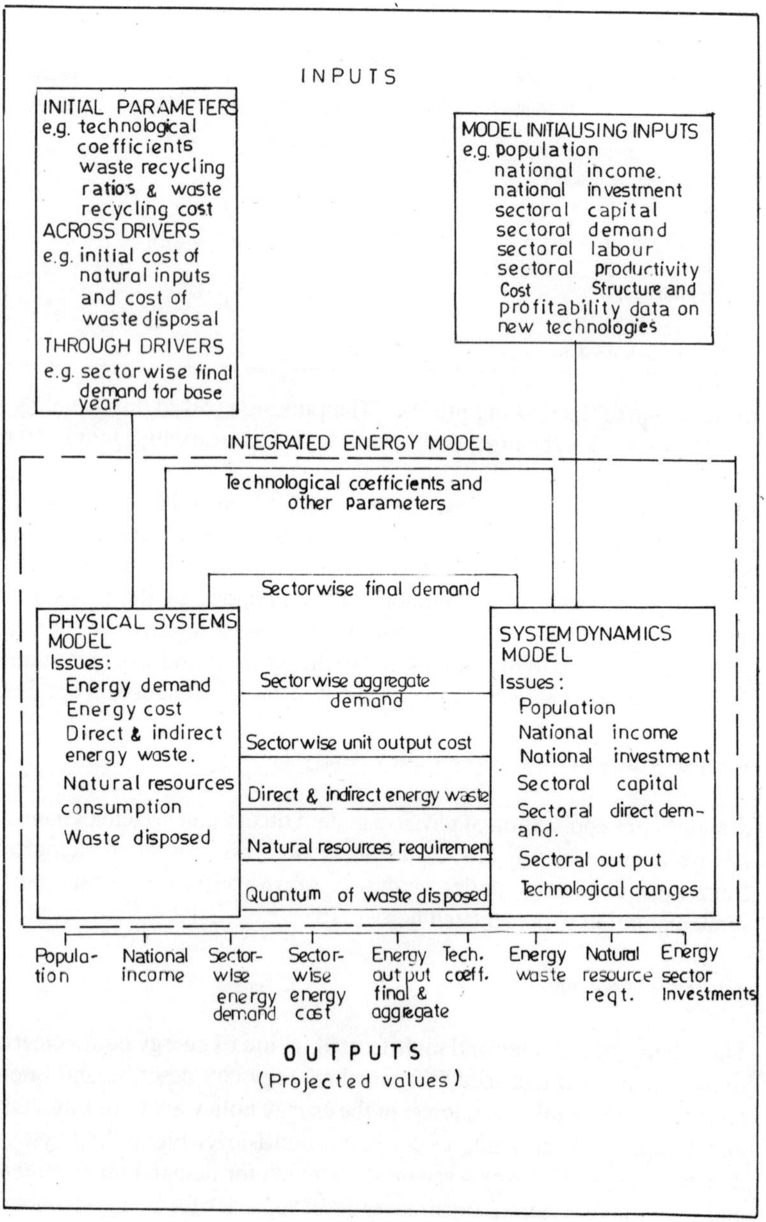

FIG. 21.7: Schematic Diagram showing Integration of the PS and SD Models

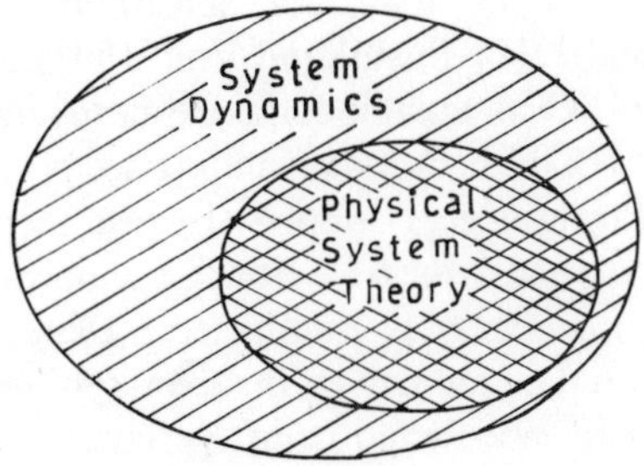

FIG. 21.8: Integration of Techniques for Case Study on Energy Policy Analysis.

Integration of the physical system (PS) and system dynamics (SD) models is shown in Figure 21.7, which is based on the submerging of the PS model in the SD model as shown in Figure 21.8. The main inputs to the PS model are sectorwise final demands, technological coefficients, waste recycling ratios, cost of waste recycling, natural inputs and wastes disposal. Initial values of these parameters and variables for a base year are fed exogenously.

SD model needs initialising inputs on population, national income, national investment, sectorial capital, sectorial demand, sectorial labour, sectorial productivity, cost structure and profitability data on new technologies. In addition to other outputs it generates the sectorwise final demands and the technological coefficients. These data are fed to the PS model to get the values of sectorwise aggregate demands and other outputs at each time interval.

The integrated model generates the yearwise projected values of the following: population, national income, sectorwise final and aggregate energy demands, energy cost, energy investments, technological coefficients, direct and indirect energy wastes and natural resources requirement.

4.2 *Policy Implications*

The integrated energy model developed and tested in this study may be used for policy analysis and planning in the following areas:

Energy demand and supply balance: Sensitivity analysis runs of the integrated energy model (Vij, Sushil and Vrat, 1993) show that macro-economic parameters like national income are more sensitive to demand management policies in the energy-consuming sectors than the policies aimed only at increasing energy supply. In case the effect of energy constraints can be restricted to the final flow, i.e. supply to the household, the national income is relatively unaffected. Demand management through improved material productivity in the energy-consuming sectors, coupled with increased labour and capital productivity of the energy supply sectors may have a significant impact on the overall growth of the economy.

Resource allocation: Model results show that higher priorities in investment to energy sectors do not lead to a significant increase in the national income. On the other hand, such sectorial priorities may be at the cost of investment in other production sectors. This could mean a deceleration in the growth of those production sectors where lower priorities are assigned. It is imperative to link the sectorial priorities to the basic needs of the people.

Energy conservation: Sensitivity analysis shows that energy conservation has a significant relevance for the developing economies. The impact of waste on the natural resource requirements warrants a serious consideration and should be an important policy parameter in the national energy planning.

Construction delays and lead times: Sensitivity runs show that reduction of construction and lead times of energy projects leads to a faster capital formation in the energy sectors, and consequently an increased energy output. However, the increased energy supply should be accompanied by a productivity increase in other production sectors where energy is one of the inputs.

Energy cost: Energy cost shows a higher sensitivity to the material productivity changes than the natural resources prices. Waste in the energy-consuming sectors has more crucial effect on the cost of energy output.

5. Concluding Observations

The analysis and design of public policy requires a methodological support that can cater to its varied requirements. Flexible systems methodology provides a comprehensive framework for using existing systems based techniques in an integrative manner to suit the need of different policy design situations. The methodology either can be applied at a fully creative level or some support can be provided to reduce the burden on the user by designing suitable expert systems for this purpose. Two case studies on agricultural waste management and energy policy analysis have illustrated the utility of such an integrative paradigm. Some more applications have been tried out at I.I.T., Delhi, and the response is very encouraging. However, this can at best be treated as a good beginning point for using the existing systems based techniques in a more pragmatic manner for policy analysis and design.

REFERENCES

Bertalanffy, L, Von (1972) 'History and status of general system theory'. In Klir, G.J. (ed), *Trends in General System Theory,* John Wiley & .Sons, Inc., New York. 21-38.

Bora, M.C. (1981) *A System Dynamics Study on Policy Design for Price Stabilization and Long Term Growth of Indian Tea Industry.* Ph.D. Thesis, IIT, Kharagpur.

Boulding, K.L. (1956), 'General Systems Theory - The Skeleton of Science', *Management Science,* 2,193-199, Reprinted in General Systems, 1,11-17.

Checkland, P.B. (1981a) 'Rethinking a Systems Approach', *Journal of Applied Systems Analysis,* 8, 3-14.

Checkland, P. (1981b) *System Thinking, Systems Practice,* John Wiley & Sons, New York.

Flood, R.L., and Jackson, M. (1991) *Creative Problem Solving: Total System Intervention,* John Wiley & Sons, NY.

Forrester, J.W. (1961) *Industrial Dynamics,* MIT Press, Cambridge, Massachusetts.

Godet, M. (1987) *Scenarios and Strategic Management,* Butterworths, New York.

Klir, G.J. (1969) *An Approach to General Systems Theory.* Van Nostrand Reinhold Co., New York.

Koenig, H.E., Tokad, Y., and Kesavan, H.K (1967) *Analysis of Discrete Physical Systems,* McGraw-Hill, NY.

Kumar, S., and Satsangi, P.S. (1993) 'System Dynamics Simulation of Physical Systems with Application to Hopfield Neural Networks', In Sushil (ed), *System Dynamics for Management Support,* Wiley Eastern Ltd., New Delhi.

Luconie, F.L. Malone, T.W., and Scott Morton, M.S., (1986) 'Expert Systems: Next Challenge for Managers', *Sloan Management Review Summer,* 3-13.

Luthans, F., and Steward, T.I.,(1977) 'A General Contingency Theory of Management', *Academy of Management Review,* April, 181-194.

Pankaj (1992) *'On Designing Expert Support Systems Using System Dynamics and Fuzzy Sets'*, Ph.D. Thesis, IIT Delhi.

Pankaj, Seth, K. and Sushil (1993) 'A fuzzy set theoretic Approach to Qualitative Analysis of Causal Loops in System Dynamics'; *European Journal of Operational Research*, Forthcoming.

Saaty, T.L. (1980) *The Analytic Hierarchy Process*, McGraw-Hill, New York.

Saxena, J.P., Sushil and Vrat, P. (1990) 'Impact of Indirect Relationships in Classification of Variables: A MICMAC Analysis for Energy Conservation', *Systems Research*, 7 (4), 245-253.

Sharma, H.D., (1992) *A Multilevel Futures Research Study of Management of System Waste in India*, Ph.D. Thesis, I.I.T. Delhi.

Sharma, H.D., Gupta, A.D. and Sushil (1993) 'System Waste in Socio-Technical Systems: Overview of a National Study'. In A. Ghosal and P.N. Murthy (eds.) *Recent Advances in Cybernetics and Systems*, Tata McGraw-Hill Pub. Co., N. Delhi, 131-139.

Singh, N., and Sushil (1990) 'Technology Selection Models for Multistage Production Systems: Joint Application of Physical System Theory and Mathematical Programming', *European Journal of Operational Research*, 47, 248-261.

Sushil (1993) 'Flexible Systems Methodology', *Key Note Address Presented at Ninth International Congress of Cybernetics and Systems*, January 18-23, N. Delhi, also Invited by Systems Practice.

Troncale, L. (1988) 'The Systems Sciences : What are they? Are They One, or Many?', *European Journal of Operational Research*, 37, 8-33.

Vij, A.K. (1990) *Energy Policy Modelling and Analysis for the Indian Economy*, Ph.D. Thesis, I.I.T., Delhi.

Vij, A.K., Vrat. P, and Sushil (1988) 'Energy Modelling Through Integration of System Dynamics with Physical System Theory', *System Dynamics: An International Journal of Policy Modelling*, 1(1),1-9.

Vij, A.K., Sushil and Vrat, P. (1993) 'Energy Policy Analysis for the Indian Economy Through Integration of System Dynamics with Physical System Theory'. In Sushil (ed.) *System Dynamics for Management Support*, Wiley Eastern Ltd., N. Delhi, 371-383.

Vizayakumar, K. (1990) *A Study on Some Aspects of Environmental Impact Analysis*, Ph.D. Thesis, I.I.T., Kharagpur.

Warfield, J.N. (1990) *A Science of Generic Design: Managing Complexity Through Systems Design* Vol I & II, Inter Systems Publication, USA.

Zadeh, L.A. (1965) 'Fuzzy sets', *Information and Control*, 8, 338-353.

22. GUIDELINES FOR POLICY ON VOCATIONAL TRAINING IN ADVANCED TECHNOLOGY

S.K. Batra

1. Introduction

There has been a sharp increase in the application of advanced technology (AT) in the manufacturing and service industries of various countries in the recent years. Consequently the need for human resources development to meet the new challenges passed by AT applications has increased manifolds. Specifically, it has become increasingly important to strengthen the AT training capabilities in various countries, so that they do not lag behind in utilising the advantages offered by AT. Merely because the personnel engaged in the manufacturing and service industries have not been able to update their knowledge and skills and keep pace with the demands of AT.

It has been increasingly felt that one reason for a gap between the needs and actual availability of AT training in various countries is the lack of a policy document. Activities related to AT training can always take place even in absence of any policy documents. However, if these activities are guided by a well defended policy document, which clearly defines the direction in which advanced technology training should move, then the overall effectiveness of such a training for the country, as a whole, can significantly increase. A policy document can help minimise counter-productive, conflicting and redundant efforts by different types of institutions engaged in AT training and can help enhance the synergy of such efforts.

The Experts Group Meeting convened by APSDEP at Phuket, Thailand in August 1991 discussed at great length, the issue of formulating a policy document on AT training for the member countries. It has recognised by the group that owing to socio-political, economic and cultural differences amongst various countries, it is not practicable to design a single policy document applicable to all countries. However, it is possible to formulate broad policy guidelines which can be used to develop country specific policy documents. These policy guidelines serve the purpose of outlining a range of desirable features, which the country specific documents should attempt to incorporate.

The Experts Group proposed a set of policy guidelines for AT training which could be adapted to the specific needs and circumstances of individual countries. A sample policy document for XYZ country based on these policy guidelines was also proposed.

The high-level seminar convened by ILO/APSDEP/JAPAN at Chiba, Japan in October 1991 considered the above policy guidelines and the sample policy document for XYZ country. After discussions, the participants of the seminar accepted the policy guidelines and the sample policy document with certain amendments.

The revised policy guidelines based on the changes suggested by the High Level Seminar have been presented in the following paragraphs. The revised sample policy document for XYZ country is placed at Annexure.

2. Objectives of Policy Guidelines

The policy aim at achieving the following objectives:

a) to provide a basic framework within which all activities related to AT training will be carried out.
b) to establish a reference for planning and co-ordination of all activities related to AT training.
c) to facilitate autonomous action by all concerned within limits defined by policy guidelines.

3. Characteristics of Policy

For a policy document to have long-term perspective, it is essential that it possesses certain key characteristics, which make the AT training system viable. Some of these characteristics are as follows:

a) The policy should not be static but should be periodically updated.
b) It should have features which promote rather than inhibit growth of AT training.
c) It should be outward looking, feedforward based and not merely feedback based.

d) It should be consistent with the wider policy framework of the country, such as the policies related to economic development, industrial growth, technology development and induction, employment and vocational training, in general.

e) It may or may not have a legislative support.

4. Components of Advanced Technology Training System

The following key components of the AT training system have been identified:

a) Institutional framework
b) Resources
c) Co-ordination and Desired Interactions
d) Monitoring and Control
e) Quality
f) R&D and Innovation

The suggested guidelines for each of the above components have been discussed below.

4.1 *Institutional Framework*

Typically, the institutional framework for at training in any country comprises of the following:

— National Training Authorities
— Other concerned departments in the national Government, such as industry, employment, technology, human resources, etc.
— State/provincial Governments
— Enterprises providing enterprise based training
— External training institutions providing AT training
— Employers organisations
— Workers organisations
— Any other agencies, which may be identified by the country

It is important that all the agencies in the country, whose activities have some bearing on AT training, should be identified. This will help in ensuring that all facets of the AT training system are represented in the policy framework.

4.2 *Resources*

The national training authority should ensure that all the requisite resources are identified, obtained, allocated and utilised for AT training related activities in the country. Some of these resources include:

- Training Infrastructure
- Training Personnel
- Training Equipment
- Technical support from international funding agencies
- Financial resources for meeting the costs of AT training

In view of the fact that resources are invariably limited, it is important that appropriate criteria for setting the priorities are pre-determined and applied. As far as possible, financial resources should be generated within the AT training system. Wherever financial assistance and technical support is sought from international agencies, it should be ensured that the request and utilisation of such resources is in accordance with the national priorities and not necessarily in accordance with the preferences of the funding agencies.

4.3 *Co-ordination and Interactions*

For the AT training system to operate smoothly, formal interactive mechanisms should be provided for and made use of by all concerned. These interactions will help the concerned institutions in dovetailing each other's activities and avoid gaps and redundancies. They will also help in providing extension and propagation services related to AT. It is suggested that formal interactive mechanisms should be specified for the following:

- Apex level participation of all Government authorities identified in the institutional framework, as well as employers' organisations and workers' organisations
- Interaction between the national training authorities and the corresponding state/provincial Government departments
- Interactions between enterprises and external training institutions
- Interactions amongst enterprises in the same industry/industries using similar advanced technologies
- Interactions amongst external training institutions

— Interactions of the enterprises and external training institutions with educational and research institutions concerned with the same or similar AT areas.

The formal interactive mechanisms should also be supported by informal modes of interaction to enable gaining additional insight into problems/concerns, if any.

4.4 *Monitoring and Control*

The policy document should aim at setting up monitoring and control systems which help in taking corrective actions in case the activities of various agencies signal some deviations from the stated policy or in case the pace of their activities is not as fast as it is desired to be. However, monitoring and control should not lead to undue interference in the day to day functioning of these agencies. Further, it is also stipulated that the monitoring and control functions are carried out at different levels in the AT training system. Some of these levels may be the following:

— Heads of the external training institutions
— Managers of enterprise-based training
— Top managements of enterprises
— Industry associations
— Employers' organisations
— Workers' organisations

The apex level agency for monitoring and control, of course, is the national training authority.

4.5 *Quality*

It is necessary to establish, disseminate, use and update standards for various aspects of advanced technology training. Some of the areas for which standards/norms can be established, include the following:

— Faculty-trainee ratio
— Training infrastructure
— Eligibility and selection criteria for admission to the training institutions
— Delivery of training
— Evaluation criteria

— Effectiveness of training

These standards/norms should be in accordance with international standards, wherever applicable. Further, they should be consistent in similar fields with in the country. To ensure conformity with international standards and internal consistency, they should benevetted by the national training authority.

4.6 *R&D and Evaluation*

Since the policy for AT training can not remain isolated from the dynamic interactions taking place in the society at large and in the industry in particular, it is necessary to have continual R&D in areas on which AT has an impact, and use the results of such R&D efforts to evaluate and update the policy. Some of the suggested areas for R&D in this context are as follows:

- Continual exploration of the frontier areas of AT to make a realistic assessment of the anticipated technologies
- Effectiveness of training methodologies
- Macro and micro level studies related to the impact of AT applications on factors such as productivity, employment, labour market, salary structure, career paths and quality of life etc.

Each country will have to identify its own priority areas for research, depending upon the socio-economic and development issues confronting it. Further, each country will need to define its own time frame for trying out a given policy for relevance and effectiveness and for making structural changes in the same, if required.

5. Other Relevant Factors

The above components are the key components of a typical policy document. However, it is desirable to incorporate the following additional features to make the document more meaningful:

a) Background to the Policy
b) Objectives of the Policy
c) Definitions
d) Philosophy
e) Strategies

f) Linkages with other policies in related areas
g) Conformity with international forms/conventions.

It should also be ensured that legislative support, levies, obligations, restrictions, concessions, incentives, preferences and subsidies etc. are specifically and explicitly covered under appropriate headings, if provided for as a part of the policy framework of the country.

6. Conclusion

The guidelines provided in this document are intended to provide some kind of a check list, using which country-specific policy documents can be designed by each country. The policy documents emerging with such an approach are expected to have the features of conformity with international norms, as well as adaptability to unique requirements of the country.

PROPOSED POLICY ON VOCATIONAL TRAINING FOR ADVANCED TECHNOLOGY IN XYZ COUNTRY

1. Introduction

This document outlines the proposed policy on vocational training for advanced technology (AT) in XYZ country. Key components of the policy include institutional framework, resources, co-ordination and desired interactions, monitoring and control, quality, R&D and evaluation.

2. Institutional Framework

The institutional framework for institutional training for advanced technology will include the following institutions/agencies:

a) ***Apex Government Authority (AGA)***

The overall responsibility for policy-making, planning and Co-ordination of AT training in the country will lie with AGA.

b) ***Advisory Board***

AGA will be guided by an Advisory Board comprising representatives of the Government, employers organisations and workers organisations.

This Board will have an advisory role and will examine all aspects relating to vocational and advanced technology training.

The Ministry of Human Resources Development, Ministry of Finance, Ministry of Planning, Department of Electronics, Directorate General of Technology Development, Technology Information Forecasting and Assessment Council, Department of Industry (and any other concerned departments) will be represented in the above board.

c) *State Governments*

The State Government (Appropriate Department) will be responsible for implementation of training policy for advanced technology in their respective states.

d) *Training Institutions*

Training for advanced technology will be provided by a network of Government and private training institutions. Besides, the enterprises will also provide AT training in several areas, specific to their own requirements and not catered to by external training institutions.

The Government run training institutions for advanced technology include, amongst others, the following:

(i) Industrial Training Institutes (ITI's) for craftsmen training.
(ii) Advanced Training Institutes for providing training under Advanced Technology Training Scheme.
(iii) Advanced Training Institutes for electronics and process instrumentation for providing advanced courses in the field of electronics and process instrumentation.
(iv) National Vocational Training Institutes for Woman for providing training in basic and advanced skills to women.
(v) Model ITIs for organising craftsmen training programmes on modular basis.
(vi) Foremen Training Institute for meeting the training requirements of industry at lower or middle levels of management.
(vii) Central Staff Training Institute for carrying out staff training and R&D in concerned areas.

e) *Employers' Organisations*

These will be responsible for representing the views and interest of the employers at various state, national and international forums for AT training.

f) ***Workers' Organisations***

These will be responsible for presenting the views and interest of the workers at various state, national and international forums and at the level of enterprises for AT training.

g) ***Other Government Departments***

For providing more focussed attention on several areas of AT training, other Government departments will have a specific role. These include, amongst others,

(i) Department of Electronics, for providing training in computer hardware and software

(ii) Ministry of Human Resources Development for Vocational Education under the New Education Policy and implementation of the Apprenticeship Act for engineering degree and diploma holders.

3. Resources

a) AGA will play a catalytic role in ensuring that appropriate and adequate finances are provided to various institutions identified above for meeting the needs of AT training.

b) AGA will interact with International Funding Agencies to obtain requisite technical assistance and financial support for strengthening AT training capabilities in the country, both in enterprises and external training institutions.

c) AGA will keep a track of training resources available with various institutions (including enterprises) engaged in AT training. These include amongst other training equipment, training infrastructure, training faculty and delivery systems for training. For this purpose, AGA may set up and maintain a comprehensive data base on training resources.

4. Co-ordination and Interactions

a) AGA will ensure that the advisory board meets at least on a quarterly basis to keep a track of problems and lacunae in AT training.

b) AGA will also prescribe modes of formal interaction on a regular basis between enterprises and external training institutions and amongst external training institutions.

c) AGA will also maintain continual liaison and interactions with international funding agencies for monitoring and promoting availability of technical assistance from them for AT training.

d) The training institutions will be responsible for planning their activities in line with the market demands and will continually interact with the industry to identify specific measures using which they can provide relevant training services to the enterprises.

e) AGA will organise seminars and workshops on AT training for various industries on a regular basis. It will promote exchange programmes between enterprises and training institutions, including promotion of the concept of adoption of training institutions by enterprises.

f) AGA will promote greater participation of the representatives of employers organisations and workers organisations in planning and review of various activities related to AT training.

5. Monitoring and Control

a) AGA will monitor the performance of training institutions (including enterprise based training) and suggest corrective actions to the concerned heads of such institutions. For this purpose, it may prescribe periodic reports/returns from training institutions and enterprises engaged in AT training.

b) AGA will undertake field visits on a selective basis to obtain in-depth information on the status of AT induction and adequacy of training system for the same.

c) AGA will introduce a comprehensive management information system to facilitate planning and control of AT training. It will maintain computerised data bases on industry wise employment status, output of universities and vocational education institutions, supply of trained manpower from training institutions, technology changes, anticipated demand for trained manpower and current and projected status on availability of AT training. These data banks will be continually updated.

d) AGA will develop appropriate system for monitoring the employment and occupation status of pass-outs from training institutions.

e) AGA will monitor the process of regular annual review and updating of training curricula and training packages by the training institutions and the enterprises.

f) AGA will review the effectiveness of various training programmes being conducted by developing appropriate performance indicators.

6. Quality of AT Training

In order to ensure that a high quality of AT Training is consistently maintained. AGA will play a catalytic role in establishment of requisite standards and norms for various aspects of AT Training. Some of these aspects are:

a) Faculty-trainee ratios for various types of AT Training
b) Specifications of training infrastructure required
c) Qualifications of faculty members
d) Availability of training equipment and other physical resources
e) Admission and evaluation of potential/current trainees
f) Delivery of AT training

These standards and norms will need to be set up by appropriate expert groups, keeping into consideration international norms, industry norms or any other bench marks and the local conditions.

7. R&D and Evaluation

a) AGA will continually identify sectors/areas in which there is a substantial demand for AT training but which are currently not supported by training institutions or enterprises.

b) AGA will undertake periodic industry-wide surveys to assess the changes taking place in employment patterns, occupational profiles and job descriptions.

c) AGA will arrange to carry out research studies on the impact of financial support provided by international funding agencies on the institutional capabilities of the beneficiaries of AT training.

d) AGA will arrange to conduct studies for developing innovative methods to create awareness about the benefits of AT training and increasing the involvement of employers and workers organisations.

e) R&D shall be organised with the active participation of beneficiaries and other social partners of the community.

f) This policy will be evaluated every five years to reassess its relevance in providing a conducive framework for promoting AT training in the country. The evaluation will be carried out by an independent objective agency.

REFERENCES

Beer, Stafford, (1979) *The Heart of Enterprise,* John Wiley London.

Jamal-ul Din (Ed), (1992) *New Perspectives in Vocational Training for Advanced Technology,* International Labour Organisation (ILO), Asian and Pacific Skill Development Programme (APSDEP), Bangkok, Thailand.

APSDEP/ILO, 1-9 October, (1991) *Proceedings of the High-Level Seminar on Advanced Technology Training,* held at Chiba, Japan.

Batra, S.K., 16-22 September, (1992) *Policy Issues in Apprenticeship System,* a paper presented at the Regional Workshop on Trainers/Instructors Training conducted by APSDEP/ILO at Chiba, Japan.

Batra, S.K., 1-9 October, (1991) *Policy Guidelines for Advanced Technology Training,* a paper presented at High Level Seminar on Advanced Technology Training, conducted by APSDEP/ILO at Chiba, Japan.

Batra, S.K., 19-23 August, (1991) *Policy Guidelines on Vocational Training for Advanced Technology,* a paper presented at the Experts Group Meeting, convened by APSDEP/ILO at Phuket Thailand.

23. ANALYSIS OF OPTIONS FOR ENERGY CONSERVATION POLICY IN INDIAN CEMENT INDUSTRY

J.P. Saxena

1. Introduction

The success of any programme such as the one on energy conservation greatly depends upon correct identification of various program plan sub-elements, specially the objectives and consequently evolving appropriate policy options to fulfil those objectives. In a large system, different options may relate to different areas. In some cases one option may related to one or even more than one area. Thus, these options must come from the think tank of the system involving various experts related to different areas, each associated with one objective or even more objectives out of the various objectives of the programme plan. Unification of the diversified options associated with various experts is essential for evolving an integrated policy. The options of the policy, therefore, must have linkages with one or more programme plan objective. Based on the options finalised, activities are identified and scheduled.

The options, therefore, revolve around objectives, and their importance can be decided by using certain features having linkages with the objective measures and the activity measures of the programme plan.

Given various options, the decision maker faces the problem of making up his mind for choosing the one or more than one option from the various options available to him. The considerations in arriving at a decision may be related to technological, political, economical and social factors or a combination of these factors. Evolving policy for achieving the objectives, therefore constitutes multi-criteria decision making. The policy formulation for energy conservation in an industrial sector depends on many considerations, such as: the present technological status, new developments, quality of inputs like coal and raw materials; availability of power, transportation facilities, manpower, managerial skills, financial resources, the product, the market dynamics, government regulations and the local factors.

2. Methodology for Development of Policy

The aim of a systematic methodology for development of policy is to reduce subjectivity and bring in objectivity as much as possible. Identification of options for achieving the desired objectives in itself is the most difficult and important task. Policy formulation is the process of generating a framework of preferences of options for the given objectives. It needs prioritisation amongst various options available. Options are to be evaluated, based on certain criteria or features. Delphi methodology can be used to identify features and options, including deciding on the weightages to each one for selecting important features and options for further detailed analysis.

The Analytic Hierarchy Process (AHP) (Harker, 1987) is used for an indepth study to decide on the weightages attached to each feature selected through the Delphi exercise. Thus the Delphi method is used for identifying the important features and AHP technique is used for deciding the weightages of each feature. Integration of the Delphi exercise and the AHP is known as Delphic Hierarchy Process (DHP) (Khorramshahgol and Moustakis, 1988; Rodekohr, 1981). Fuzzy Set Methodology (FSM) (Bellman and Zadeh, 1970) is a useful multi-criteria decision making technique for systematic analysis of the importance of the various policy options and determining their ranks. However, the features and their weightage as found out from DHP are used for identifying and ranking of the options. Thus the proposed methodology DHP-FSM (Fig. 23.1 for policy formulations is a combination of Delphi methodology, Analytic Hierarchy Process and Fuzzy Set methodology.

2.1 Delphic Hierarchy Process

2.1.1 *Delphi Method:* Delphi methodology is a systematic method for obtaining the experts' views on a subject. According to Dalkey, (1969), three features of the Delphi methodology are (i) anonymity, (ii) controlled feedback, and (iii) statistical group response. The exercise is monitored by a monitor team, which formulates a note bringing out the relevant information on the subject matter. The monitor team prepares a questionnaire for obtaining response of the experts engaged in different but related activities to the subject. The experts, though they may be physically located far away, contribute to the issues under consideration

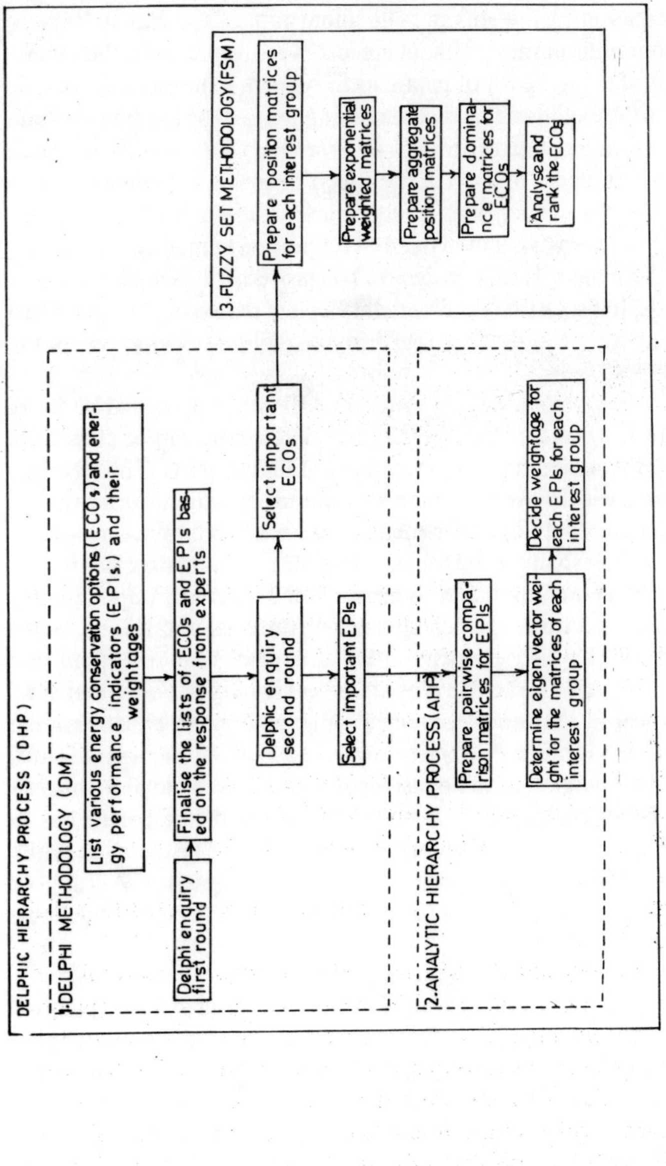

FIG. 23.1: Schematic Diagram of Delphi Hierachy Process and Fuzzy Set Methodology (DHP-FSM)

by providing their valuable opinions through questionnaire. The important aspect of this technique is that each expert has enough time to give their considered views on the subject without being influenced by others who are participating in the survey. The anonymity of the expert helps in bringing out frank opinion without the fear of being quoted for their views or the fear of being heard in public as in seminars and workshops. The response of the experts when received are aggregated by the monitor team using statistical methods of analysis. The monitor team gives the feedback of the group response to each of the expert to enable them to know how others feel on the subject. This feedback helps the experts to review their stand already taken by them in the first round, and to modify their earlier stand on the subject, if they so desire. The process is repeated in three or four rounds. It is seen that the divergent views of the experts narrow down and at the end of the third or fourth round, consensus emerges on the various issues.

2.1.2 *Analytic Hierarchy Process:* AHP was introduced by Saaty (1980) and is based on the idea that a complex issue can be effectively examined if it is hierarchically decomposed into its parts. The elements are compared with each other thus providing an opportunity for a pairwise comparison for evolving the structure into *n* x *n* reciprocal judgment matrix (Khorramshahgol and Moustakis, 1981). In the matrix, one begins with an element on the left and compares how much more important it is than an element on top. when compared with itself, the ratio is one. When compared with another element, either it is more important than that element (then an integer value is used), or less important and in that case, the reciprocal of the previous integer value is used. In either case the reciprocal ratio is entered in the transpose position of the matrix. Thus, only *n* (*n*-1)/2 judgments are considered where n is the total number of elements being compared. It is to be noted that the respondent is to concentrate on only two elements at a time under consideration while giving his judgment in the box on their pairwise comparison. A scale 1 to 9 is used for giving judgment value according to the following guidelines:

a *(ij)* = 1 if *i* and *j* are equally important
= 3 if *i* is weekly more important element as compared to *j*.
= 5 if *i* is strongly more important element as compared to *j*.
= 7 if *i* is very strongly more important element as compared to *j*.
= 9 if *i* is absolutely more important element as compared to *j*.
= 2,4,6,8 used to compromise between two judgments.
= Reciprocals of above non-zero numbers, if an element has one

of the above numbers (e.g. 3) compared with a second activity has the reciprocal value (e.g. 1/3) when compared with the first.

The weightages of the features are obtained by calculating the Eigen Vector Weights for the judgments matrix.

An index of consistency is calculated to provide information on how serious are violations of numerical and transitive consistency. The result could be used to seek additional information and re-examine the data used in constructing the scale in order to improve consistency. The Consistency Index (C.I) is obtained by CI= (λ max-n)/(n-1) where n is the number of elements being compared and λ max is the largest eigen value of the judgment matrix. For a reciprocal matrix λ max- $\geqslant$ always. Dividing C.I. by the random consistency number for the same size matrix, the consistency ratio CR is obtained. The value of CR should be around 10 per cent or less to be acceptable. In some cases, 20 per cent may be toterated but never more. If the CR is not within this range, the participants should study the problem and revise their judgment. The average consistencies for different order random matrices are given below:

Size of Matrix	1	2	3	4	5	6	7	8	9	10
Random Consistency	0	0	0.58	0.9	1.12	1.24	1.32	1.41	1.45	1.49

2.2 Fuzzy Set Methodology

The Fuzzy set methodology (Bellman and Zadeh, 1970; Zadeh, 1965) for multi-criteria decision making is used to analyse various options. The fuzzy set techniques (Alley *et al.*, 1978; Jain, 1976) are designed such that quantitative and non-quantitative factors, and the view points of the interest groups can be readily incorporated into the decision-making process. Ranks of the options are achieved through a dominance matrix designed for the purpose.

In order to represent the views of each of the interest group, a position matrix is prepared from the response of all the experts in the group by giving the values to the qualitative assessment. The average value of each element is worked out representing the group response. By raising the membership values to the power of the assigned weight, i.e., the eigen vector weight, some of the biases in the matrix can be eliminated. The weighted matrices for each of the interest groups are then prepared. The most useful aggregation of the interest group are then prepared. The most useful aggregation of the various matrices is the pessimistic aggregation.

This results in a matrix of 'worst-case' membership values and is the intersection operation. Some use the optimistic aggregation, which is the union operation and some other use 'mean aggregation' which is an averaging calculation. For this purpose, the values assigned for each feature by each group relating to each option are tabulated. The highest value among the various group responses represents the optimistic value, the lowest value represents the pessimistic value and the average of all the values represent the mean value. Taking these values, three separately weighted position matrices, the optimistic weighted position matrix, the pessimistic weighted position matrix and the mean weighted position matrix are prepared.

An n x n matrix 'D' called dominance matrix is prepared to display the dominance structure between all possible pairs of options. The element d_{ij} is the number of features for which membership value of option j dominates or is greater than option i. A dash is entered for the diagonal d_{ij} elements. If the Kth column is summed, the total number of dominances of option K over all other options is obtained. Similarly, if the Kth row is summed, the number of times the Kth option is being dominated by all the other options is determined. More favourable outcomes have higher column sums and lower row totals. In cases where an option is very close to another option on the basis of aggregation weighted position matrix, the dominance among the options exist only if the membership value of the second option is outside the specified limit. The options can be considered equivalent with respect to that feature. This range may be set for each problem (for example + 5 per cent of the membership value) but should not be too large, otherwise a lot of information is likely to be lost. As in the case of weighted position matrices, three dominance matrices: optimistic dominance matrix, pessimistic dominance matrix and mean dominance matrix: are prepared. The ranks of the options is normally decided by examining the ranks obtained from the extent of dominance and also the extent of being dominated by other options.

One could adopt any of the alternatives of dominance, i.e. pessimistic, the safest course of action; the optimistic, the most wanted course of action and the mean, the middle course of action. Each course of action has points both in favour and against. While one could like to adopt the optimistic course of action, the approach may be far from reality. In real life situation, the top management do take decisions based on their understanding of the situation and their own judgment which may be different from any of the courses of action determined from mathematical exercises. The best course of action for the decision-maker in such a situation may be to use the Hadley Criterion of 'cautious' optimism (Hadley, 1967)'. The decision-maker may choose different coefficient of optimism (α). If A is the dominance weight of the option as determined from optimistic dominance matrix and B the dominance weight of the option as determined from the pessimistic dominance matrix, the weight of the option according the Hadley criterion is determined by the relationship:

$$W = \alpha A + (1-\alpha) B$$

The ranks of the option are then determined on the basis of the weights thus obtained form Hadley Criterion. Since the process of choosing the co-efficient of optimism (α) in the Hadley Criterion of 'cautious optimism' is a judgment based approach, the ranks of the options from the dominance matrix is considered on the basis of dominance and ignoring the considerations of being dominated.

A sensitivity analysis is made by taking different values of α and considering different alternatives. Sensitivity analysis provides various schemes for the hierarchy of options. The most appealing scheme is selected and referred to the experts for a feedback. The scheme is adopted as a policy framework if the experts agree with it or have no serious objections.

3. The Case of the Indian Cement Industry—Energy Conservation Policy

The proposed methodology—The Delphic Hierarchy Process and Fuzzy Set Methodology (DHP-FSM)—has been used to decide on the ranks of the options, adoption of which will result in reduction of energy consumption in the Indian Cement Industry. The steps adopted are:

i. *Identification of Energy Conservation Options and Energy Performance Indicators using Delphi*

To begin with, the monitor team identified twenty one Energy Conservation Options (ECOs) keeping in view the objectives of program plan. Fourteen features called Energy Performance Indicators (EPIs) were separately identified by keeping in view the objective measures and activities measures of the program plan. 34 experts were identified from the following six interest groups:

(i) Cement Producers
(ii) Cement Machinery Manufacturers

(iii) Research Institutes.
(iv) Consultants
(v) Technological Institutes
(vi) Government Departments.

The questionnaires were sent to them alongwith a status note on the subject. The experts were given two questionnaires : first for the Energy Conservation Options (ECOs):and second for the Energy Performance Indicators (EPI's) with a choice to delete or modify any of the ECO's and EPI's listed in the questionnaires or to add any new ECO and EPI as they consider appropriate. The experts were also requested to give weightage to each of the ECOs and EPIs using a scale 0-10. The ECO's and EPI's considered to be the most important were to be assigned 10 points and other were to be judged accordingly and given appropriate weightage. The response from the first round of the survey indicated that the experts took a keen interest and added a good number of ECOs and EPIs.

The maximum, minimum and average weightages of the responses were worked out as related to each ECO and EPI and a revised list of 30 ECOs (Table 23.1) and 22 EPIs (Table 23.2) with their maximum, minimum and average weightages were sent to the experts. The responses as given by each expert to the questionnaires in the first round of the Delphi exercise were also indicated to provide them with the opportunity of comparing their won response with that of the group response. The experts were free to retain or modify the ECOs and EPIs including the weightages given by them, as they desired. The responses received from the second round of Delphi exercise indicated that all the ECOs (Table 23.1) and EPIs (Table 23.2) as finalised after the first round of Delphi survey were retained by the experts. Five (20%) experts retained their earlier response as given in the first round of Delphi survey. According to importance of the ECOs and EPIs, first twenty ECOs and fourteen EPIs are selected for detailed analysis.

ii. *Determination of Eigen Vector Weight*

The monitor team conducted another Delphi enquiry to obtain the judgment matrices for pairwise comparison of first fourteen of the selected EPIs as determined from second round of the Delphi survey. The enquiry was made from each expert from all the interest groups. The value judgment, provided by the expert 1 of the interest group 'Cement Machinery manufacturers' is given in Appendix-I.

TABLE 23.1 : Energy Conservation Options

Sl. No.	Item	Identi-fied by	Delphi Round 1		Delphi Round 2	
			Average Weight	Rank	Average Weight	Rank
1.	Use of Energy Efficient Equipment	M	8.12	3	8.04	1
2.	Energy Audit	M	7.88	4	8.20	2
3.	Top Management Involvement	D	10	1	7.77	3
4.	Fiscal incentives for energy conservation	M	7.24	6.	7.42	4
5.	Development of Energy Efficient Technology	M	7.24	6	7.22	5
6.	Management of Direct Energy Waste	M	7.28	5	7.22	5
7.	Upgradation of Technology	M	7.16	8	7.2	6
8.	Energy Performance Monitoring on a Continuous Basis	M	7.20	7	7.16	7
9.	Load Management and Load Scheduling	D	10	1	7.0	8
10.	Operational Improvement at Unit	M	6.84	10	6.9	9
11.	Creation of Funds on Soft Terms for Energy Conservation Activities	M	7.0	9	6.7	10
12.	Instrumentation and Automation	M	6.66	12	6.66	11
13.	Creation of posts of Chief, Energy Conservation/Audit Officer at Corporate Level	D	9	2	6.59	12
14.	Control and Monitoring of Quality of Coal and Power and Installation of Captive Power	M	6.84	10	6.58	13
15.	Retionalisation and Standardization	M	6.72	11	6.58	13
16.	Organization of Energy Management	D	10	1	6.54	14
17.	Preparation of Energy Conservation plan for the year and 5 year Period	M	6.44	15	6.52	15
18.	Training of Personnel	M	6.56	13	6.52	15
19.	Increasing Awareness for Energy Conservation through Workshops, Seminars, Newsletter, use of Media etc.	M	6.48	14	6.52	15

Sl. No.	Item	Identified by	Delphi Round 1		Delphi Round 2	
			Average Weight	Rank	Average Weight	Rank
20.	Management of Indirect Energy Waste	M	6.16	16	6.38	16
21.	Licencing Policy Conforming to Minimum Energy Efficiency Standards	M	6.16	16	6.2	17
22.	Creation of Motivation by Institution of Awards	M	6.08	17	5.94	18
23.	Development of Energy Efficient Model Plants	D	8	4	5.93	19
24.	Creation of Data Bank and Institution of Awards	M	5.72	19	5.78	20
25.	Adoption of Energy Conservation Law	M	5.69	20	5.4	21
26.	Basic Technical Education in Energy Management as a Specific Discipline	D	6	18	5.11	22
27.	Implant R&D	D	6	18	4.86	23
28.	Use of Appropriate Guide Norms	D	4	22	4.86	23
29.	Substitution of Source of Energy in Cement Manufacturing	M	4.6	21	4.76	24
30.	Institutional R&D	D	6.0	18	4.73	25

M : Identified by monitoring team
D : Added through Delphi Round

TABLE 23.2: Energy Performance Indicator

Sl. No.	Item	Identified by	Delphi Round 1 Average Weight	Delphi Round 1 Rank	Delphi Round 2 Average Weight	Delphi Round 2 Rank
1.	Reduction of Energy Cost per Tonne of Cement Produced	M	7.56	2	8.5	1
2.	Increase in Capacity Utilization	M	6.96	6	7.68	2
3.	Reduction in Energy Demand	M	7.95	1	7.66	3
4.	Reduction in Cost of Cement per Tonne	M	7.20	4	7.58	4
5.	Meeting Standards	D	—	—	7.36	5
6.	Thermal Energy Efficiency	D	—	—	7.09	6
7.	Electrical Energy Efficiency	D	—	—	7.00	7
8.	Improved Power Factor	M	7.39	3	6.92	8
9.	Improved Load Factor	M	7.04	5	6.70	9
10.	Good Housekeeping and Cleanliness	M	6.34	8	6.48	10
11.	Energy Consciousness	M	6.95	7	6.40	11
12.	Induction of Technology (Cost Effective	D	—	—	6.20	12
13.	Target Setting and Achievement of Targets	D	—	—	6.18	13
14.	Effective Utilization of Waste Heat	D	—	—	6.11	14
15.	Profitability of Cement Unit	M	5.68	10	5.4	15
16.	Use of materials Like Slag	D	—	—	5.38	16
17.	Participative Culture	M	5.04	13	5.28	17
18.	Longer Availability of Fuel Reserves	M	6.33	9	5.04	18
19.	Growth of Cement Industry	M	5.55	11	4.96	19
20.	Possibility of use of Alternate Fuels	M	5.04	13	4.92	20
21.	Total Energy Concept (Efficiency based on it)	D	—	—	4.91	21
22.	Impact on Environment	M	5.17	12	4.76	22

M : Identified by monitoring team
D : Added through DELPHI Round

iii. *Position Matrices*

For determining the ranks of the ECOs, the monitor team used Delphi technique to obtain the responses from the experts of each group in the form of position matrices. The experts were asked to indicate their assessment for the Energy Performance Indicators (EPIs) indicating the extent of energy conservation expected to be achieved from each energy conservation option (ECO), by using the following scale:

Very Low	Low	Medium	High	Very High	Full
VL	L	M	H	VH	F

iv. *Ranking of the Energy Conservation Options Using Fuzzy Set Methodology*

The qualitative judgments in the position matrices as obtained by Delphi technique are converted in quantitative values by following a scale 0-1.

Qualitative Assessment	Nil	Very low (VL)	Low (L)	Medium (M)	High (H)	Very High (VH)	Full (F)
Quantitative Values	0	0.1	0.3	0.5	0.7	0.9	1.0

The value of each box for the group position matrix is obtained by averaging the responses in all the position matrices under each group. The Cement Machinery Manufacturers group position matrix is given in Appendix II. It can be seen from the Table 23.3 that ECO III ranks first in accordance of importance as it has the highest dominance 219, the sum of the values in column I. The ranks of all the ECOs are determined accordingly as shown in Table 23.3. Following the analysis on this line, the optimistic dominance matrix (Table 23.3), the pessimistic dominance matrix (Table 23.4) and the mean dominance matrix (Table 23.5) are prepared from the corresponding aggregation matrices.

v. *Sensitivity Analysis for for the Ranks of Energy Conservation Options*

A sensitivity analysis is done by working out the weightage of the options with different weightages of optimistic dominance along with related pessimistic dominance, say, 20, 40, 50, 60, 80, and 100 per cent, through

OPTIONS	Dominates I	II	III	IV	V	VI	VII	VIII	IX	X	XI	XII	XIII	XIV	XV	XVI	XVII	XVIII	XIX	XX	Sum of Rows	Ranks
I	-	3	7	3	3	3	3	1	1	2	2	2	3	3	3	1	1	1	2	2	46	19
II	7	-	12	6	5	7	6	4	2	6	1	3	6	5	7	4	1	3	2	5	92	10
III	1	0	-	0	0	1	0	0	0	0	0	0	1	0	0	0	0	0	0	0	3	20
IV	7	5	12	-	8	5	6	6	3	1	0	3	4	6	7	4	2	3	2	4	88	12
V	7	1	9	3	-	2	4	3	2	2	1	3	4	4	2	1	2	2	2	2	56	19
VI	8	8	11	3	6	-	5	4	5	3	2	4	8	3	6	5	2	2	3	3	91	11
VII	7	7	10	2	6	5	-	2	2	1	0	5	5	5	6	2	1	2	1	2	71	15
VIII	8	8	12	5	8	7	6	-	2	0	1	3	7	6	8	4	0	2	2	4	93	9
IX	7	7	13	5	8	7	7	5	-	3	1	5	7	7	8	5	3	3	3	4	106	7
X	10	7	14	6	11	6	10	8	8	-	2	8	9	8	9	7	4	5	5	6	143	2
XI	11	7	13	10	9	11	11	10	7	7	-	9	10	9	10	9	6	8	5	7	169	1
XII	9	7	13	4	9	6	8	7	5	3	1	-	6	7	7	7	2	5	2	5	113	6
XIII	5	4	12	2	4	4	4	4	1	2	1	2	-	6	4	1	1	2	2	2	68	16
XIV	6	4	10	4	4	5	4	3	2	2	3	5	6	-	5	3	2	2	4	4	78	14
XV	7	4	11	3	4	4	3	3	2	1	1	4	5	4	-	2	2	2	3	1	66	17
XVI	7	4	12	4	7	6	4	3	2	2	1	5	6	7	6	-	0	1	1	3	81	13
XVII	10	5	13	8	10	8	9	7	5	5	1	5	9	9	9	5	-	4	1	6	128	4
XVIII	8	5	11	5	9	6	5	5	4	3	2	5	7	7	8	3	1	-	1	5	100	8
XIX	10	7	12	8	9	10	7	9	5	6	0	5	7	9	8	5	3	5	-	4	129	3
XX	9	7	12	7	7	8	6	8	8	3	1	5	8	9	6	6	5	5	4	-	124	5
Sum of Columns	144	100	219	78	127	111	108	92	66	52	21	81	118	114	119	74	38	57	45	69		
Ranks	2	9	1	12	3	7	8	10	15	17	20	11	5	6	4	13	19	16	18	14		

TABLE 23.3: Optimistic Dominance Matrix for Energy Conservations Options

optimistic and remaining weightage through pessimistic dominance matrices. Eight alternative schemes for cautious optimism including schemes with 100 per cent pessimism and mean dominance weight (Table 23.6) are considered.

From Table 23.6, two patterns are noticed by studying schemes I to VII. The dominances are of reducing order as one moves from left to right, i.e. 100 per cent optimistic to 100 per cent pessimistic. This is applicable to 14 ECOs at Sl. No. I, II, IV, V, VI, VII, IX, XII, XIII, XIV, XVI, XVII, XIX, and XX. This implies that these ECOs gain importance as the policy is framed more and more optimistically. The other pattern is visible in which weights of dominance are of increasing order as one moves from left to right, i.e. 100 per cent optimism to 100 per cent pessimism and is applicable to ECOs at Sl No. II, VIII, X, XI and XVIII. This implies that these ECOs gain importance as the policy is framed more and more pessimistically.

Ranks of various ECOs are then worked out under different schemes (Table 23.7). It can be seen that any scheme with cautious optimism II to VI provides very decisive ranks for first three ranking ECOs. These being 'top management involvement' (first rank), use of energy efficient equipment (second rank) and, 'control and monitor quality of coal and power and installation of captive power' (third rank). The most appropriate scheme has been found to be Scheme III, i.e. 60 per cent optimism and 40 per cent pessimism. The hierarchy of ECOs selected for policy framework is therefore based on this scheme.

An examination of the hierarchy of the top twenty ECOs as obtained from DHP-FSM (Table 23.8) and from the Delphi second round (Table 23.1) shows that DHP-FSM analysis has resulted in higher priority to ECOs 'Top Management Involvement', 'Use of Energy Efficient Equipment', 'Control and Monitor Quality of Coal and Power and Installation of Captive Power', and 'Creation of Posts of Chief Energy Conservation/Audit Officer at Corporate Level' as compared to results obtained from Delphi second round where higher priority is associated with the 'Use of Energy Efficient Equipment', 'Energy Audit', 'Fiscal Incentives for Energy Conservation', and 'Operational Improvements at Unit Level', etc. It can be observed that the priorities as emerged from DHP-FSM methodology give a thrust to energy management aspects and tackling one of the basic problem of the Indian cement industry of poor quality of coal and power and appears to be more convincing to achieve better results. Further, DHP-FSM takes into account the multi-criteria decision-making in evolving the policy framework, while Delphi exercise lacks in this aspect. The choice for the methodology in determining the

Options (j) (i)	I	II	III	IV	V	VI	VII	VIII	IX	X	XI	XII	XIII	XIV	XV	XVI	XVII	XVIII	XIX	X X	Sum of Rows	Ranks
	Dominates																					
I	-	5	8	3	3	3	3	7	4	5	3	5	6	5	7	4	2	3	2	2	80	10
II	4	-	7	0	2	3	1	3	1	2	1	2	3	2	4	3	1	3	2	2	46	17
III	5	4	-	0	0	3	4	2	2	5	1	2	2	0	2	2	2	1	2	0	39	18
IV	6	6	6	-	3	4	5	6	1	4	0	4	5	2	7	4	2	3	2	1	70	12
V	5	8	8	4	-	3	6	7	3	6	2	6	6	2	7	3	1	4	3	1	85	8
VI	7	9	7	6	4	-	7	8	5	7	3	5	7	6	9	6	2	3	3	3	107	3
VII	5	5	7	1	3	1	-	5	2	2	1	3	4	1	5	4	0	2	1	1	50	16
VIII	4	4	5	0	0	4	3	-	1	3	0	3	1	0	4	0	0	2	1	0	35	20
IX	8	8	7	5	3	4	7	8	-	4	0	1	6	4	8	5	1	4	3	3	89	7
X	6	6	7	3	3	1	4	5	1	-	0	2	4	3	6	4	1	3	2	1	62	13
XI	8	8	8	7	4	5	8	9	3	8	-	4	7	5	8	6	3	7	4	5	117	1
XII	8	8	5	4	3	1	7	6	3	3	1	-	5	4	5	4	2	0	1	2	72	11
XIII	6	6	6	2	1	4	6	5	2	4	0	3	-	1	3	2	1	3	3	2	60	15
XIV	7	7	8	4	2	4	6	7	2	5	1	5	5	-	7	4	1	4	3	2	84	9
XV	5	5	4	1	1	2	4	2	2	3	1	1	1	1	-	1	1	1	2	0	38	19
XVI	6	6	7	2	1	4	4	5	2	4	1	4	3	1	6	-	0	2	2	1	16	14
XVII	8	8	9	6	3	3	8	10	3	6	2	6	8	4	9	6	-	4	3	3	109	2
XVIII	8	8	7	5	3	2	7	7	4	5	3	4	7	4	8	5	2	-	1	1	91	6
XIX	7	7	9	6	4	4	6	8	3	5	2	6	7	4	8	5	1	4	-	1	97	4
XX	6	6	9	5	2	4	6	8	3	6	2	5	8	3	9	5	2	4	2	-	95	5

Sum of Columns	119	116	139	64	45	59	102	118	47	87	24	71	95	52	121	70	24	57	42	31
Ranks	3	5	1	11	16	12	6	4	15	8	19	9	7	14	2	10	19	13	17	18

TABLE 23.4 : Pessimistic Dominance Matrix for Energy Conservation Options

Options (j) (i)	I	II	III	IV	V	VI	VII	VIII	IX	X	XI	XII	XIII	XIV	XV	XVI	XVII	XVIII	XIX	X X	Sum of Rows	Ranks
	Dominates																					
I	-	6	8	4	4	1	3	7	2	3	1	3	4	3	5	3	3	3	3	1	67	13
II	5	-	7	0	0	1	2	0	1	3	0	3	0	2	2	0	0	1	1	1	29	18
III	4	2	-	0	0	1	0	0	0	0	0	0	0	0	0	0	0	0	0	0	7	19
IV	5	9	12	-	4	5	7	8	3	4	0	6	5	1	5	0	1	3	0	2	80	9
V	5	6	8	3	-	2	3	4	3	4	1	3	2	2	1	2	2	4	4	0	60	14
VI	6	12	9	3	4	-	4	6	1	6	1	3	5	1	5	5	3	4	4	1	83	7
VII	6	7	10	2	1	1	-	2	1	2	1	1	3	0	0	2	1	3	2	0	45	16
VIII	5	2	8	0	1	1	4	-	2	4	0	2	1	1	2	0	0	1	1	1	36	17
IX	9	10	11	7	9	6	9	8	-	6	3	7	10	4	6	8	7	7	6	4	138	3
X	6	10	13	4	5	2	3	7	1	-	3	2	5	0	5	5	4	3	2	1	81	8
XI	6	11	13	6	7	7	10	10	6	8	-	8	8	5	8	9	8	6	6	4	146	1
XII	6	10	12	4	4	1	2	7	2	1	1	-	4	0	3	4	3	3	2	1	70	12
XIII	5	6	12	3	3	3	3	3	2	2	0	4	-	2	4	0	0	2	0	1	55	15
XIV	8	11	13	4	8	5	9	10	4	4	3	6	7	-	7	6	4	5	6	4	124	4
XV	6	8	10	2	4	2	5	6	2	4	1	4	6	2	-	3	3	3	3	1	75	10
XVI	5	8	12	1	6	4	4	4	3	4	0	5	3	2	3	-	0	2	1	0	67	13
XVII	6	6	13	1	7	4	7	7	2	5	0	6	2	2	5	0	-	1	1	1	76	11
XVIII	7	6	13	4	7	3	7	8	3	4	1	4	4	1	6	4	1	-	1	1	85	6
XIX	7	7	14	4	7	5	8	10	3	6	2	6	8	3	6	8	4	4	-	2	114	5
XX	8	8	14	6	8	7	8	10	5	8	3	9	10	6	7	7	6	10	5	-	145	2
Sum of Columns	115	145	212	58	89	61	98	117	46	78	21	82	87	37	80	66	50	65	48	26		
Ranks	4	2	1	14	6	13	5	3	17	10	20	8	7	18	9	11	15	12	16	19		

TABLE 23.5 : Mean Dominance Matrix for Energy Conservation Options

Schemes-> ECOs	I		II		III		IV		V		VI		VII	VIII
	100%	opt	80% 20%	opt + pess	60% 40%	opt + pess	50% 50%	opt + pess	40% 60%	opt + pess	20% 80%	opt + pess	100% pess	Avg
I	144		139		134		131.5		129		124		119	115
II	100		103.2		106.4		108		109.6		112.8		116	145
III	219		203		187		179		171		155		139	212
IV	78		75.2		72.4		71		69.6		66.8		64	58
V	127		110.6		94.2		86		77.8		61.4		45	89
VI	111		100.6		90.2		85		79.8		69.4		59	61
VII	108		106.8		105.6		105		104.4		103.2		102	98
VIII	92		97.2		102.4		105		107.6		112.8		118	117
IX	66		62.2		58.4		56.5		54.6		50.8		47	46
X	52		59		66		69.5		73		80		87	78
XI	21		21.6		22.2		22.5		22.8		23.4		24	21
XII	81		79		77		76		75		73		71	82
XIII	118		113.4		108.8		106.5		104.2		99.6		95	87
XIV	114		101.6		89.2		83		76.8		64.4		52	37
XV	119		119.4		119.8		120		120.2		120.6		121	80
XVI	74		73.2		72.4		72		71.6		70.8		70	66
XVII	38		35.2		32.4		31		29.6		26.8		24	50
XVIII	57		57		57		57		57		57		57	65
XIX	45		44.4		43.8		43.5		43.2		42.6		42	48
XX	69		61.4		53.8		50		46.2		38.6		31	26

Opt : Optimistic
Pess : Pessimisstic
Avg : Average

TABLE 23.6 : Dominance Weights for Alternative Schems for Hierarchy of ECOs

Schemes-> ECOs	I		II		III		IV		V		VI		VII	VIII
	100%	opt	80% 20%	opt + pess	60% 40%	opt + pess	50% 50%	opt + pess	40% 60%	opt + pess	20% 80%	opt + pess	100% pess	Avg
I	2		2		2		2		2		2		3	4
II	9		7		5		4		4		4		5	2
III	1		1		1		1		1		1		1	1
IV	12		12		12		12		14		11		11	14
V	3		5		8		7		9		13		16	6
VI	7		9		9		8		8		10		12	13
VII	8		6		6		6		6		5		6	5
VIII	10		10		7		6		5		4		4	3
IX	15		14		14		15		16		15		15	17
X	17		16		13		13		12		7		8	10
XI	20		20		19		19		20		19		19	20
XII	11		11		11		10		11		8		9	8
XIII	5		4		4		5		7		6		7	7
XIV	6		8		10		9		10		12		14	18
XV	4		3		3		3		3		3		2	9
XVI	13		13		12		11		13		9		10	11
XVII	19		19		18		18		19		18		19	15
XVIII	16		17		15		14		15		14		13	12
XIX	18		18		17		17		18		16		17	16
XX	14		15		16		16		17		17		18	19

Opt : Optimistic
Pess : Pessimisstic
Avg : Average

TABLE 23.7 : Ranks of Options in Various Schemes

hierarchy of ECOs for development of policy framework becomes obvious in favour of the methodology of DHP-FSM. However, the remaining ten ECOs, which were identified through DELPHI but not taken up for an indepth analysis are also included in the list to form a comprehensive policy framework and are listed after the ECOs already prioritised by DHP-FSM methodology. Taking together the ECOs as determined from DHP-FSM and adding the remaining ECOs ranked with the responses from DELPHI, the comprehensive policy framework is presented in Table 23.8.

vi. *Feedback on the Evolved Policy Framework*

Results as obtained from the DHP-FSM methodology and moderating the same by cautious optimism approach were sent to all the experts for their information and views with an opportunity that they may suggest changes in the priorities amongst ECOs if they think so. Analysis of the twelve feedbacks received is given below:

a) Six experts agreed in toto to the policy framework so arrived by DHP-FSM methodology.
b) One expert suggested that 'top management involvement' may not be given 1st rank and another suggested that the top management involvement should not have been included as an option along with others. However, he agreed that the 'top management involvement' is useful in implementing the other options.
c) Two experts suggested higher priority to 'creation of awareness for energy conservation through workshops and seminars, etc'. One expert suggested even lower priority to this option.
d) One expert suggested higher priority to 'training of personnel', another suggested even lower priority as obtained from analysis.
e) Two experts suggested higher priority to 'energy conservation plans'.
f) Three experts suggested interchanging the ranks between 2 or 3 adjacent ECOs while on expert suggested higher ranks for the options relating control and monitoring aspects of energy conservation, the other suggested higher ranks for aspects relating to technological aspects of energy conservation.

Thus, suggestions received did not call for any major change in the policy framework arrived at by the approach followed. A large number of

TABLE 23.8: Policy Framework of Energy Conservation in Indian Cement Industry

Sl. No.	Energy Conservation Options	Ranks
1.	Top Management Involvement	1
2.	Use of Energy Efficient Equipment	2
3.	Control and Monitor Quality of Coal and Power and Installation of Captive Power	3
4.	Creation of Posts of Chief Energy Conservation/Audit Officer at Corporate Level	4
5.	Energy Audit	5
6.	Upgradation of Technology	6
7.	Energy Performance Monitoring on a Continuous Basis	7
8.	Development of Energy Efficient Technology	8
9.	Management of Direct Energy Waste	9
10.	Rationalization and Standardisation of Plant and Machinery for Energy Performance	10
11.	Instrumentation and Automation	11
12.	Organization of Energy Management both at Plant and Carport Level	12
13.	Fiscal Incentives for Energy Conservation	12
14.	Operational Improvement at Unit Level	13
15.	Load Management and Load Scheduling	14
16.	Training of Personnel	15
17.	Management of Indirect Energy Waste (e.g. reduction in loss of Cement, dust losses in exit gases etc.)	16
18.	Increasing Awareness for Energy Conservation Through Workshops, Seminars, Newsletter, Use of Media etc.	17
19.	Preparation of Energy Conservation Plan for the year and Five-Year Period	18
20.	Creation of Funds on Soft Terms for Energy Conservation Activities	19
21*	Licencing Policy Conforming with Minimum Energy Efficiency Standards	20
22*	Creation of Motivation by Institution of Awards	21
23*	Development of Energy Efficient (Comparable to World Standards) Model Plants	22

Sl. No.	Energy Conservation Options	Ranks
24*	Creation of Data Bank and Information System	23
25*	Adoption of Energy Conservation Law	24
26*	Basic Technical Education in Energy Management as a Specific Discipline	25
27*	Inplant R & D	26
28*	Use of Appropriate Guide Norms	26
29*	Substitution of Source of Energy in Cement Manufacturing	27
30*	Institutional R & D	28

* From DELPHI responses.

experts amongst those who responded to the feedback survey agreed to the policy framework as arrived, either totally or with a very minor modification. Hence, the policy framework generated through the DHP-FSM methodology has been considered to be valid and finally recommended.

4. Concluding Remarks

The identification of the Energy Performance Indicators and the Energy Conservation Option is of paramount importance to decision-making process for a sound policy framework for energy conservation in the Cement Industry. The joint use of Delphi Hierarchy process and Fuzzy Set Methodology (DHP-FSM) has been demonstrated through a case study to determine the ECOs and to derive priorities amongst them in a multi-person decision making situation using multiple criteria for evaluation. The methodology provides an opportunity of participation of all related experts from different interest groups. The inputs from the experts in deriving the ECOs and their priorities assist in working out the policy framework for effective energy conservation in the Indian Cement Industry, which will have the advantage of acceptance from all involved in the activity. The feedback on the policy framework confirms the suitability of the approach evolved for the purpose.

Acknowledgment

The author has freely drawn upon completed R&D work/status reports of NCM and some of the unpublished work in NCB. This paper is being published with the permission of Director General, NCB.

REFERENCES

Alley, H., Bacinello, C.P. and Hipel, K.W., (1978) 'Fuzzy Set Approaches to Planning in the Grand River Basin', *Advances Water Resources,* 1-36.

Bellman, R.F. and Zadeh, L.A., (1970) 'Decision-Making in Fuzzy Environment', *Management Science,* 17 (4), B-141-164.

Dalkey, N.C., (1969) *The Delphi Method : A Experimental Study of Group Opinion,* Santa Monica, CA: The Rand Corporation, RM-888R.

Hadley, G., (1967) *Introduction of Probability and Statistical Decision Theory.* San Francisco: Holden-Day.

Harker, P.T., (1987) 'Alternative of Questioning in the Analytic Hierarchy Process', *Mathematical Modelling,* 9(3-5), 353-360.

Jain, R., (1976) 'Outlines of an Approach for the Analysis on Fuzzy Systems', *Int'l J. Control,* 23,627-640.

Khorramshahgol, R. and Moustakis, S. (1988) 'Delphic Hierarchy Process (DHP): A Methodology for Priority Setting Derived from the Delphi Method and Analytical Hierarchy Process', *European Journal of Operational Res.,* 37 (3), 347-354.

Rodekohr, M., (1981) 'An Examination of Econometric Modelling and Comparison with Alternative Methodologies'. In Bayraktar, B.A., Cherniavsky, E.A., and Laughton, M.A. (eds.) *Energy Policy Planning,* Plenum Press, New York, 387-397.

Saaty, T.L., (1980) *The Analytic Hierarchy Process,* McGraw-Hill, New York.

Zedeh, L.A., (1965) 'Fuzzy Sets', *Information and Control,* 338-353.

Appendix. 1

ENERGY PERFORMANCE INDICATORS (i) (EPLs)	Energy performance indicators (EPLs) (j) — Interest group cement machinery manufacturers expert 1													
	1. Reduction in energy cost per tonne of cement produced	2. Increase in capacity utilization	3. Reduction in energy demand	4. Reduction in cost of product Le per tonne of cement.	5. Meeting standards	6. Thermal energy efficiency	7. Electrical energy efficiency	8. Improved power factor	9. Improved load factor	10. Good house keeping and cleanliness	11. Energy consciousness	12. Introduction of cost effective technologies	13. Target setting and achievement of targets.	14. Effective utilisation of internal waste heat.
1. Reduction in energy cost per tonne of cement produced	1	1	1	1	1	1	1	5	3	3	3	3	3	1
2. Increase in capacity utilization		1	1	1	1	1	1	5	3	3	3	1	3	1
3. Reduction in energy demand			1	1/3	1/3	1/3	1/3	5	3	3	3	1	3	3
4. Reduction in cost of product Le per tonne of cement				1	1	1	1	5	3	3	3	3	3	3
5. Meeting standards					1	1	1	5	5	3	3	3	3	3
6. Thermal energy efficiency						1	1	7	7	3	3	3	3	1
7. Electrical energy efficiency							1	5	5	3	3	3	3	3
8. Improved power factor								1	1	1	1/3	1/3	1	1/3
9. Improved load factor									1	1	1/3	1/3	1	1/3
10. Good house keeping and cleanliness										1	1/3	1/3	1/3	1/3
11. Energy consciousness											1	3	3	3
12. Introduction of cost effective technology												1	3	3
13. Target setting and achievement of targets													1	3
14. Effective utilisation of internal waste heat														1

JUDGEMENT MATRIX FOR PAIRWISE COMPARISON OF ENERGY PERFORMANCE INDICATORS.

24. ROLE OF MODELS IN PUBLIC POLICY ANALYSIS AND DESIGN

A.K. Vij

Introduction

The inherently complex and multifaceted nature of public policy issue calls for an eclectic approach to modelling. A variety of quantitative and qualitative techniques have been used for policy modelling, such as econometrics, input-output, optimisation, physical systems theory and system dynamics in the former category, and programme planning, interpretive structural modelling (ISM), analytic hierarchy process (AHP), fuzzy set theory (FST) and delphi belonging to the later category of qualitative techniques. Some of the latest technique emerging from the discipline of artificial intelligence (AI), e.g. neural networks have also been used for public policy modelling. Contemporary trends in modelling also suggest attempts towards unification of modelling approaches. Culmination of integrative research at Indian Institute of Technology, Delhi has led to the emergence of a new paradigm 'Flexible Systems Methodology' which provides a framework for the selection and application of suitable modelling methodologies for any public policy problem in a spectral and integrative manner.

This paper provides an overview of these modelling techniques, describing the situation where they may be applied and their limitations. The review has been conducted selectively in the background of the world and Indian energy scene. As part of the integrative research, we have developed a multi-level hierarchical system dynamics model by using a sectorial approach for demand and conservation of energy and a macro-level approach for energy-economy interactions and transition dynamics. The micro-model combines the input-output approach with waste management using physical systems theory, whereas the macro-model is based on system dynamics. Salient features of this model, its results and policy implications signifying the benefits of integration are also described.

Quantitative Approaches

Research on the use of quantitative modelling to support policy making and planning process is nearly four decades old and publications in this area indicate a great deal of enormity and diversity of scope. Emergence of mathematical modelling techniques may be traced back to the efforts of the British and U.S. defense departments during the Second World War, and their foundations lie in the engineering and military fields. These techniques came to be known under such diverse names as operational research, operations analysis, operations research, systems analysis, systems engineering and management science etc. These names were used more or less interchangeably for various techniques used in the design and control of military systems. The initial application of these techniques was limited to industrial and business problems. However, very soon the models came to be applied to a variety of socio-economic problems, the most noteworthy example being the use of econometric models for policy planning.

Econometric Models: Econometrics was founded in the 1930s by the Dutch economist Tinbergen. At the heart of econometrics is the use of statistical analysis to estimate the values of the parameters in a mathematical economic model. Most of the econometric models consist of linear difference equations and are of a discrete deterministic macro type.

Econometric modelling is primarily deductive in nature, and has been the principal method for fuel and sectorial demand estimates, energy elasticities, supply-demand linkages and trade analysis for short and medium-term planning.

In most of the earlier econometric studies, energy problem was perceived as a supply problem. The task of these initial energy models was to explore ways to increase production to meet the final demand. Many energy-economy models developed later, combined macro-economic theory and econometrics with input-output approach, optimisation methods and process analysis. These integrated models are discussed in the later paragraphs. Some of the well known econometric studies for energy analysis are: 'Project Independence Evaluation System' (PIES) launched by Federal Energy Administration of U.S.A. [FEA (1974)], by Schwartz (1974) to measure the relative impacts of higher oil prices on OECD countries, and by Kashihara (1986) for the energy model of Japan.

In India econometric techniques have been the most popular among all the methods of projections. Fuel Policy Committee (1974) used linear and log-linear regression models, and projected the future demand for commercial energy on the basis of national income. Parikh (1976) started with the regression carried by the Fuel Policy Group and later adopted the scenario approach. The Working Group of Energy Policy (1979) also adopted the Scenario approach. Parikh (1980) formulated an econometric simulation model to project the end-use energy consumption in various sectors. The model was used to project macro-economic parameters like GDP, private consumption and industrial GOP, which alongwith demographic projections were used as inputs to another model which estimated energy consumption. The model was used to forecast demand for energy in India up to 2004-05.

Limitations of Econometric Models: Notwithstanding their popularity and widespread use, econometric models suffer from the unrealistic assumptions about the motivations of people and the information available to make decisions in the real world. These faults are inherent in the economy theory, primarily based on the modern neoclassical theory and rational expectations schools (Sterman, (1988). Some of the limitations of econometric models are listed below:

a) Econometric models are based on the assumptions of perfect information, optimisation and equilibrium of the market or the economy. These simplifying assumptions ignore the complexities of real world like dynamic processes, disequilibrium and the physical basis for delays between actions and results.
b) Econometric models use the historical data to find the parameter values. Such estimation techniques reveal only the degree of past correlation between the variables. Such correlations cannot accurately represent the future because these correlations may change or shift as the system evoles.
c) Aggregate statistical data measure only the results of the decisions made, not the process of making those decisions. Statistical data do not reveal the nature and quality of information used in decision-making. Hence the models based on such data cannot be used to indicate how changes in that information will alter future decisions.
d) Econometric models ignore soft variables and immeasurable quantities. At best, these variables are handled with proxy variables.
e) Causal relationships between model variables and feedback are not considered. The feedback relationships between environmental, social and demographic factors are usually as important as economic influences.

f) These models are based on the limited range of historical data. Aggregate statistical data do not provide a guide to behaviour outside the historical range of experience or under a different set of policies or incentives. Consequently, most of the econometric models are not robust, and any changes in policies or conditions cause the models to break down.

g) Many econometric models suffer from narrow model boundaries. These models ignore factors outside the expertise of the model builders or the mandate of the sponsoring organisation.

h) Presence of a large number of exogenous variables (which in real life are interrelated) leads to internal inconsistency in the econometric models.

Optimisation Models: The theories of mathematical optimisation provide a robust methodological basis for the use of analytical models in policy planning. Optimisation models are normative in approach. These are aimed at identifying the efficient trade-offs among a set of attributes which quantify the consequences of alternative policies. The techniques of linear and non-linear programming, integer programming, statistical design theory, and the theory of optimal control have played a major role in optimisation models.

The traditional form of an optimisation model is a linear programming model with objective functions of minimising costs of meeting the established energy demands from known suppliers. The World Energy Model of Queen Mary College (Deam *et al.*, 1974) is a well known example of optimisation model. The model presented the world distribution of petroleum, given producing—capabilities and a structure of product demand by regions, and examined issues such as world's oil and gas production, supply, refining and product-demand situations and highlighted the global effects of policy changes within the United States. The Brookhaven Energy System Optimisation Model (BESOM) is another famous linear programming model which provided a framework for planning and technology assessment of the entire U.S. energy system (Cherniavsky, 1974). Another well known energy model based on optimisation the ETA-Macro model developed by Electric Power Research Institute Manne (1977). An energy forecasting model for India, developed at the Centre for Energy Management, Indian Institute of Management, Bangalore is based on a combination of regression analysis with linear programming. Sushil (1987) has demonstrated a goal-programming model for energy source selection to meet the energy needs of a village cluster.

Limitations of Optimisation Models: Optimisation models also suffer from certain limitations, some inherent in the basic assumptions of these models, and others from the practical viewpoint of the policy-maker. Some major limitations are outlined as follows:

a) One common simplication in the optimisation models is to assume that all the relationships in the system are linear. In the real life, linearity is almost always unrealistic. There are some techniques available to solve non-linear optimisation problems, but in general, the vast majority of optimisation models assume linearity.
b) Although, it is possible to incorporate feedback in optimisation models, yet in practice, the resulting complexity and non-linearity usually renders the optimisation problems insoluble. As a result, many optimisation models ignore most of the feedback effects.
c) Many optimisation models are static. These are designed to determine the optimal solution for a particular moment in time without regard for how the optimal state is reached. Even the dynamic optimisation models don't explain how the system moves from one optimal state to another.
d) From the viewpoint of the model user, the optimisation models are large, cumbersome and complex. As a result, the policy-maker tends to be sceptial about the answers that these models provide.

Input-Output Models: Input-output models are based on the economic reality of highly inter-connected and inter-dependent production systems. These models attempt to explain ways through which demands are met by the existing technological structure and the determination of changes that a demand shock tends to generate on that structure.

The input-output modelling technique dates back to 1930s and 1940s and was developed by W.W. Leontief. Earlier input-output model were static, i.e. they were based on the assumption of fixed technological coefficients. Technological change in the dynamic input-output model is represented in terms of a dynamic input-output index, which Leontief formulated (1953), implemented (1970), and used for analysing the choice of technology in a linear programming framework.

In the case of energy analysis, two types of multisector models have been used: those built around the inter-industry or input-output models of the Leontief type, and those which integrate inter-industry framework with process analysis and optimisation to evaluate the substitution of energy technologies. The long-term Wharton Annual and Industry Model (Preston, 1972) based on sixty-three sector input-output structure of the U.S. economy is one of the early examples of multi-sector energy models. Other well-known multisector models are the Hudson-Jorgenson (HJ) model of the U.S. economy (Hudson and Jorgenson, 1974), Optimisation Model for Energy Resources (OMER Model) for the energy issues of Israel (Avriel *et al.*, 1982), and the energy economy input-output model with a linear programming technology model of the Australian economy (James *et al.*, 1986).

Input-output models of different variants, basically belonging to the Leontief group, have come into increasing use in India's five year plans, since the third plan. These models focused on the need for establishing inter-sectorial consistencies in building the production targets, mainly estimated from the demand side. In the earlier models, supply side was rather neglected in the sense that no sectorial supply constraints were formulated. However, the models were increasingly articulated by making them 'closed', i.e. by endogenising imports and consumption in the final demand vector. Since the sixth plan (Government of India, Planning Commission, 1980, attempt has been made to integrate Harrod-Domar and input-output approaches in a demand-supply framework. Sushil (1984) has attempted to integrate vast management with input-output approach (input-output-waste model) by using the graph-theoretic approach of physical system theory.

Limitations of Input-Output Models: Some major limitations of the input-output models are,

a) Traditional input-output analysis, as in the Brookhaven Energy System Optimisation Model (BESOM) is based on the assumption of fixed technological coefficients. The producer behaviour, consumer demand and capital accumulation are treated exogenously.

b) Dynamic input-output models like the Hudson-Jorgenson (HJ) are free from these difficulties. However, the equilibrium orientation of these models and the lack of behavioral decision-making structure, limit their utility for the transitional analysis.

c) In general, rigid structural requirements of the input-output models prove to be restrictive in the analysis of real-life systems. These approaches lack the much needed flexibility in the dynamic analysis of socio-economic systems.

d) The existing approaches to the input-output modelling give no explicit representation to waste in the policy analysis. Input-output analysis, due to its emphasis on inter-dependency among sectors, is ideally suited for such an analysis but the existing approaches miss this crucial aspect.

System Dynamics Models: System Dynamics was pioneered in 1959 by Forester, who combined the cybernetics and information feedback concepts put forth by Wiener and Tustin, and showed how the new methodology could be applied to problems which could not have been solved earlier. Because of its specific features, like long-term view of the problem, importance of feedback to analyse the system behaviour in terms of its internal causal structure, and its central focus on policy, the system dynamics methodology has found applications in diverse socio-economic areas, such as societal dynamics, urban dynamics, economic growth, energy and even world dynamics.

Significant work on energy modelling using system dynamics methodology has been done at Thayer School of Engineering, Dartmouth College, Hanover, U.S.A., and the pioneer System Dynamics Group, Massachusetts Institute of Technology, U.S.A., where energy-related work was taken up as part of the System Dynamics National Project. An important energy-economy interaction model based on system dynamics is by Sterman (1981). The model is designed to provide a vehicle for understanding the role of energy in the economy and for understanding the macro-economic consequences of energy policies. Raghavendran (1983) has developed a similar model for the Indian economy which captures the important linkages between economic growth and the development of various forms of energy. In India, a significant work on system dynamics modelling is being done at Indian Institute of Technology, Delhi and Kharagpur. The applications range from manufacturing in the steel plant to tea industry, agriculture, transportation and energy.

Limitations of System Dynamics Models: System dynamics models circumvent most of the barriers imposed by traditional approaches to economic analysis. These models have many strengths, e.g. an emphasis on the causal structure, search for a high-leverage internal policy, recognition of disequilibrium, delays and bounded rationality in decision-making, free use of mental data-bases, and incorporation of non-linear relationships.

However, despite its many strengths, system dynamics has been subjected to severe criticism and controversy in the past. Some main objections to SD models are listed below:

a) The internal structure of the earlier SD models was impenetrable, because too many variables were connected in a way which made any trace back of causal behaviour futile.

b) Many external assumptions were made on too few and ill-documented data.

c) The SD models lacked mathematical sophistication, because DYNAMO a simulation language did not make use of mathematics beyond addition and subtraction.

d) The concept of "one world-one model" was thought to be misleading. The real world showed some serious structural differences with respect to the main indicators of different world regions, whether these are national entities or higher aggregates. These models were not multi-levelled or hierarchically organised (Mesarovic and Pestel, 1974).

e) System dynamics methodology is difficult for the uninitiated and it makes a higher demand on professionalism than other methodologies (Keloharju, 1983).

Qualitative Techniques

In large-scale and complex societal systems, problem definition, design and synthesis of objectives and policies is very crucial. Public policy issues are not well structured; instead these are complex and amorphous. Qualitative techniques of modelling may act as complementary to the hitherto used quantitative modelling techniques. These techniques incorporate judgment so important to be considered while deciding on important policy issues.

Some of the well known qualitative techniques are: Programme planning, interpretive structural modelling (ISM), analytic hierarchy process (AHP), fuzzy set theory (FST), delphi etc. Sage (1977) placed considerable emphasis the use of graphical approaches for programme planning. He illustrated the use of Hall Activity Matrix approach through an energy demand and supply problem.

Sage (1977) also recommended the application of Digraph modelling to the complex societal problems. A digraph model can be converted into an interpretive structural model (ISM) using various alogorithms based on the concept of reachability matrix for organising the data acquired for developing a structural model, and presented a methodology for interpretation of complex structural models by partitioning a reachability matrix. Analytic Hierarchy Process (AHP) is a decision planning tool developed by Saaty in 1970s. AHP serves as a framework for people to structure their own problems and provide judgments based on knowledge, reasons or feelings to derive a set of priorities for an optimal solution to a decision problem. The concept of Fuzzy Set Theory (FST) was introduced by Zadeh to overcome the need for undue precision in the study of systems involving humans. A considerable amount of work has been done both in respect of theory and application of fuzzy-sets since 1965, and it has improved the quality of decision-making, bringing the input of judgment based on the experience and feelings of decision-makers. The results of decisions using FST are nearer to the real-life situations.

DELPHI is another qualitative technique which has been used for energy forecasting. DELPHI is a method of obtaining expert opinion from large groups of people in a systematic way. The technique which was first used by Rand Corporation is a modification of the panel or committee approach, while it eliminates some of the disadvantages of the classical committees. One famous study conducted on the energy system of India is by Rohtagi *et al.* (1979). Satsangi *et al.* (1986) have used DELPHI and HARVA techniques in the context of rural energy in India. Srinivasan *et. al.* (1987) have conducted a DELPHI study for energy conservation policies in the Indian context.

Acceptance of qualitative techniques of modelling is high among the policy-makers, because these techniques permit the role of subjective judgment in model-building. However, the conclusions derived from qualitative studies should be substantiated through detailed quantitative studies.

Current Trends in Modelling

Current literature on policy modelling suggests three emerging trends, viz. interactive modelling based on the concept of decision support systems, attempts towards integration of modelling approaches, and the role of policy models in changing the mental models of policy-makers i.e. the learning aspect of modelling process.

Interactive Modelling: Recent advances in computer technology favour interactive modelling based on the concept of decision support systems (DSS) and micro-computer based models for the reasons of portability. The modelling software also incorporates many user-friendly features like menu help, graphic-user-interface (GUI) and on-line, validation. An excellent example of interactive modelling software is STELLA from High Performance Systems, U.S.A. for system dynamics modelling. Medsker (1984) has described an ongoing project at the National Audobon Society (NAS), namely the development of an interactive computer system (EPLAN) or Energy PLAN). It models the impacts of various public policies on U.S. energy demand from a DSS viewpoint. Raskin (1985) has described a micro-computer based LDC (Lesser Developed Countries) Energy Alternatives Planning System (LEAP). The model deals with end-use fuel requirements, energy production and distribution, and pressure on land-use and bio-mass.

The attempts at interactive modelling with micro-computer support have greatly facilitated the developments towards group model building process (Richardson *et al.* 1993).

Integration of Modelling Approaches: The ever-increasing complexity of socio-economic and managerial systems has led to a proliferation of system based techniques for understanding the complex problem situations in multiple ways. In the past, there have been futile debates and controversies to judge the supremacy of one technique or approach over the others. There are many paradoxical schools of thought such as hard versus soft systems, quantitative versus qualitative analysis, exogenous versus endogenous (or open versus closed) models, individual versus system structure etc. Such controversies have generated only confusion and skepticism amongst the end-users of the policy models, i.e. the policy makers. The task of designing or selecting a methodology for a particular problem situation is becoming more difficult with ever-increasing choice.

Current trends in modelling suggest an attempt towards integration. Integration of macro-econometrics or input-output models with optimisation has been successfully achieved in earlier large-scale models like ETA-MACRO, BESOM, Hudson-Jorgenson, and OMER studies. Integration approach has been strongly propagated by many authors including Troncale (1988), Warfield (1990), Flood and Jackson (1991) etc. Integration of system dynamics with parametric optimisation has been attempted Keloharju (1983). Many examples of integrated models in the Indian context have been given by Sushil (1993). Further, a new paradigm, which has its foundations in the research work of nearly a decade at Indian Institute of Technology has also been put forth under the title 'Flexible Systems Methodology' (Sushil, 1993). The aim of this integrative approach has also been put forth under the title 'Flexible Systems Methodology' is to resolve the end of continuum paradoxes in literature and providing a unifying framework for the selection and application of suitable modelling methodologies for any public policy problem.

Recent studies also show the application of advanced methodologies from the discipline of artificial intelligence, e.g. neural networks to policy modelling (Kumar and Satsangi, 1993).

Learning Aspects of Policy Models: The available literature on the impact of computer models on policy-making suggests that the early applications, though marked by great enthusiasm and optimism on the part of policy-modellers, almost singularly filled in there utility as policy support systems. In fact these policy models indicated that the modelling was more effective in educating the policy-modellers rather than the policy-makers.

However, recent developments in the quantitative modelling, e.g. improvements in modelling methodology, user-friendly and interactive software, adoption of new ideas from behavioural decision theory and experiments with group-modelling have helped in creating computer-based learning environments (or microworlds) for policy-makers to 'play with' their knowledge of business and social systems and to debate policy and strategy change (Morecroft, 1988).

The emphasis of the current modelling trend is on small transparent models, on games, and on dialogue between mental models and computer simulations (Vennix, 1990).

Significant efforts have also been made to foster better communication between the model-builders and the policy-makers through forum approach. The Energy Modelling Forum of Stanford University, U.S.A., has made a significant contribution in this area (Huntington *et al.*, 1982). In India, the System Research Institute, Bangalore has done similar work by holding energy workshops, through documentation and analysis of policy models.

Integrated Energy Model—An Indian Case

Purpose of this research study has been to develop a methodology based on systems theory to analyse the energy policy issues of the Indian economy in a dynamic and multi-sectorial framework, with prime focus on energy conservation and waste management. The integrated energy model combines two systems paradigms which have traditionally been opposing each other. The integrated model combines the advantage of sectorial interlinkage of input-output economics with causality and feedback features of system dynamics (Vij, 1990).

The Physical Systems Model: A generalised multisector model which combines input output economics with waste management (input-output-waste energy model) has first been developed.

In this model, the national economy has been considered to consist of the following six aggregated sectors: (i) Petroleum, (ii) non-petroleum energy i.e. power, (iii) industry, (iv) transport, (v) agriculture, (vi) commercial, residential and public services.

The model is based on Leontief's concept of input output economics with a modification

$$\text{Input} = \text{Output} + \text{Waste}$$

In terms of the modified concept, the total energy demand of the economy consists of direct energy demand of the human population, the intermediate demand of other sectors, and the direct as well as indirect energy wastes which cannot be recycled and have to be rejected to nature.

The model has been developed by using the graph-theoretic approach of physical systems theory in a branch-chord framework.

Integration of the Input-Output-waste Model with System Dynamics: The aforesaid input-out-waste (I.O.W.) model is static and the impact of various macro-economic variables, e.g. population, national income, national investment sectorial capital, sectorial demand, sectorial output and technological changes can be studied only through a dynamic model. This objective has been achieved by integrating the I.O.W. model with system dynamics (SD).

The integration has been achieved in such a way that both the models maintain their individual identity, but at each iterative step the output of SD model is fed as an input to the I.O.W. model and *vice versa*.

The integrated model generates the year-wise projected values of the following: population, national income, sectorwise final and aggregate energy demands, energy cost, energy investments, technological coefficients, direct and indirect energy wastes and natural resources requirement.

Significance of the Integration: The integration of physical system theory with system dynamics is a step forward in developing a multi-level hierarchical approach in the SD modelling. The integrated energy model is a two-level approach, i.e. sectorial approach for I-O-W modelling and the micro-economic approach for SD modelling. These are inter-linked with each other. A comparison of micro-model (I.O.W.), macro-model (S.D.) and the integrated model is given in Table 24.1.

TABLE 24.1 : Comparison of Micro (I.O.W.), Macro (S.D.) and Integrated Models

	MICRO (I.O.W.) MODEL	MACRO (S.D.) MODEL	INTEGRATED MODEL
1. PURPOSE	To study the issues related to energy demand, energy conservation, natural input requirements, energy waste disposal to nature and cost of energy output in the context of sectoral inter-linkages in the economic and their resulting cascading effect.	To study energy issues in relation to other economic variables and their causality e.g. population, national income, capital formation rate, sectoral demand, waste management, technology, natural resources etc. a dynamic environment.	To study the following inter-related energy issues in a dynamic, multisectoral environ-ment: Sector-wise energy demand, energy output, direct and inindirect energy waste the effect of energy waste on unit cost of energy available to the consumer consumption of natural resources, population growth, technological changes and their impact on the energy sector.
2.METHODOLOGY & MODELLING CHARACTERI-STICS	Input-output economics comb-ined with waste management, using graph-theoretic approach of physical systems theory	System Dynamics	Input-output economics and waste management integrated with System Dynamics.
3. SIGNIFICANCE	a) I.O.W. model is a multi-sector energy model with waste parameter incorporated explicitly.	a) System Dynamics Methodo-logy provides an ideal frame-work for studying complex, dynamic and non-linear interactions in socio-econo-mic systems such as energy.	a) Integrated model is a multi-sectoral, dynamic energy model incorpor-ating the advantages of both, Input-Output economics and System Dynamics.
	b) Energy conservation has been defined in a broader perspective covering the direct as well as indirect energy waste.	b) Long-term view of the energy problems.	b) Two-level approach, i.e. sectoral approach I.O.W. modelling and the macro-economic approach for S.D. modelling. These are inter-linked with each other.
	c) Impact of waste generation and recycling in energy cons-uming sectors on aggregate energy demand, energy pri cing ecological and environ-mental issues and national accounting policies, clearly demonstrated.	c) Feedback effects are considered. d) Non-linear relationships, which are typical in real-life systems, are incorporated.	c) Main features of S.D. models like feedback, non-linearity, flexi-bility and use of mental data base for policy analysis and design have been incorporated.
		e) Emphasis is on micro-structure of causal rela-tionship which generates macro behaviour.	d) Computational effort is a compromise between the typical input-

	MICRO (I.O.W.) MODEL	MACRO (S.D.) MODEL	INTEGRATED MODEL
		f) Provides the much needed flexibility in the dynamic analysis of energy systems.	output modelling approach and S.D.
		g) The model emphasises policy analysis rather than mathematical sophistication.	
		h) Data limitations are not a serious problem in S.D. models.	
4. LIMITATIONS	a) Static model, gives only a snapshot view of the energy problem.	a) Multi-sectoral features and the multiplier effects due to inter-relatedness of sectors is more difficult in S.D. models.	a) The integrated model combines two scientific paradigms which have traditionally been opposing each other. Their "marriage" needs the sanction and approval of these professional communities.
	b) Rigid structure.	b) S.D. models have been criticised for lack of mathematical sophistication, many external assumptions are made based on too few and ill-documented data.	b) The model is relatively 'open' compared to the typical S.D. models, i.e. it incorporates manyexogeno variab-. les world shows some
	c) Computational effort is more due to matrix-inversions.	c) The concept of "one world-one model" has been thought as misleading. The real serious structural differences with respect to different "regions" which constitute the "world".	c) The present model is based on simple neo-classical structure. More sophistication can be incorporated by adding a monetary sector and foreign trade sector.
	d) Data limitations especially those related to sectorwise waste generation and recycling because waste is not incorporated as an explicit parameter in national accounting.	d) S.D. methodology is difficult for the uninitiated and makes a higher demand on professionalism than other methodologies.	d) Policy design based on an optimum selection of policy options will be a natural extension to the model.

Model Results

The integrated model developed and tested in this study has been used for policy analysis and planning in the following areas:

a) *Energy Demand and Supply Balance:* Sensitivity analysis runs of the integrated energy model show that the parameters like national income are more sensitive to demand management policies in the energy consuming sectors than the policies aimed only at increasing the energy supply. The model results show that if the energy constraints could be restricted only to household-supply, the national income is relatively unaffected because energy sector forms a small fraction of the national income. However, if these shortages are passed to production sectors as well, it leads to a vicious circle of decline in the national income, leading to a complete collapse of the economy. Demand management through improved material productivity in the energy consuming sectors, coupled with high capacity utilisation in the energy sectors may have a significant impact on the overall growth of the economy.

b) *Resource Allocation:* Model results show that higher sectorial priorities in investment to energy sectors do not lead to a significant increase in the national income. On the other hand, such priorities may lead to changes in the GDP-mix in the form of increased share of energy in the overall national income. This could mean a declaration in the growth of other production sectors where lower priorities are assigned. It is imperative to link the sectorial to the basic-needs of people.

c) Sensitivity analysis in respect of I-O-W model shows that energy conservation has a significant relevance for the developing economies. Waste has a multiplier effect in the economy. When the waste generation in the economy goes up by 25 per cent, petroleum requirements increase above 400 per cent, i.e. an average increase of over 12 per cent for every one per cent increase in waste generation. The impact of waste on the natural resource requirements warrants a serious consideration and should be an important policy parameter in the national energy planning.

d) *Construction Delays and Lead Times:* Sensitivity runs show that reduction of construction lead times of energy projects leads to a faster capital formation in the energy sectors, and consequently an increased energy output. This is an important policy dimension for the transition dynamics. However, the impact of increased energy supply on the national income may be felt only if it is accompanied by a productivity increase in the energy consuming sectors.

e) *Energy Cost:* Energy cost shows a higher sensitivity to the material productivity changes than the natural resources prices.

Indirect effects of waste in the energy consuming sectors have a more serious impact on the cost of energy output.

Policy Implications of the Study

Many lessons from the viewpoint of energy policy planning can be drawn from this research study. Some of the thrust areas are identified as follows:

a) It is necessary to establish the relationship of energy with other national priorities like food, clothing, health, family welfare etc. Energy, being an essential input to all the production sectors, plays a key role in the growth and prosperity of the nation. Hence, sectorial inter-dependencies should be clearly recognised and should be the basis of energy planning at the national level.

b) Conservation of resources is a key policy issue in a developing country, where population pressure and the requirements of economic growth place a heavy demand on the scarce natural resources. Waste management should be considered as a policy parameter and it should be studied in the context of sectorial interlinkages in the economy.

c) Emissions related to energy serious environmental implications. Waste management has linkages not only to resource conservation, but also pollution control policies. in the context of energy planning, it is imperative to consider the consumption of non-renewable resources, energy conservation, waste management and environmental issues in an integrated manner.

d) Delays are inherent in any economic system, in terms of information, perception, development and construction leads time. Such delay imply that the response of the economy to the energy crisis, in terms of inter-fuel substitution, development of energy resources and relatively newer technologies taking over the conventional ones, is expected to be sluggish. Hence transition dynamics, rather than long-term equilibrium should be the focus of energy policy analysis.

e) Optimisation approach to assessment of new technologies is normative in nature, but it does not explain why a new technology, even if superior, is not taken up immediately by all the potential uses. The study of the diffusion process of new energy technologies is necessary for long-term analysis of energy problems.

Conclusion

The computer models have been applied to a variety of socio-economic problems ranging from business and industry to economic growth, energy, education, health, army and police, urban planning, societal dynamics and even world dynamics. However, the impact of the earlier computer models on the policy making process was rather marginal. Proliferation of modelling methodologies and the debates and controversies relating to the supremacy of one technique over the other in the past, have also eroded the faith of policy-makers on the utility of models. However, recent trends in modelling towards user-friendly, transparent models with interactive software, unification of modelling approaches and emphasis on learning and communication aspects indicate a definite and positive role of models in the future policy making process.

REFERENCES

Avriel, M., Briener, A., and Karni, R. (1982) 'Energy-Economic Planning in Israel': The OMER Study. In Amit, R., Avriel, M. (eds.), (1982) *Perspectives in Resource Policy Modelling*, Ballinger Publishing Company, Cambridge, MA.

Cherniavsky, E.A. (1975) *Brookhaven Energy System Optimisation Model*, BNL 19569, Upto, New York: Brookhaven National Laboratory.

Deam, R.S., *et. al.*, (1974) *World Energy Model-Description and Results*, Special Energy Policy Publication on Energy Modelling. Guilford, Surrey, England: IPC Science and Technology Press Limited.

— — (1974) 'Federal Energy Administration', *Project Independence Report*, Washington, D.C.: FEA.

Flood, R.L. and Jackson, M. (1991) *Creative Problem Solving: Total System Intervention*, John Wiley and Sons, NY.

Government of India.(1974) *Report of the Fuel Policy Committee*, New Delhi.

Government of India. (1979) *Report of the Working Group on Energy Policy*, Planning Commission, New Delhi.

Hudson, E.A., and Jorgenson, D.W. (1974) 'Energy Policy and Economic Growth,: 1975-2000', *Bell Journal of Economics*, 5, 461-514, Autumn.

Huntington, H.G., Weyant, J.P. Sweeney, J.L. (1982) 'Modelling for Insights, Not Numbers: The Experiences of the Energy Modelling Forum', *OMEGA*, Vol 10, No. 5, pp. 449-462.

James, D.E., Musgrove, A.R. de L., Stocks, K.J. April (1986) 'Integration of an Economic Input-Output Model and a Linear Programming Technological Model for Energy System Analysis', *Energy Econ*, V8, n2 pp 99-112.

Kashihara, T., Wakamatu, S. (1986) 'The Study of the Computer Model for the Energy Systems Demands', *Denshi Gijutu Sogo Kenkyusho Iho*, V50, n4, pp 264-285, 1986.

Keloharju, R.(1983) *Relativity Dynamics, ACTA Series,* The Helsinki School of Economics, Helsinki.

Koenig, H.E., Tokad, Y., Kesavan, H. (1967) *Analysis of Discrete Physical Systems.* New York: McGraw Hill.

Koenig, H.E., Cooper, W.E., and Falney, J.M. (1972), 'Engineering for Ecological, Sociological and Economic Compatibility', IEEE Transactions: Systems, *Man and Cybenetics,* Vol. SMC-2, no. 3, pp 319.

Kumar, S., and Satsangi, P.S. (1993) 'System Dynamics Simulation of Physical Systems with Application to Hopfield Neural Networks' Proc. Fifth National Conference on System Dynamics', in Sushil (ed.). *System Dynamics for Management Support,* Wiley Eastern Limited.

Leontief, W.W. (1953) *Studies in the Structure of the American Economy.* New York: Oxford University Press.

Leontief, W.W.(1966), *Input-Output Economics.* New York: Oxford University Press.

Leontief, W.W. (1970) 'Contributions to Input-Output Analysis'. *Proc. of the Fourth International Conference on Input-Output Techniques,* Geneva, Jeneva 8-12, 1968, North Holland.

Manne, A.S. (1977), ETA-MACRO: 'A Model of Energy Economy Interactions'. In Hitch, C.J. (ed.) *Modelling Energy Economy Interactions,* Washington, DC: Resources for the Future.

Medsker, L.R., November (1984) 'Interactive Decision Support System for Energy Policy Analysis', *Common ACM,* V27, n11, pp 1122-1128.

Mesarovic, M. and Pestel, E. (1974) *Multilevel Computer Model of World Development System,* Vols. 1-6, Laxenberg, Austria.

Morecroft, J.D.W. (1988) 'System Dynamics and Microworld for Policy-makers', European *Journal of Operational Research,* North Holland, 35, 301-320.

Parekh, Jyoti (1979) *Modelling Energy Demand for Policy Analysis,* Planning Commission, India.

Parikh, Kirit, (1976) *Second India Studies: Energy.* Delhi: Macmillan.

Preston, R.S.,(1972) *The Wharton Annual and Industry Forecasting Model,* Philadelphia, Economic Research Unit, University of Pennsylvania.

Raghavendran, P. (1985) Energy Development and Economic Growth- A Dynamic Model for India, *Proc. Workshop on Energy Modelling,* National Productivity Council, New Delhi.

Raskin, P.D., (1985) 'Integrated Energy Planning in Developing Countries: *The Role of Computer Systems, Ambio,* V14, n4-5, pp 210-213.

Rohtagi, P.K., Rohtagi, K., and Bowonder, B.,(1979) *Technological Forecasting,* New Dehli: Tata McGraw Hill.

Richardson, G.P., Anderson, D.F., Rohrbaugh, J. and Steinhurst, W. (1993) 'Group Model Building. Proc. Fifth National Conference on System Dynamics in Sushil (ed.) *System Dynamics for Management Support,* Wiley Eastern Limited.

Sage, A.P.,(1977) *Methodology for Large Scale Systems,* McGraw Hill Inc.

Satsangi, P.S.,(1986) *Energy Planning Model for Rural India,* I.I.T. Delhi.

Schwartz, A.N.R., (1974) *The Effect of Rise in Oil Prices on the Economy of Industrialised Countries.* Monograph No. 17, The Netherlands Central Planning Bureau.

Srinivasan Setty, K.P., Padmanabhan, S., Natarajan, R., May (1987) 'National Energy-Conservation Policy DELPHI: Report of the Findings', *Technol. Forecast Soc. Change,* V31, n3, pp 257-267.

Sterman, J.D., (1981) 'The Energy, Transition and the Economy: A System Dynamics Approach, Ph.D. Dissertation, A.P. Sloan School of Management, MIT, Cambridge, MA.

Sterman, J.D., (1988) *A Skeptics Guide to Computer Models, Foresigh and National Decisions,* Grant, L., University Press of America.

Sushil, (1984) Systems Modelling of Waste Management in National Planning, Ph.D. Thesis, Indian Institute of Technology, New Delhi.

Sushil, January (1987) 'Energy Source Selection in the Rural Area, A Goal Programming Application', *Proc. XXIX National Convention of IIIE,* Calcutta, India.

Sushil, January 18-23, (1993) Flexible Systems Methodology, Keynote Address. *Ninth International Congress of Cybernetics and Systems,* New Delhi.

Troncale, L., (1988) 'The Systems Sciences: What are they? Are they one or Many'? *European Journal of Operational Research,* 37, 8-33.

Vennix, J.A.M., (1990) *Mental Models and Computer Models: Design and Evaluation of Computer-based Learning Environment for Policy-Making*. University of Nigmegen, Netherlands.

Vij, A.K., (1990) Energy Policy Modelling and Analysis for the Indian Economy, Ph.D. Thesis, Indian Institute of Technology, Delhi.

Warfield, J.N. (1982) 'Internal Structures', *IEEE Trans. Systems, Man and Cybernetics,* Vol SMC-2, pp 133-140, March.

Warfield, J.N., (1990) *A Science of Generic Design: Managing Complexity Through Systems Design,* Vol. I & II, Inter Systems Publication, U.S.A..

25. AN INTEGRATED APPROACH TO PUBLIC POLICY DESIGN

V.K. Agnihotri

1. Statements on Public Policy

In recent years there has been an upsurge in formal policy documents issued by the Government of India. They have come to be usually captioned "Statement on (whatever) Policy". The main content of these statements is a set of objectives that inform government action (and inaction) in different areas of concern to the welfare state, such as health, industry, technology, environment, education, housing, telecommunication and so on. Their wording style is comparable to manifestoes issued by political parties. For example, let us look at the following stipulation in the Statement on Industrial Policy (Ministry of Industry, 1991, para 12):

> "Government will provide enhanced support to the small-scale sector so that it flourishes in an environment of economic efficiency and continuous technological upgradation."

and compare it with the corresponding provision in the election manifesto of the Congress Party (Indian National Congress -I, 1991, p.36):

> "The Congress will continue to provide support to the small scale sector so that it flourishes in an environment of economic efficiency and continuous technological upgradation."

Or take the BJP manifesto, for that matter, (Bhartiya Janata Party, 1991, p.16):

> "Small scale sector will be given due importance and encouragement."

The Government of India have resorted to issuing statements on public policy for several reasons, including the need to make a formal declaration of their intentions, to tackle complexity in decision-making or to make a clean break from the past. In their origination, they are preceded sometimes by a study or a committee, the report of which forms the basis of the Statement on Policy (e.g. Statement on Textile Policy, 1985). At other times, they are issued periodically since a time limit is prescribed to their currency (e.g. Import-Export Policy). Some others are issued and/or revised as and when government changes or decides upon new initiatives due to endogenous and exogenous factors (e.g. Statements on Industrial Policy, Science Policy, Technology Policy, Computer Policy, Education Policy, Sports Policy etc.). Some others attempt to put together the essence of policy decisions taken by the government on the subject from time to time, especially in the recent past (e.g. Statement on Trade Policy, 1991).

1.1 *Pros and Cons of Statements of Policy*

A formal statement of policy has its plus and minus points. On the positive side, it helps provide a definite focus to government activity. It also establishes norms for assessing success in achievement of goals.

On the negative side, it binds the government to certain courses of action and thereby, to some extent, reduces flexibility in policy responses to the solution of social problems. Once a statement of policy is issued on a particular subject, it tends to perpetuate and it is not normally possible to withdraw it totally and revert to a more flexible "no-policy-statement" situation, although the document may be marginally or even radically revised. All subsequent comprehensive policy responses have to take the form of a fresh statement of policy or a modification thereof. More importantly, underlying or unresolved contradictions in the objectives contained in a statement on policy cause avoidable embarassment to the government and are grist to the opposition mill. Inability to implement any of the policy objectives too could be a source of similar discomfiture. Statements on health, textile and education policies have, therefore, periodically run into rough weather.

1.2 *Basic Characteristics of Policy Statements*

One of the fundamental characteristics of these statements is that they string together a set of objectives which inform government intervention in a given field; the syntactical definition of an objective being: to (active word)+(object)+(qualifying phrase) (Sage, 1977). One finds these objectives practically in every sentence. An example from the Textile Policy (Department of Textiles, 1985) is listed below to illustrate this point. The original phrasing is given first, followed by restated objective contained within brackets.

PARA 7

1. In the spinning sector, all steps will be taken to ensure optimum utilisation of the spinning capacity. (To ensure optimum utilisation of the spinning capacity).
2. The availability of raw materials for the spinning sector would be augmented. (To augment the availability of raw materials for the spinning sector).
3. The infrastructure for the distribution of yarn would be strengthened. (To strengthen the infrastructure for the distribution of yarn).
4. At the same time, necessary measures to encourage and increase spinning in the Khadi sector would be taken in view of its large employment potential. (To encourage and increase spinning in the Khadi sector).

Another feature of these statements is that often these objectives are listed/discussed under several headings/sub-headings which are identifiable as the horizontal dimensions of the policy in question. For example, the Industrial Policy (Ministry of Industry, 1991) has the following broad subject heading/dimensions:

A Industrial Licensing Policy;
B Foreign Investment;
C Foreign Technology Agreement;
D Public Sector Policy; and
E Monopolies and Restrictive Trade Practices Act (MRTP Act).

The National Sports Policy (Department of Youth Affairs and Sports, 1992) has the following main headings:

* Creating a Sports Environment;
* Broadbasin;
* Improving Competitive Standards;
* Sports Management; and

* Referees and Other Technical Officials.

A further important characteristic of the policy statements is that the objectives contained in them have a vertical hierarchy specially in terms of the degree of abstraction/specificity implied in them. For example, consider the following objectives of the Textile Policy (Department of Textiles, 1985):

1. To meet the clothing requirements of a growing population (para 4);
2. To preserve the distinct and unique role of the handlooms in the weaving sector (para 8); and
3. To introduce a Contributory Thrift-Fund Scheme to provide assistance to the handloom weavers during times of need (para 15).

By no stretch of imagination could these three objectives be said to belong to same category/level. The basic difference among them is in terms of the degree of abstraction/specificity. While the first one is stated in a more broad and general terms and encompasses a larger field of societal concern, the second one is comparatively less abstract and the third one is relatively very specific. Thus, these objectives could be said to be part of a vertical hierarchy.

1.3 *Shortcomings*

Even though the policy statements are a set objectives having dimensions and hierarchy, this is not explicitly so recognised. An examination of some of these policy statements further reveals the following general shortcomings:

(1) absence of a standard approach to documenting public policy;

(2) absence of a systematic procedure for arriving at an optimal set of policy objectives in a given policy area and identifying its dimensions and the hierarchy of its objectives;

(3) no explicit attempt to identify conflicts among various policy objectives and to prescribe specific procedures for their resolution; and

(4) absence of a mechanism for measuring objectives through verifiable indicators.

It is hypothesised that these deficiencies are largely responsible for much of governmental failure in successfully implementing, monitoring and evaluating public policy.

2. Objectives Paradigm

If the policy statements of the Government of India comprise a set of objectives which have horizontal dimensions and a vertical hierarchy, methods have to be devised for arriving at an optimal set of policy objectives, extracting their dimensions and arranging them in a vertical hierarchy in order to be able to properly appreciate the means-ends relationship among them.

Among the available methodologies, Brainwriting/Ideawriting and Nominal Group Technique (NGT) combined with Options Field Methodology, Options Profile Methodology and Interpretive Structural Modelling (ISM) provide the means for generating an optimal set of policy options and arranging them into categories and dimensions. This approach was adopted by the author for analysing and designing handloom policy (Agnihotri and Satsangi, 1993a, 1993b).

For arranging objectives in a hierarchy, Warfield (1973a, b, c) has suggested a Methodology for constructing an intent structure which describes a mathematical or graphical arrangement of objectives or goals to be attained. One type of intent structure is called an objective graph which when presented in the form of a tree is called an OBJECTIVE TREE as shown in Fig. 25.1. This facilitates visual perception of the structure of the objectives (Sage, 1977, pp.25-27).

The objective tree could be constructed by using the Interpretive Structural Modelling Methodology (Warfield, 1976). The intent structure so obtained could be used, among other things, to clarify the thinking process for complex problems, to provide a basis for decision and policy analysis and to provide a base from which objectives may be changed as more information is obtained.

However, the hierarchy of objectives obtained through Interpretive Structural Modelling is open ended even though it has been suggested that the objectives contained in an intent structure could be broadly categorised into goal reality and policy dimensions.

For purposes of structuring the objectives of public policy, however, there is need for a more definitive scheme of arranging them in a hierarchy for two basic reasons. Firstly, there is need to move gradually from abstract goals to more specific instruments designed to help in implementing the policy. Secondly, the methodology should attempt to provide a standard approach, as far as possible, for designing policy documents.

The search for a more definitively structured hierarchy of objectives leads to the Logical Framework Approach (LFA) to project planning which was originally developed by Practical Concept Incorporated for USAID in order to assist in the planning, management and evaluation of development activities and is extensively used by many development agencies (Coleman, 1987). In LFA there are four levels of project objectives, namely, Goal (or Development Objective), Purpose (or Immediate Objective), Outputs and Inputs. Some agencies insert another level between Outputs and Inputs called Activities.

In Management literature also, one finds a hierarchy of organisational plans. Koontz and Weihrich (1988, pp. 61-69) have provided the following classification:

(1) purposes or missions;
(2) objectives or goals;
(3) strategies;
(4) policies;
(5) procedures;
(6) rules;
(7) programmes; and
(8) budget.

They also talk of a hierarchy of organisational objectives (pp. 81-83) ranging from the broad aim to specific individual objectives. This hierarchy of objectives has the following levels:

1. Socio-economic purpose;
2. Mission;
3. Overall objectives of the organisation (long-range, strategic);
4. More specific overall objectives (e.g. in key result areas);
5. Division objectives;
6. Department and Unit objectives; and
7. Individual objectives (i.e. performance and personal development objectives).

Stoner and Freeman (1989, p. 146) also provide a hierarchy of organisational plans as shown in Fig. 25.2.

In the policy statements of the Government of India there is a vague recognition of a hierarchy of objectives. Some objectives are described as main, central, principal or basic objectives of policy framework. There are others which are described as objectives, policies, schemes, projects, activities, action plans, programme of action and so on. For example, the

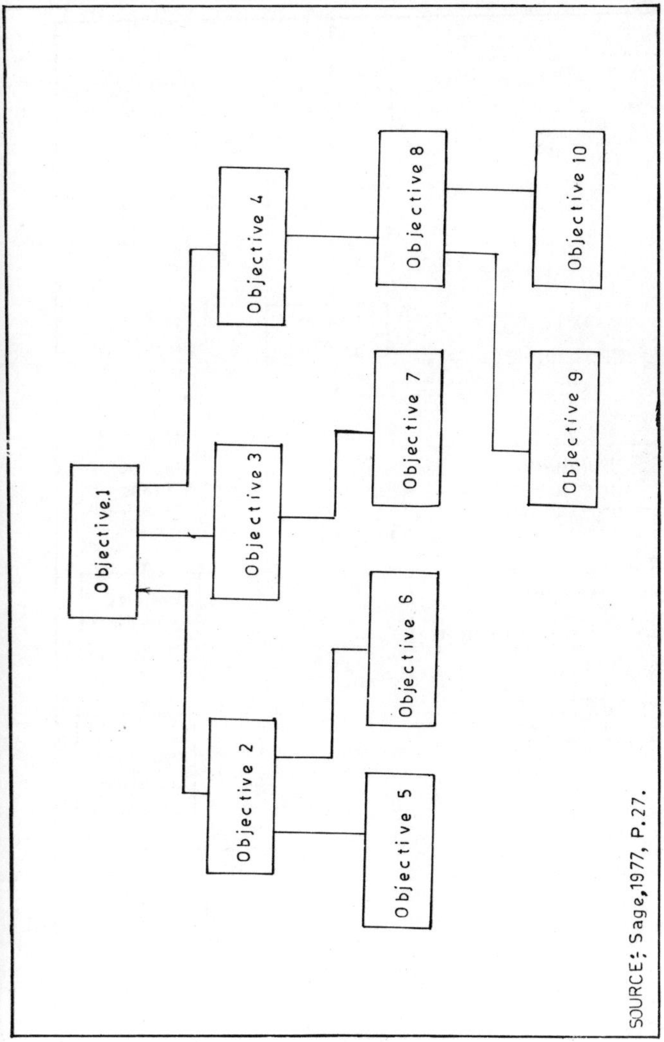

SOURCE: Sage, 1977, P.27.

FIG. 25.1: The Objective Tree

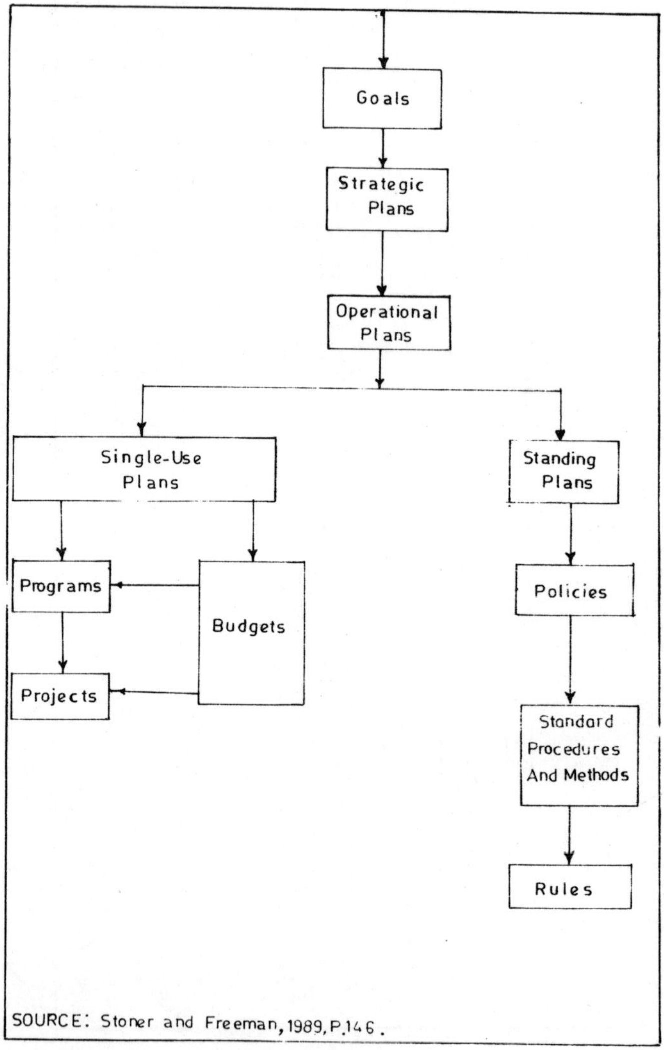

FIG. 25.2: The Hierarchy of Organisational Plans.

statement on Policy Measures for Promoting and Strengthening Small, Tiny and Village Enterprises (Department of SSI & ARI, 1991) states:

> "The primary objective of the Small Scale Industrial Policy during the nineties would be to impart more vitality and growth impetus to the sector...."

The Statement on Textile Policy (Department of Textiles, 1985) makes a very important admission:

> "The existing textile policy sets out a number of objectives. While each of these objectives is important, the multiplicity of objectives has inhibited the achievement of the main task of the textile industry, that is to increase the production of cloth of acceptable quality at reasonable prices to meet the clothing requirements of a growing population."

It also mentions programmes and schemes. As a matter of fact, the National Sports Policy document (Department of Youth Affairs and Sports, 1992) is entitled "Programme of Action". Similarly, the tourism policy statement (Ministry of Civil Aviation and Tourism, 1992) has been given the title "National Action Plan for Tourism".

In order to sort out this semantic confusion concerning the hierarchy of objectives in policy documents, it is sought to adapt the ideas of LFA and management for purposes of describing the levels of objectives in them. A five-level optimal/adequate hierarchy of objectives of public policy is suggested as follows:

(1) *Aim or Mission:* The ultimate aim of government intervention in a policy area. The main objective of a government ministry or Department which sets it apart from other government ministries or departments.

(2) *Goals:* The break up of the Aim or Mission into more specific objectives, sometimes called "main", "central" or "basic" objectives of public policy for a particular policy area/space. These may often be primary objectives of different divisions, sub-units of a Ministry or Department and are relatable to horizontal dimensions discussed earlier. Alternatively, these are the ends towards which policies are aimed.

(3) *Policies:* General statements or understandings which guide the thinking and decision-making in the concerned government

Ministry or Department. These can also be described in terms of policy options.

(4) *Programmes:* Packages of measures devised to operationalise policies.

(5) *Schemes or Projects:* Specific and detailed components of programme packages.

Table 25.1 below gives the conceptual framework of this hierarchy of objectives:

TABLE 25.1: Policy Objective Hierarchy

Objective Type	Objective Characteristic	Objective Hierarchy
Conceptualising or Axiomatic	Long-term, largely a political, consensual	1. Aim or Mission 2. Goals
Paradigmatic	Medium-term, political party specific	3. Policies
Actualising or Implementing	Relatively short-term, often time bound, political party/ bureaucracy specific	4. Programmes 5. Schemes or Projects

This hierarchy of objectives also reflects the degree of abstraction of objectives. The conceptualising objectives have a greater degree of abstraction while implementing objectives are more concrete. This gradual descent from axiomatic precepts to actual schemes also provides scope for adequate conceptualisation.

Formulation of the Aim or Mission statement helps provide a specific focus to public policy document and the concerned Government Ministry/Department. Osborn and Gaebler (1992) have extolled the virtues of mission-driven Government. The break-up of the Aim into more specific goals leads to a more concrete spelling out of the main or basic objectives of the policy/ Ministry. A stage is thus reached where thinking in terms of working out policy norms could be fruitfully begun. Once the policies have been spelt out, it is time to develop packages of programmes to integrate the policies and work out specific action plans which facilitate allocation of quantifiable and objectively verifiable schemes and projects to the implementing agencies. This could be regarded as providing for adequate levels of hierarchy in policy design.

It is important to point out at this stage that the work does not begin or end with the structuring of a five level hierarchy of policy objective. The concept of programme planning linkages developed by Hill and Warfield

(1972) provides a useful guide to the type of backward and forward linkages required for proper policy design and implementation. Thus consideration of needs, alterables and constraints should precede the development of five-level hierarchy of policy objectives. Again, the formulation of programmes and schemes should be succeeded by detailing of specific activities (e.g. legislation, issuing of Government orders and circulars announcing the programmes and schemes, establishing rules and procedures, executive instructions, guidelines, action plans, etc. for implementation). This should be coupled with identification of agencies to be vested with the responsibility of undertaking each of the activities.

It should also be borne in mind that Policy Design is only one sub-system of the Policy System which *inter alia* subsumes other sub-systems such as Implementation Design and Impact Design. (It is also closely linked with other systems such as the Delivery Systems). Each one of these is an important link in the chain which ultimately helps ensure that the Aim of the policy actually delivers the intended benefits to the target group(s) in an appropriate manner to the satisfaction of all the stakeholders. However, here the discussion is focused on policy design.

The vertical logic in the five-level hierarchy of policy objectives is based on a means-ends relationship. From Schemes/Projects to Aim/Mission there is a sequence of four relationships in which a given level is related to the level above. This means-ends linkage can be expressed in terms of the contextual relation in an intent structure. Thus we can say that implementation of Schemes "Contributes to" or "Facilitates" or "Helps Achieve" the concerned Programme objective.

It should, however, be noted that in the nature of things this vertical logic is stronger at the base of the structure and becomes somewhat feeble as we move up. Thus the Schemes contribute to achievement of Programme to a greater degree than Programmes do to Policies or Policies do to Goals.

This nature and characteristic of relationship between different levels of policy hierarchy needs to be reckoned with while evaluating public policy.

3. A New Approach to Public Policy Design

In the context of the foregoing discussion and taking note of the shortcomings of public policy documents, a set of procedures called Logical Processual Framework is suggested in order to aid the Government's policy design process. This approach is largely built around the objectives paradigm and requires following certain logical steps for designing and/or redesigning public policy as per the requirements of a given Ministry/

Department. A processual or step-by-step framework for public policy design has been suggested especially in the context of prevailing government/bureaucratic systems based on procedures.

The aim of the methodology is to provide dynamic policy support to central minds of Government for designing and redesigning public policy through units located near or close to them (Dror, 1986). *Inter alia,* it attempts to infuse in public policy documents, some of the rigour of project management mechanisms evolved by national and international agencies.

3.1 *Conceptual Framework*

Following concepts are integral to and provide the theoretical underpinnings of the approach:

(1) Objective Tree (Sage, 1977);
(2) Interpretive Structural Modelling (Warfield, 1976);
(3) Programme Planning Linkages (Hill and Warfield, 1972);
(4) Consensus Methodologies (Warfield, 1990a, 1990b);
(5) Fuzzy Set Evaluation Procedures (Alley *et al,* 1979);
(6) Hierarchy of Objectives (Koontz and Weihrich, 1988; Stoner and Freeman, 1989); and
(7) Logical Framework Approach (Coleman, 1987; GTZ, 1988; Gasper, 1991).

3.2 *Assumptions and Hypotheses*

(1) The main thrust of the new approach is the preparation, modification and maintenance of the Objective Tree, the importance of which is underscored by the following factors:
(a) It (especially the developing of hierarchical structure) clarifies thinking about objectives which constitute the core of public policy;
(b) In attempting to word the objectives accurately and concisely, the concepts get further clarified. Attempting narrative text straightway promotes fuzziness and conceals conflicts;
(c) The listing of objectives converts them into symbols amenable to various types of operations (e.g. ISM); and
(d) Drawing up of the Objective Tree improves communicability of policy and helps speed up thinking process. (It could be displayed in a central policy room and elsewhere for the guidance of policy makers and implementors).

(2) The hierarchy of objectives also reflects the degree of abstraction of objectives which are sought to be arranged in a descending order of abstraction, moving from abstract/general objectives to concrete/specific objectives. It gradually leads from axiomatic principles to action points, thus ensuring provision of policy implementation mechanisms. By prescribing five specific levels, the process is sought to be given a definite focus and direction.

(3) The step by step process of policy design underscores the importance of thinking things through with the help of domain experts in tackling complexity.

(4) Improvement in public policy is not possible without the active cooperation of main policy actors in democratic societies, viz. the political executive and the government bureaucracy, and hence the policy design methodology must be Psychological owned by them. The tools to be acceptable to and operable by them, must be user-friendly and transparent.

(5) The methodology belongs to the genre of Group Decision Support Systems and emphasises the participation of domain experts and stakeholders in public policy design in the context of the crucial role they play in public policy making process in democratic states, the importance of developing consensus among main policy actors, and the complexity of the problem situation which does not always lend itself to finding satisfactory solutions through standard management science approaches.

(6) The methodology will help incorporate various pressure group interests in public policy while maintaining a modicum of rationality and without losing sight of basic objectives. Currently public policy appears to be a "patchwork quilt" of various interest group positions very much like the manifestoes of political parties.

(7) The suggested policy support methodology inter alia would be able to:

- strengthen the logical fiber of the policy documents;
- provide a way for articulating and resolving conflicts whose existence in policy documents makes the latter suspect in the eyes of the public and open to criticism by the opposition; and
- provide a mechanism for measuring the achievement of objectives.

(8) The methodology may in some cases lead to only marginal

improvement in the situation; but given the current state of affairs, any improvement is better than none at all.

4. Logical Processual Framework

It consists of a set of step-by-step procedures as an aid to thinking in policy making. Not all steps may be warranted in every situation. The full or a smaller set of steps may be invoked depending upon the nature and scope of public policy under consideration and the requirements of the policy makers/stakeholders. The process is both iterative and cyclical. The discussion of the steps will be illustrated with references to the handloom policy of the Government of India.

The Logical Processual Framework consists of the following steps:

4.1 *STEP 1: Decomposition*

This preliminary step requires breaking down the existing policy statement into a set objectives and rephrasing them appropriately, following the syntactical definition of an objective. Warfield (1976, pp. 456-470) has at length demonstrated this process by converting the United Nations document entitled "Towards Accelerated Development: Proposals for the Second United Nations Development Decade" into a set of objectives.

If a specific policy document is not available on a particular subject, this exercise could be undertaken through content analysis of policy-related literature (statements made in Parliament, circulars, executive instructions, programmes, schemes etc.), supplemented by discussions with the concerned officials.

Alternatively, as suggested in STEP 3 later, a list of objectives could also be generated by using the Ideawriting and Nominal Group Technique methodologies with the help of the stakeholders. This may also be done even if a policy document is available, but the circumstances warrant a fresh start to the process. Such an approach will specially suit the Ministries/Departments which feel that their attempts to revise the existing policy document are getting stuck (e.g. Health and Textiles). This could also help in tackling the problem associated with the multiplicity of objectives, as during this process a smaller set of critical objectives could be identified through Nominal Group Technique. However, before proceeding with this alternative, the exercise of decomposition of existing policy document/literature should be undertaken in order to provide a learning opportunity in writing objectives as well as generate a basic set of objectives to refer to/work upon.

A decomposed set of objectives of handloom policy of the Government of India (already arranged under first three levels, viz. Aim, Goals and Policies following Step 2 below) is given in Appendix I.

4.2 *STEP 2: Preparing a Descriptive Objective Tree*

This step entails arranging the objectives into a five level hierarchy, namely, Aim, Goals, Policies, Programmes and Schemes. This could be done with the help of ISM which generates a basic hierarchy and identifies the Goals and Policies. The Goals could be also identified through Options Field Methodology which *inter alia* generates a set of dimensions. Each dimension suggests a Goal objective.

Identification of objectives at various levels need not be done sequentially from top to down. For instance, it may be easier, in the first place, to list the programmes along with their component Schemes or Projects. If a formal policy document for the organisation is not available, Policies could be deduced from Programmes, and Goals can then be deduced from the Policies. However, it is advisable to determine the Aim of the organisation independently after careful thinking, from which Goals and Policies could then be derived. In the Indian policy making scenario, this task could be undertaken by the Cabinet and/or the Planning Commission. A list of objectives arranged in a five level hierarchy could thus be prepared through backward and forward iterations.

There is inter-connectivity at the interfaces of the three categories of objectives, namely, Axiomatic, Paradigmatic and Implementing objectives. Thus a Goal, alone or in conjunction with other Goals, may lead to two or more Policies and, conversely, a Policy, alone or in conjunction with other Policies, may sometimes serve two or more Goals. The same type of inter-connectivity may exist between Policies and Programmes.

During this process of arranging objectives in a hierarchy, it would be often found that in addition to the absence of the Aim statement, the Policy and Programme objectives are also not always clearly articulated. There is a tendency to rush to devise Schemes to implement Goals or Policies without going through the stages of conceptualising specific policies and/or packages of comprehensive Programmes, which results in multiplicity of Schemes or Projects with the attendant duplication of effort and of instruments for implementing Policies. There is clearly a need for adopting an integrative approach here in order to counter-balance the differentiation implied in the drawing up of an Objective Tree.

The Objective Tree of the handloom policy prepared on the basis of the decomposed set of objectives (Appendix I) is given in Appendix II.

In order to ensure that a given policy is thought through in all its details, including its implementation, the five level hierarchy should be meticulously developed as a departmental document for internal use. However, for purposes of preparation of the policy document, especially for public consumption, only the first three levels (i.e. Aim, Goals and Policies) are relevant. This approach is advocated for the following reasons:

(1) to concentrate on broad policy related issues in the policy document;
(2) to speed up the process of preparation of policy document (working out complete details of Programmes and Schemes takes time);
(3) to obtain a concise and compact policy document and avoid cluttering it up with multiplicity of objectives; and
(4) to avoid the necessity of changing/revising the policy document very often, since Programmes and Schemes/ Projects get added, altered, revised and deleted of tener than broad policy pronouncements.

4.3 *STEP 3: Policy Research and Debate*

During this step, in the first place, in consultation with policy-makers and other stakeholders (if possible and desirable), the following exercises of Programme Planning (Hill and Warfield, 1972) may be undertaken in order to identify backward policy planning linkages:

(a) Problem definition;
(b) Needs identification; and
(c) Alterables and Constraints demarcation.

Thereafter, wherever necessary, surveys and studies (internally or through external agencies) of various types and degrees of sophistication, appropriate to the issue under consideration, may be undertaken. These must take into account the problem, needs and constrains identified earlier and make recommendations in their light. The findings of these survey and studies may be then discussed with the policy makers and stakeholders, including formal consultations, in preparation for the next step.

Judicious use of Brainstorming, Ideawriting and Nominal Group Technique is recommended during this stage to generate policy options. Thereafter, Options Field and Options Profile methodologies (Warfield,

1990a, 1990b) and Fuzzy Set Evaluation Procedures (Alley *et al,* 1979) could be used to obtain the essential dimensions of the policy and arrive at a satisficing policy alternative containing an optimal set of policy options.

In respect of the handloom policy of the Government of India, following these procedures, an export-oriented policy was developed (Agnihotri and Satsangi, 1993b). The list of objectives rewritten to conform to syntactical definition of this policy along with their dimensions is given in Appendix III. It has 12 dimensions and 27 policy options arranged under them. If considered necessary, a few more relevant policy options out of the list generated could be added to make this set of objective more comprehensive. Thus, for instance, under the dimension MARKETING AND EXPORT, one could add the following:

(i) to concentrate on marketing of furnishings and other non-apparel items in export markets [NON-APPAREL EXPORT]; and
(ii) to introduce "handloom mark" to upgrade the image of handloom products [HANDLOOM MARK].

4.4 *STEP 4: Preparing a Normative Objective Tree*

On the basis of the dimensions and the set of objectives obtained during the previous step, a normative objective tree could now be drawn. ISM may be used to identify the Aim or the top level objective of the policy. The Goals should broadly conform to the dimensions and the rest of the objectives should be arranged at the third level as Policies under their respective Goals. If necessary, some editing/deletion of objectives may be done to obtain a satisficing structure with the help of policy makers/ stakeholders.

In order to combine an integrative approach with differentiation involved in drawing the Objective Tree, it is necessary to look integratively when moving from Goals to Policies and again when Policies are sought to be converted into Programmes. Thus when attempting to outline Policies to achieve the Goals, one should try to see whether it is possible to meet the needs of two or more Goals, wholly or partially, through the instrument of a single Policy. Similar integration should be attempted by developing flexible Programme packages which would help translate several Policies into a comprehensive Programme. This would ensure that multiplicity of Programmes, Schemes and the attendant duplication of effort and inter-scheme conflict is avoided.

Drawing the Objective Tree horizontally, like a Value or Decision Tree, may help think integratively.

In the case of the handloom policy of the Government of India, using the set of objectives given in Appendix III and adding two more objectives under the dimension MARKETING AND EXPORT as suggested in the previous step, ISM was used to identify the Aim of the policy. Two candidates for the Aim level were thus identified as follows:

(1) to launch a drive to increase exports of handloom products ten-fold in next five years [EXPORT DRIVE]; and
(2) to give a slogan to handlooms to produce competitively or perish [COMPETE OR PERISH].

Of these two, the first one (EXPORT DRIVE) was considered to be a better Aim on account of its clarity and better measurability. It was, therefore, selected as the Aim of the handloom policy. Thereafter, taking into account the identified dimensions, the Goals were described as shown in Table 25.2.

TABLE 25.2: Goals of Handloom Policy

Sl.No.	GOAL
1	To promote exports of handloom products [PROMOTE EXPORTS]
2	To make raw materials available to handloom industry in adequate quantity and at reasonable prices [RAW MATERIALS]
3	To ensure involvement of weavers in handloom development programmes and schemes [WEAVERS' INVOLVEMENT]
4	To undertake measures for welfare of handloom weavers [WELFARE MEASURES]
5	To protect handlooms from unfair competition [PROTECTIVE MEASURES]
6	To provide technical inputs for improving the quality and range of handloom products [TECHNICAL INPUTS]
7	To strengthen organisational support for promoting handloom activity [ORGANISATIONAL ARRANGEMENTS]
8	To undertake fiscal measures to provide competitive edge to handloom products [FISCAL MEASURES]
9	To make adequate credit available to handloom weavers at reasonable rates of interest [CREDIT]
10	To provide training to handloom weavers and other personnel responsible for implementing handloom development programmes and schemes [TRAINING]

The objective tree comprising the first three levels (Aim, Goals and

Policies) thus prepared for the handloom policy is given in Appendix IV.

Working integratively, it is possible to combine two or more Policies to develop a Programme. Thus, for instance, one can think of an "Export Production and Marketing Programme" which would integrate Policies:

> G1P1, G1P3, G1P5, G1P6, G2P8, G2P12, G2P13, G6P18, G6P19, G6P20, G6P21, G9P26 and G10P28.

Similarly, a "Weavers' Development Programme" could encompass policies G3P14, G4P15, G4P16 and G10P27.

Each Programme would be supported by a set of specific Schemes in keeping with various facets of the underlying Policies/Goals. Thus the "Export Production and Marketing Programme" would inter alia have Schemes for:

(i) supply of quality yarn, dyes and chemicals to handloom weavers through their organisations [SUPPLY RAW MATERIALS];
(ii) supplying yarn to identified agencies to undertake reeling of hank yarn outside mill premises subject to certain quality standards [DECENTRALISED REELING];
(iii) developing a system for identifying appropriate export markets and targeting them through publicity etc. [TARGETING EXPORT MARKETS]; and
(iv) developing and enforcing handloom mark [DEVELOP HANDLOOM MARK], and so on.

While devising Programmes and Schemes, it is also possible to think spatially rather than sectorally. Thus, a group of integrated and supportive facilities to ensure production of export quality handloom products could be provided to certain geographical locations having a large population of appropriate weavers.

This step should be taken to its logical conclusion by developing a list of specific activities to be undertaken in order to implement the Programme and its Schemes and by identifying the agencies responsible for executing them. Thus in the case of handloom policy the Scheme of "Developing and enforcing handloom mark" would, prima facie require three activities to be undertaken, namely:

(i) developing handloom mark;
(ii) enforcing handloom mark, and
(iii) preparing the budget for the above mentioned activities.

The agency for developing handloom mark could be identified through a national or international competition organised for the purpose. The job of enforcing the handloom mark could be entrusted to the National Handloom Development Corporation or some other suitable agency.

The activity of preparing the budget would be common to almost all Schemes and could be undertaken together to arrive at the total cost of all Programmes and Schemes. This, in turn, may point to the need to abandon or scale down some Programmes and Schemes on account of resource constraints. If this happens, it may become necessary to take a fresh look at the Objective Tree to priorities the objectives and, if necessary, keep some Goal(s), Policies, Programme(s) or Scheme(s) in abeyance while recording the effect of doing so explicitly in the internal policy document.

If for some reason it is not possible to complete the objective tree in terms of specific Programmes and Schemes or otherwise, guidelines for action to be taken in future to work them out should be incorporated in the internal policy document.

The policy monitoring, termination and redesign parameters also need to be spelled out.

4.5 *STEP 5: Conflict Articulation and Resolution and Redrawing the Normative Objective Tree*

In public policy making situations it is a common experience to find the government seeking to achieve conflicting objectives, resulting in non-achievement or sub-optimal realisation of the concerned policy objectives. During this step, therefore, an attempt is made to articulate such conflicting objectives and to prescribe a procedure for conflict resolution.

For this purpose, an enlarged list of objectives comprising the conceptualising and paradigmatic objectives of the particular policy under consideration already listed during the previous step, the important interacting/impinging conceptualising and/or paradigmatic objectives of national and other policies, is prepared by the policy makers using their domain expertise. Identification of the set of negatively related objectives among them could be done either through a careful examination of those objectives or by generating a Negative Impact Structure using Interpretive Structural Modelling technique (Warfield, 1976).

Conflict resolution takes place by either eliminating negatively related objectives or prioritising them (Warfield, 1976) and making necessary institutional arrangements.

As far as the handloom policy is concerned, the list of its objective identified earlier (Appendix IV) was compared with a list of relevant national and textile policy objectives generated by domain and other experts and the Negative Impact Structure developed by them (Satsangi *et al,* 1991). The list of these national and textile policy objectives is given in Appendix V. No conflicting objectives among the objectives of handloom policy were found. This may be largely attributed to the procedure adopted for generating those objectives. The salient conflicts between the objectives of the handloom policy, on the one hand, and those of national and textile policies, on the other, may be summarised as follows:

(1) The national objective of increasing productivity of national economy is in conflict with the objective of promoting handlooms because of their underdeveloped technology and low productivity;
(2) Promotion of handloom exports has to be supported by several measures which require subsidisation which does not quite gel with the national objective of rationalising subsidies;
(3) The handloom policy objective of protecting handlooms by controlling powerlooms is not quite in conformity with the national objective of liberalisation and deregulation;
(4) The objective of ensuring economic viability of decentralised powerlooms is in conflict with the objective of promoting handlooms, in general, and promoting exports of handloom products, in particular;
(5) The textile policy objective of augmenting the availability of cloth at affordable prices is, at present, better served by powerlooms than handlooms;
(6) Ensuring remunerative prices for cotton growers does not bode well for handloom weavers;
(7) Modernisation of handloom industry is not quite in tune with the modernisation of other sectors of textile industry; and
(8) The textile policy objective of improving the quality of textile industry products is way ahead of the handloom policy objective of providing technical inputs for improving the quality and range of handloom products.

These conflicts could be resolved either by abandoning one of the concerned objective or by prescribing some procedure to resolve the conflict. For example, it is obvious that the twin objectives of promoting handlooms and decentralised powerlooms cannot be pursued together. Instead of going through the charade any longer, one of the two objectives given priority has to be actively promoted as a policy prescription.

On the other hand, depending on the availability of resources, modernisation of textile industry in general may get priority over a large scale modernisation of handlooms. In such a situation, inter alia, an institutional arrangement for conflict resolution could be made whereby the policy makers and other stakeholders meet on appropriate occasions to discuss and recommend allocation of funds for the two divergent objectives in the context of the overall concerns, such as increasing productivity of the national economy, promoting textile exports, raise resources for financing development, generating employment and so on.

Taking into account the modifications in and/or abandoning of objectives during the previous and the present step, the Normative Objective Tree could be given its final shape.

4.6 *STEP 6: Objective Measures*

The attainment of objectives needs to be assessed in order to verify whether they have actually been accomplished. This is of great significance from the point of view of successful implementation of public policy. To this end a set of objective measures has to be defined. This concept of objective measures is supported both by Unified Programme Planning (Warfield, 1976, p. 157; Sage, 1977, pp. 83-84) and Logical Framework Approach (LFA)(Coleman, 1987). According to LFA, it has two components, namely, Objectively Verifiable Indicators (OVI) and Means of Verification (MOV).

4.6.1 *Objectively Verifiable Indicators (OVI):* OVI represent a set of criteria which indicate in concrete terms that expected results have been achieved. To be valid and useful, the OVI must have the following qualities:

(i) *Criteria:* They must clearly indicate the criteria for the success of the policy objective.
(ii) *Importance:* They must focus on what is important in the objective from the point of view of the policy area concerned.
(iii) *Plausibility:* They must be plausible and clearly related to the objective with which they are associated.
(iv) *Sufficient Number:* There must be a sufficient number of indicators of sufficient detail to allow adequate measurements of achievement of objectives.
(v) *Independence:* They must be independent—a given indicator should not signal achievement at two distinct levels of the

hierarchy of objectives, nor should one indicator simply be a different way of expressing another indicator.

(vi) *Objective Verification:* The OVI must be objectively verifiable so that two independent observers would come to more or less the same conclusion regarding the status of the objective. The measures, however, could be quantitative as well as qualitative.

(vii) *Indirect Indicators:* It may not always be possible to define OVI which will give a direct verifiable indication of achievement at a given level of objective. In such cases it may be necessary to resort to indirect indicators.

(viii) *Precise Definition:* They must also be defined as precisely as possible in the given circumstances. An attempt should be made to specify the nature of the OVI, its quantity, its quality and the time required for the objective to be achieved, specially in respect of Actualising or Implementing Objectives (i.e. Programmes and Schemes).

4.6.2 *Means of Verification (MOV):* The means of verification (MOV) ensure that the previously defined OVI can be measured effectively. The MOV have two roles:

(a) They confirm that the indicators chosen are realistic, since they specify how the indicators can be verified, and

(b) They facilitate policy evaluation by establishing in advance how the criteria for success in accomplishment of policy objectives should be verified.

Each OVI must have one or more MOV associated with it. The MOV could be classified according to:

(i) *Types of Data to be gathered:* This refers to the information required to measure each OVI; it may be quantitative or qualitative data.

(ii) *Sources of Information:* The MOV should also identify the sources from which the desired information can be obtained. The sources may be grouped into three categories - physical location, people and documents.

(iii) *Data Collection Techniques:* The MOV must also identify how the desired information will be obtained.

Identifying OVI and MOV may not be necessary for Axiomatic or Conceptualising Objectives (i.e. Aim and Goals). It is, however, important to specify them for the remaining three levels of the hierarchy of policy objectives, viz. Policies, Programmes and Schemes. The following Table 25.3 illustrates the process in respect of some of the objectives of handloom policy:

TABLE 25.3: OVI and MOV of Handloom Policy Objectives

	Objective	OVI	MOV i) Type of data ii) Source of Information iii) Data Collection Technique
	Policies		
1	Rationalise Hank Yarn Obligation	Availability of hank yarn of different counts	i) Kg. of hank yarn of different counts ii) Data of production of hank yarn by textile/ spinning mills prepared by Textile Commissioner iii) Obtain copy of textile Commissioner's report every year
2	Minimum Wages	Rates of minimum wages for handloom weaving and allied activities	i) Wages per hour/piece ii) Minimum wages notifications of State Govts. iii) Obtain copies of State Governments' notifications as and when issued.
	Programmes		
3	Export Production and Marketing Programme	Quantity and value of handloom products exported	i) Quantity in sq. metres and value in dollars ii) Export data maintained by various commodity export promotion councils especially Handloom Export Promotion Council iii) Obtain export data from Export Promotion Councils on an annual basis
	Schemes		
4	Targeting Export Markets	(a) Amount spent on external	i) Amount in dollars ii) Annual budgets of

	publicity by handloom agencies as a percentage of their turn over	selected handloom agencies iii) Obtain copies of annual budgets
	(b) Quality of external publicity	i) Clients' perceptions ii) A consultancy agency to be engaged for the purpose iii) Sample surveys in USA and UK

Measuring of objectives has its costs which may range from the cost of a letter or the visit of an official to the location, to the contractual cost of a consultancy organisation engaged on a temporary or permanent basis to carry out a survey, a study or an activity. These costs also need to be built into the total objective cost for purposes of budgeting.

4.7 *STEP 7: Decomposition or Policy Documentation*

The stage is now set to put together the products of the preceding steps in the form of a policy document or statement. As suggested earlier, two types of documents could be attempted as follows:

(1) A total internal policy document containing all the information needed by policy-makers as well as implementors. It would inter alia include the complete five level hierarchy of policy objectives, the details of costing of Programmes and Schemes, conflict resolution procedures, objective measures etc.

(2) A simplified version containing only the essential details such as the background to policy documentation, the first three levels of policy objectives, a discussion of various dimensions, policy monitoring, termination and redesign parameters.

The following scheme is recommended for drafting the internal policy document:

Section 1: Introduction: Detailing the previous documentation history, if necessary, and the policy design/redesign process.

Section 2: Policy Scenario: Containing a discussion of the Problem, the Needs, the Alterables and the Constraints.

Section 3: Policy Objectives: A detailed discussion of the final Objective Tree comprising:

(a) Conceptualising or Axiomatic Objectives;
(b) Paradigmatic Objectives; and
(c) Actualising or Implementing Objectives.

The latter two may be discussed under various Goal dimensions.

Section 4: Policy Operationalising Procedures: This would include a discussion of activities to be undertaken for implementing the Policies, Programmes and Schemes, and the agencies responsible for executing them. It may also include guidelines for future action to complete the Objective Tree, if some part of it remains incomplete.

Section 5: Conflict Resolution Procedures: Outlining the steps to be taken in case of conflicts arising during implementation (vide Step 5).

Section 6: Monitoring and Control: A discussion of objective measures and related procedures for carrying out policy monitoring and evaluation.

Section 7: Costing and Budgeting: The details of Costing of Programmes and Schemes if worked out during STEP 4, may be incorporated separately here.

Section 8: Policy Termination and Redesign: It may be appropriate to set a life span for a policy document so that it is periodically reviewed. A more sophisticated method of doing so would be to prescribe certain policy redesign parameters or certain events, the occurrence of which would trigger policy redesign activity. Thus, for example, fall in volume of exports of handloom products, decline in the availability of hank yarn etc. should provide an occasion for reviewing the handloom policy.

Section 9: Conclusion: This portion may contain a discussion of policy limitations and guidelines for future policy design.

Section 10: Appendices: The policy document should have the following appendices:

(a) Objective Tree (Section 3);
(b) List of Agencies (Section 4);

(c) Physical and Financial Targets (Section 7);
(d) Glossary of Terms;
(e) List of Participants;
(f) Acknowledgments; and
(g) Bibliography.

The "manifesto style" simplified versions of the policy document may be prepared keeping in view the audience. The essentials of internal document contained in Sections 1, 2, 3 (only the first three levels of the hierarchy), 8 and 9 and the relevant appendices, may form part of the policy document for public consumption. It could also incorporate material relating to initiatives of the government, data relating to past achievements, photographs of schemes completed or under implementation etc. to match glossy corporate-style brochures. Alternatively, an Action Plan comprising only the Programmes and Schemes could also be prepared (Vide National Action Plan for Tourism, Ministry of Civil Aviation and Tourism, 1992).

5. Evaluation and Conclusion

The Logical Processual Framework described above is iterative and cyclical and may be used for designing and redesigning statements of public policy. In actual policy making situations, it needs to be institutionalised in order to provide dynamic policy support to Central Government's Ministries/Departments.

The essence of the methodology lies in the preparation of the Objective Tree and thinking things through in a logical manner. The number of steps followed and the degree of sophistication of procedures applied therein will depend on the nature and requirements of the organisation and the abilities of its personnel.

The main advantages of this model are that it:

* is consumer (policy-maker) oriented and could be easily internalised;
* clarifies thinking in respect of hierarchy of policy objectives;
* addresses the need for operationalising policy;
* ensures generation of adequate variety of policy options and alternatives;
* makes provision for conflict articulation and conflict resolution;

* provides visibility;
* satisfies the need for incrementalism in public policy design; and
* helps monitor achievement of policy objectives.

The main problem with this integrated approach to public policy design is that it is elaborate and time consuming. However, as it is, the Ministries of Government of India spend considerable time in the preparation of policy statements mainly on account of several stages of consultations involved in the process. The more elaborate steps of the Logical Processual Framework could be simultaneously attempted in house while the consultations are on.

The other problem of this approach is that it would inevitably result in a large number of objectives which the Ministries/Departments would like to deal with. This in turn will have implications in terms of having to cope with a large number of elements. One solution to this problem would be for the Ministries/Departments to voluntarily choose to deal with a core set of objectives which could be identified through a prioritising process.

Finally, based as it is on application of consensus methodologies, this approach inherits limitations associated with them and has utility only for analysis and design of broad-based social and welfare public policies where these are no clear cut and neat solutions and the need for building consensus is perceived by the policy makers. Further, designing of implementation and impact of public policies is largely outside its purview.

REFERENCES

Agnihotri, V.K. and Satsangi, P.S. (1993a) 'Policy Analysis Through Structural Modelling: Indian Handloom Policy', Paritantra: *A Journal of Systems Science and Engineering,* 1:1, pp.53-65.

Agnihotri, V.K. and Satsangi, P.S. (1993b) 'Indian Handloom Policy Design: A Consensus Methodological Approach'. In Ghosal, A and Murthy, P.N. (eds.) *Recent Advances in Cybernetics and Systems,* Proceedings of the Ninth International Congress of Cybernetics and Systems (New Delhi: January 18-23, 1993), New Delhi: Tata McGraw-Hill.

Alley, H., Bacinello, C.P. and Hipel, K.W (1979) 'Fuzzy Set Approaches to Planning in the Grand River Basin', *Advances in Water Resources,* 2:1, pp.3-12.

Bharatiya Janata Party (1991) *Towards Ram Rajya; Mid-Term Poll to Lok Sabha,* May 1991; Our Commitments, New Delhi: Bharatiya Janata Party Publication.

Coleman, G. (1987) 'Logical Framework Approach to the Monitoring and Evaluation of Agricultural and Rural Development Projects', *Project Appraisal,* 2:4, pp.251-259.

Department of SSI&ARI (1991) Policy Measures for Promoting and Strengthening Smıll, Tiny and Village Enterprises. New Delhi: Ministry of Industry, GOI.

Department of Textiles (1985) *Statement on Textile Policy,* New Delhi: Ministry of Supply and Textiles, GOI.

Department of Youth Affairs and Sports (1992) *Programme of Action* (August, 1992): National Sports Policy. New Delhi: Ministry of Human Resource Development,GOI.

Dror, Y. (1986) *Policy-making Under Adversity,* Brunswick: Transaction Books.

Gasper, D.R. (1991) *Notes on the Logical Framework Approach,* The Hague: Institute of Social Studies.

GTZ (Deutsche Gesellschaft fur Technische Zusammenarbeit) GmbH (1980) *ZOPP Planning Method: An Introduction to the Method,* Frankfurt: GTZ.

Hill, J.D. and Warfield, J.N. (1972) 'Unified Programme Planning', *IEEE Transactions on Systems, Man and Cybernetics,* SMC 2:5, p.610-621.

Indian National Congress(I) (1991) *Election Manifesto: General Election 1991,* New Delhi: All India Congress Committee(I).

Koontz, H. and Weihrich, H. (1988) *Management.* New York: McGraw-Hill.

Ministry of Civil Aviation and Tourism (1992) *National Action Plan for Tourism,* New Delhi: GOI.

Ministry of Industry (1991) *Statement on Industrial Policy.* New Delhi. GOI.

Osborn, D. and Gaebler, T. (1992) *Reinventing Government: How the Entrepreneurial Spirit is Transforming the Public Sector,* New Delhi: Prentice-Hall.

Sage, A.P. (1977) *Methodology for Large Scale Systems.* New York: McGraw-Hill.

Satsangi, P.S., Swani, N.M., Mathur,M.C. and Agnihotri, V.K. (1991) *Handloom Policy Analysis: An Interpretive Structural Modelling Approach.* New Delhi: Indian Institute of Technology Delhi.

Stoner, J.A.F. and Freeman, R.E. (1989) *Management,* Englewood Cliffs, N.J.: Prentice-Hall.

Warfield, J.N. (1973a) 'On Arranging Elements of a Hierarchy in Graphic Form, IEEE Transactions on Systems, *Man and Cybernetics,* SMC 3:2, pp.121-132.

Warfield, J.N. (1973b) 'Intent Structures', *IEEE Transactions on Systems, Man and Cybernetics,* SMC 3:2, pp.133-40.

Warfield, J.N. (1973c) *An Assault on Complexity.* Battelle Monograph No.3. Columbus, O.: Battelle Memorial Institute.

Warfield, J.N. (1976) *Societal Systems: Planning Policy and Complexity.* New York: Wiley (Reprinted, Salinas, CA: Intersystems, 1989).

Warfield, J.N. (1990a) *A Science of Generic Design: Managing Complexity through Systems Design,* Vol.1. Salinas, CA: Intersystems Publication.

Warfield, J.N. (1990b) *A Science of Generic Design: Managing Complexity through Systems Design,* Vol.2. Salinas, CA: Intersystems Publication.

APPENDIX I

DECOMPOSED SET OF OBJECTIVES OF HANDLOOM POLICY OF THE GOVERNMENT OF INDIA

Aim

To enable the handlooms to realise their full potential [FULL POTENTIAL]

Goals

G1	To preserve the distinct and unique role of handloom sector in the textile industry [PRESERVE HANDLOOMS]
G2	To ensure higher earnings for handloom weavers [HIGHER EARNINGS]
G3	To improve the delivery of handloom programmes and schemes [IMPROVE DELIVERY]

Policies

G1P1	To sustain employment in the handloom sector [SUSTAIN EMPLOYMENT]
G1P2	To ensure availability of yarn and other raw materials to handloom industry [RAW MATERIAL AVAILABILITY]
G1P3	To make adequate credit available for production and marketing of handloom goods [CREDIT AVAILABILITY]
G1P4	To improve cost competitiveness of handloom products [COST COMPETITIVENESS]
G1P5	To improve working and living conditions of handloom weavers [WORKING AND LIVING CONDITIONS]
G1P6	To protect the production base of handloom industry [PRODUCTION BASE]
G1P7	To provide adequate financial support for handloom programmes and schemes [FINANCIAL SUPPORT]
G1P8	To encourage handloom sector to realise its potential for exports [HANDLOOM EXPORTS]
G2P9	To improve marketing of handloom products [MARKETING]
G2P10	To provide technological inputs for improving productivity, design, quality and finish of handloom products [TECHNOLOGICAL INPUTS]
G2P11	To encourage production of mixed and blended fabrics in

	the handloom sector [MIXED AND BLENDED FABRICS]
G2P12	To provide raw materials at reasonable prices to handloom weavers [RAW MATERIAL PRICES]
G2P13	To ensure availability of credit at cheaper interest rates to handloom weavers [CHEAPER CREDIT]
G2P14	To ensure availability of adequate and appropriate facilities for processing of handloom cloth at reasonable prices [PROCESSING FACILITIES]
G2P15	To develop handlooms through the institutions of cooperatives and corporations [COOPERATIVES AND CORPORATIONS]
G2P16	To create productive assets with handloom weavers [PRODUCTIVE ASSETS]
G2P17	To motivate weavers to engage in cultural heritage related handloom activity [CULTURAL HERITAGE]
G2P18	To train handloom weavers in production of better quality and high value-added items [TRAINING OF WEAVERS]
G2P19	To relieve the distress caused to weavers by periodic visitations of natural calamities [NATURAL CALAMITIES]
G2P20	To implement special programmes for disadvantaged weavers [DISADVANTAGED WEAVERS]
G3P21	To upgrade the technical, managerial and administrative skills of personnel employed in the handloom sector [UPGRADE PERSONNEL SKILLS]
G3P22	To strengthen the database for better planning and execution of handloom development programmes [DATABASE]
G3P23	To strengthen the machinery for implementation, supervision and evaluation of handloom programmes [MONITORING AND EVALUATION]
G3P24	To train cooperators in managing cooperatives [TRAINING OF COOPERATORS]

APPENDIX II

OBJECTIVE TREE OF HANDLOOM POLICY (DESCRIPTIVE)

Aim	Goals	Policies
Full Potential	G1 Preserve Handlooms	P1 Sustain Employment
		P2 Raw Material Availability (with P12)
		P3 Credit Availability
		P4 Cost Competitiveness
		P5 Working and Living Conditions
		P6 Production Base
		P7 Financial Support
		P8 Handloom Export
	G2 Higher Earnings	P9 Marketing
		P10 Technological Inputs
		P11 Mixed and Blended Fabrics
		P12 Raw Material Prices
		P13 Cheaper Credit
		P14 Processing Facilities (with P10)
		P15 Cooperative and Corporations
		P16 Productive Assets
		P17 Cultural heritage
		P18 Training of Weavers
		P19 Natural Calamities
		P20 Disadvantaged Weavers
	G3 Improve Delivery	P21 Upgrade Personnel Skills
		P22 Database
		P23 Monitoring and Evaluation
		P24 Training Cooperators

APPENDIX III

OBJECTICES OF EXPORT-ORIENTED HANDLOOM POLICY

Sl. No.	Dimension/Policy Option
	Marketing and Export
1	To launch a drive to increase exports of handloom products ten-fold in next five years [EXPORT DRIVE]
2	To energise handloom export efforts in international markets with preference for handloom designs [EXPORT MARKET SEGMENTATION]
3	To provide special incentives for exports of handloom products including input cost stabilisation subsidy [EXPORT INCENTIVES]
4	To give a slogan for handlooms to produce competitively or perish [COMPETE OR PERISH]
5	To give tax incentives to industrial houses for adopting clusters of weavers for improving and exporting their products [INDUSTRIAL HOUSES]
	Yarn Production
6	To rationalise hank yarn obligation to ensure easy and continuous availability of critical counts of yarn to handloom weavers [RATIONALISE HANK YARN OBLIGATION]
7	To permit reeling of hank yarn outside mill premises at weaver locations to ensure availability of hank yarn to them of desired specifications at lesser price [DECENTRALISED HANK YARN REELING]
8	To arrange supply of cotton at stable prices for a reasonable period to identified spinning mills to manufacture yarn for NHDC on agreed terms [COTTON FOR YARN]
	Yarn Supply
9	To supply yarn at mill gate prices to handloom weavers [MILL GATE PRICE]

10 To eliminate taxes and duties on movement of hank yarn and dyes and chemicals from state to state by National Handloom Development Corporation [NO DUTIES ON NHDC]

Dyes and Chemicals

11 To make improved dyes and chemicals available to the handloom sector at reasonable prices [DYES AND CHEMICALS]

12 To make available dyes and chemicals in packagings of one kg and one x five lots for handloom sector [SMALL PACKAGING OF DYES]

Weavers' Involvement

13 To develop strong weavers' associations to demand effective design and technological services from the government at marginal cost [STRONG WEAVERS' ASSOCIATIONS]

Welfare Measures

14 To undertake measures for the welfare and social security of handloom weavers [WELFARE AND SECURITY]

15 To ensure payment of minimum wages to handloom weavers and allied workers [MINIMUM WAGES]

Protective Measures

16 To control unplanned growth of powerlooms and allow only alimited increase each year [CONTROL POWERLOOMS]

Technical Inputs

17 To launch a massive design input drive for the handloom sector including computer-aided design [DESIGN INPUT DRIVE]

18 To cover improvements in equipment as well as environment under handloom modernisation [MODERNISATION COVERAGE]

19 To sensitise technologists and designers to the needs of handloom weavers [SENSITISE]

20 To upgrade facilities in Weavers' Service Centres [UPGRADE WSCs]

Organisational Arrangement

21 To provide adequate, location-specific and effective delivery systems [DELIVERY SYSTEMS]

22 To man handloom executive posts with aspiring and motivated personnel [MOTIVATED PERSONNEL]

Fiscal Measures

23 To equalise prices through fiscal measures of cone and hank yarn of those counts for which hank yarn prices are higher [EQUALISE CONE-HANK PRICES]

24 To make cone yarn available to handloom weavers without excise duty [CONE YARN EXEMPTION]

Credit

25 To make credit available to all handloom weavers at interest rates below bank rate [CHEAPER CREDIT COVERAGE]

Training

26 To provide financial support for one year to handloom weavers during training [TRAINING COMPENSATION]

27 To provide facilities and incentives for training of handloom personnel [PERSONNEL TRAINING]

APPENDIX IV

OBJECTIVE TREE OF HANDLOOM POLICY (NORMATIVE)

Aim	Goals	Policies
Export Drive	G1 Promote Export	G1P1 Export Market Segments
		G1P2 Export Incentives
		G1P3 Industrial Houses
		G1P5 Non-Apparel Export
		G1P6 Handloom Mark
	G2 Raw Materials	G2P7 Rationalise Hank Yarn Obligation
		G2P8 Decentralise Hank Yarn Reeling
		G2P9 Cotton for Yarn
		G2P10 Mill Gate Price
		G2P11 On Duties on NHDC
		G2P12 Dyes and Chemicals
		G2P13 Small Packaging of Dyes
	G3 Weavers' Involvement	G3P14 Strong Weavers' Associations
	G4 Welfare Measures	G4P15 Welfare and Security
		G4P16 Minimum Wages
	G5 Proctive Measures	G5P17 Control Powerlooms
	G6 Technical Inputs	G6P18 Design Input Drive
		G6P19 Modernisation Coverage
		G6P20 Sensitise
		G6P21 Upgrade WSCs
	G7 Organisational Arrangements	G7P22 Delivery Systems
		G7P23 Motivated Personnel
	G8 Fiscal Measures	G8P24 Equalise cone-hank
		G8P25 Cone Yarn Exemption
	G9 Credit	G9P26 Cheaper Credit Coverage
	G10 Training	G10P27 Training Compensation
		G10P28 Personnel Training

APPENDIX V

OBJECTIVES OF NATIONAL AND TEXTILE POLICIES

1. Objective of National Policy

1. To promote exports [EXPORTS]
2. To increase productivity of the national economy [PRODUCTIVE ECONOMY]
3. To promote and support village and small-scale industries [SMALL-SCALE]
4. To promote industrialisation [INDUSTRIALISATION]
5. To meet the basic needs of the people [BASIC NEEDS]
6. To generate employment [EMPLOYMENT]
7. To improve the quality of life of the people in terms of health, education and family welfare [QUALITY OF LIFE]
8. To maintain stability of prices [PRICE STABILITY]
9. To promote and develop appropriate technology [APPROPRIATE TECHNOLOGY]
10. To maintain a reasonable balance of payments [BOP]
11. To provide clean environment [ENVIRONMENT]
12. To make the economy self-reliant [SELF-RELIANCE]
13. To raise resources for financing development [RAISE RESOURCES]
14. To rationalise subsidies [RATIONALISE SUBSIDIES]
15. To accelerate the development of rural areas [RURAL DEVELOPMENT]
16. To make the public sector contribute more effective to development [PUBLIC SECTOR]
17. To decentralise the process of planning and implementation [DECENTRALISATION]
18. To ensure efficient utilisation and conservation of energy [ENERGY EFFICIENCY AND CONSERVATION]
19. To have a balanced growth rate of the economy [GROWTH RATE]
20. To liberalise the economy [LIBERALISATION]
21. To ensure equitable distribution of income [EQUITABLE INCOME]
22. To promote balanced urban development [BALANCED URBAN DEVELOPMENT]

2. Objectives of Textile Policy

1. To ensure the welfare, sustain employment and improve the earnings of handloom weavers [HANDLOOMS]
2. To make available good quality input in adequate quantity to the textile industry at reasonable prices [INPUTS]
3. To ensure planned development of powerloom sector [POWERLOOMS]
4. To ensure economic viability of weaving operations of decentralised/non-factory powerlooms [VIABILITY OF POWERLOOMS]
5. To encourage expansion of the khadi sector [KHADI]
6. To increase productivity of the textile industry [PRODUCT-IVITY]
7. To make available synthetic and blended fabrics to the consumers at lower/reasonable prices [MAN-MADE FABRICS]
8. To evolve an efficient marketing and distribution system in the textile industry [DISTRIBUTION SYSTEM]
9. To maintain stability of cotton prices [COTTON PRICE STABILITY]
10. To augment availability of cloth at affordable prices to the poorer sections of the population [AFFORDABLE CLOTH FOR THE POOR]
11. To sustain employment in the textile industry [SUSTAIN EMPLOYMENT]
12. To promote development and dissemination of appropriate technology in textile industry [TEXTILE TECHNOLOGY]
13. To encourage and promote sericulture industry [SERICULTURE]
14. To protect the interests of textile mill workers [MILL WORKERS]
15. To ensure remunerative prices to cotton growers [COTTON GROWERS]
16. To encourage and support modernisation of textile and allied industries [MODERNISATION]
17. To restructure the textile industry for its integrated growth [RESTRUCTURE]
18. To maintain pre-eminent role of cotton as the main raw material of textile industry [ROLE OF COTTON]
19. To rationalise policies regarding creation and expansion of textile units [CREATION AND EXPANSION]
20. To encourage and support the textile industry to realise its full

potential for exports [TEXTILE EXPORTS]

21. To make available cloth of acceptable quality and at reasonable prices to meet the growing demand of population [CLOTH FOR PEOPLE]
22. To allow full fibre flexibility [FIBRE FLEXIBILITY]
23. To ensure economic viability of textile mills [VIABILITY OF MILLS]
24. To treat the mills and decentralised/non-factory powerlooms equally in terms of fiscal levies etc. [MILLS AND POWERLOOMS AT PAR]
25. To render financial and other support to National Textile Corporation in order to enable it to provide stabilising influence and healthy competition in the textile industry [NATIONAL TEXTILE CORPORATION]
26. To maintain a database for better planning and policy-making for and monitoring and control of the textile industry [DATABASE FOR PLANNING AND MONITORING]
27. To optimise utilisation of spinning capacity [SPINNING CAPACITY]
28. To support research and development activity in the textile industry [R&D]
29. To improve quality of textile industry products [QUALITY]
30. To promote the growth of the woollen sector [WOOLLEN SECTOR]
31. To encourage indigenous manufacture of textile machinery [TEXTILE MACHINERY]
32. To avoid and discourage Government takeover of sick textile units [NO NATIONALISATION]
33. To strengthen, develop and modernise knitting and apparel manufacturing sectors [KNITTING AND APPAREL]
34. To rationalise regulations and controls in the textile industry [REGULATION AND CONTROL]
35. To reduce the incidence of sickness in the textile mills [REDUCE SICKNESS IN MILLS]
36. To treat all mechanised processing facilities at par and to protect manual processing [PROCESSING]

PROCEEDINGS OF THE SEMINAR ON PUBLIC POLICY ANALYSIS AND DESIGN HELD ON AUGUST 23-25, 1993 AT LAL BAHADUR SHASTRI NATIONAL ACADEMY OF ADMINISTRATION, MUSSOORIE

A Seminar on Public Policy and Analysis and Design was organised by the Lal Bahadur Shastri National Academy of Administration, Mussoorie between August 23-25, 1993 at Karmashila Building of the Academy. The Seminar Coordinator was Mr. V.K. Agnihotri. Mr. Sudhir Krishna, Mr. S. Mendiratta and Mr. Rajnish Karki acted as Associate Coordinators. A list of Participants is enclosed (ANNEXURE).

Inauguration

The Seminar was inaugurated by Prof. A.M. Khusro. He spoke about public policy initially in the context of Land Reforms. He described the major pillars of public policy of Government of India for the last forty years, viz, the primacy in investment decision-making of the Planning Commission; the primacy of the public sector especially in infrastructure; reliance on the private sector for consumer goods production; price controls; a subsidized economy for the poor; and import substitution. He explored how liberalisation has altered all these planks, and made several policy suggestions.

Urban Policy

In the first session of the afternoon of 23-8-1993, presentations and discussions were taken up on the issues of Urban Policy.

In this session two presentations were made-one by Mr. K. Dharmarajan and the other by Dr. Dinesh Mehta. This session was chaired by Prof. H. Ramachandran who was also its rapporteur.

The first presentation by Mr. Dharmarajan noted that we do not have a concrete urban policy for the country as such. There is, however, a felt need to evolve and put forward such a policy. He pointed out that one of the reason for the absence of a separate urban policy is the intricate interface of the urban segment with other sectors such as industry and services (e.g. water supply, urban transport etc.). Since urban processes are fully intertwined with industrial location policy as well as policies relating to location of infrastructure, urban policy is normally in response to developments related to those sectors. Secondly, urban sector falls under state subject and as such there was no national policy. However, there are specific centrally sponsored programmes relating to master plans, small and medium towns and slum improvement. In his presentation he also dwelt on the recommendations of the task force on urbanization constituted by the Planning Commission in the early 80's and the subsequent recommendations of the National Commission on Urbanization which need to be modified in the context of the changes in the macro economic policy in order to evolve the national urban policy towards this end. Mr. Dharmarajan stressed the need for consensus on the policy goals of the various states of India.

Dr. Dinesh Mehta started with some of the myths prevailing about urbanization trend and pointed out that it was not correct to believe that large towns and cities are growing rapidly or that urbanization in India was spreading rapidly. He brought out from the empirical data that there has been a decline in the rate of urbanization in India and that the rates of growth of medium towns are in fact comparable to that of large cities. He stressed the need for modifications in the Urban Land Ceilings Act and for the state to assume facilitator role in guiding and monitoring urbanization.

The discussion that followed these two presentations raised the following issues:

Firstly, a doubt was expressed as to whether a separate urban policy is at all needed since the urban process is a function of distribution of employment opportunities.

Secondly, since the changes in the macro economic policies may lead to privatisation of urban services and industrial locations may further gravitate towards existing urban centres, with consequent increase in inequities and imbalances, a national urban policy would be necessary partly in the context of urban poverty and partly in the context of imbalances. In this context, besides looking into the overall change in urban sector, there was need to address addition of large numbers of people in a few selected urban centres and the consequent pressure on urban services.

Thirdly, it was pointed out that although we do not have a national urban policy, in fact we have settlement policies at the regional level particularly around metropolitan regions.

Fourthly, the discussion also revolved around the pricing of services and municipal taxes, within which the issues relating to taxation and revenue base of newly defined urban centres were focused.

Fifthly, the issue of rural-urban migration, the nature and magnitude of the migrants and the consequent impact on urbanization were also dealt with wherein the decreasing role of rural-urban migration in the growth of urban population was underlined. In fact, it was argued that the reduction in the rural-urban stream is a cause for concern since this indicates declining urban economic base.

Sixthly, it was pointed out that the use of proportions and rates of change is misleading since the magnitudes in the Indian context are large.

Seventhly, the absence of local Government was held responsible for the poor management and urban problems and the need to strengthen such local bodies was stressed. It was also felt that the Urban Land Ceiling Act can not be modified independent of rural land ceilings.

On the whole, the general consensus was that a national urban policy is necessary to address the role of state in promoting a pattern of urbanization that is in tune with macro development policies, given the reciprocal relationship between urbanization and economic development. The consensus appeared to stress the need for urban policy which takes into account the development scenario of the rural segments and its integration with urbanization.

Environment and Forest Policy

During the afternoon of 23-8-1993, the second session was on the subject of 'Environment and Forest Policy'. In this session three speakers presented their papers — (i) Mr. Mukul Sanwal -- 'Environmental Policies', (ii) Mr. S.C. Dey — 'Bio-diversity and National Conservation Strategy', and (iii) Dr. N.C. Saxena — 'Policy Issues in Forestry'. This session was chaired by Mr. R. Rajamani. Professor Neela Mukherjee was the Rapporteur.

Mr. Mukul Sanwal explained the interaction among the environment sector and other sectors and underlined the importance of interdependence and inter-linkages of the policies. This leads to four areas of concerns which are the existing body of knowledge, set of issues, identification of problems and set of decisions on those problems. The first two concerns are relevant for assigning significance to problems while the last two are to be seen as a selection process.

The general trend in environmental policies is more towards regulation; however, in assigning significance and choosing processes, values become important i.e., the values of the analyst. The author argued that diversity is important due to the character of environment problems, their externalities, socio-economic system and what kind of things are favoured. Hence, in policies, less centralisation is required and more diversity. Here the question is how to balance costs and benefits so that there is least cost and minimum dislocation.

Regarding choice of instruments, the 'polluter pays' principle may not work in poor countries because technological capability is low and structural imbalances act as impediments. His arguments were in favour of market instruments rather than a regulatory system.

According to Mr. Sanwal we need policy tools that facilitate diversity; more of delegation is required. For trans-border environmental problems, inter-governmental relations are also important.

Since the Government has access to limited information about the costs of pollution abatement and circumstances of individuals and firms, it is important to recognise the limitations of bureaucratic solutions.

Mr. Sanwal was of the opinion that environment as a whole is affected by constant interaction and not by mega projects. Local people have to be involved instead of centralisation.

Mr. Sanwal also spoke in favour of more and more sharing of information with public, instead of making every thing confidential. A few other recommendations that could be drawn from his presentation are:

(a) Proper valuation of environmental resources;
(b) Develop institutions for bringing about policy changes; and
(c) Common but differentiated responsibilities.

In the second paper, Mr. Dey described the evolution of forest policy. Conservation and preservation of bio-diversity are of utmost significance. It is important to resolve whether population pressure is disrupting bio-diversity conservation or it is to do with our understanding of the problem.

Mr. Dey spoke of different threats to bio-diversity such as (1) Habitat destruction; (2) Extension of agriculture; (3) Filling up wastelands; (4) Conversion of rich bio-diversity; (5) Destruction of coastal areas; and (6) Uncontrolled commercial exploitation.

The elements of his main recommendations for bio-diversity

conservation were as follows:

(a) Improve policy on environment;
(b) Mobilisation of greater financial resources; and
(c) Integrating Conservation with development: economic development to launch it.

Factors which are required to be looked into for proper management of protected area system are the following :

1. Proper legal framework;
2. Institutional structures for implementation of work programmes;
3. Financial resources to back up the action plans;
4. Political commitment for conservation priority;
5. Human Resource Development; and
6. Involvement of NGOs and the local people in park management.

His recommendation was that unless we can involve people in the management of forests and they gain in the process, we can not conserve bio-diversity.

Dr. N.C. Saxena's paper at first described 3 phases in forest policy, 1875-1975 — Forests for timber; 1975-1990 — Social forestry and 1990 onwards - Joint forest management.

The present land-use policy involves mainly —

(1) forest land to produce timber; and
(2) private lands to produce fuel wood.

The major recommendations of Dr. Saxena were that Forest land should produce fuel wood and private land should produce timber. Dr. Saxena suggested that rather than look at management of forestry, the technology needs to be investigated.

Dr. Saxena also pointed out that the new forest policy does incorporate some of these things but there are a large number of contradictions.

There are different kinds of forces to explain the contradictions in the forest policy. Dr. Saxena was of the opinion that if the objective of the forest policy is to help people, one has to change not only management but also technology. This is in the context of social obligations which are very important.

Dr. Saxena suggested four kinds of policy interventions in rural areas based on types of scheme and who gains and who loses. The broad conclusion was that both rural rich and rural poor gain from these policies but not the officials.

In the question-answer session, Dr. Saxena recommended hospital or school approach to forest management where forests remain with government but are managed for people.

The main observations made by the Chairman, Mr. R. Rajamani were as follows :

1. Other sectors have to internalise environment;
2. Each person should have some knowledge of environment;
3. NOT IN MY BACKYARD SYNDROME (NIMBY) is not of much help;
4. Change in lifestyle: this cannot be done by government alone, other forces are needed. Action by people should be matched by action by policy maker;
5. Commenting on Dey's paper Sri Rajamani said that we can kill and inflict damage on bio-diversity for preserving our lifestyle but after a point homo sapiens would be affected. We, therefore, cannot afford to take chances;
6. Greatest damage will be done on forest resources from outside the rural system. The poor man's consumption is negligible when compared to our life style;
7. When we push projects we are not concerned with its damage on environment. Decision making needs to take into account its costs for bio-diversity. It is important that the policies of different sectors are integrated; and
8. There are different facets of forest policy. The kernel of it is that we have to marry our actions with out intentions.

In the plenary session, Dr. A.M. Khusro, Chairman, expressed his views that the annual rate of plantation of trees should be equal to or greater than the annual rate of denudation. Unless we tackle the demand side of the problem based on the essential need for forest resources we may not be able to tackle the problem of deforestation effectively.

Agricultural Policy

In the morning sessions of 24-8-1993, the first session was devoted to 'Agricultural Policy'. The Chairman of the session was Dr. N.C. Saxena. The rapporteur was Mr. Sudhir Krishna. During this session, a paper was presented by Prof. Ashok Gulati on 'Liberalising Indian Agriculture : An Agenda for Reforms'. The principal point made in this session was that the protection to 'Industry' sector all these years has been to the general detriment of the 'Agriculture' sector.

To help the adverse balance of trade of the country, all sectors of economy should be oriented to help exports. Agriculture is more export competitive than industry. Thus, investment in agriculture sector should be enhanced, so that sufficient agriculture surpluses are generated, which could be canalised to exports.

This would call for a review of the existing scheme of infrastructure, incentives and institutional arrangements. At the same time the adverse impact of such reforms on the poor should be carefully taken note of.

For restructuring the frame work of incentives, the following steps were proposed:

1. Inter-regional restrictions on movements of agricultural produce should be removed;
2. Levy on farmer/miller on paddy, rice, sugar etc., should be phased out;
3. State procurement of monopolistic nature should be phased out. Wherever they exist, they should still be at open market prices only;
4. The Essential Commodities Act, which was enacted during war period, should be thoroughly reviewed;
5. Quantitative restrictions on exports (quota) should be removed;
6. Export market should be treated more as priority market than a 'residuary' market;
7. Minimum export price fixation should be done away with; and
8. Imports of agricultural commodities should be decanalised. While doing so, anti-dumping laws should be kept on alert and variable import levies should be relied upon.

As regards the incentives, it was observed that the aggregate measure of subsidy/support in agriculture sector in India is negative and among the lowest in the world. However, this would not, by itself, justify subsidies. For instance, more than half of the subsidy for fertilizer sector goes to industry, rather than to agriculture.

On the subject of infrastructure, the main recommendations were :

Electricity: Pricing for electricity should be reviewed by non-gauranteed agencies and thrown open to public debate. Volumetric pricing of electricity should be considered. For electricity dues collections, farmers' involvement should be explored.

Irrigation: The existing irrigation system is not giving sufficient return; maintenance costs are not being recovered from the beneficiaries. The irrigation departments should be made autonomous bodies and farmers should be given shares.

Credit: Concessional rates of interests should be gradually withdrawn. To check on default of bank loan repayments, the group lending approach, like the Bangla Desh experiment, should be introduced.

With regard to institutional reforms, the following observations were made :

Land Reforms: Consolidation of Holdings and Protection of Tenancy rights should be the focus of Land Reforms. However, land ceiling part of these laws needs to be reviewed, as small holdings are uneconomical and non-viable for investments in modern inputs and infrastructure.

Research and Extension: A lot of effort should be put in the area of research and extention for agriculture. Corporate bodies should be encouraged and facilitated to invest in this field.

Agro-processing : Agro-processing sector needs to be given greater thrust by encouraging investment from private sector in a big way.

During the discussions, it was felt that these reforms are likely to affect the poor adversely. Several steps are needed to take care of this problem.

The PDS should be reserved only for the poor. Leakages in the PDS should be plugged. Concept of food stamps should be introduced on a pilot basis to replace the PDS.

Employment Guarantee Schemes such as that of Maharashtra, should be initiated in all the States.

Land Army of local people should be organised, and they should be assigned the task of building/constructing infrastructure.

Health and Population Policies

In the second session on the morning of 24-8-1993, papers were presented on Health and Population Policies. The key papers for this session were presented by 1) Prof. J.W. Bjorkman — 'Developmental Lessons of Sri Lanka's Health System : Instruments and Options in 'Healthy' Implementation', 2) Prof. G. Giridhar — 'Population Policy in India : A Review', and 3) Ms. Rajni Razdan, 'Population Policy'. This session was chaired by Dr. Amitava Mukherjee. The rapporteur was Mr. B. Kasinath.

The first key paper for this session was presented by Prof. J.W.

Bjorkman on 'Developmental Lessons of Sri Lanka's Health System : Instruments and Options in 'Healthy' Implementation'.

Prof. Bjorkman said that he has been studying the health policies of South Asian countries and he found that the health policy of Sri Lanka was characterised by unexceptionable results in spite of economic scarcity and uncivil violence in thc country. Therefore, he said, the need to review it so as to learn some lessons from the Sri Lankan experience.

Before embarking upon the issues related to Sri Lankan Health Policy, he dwelt upon perspectives on implementation of policies. He said that multiple actors and organisations were involved in the implementation processes that were characterised by interactive coexistence amongst themselves. He then distinguished between the macro-implementation and micro-implementation problems. He also stressed the point that a policy is not merely a statement of intentions.

Highlighting the centre-periphery problems, he said that most governments in South Asian Countries were highly centralised. The current moves to decentralise were basically aimed at deconcentration and genuine devolution was rarely found in any of the South Asian countries. He later said that centre-periphery problems occur irrespective of whether a state opts for centralised or decentralised strategies of development. He hypothesised that the centre-periphery problems would be minimised and that the desired policies would be implemented if:

- (i) services are simple but effective;
- (ii) political climate is supportive;
- (iii) intragovernmental linkages are clear and coordinated;
- (iv) adequate human capital is available; and
- (v) information is abundant.

He then focused his attention on health policy in Sri Lanka. After describing the basic parameters of the policy in terms of its administrative and organisational design, he said that Sri Lankans have access to and receive allopathic care throughout the country.

He then went on to list the problems faced by the modern health care system in Sri Lanka which are: (i) financial problems; (ii) shortage of medical personnel; (iii) division between curative and preventive services; and (iv) location of curative institutions. While dealing with other specific parameters that facilitated implementation of the policy, he summarised them under five categories, namely (i) colonial experience; (ii) investments in human capital; (iii) universal suffrage; (iv) accessible tax-base; and (v) compact geography. He then emphasised the role of education in health status, population control, etc. He said that investments in education began early in Sri Lanka and were regularly expanded.

During the discussions, following issues were raised: (i) education of women and its impact on population growth rate; (ii) age at the time of marriage; (iii) utilisation of health facilities; (iv) relationship between economic, educational and health status; (v) investment on health and education; (vi) role of NGO's; (vii) pressure on public health system; (viii) need to emphasize mental health alongside physical health; and (ix) need to have demand driven health system.

Prof. Bjorkman while replying to some of the above points, said that education was a critical factor in deciding population growth. He said that in Sri Lanka the investment on health and education was three times more than in India (in per capita terms). He said that each country should have a strong public health system supported by a market system. The chairman concluded the session by stating that we should have a demand driven health system rather than a supply driven health system.

The second key paper was presented by Dr. G. Giridhar on 'Population Policy in India:, A Review'. While presenting his paper, Dr. Giridhar said that at national level population increase was a function of number of deaths and births. To reduce the population growth, he said, the only option available was to reduce the number of births. He however said that the rapid growth of population was not due to increasing birth rates but due to decreasing death rates. Giving further details, he said that 40 per cent of total population in India was in the age group of below 14 years. As a result, he said, future parents were already born and, therefore, the growth rate would not fall even if each family were to have only two children.

He said that unlike in other sectors, population policies in India existed right from pre-independence days. The emphasis of the policies he said was on fertility reduction and that birth control was regarded as a means to control population growth. He then traced the evolution of population policy in India and highlighted major features as well as consequence of each population policy. He said that the decision to use health facilities to promote family planning was welcome, it had nevertheless led to an excessive medicalisation of family planning. This, he said, was one of the reasons for the failure of family planning programme. Talking about the Action Plan of the Ministry of Health and Family Welfare (1991), he said that its focus was on improvements in quality of services and on devising area-specific strategies.

In order to make the policy more effective and realistic he said there was a need to carry out data based planning and also to visit the field before designing the policy. He said that the emphasis of the policy should be on (i) evolving a mechanism to promote inter-departmental coordination; (ii) enlisting support of other departments in the work of family welfare departments; and (iii) improving the quality of the services provided.

The third key paper was presented by Ms. Rajni Razdan on 'Population Policy'. Ms. Razdan pointed out that over the years population explosion had become a crucial problem in India. She then highlighted the seriousness of the problem with the help of data on goals and achievements of Seventh Five Year Plan and on comparative population projection for India, China and the World. She said that some of the causes responsible for high population growth rate were: (i) social and cultural milieu of India that favoured early marriage for women; (ii) low status of women; and (iii) migration.

Reflecting on the population policy perceptions, she said that National Family Welfare Programme was the main instrument for bringing about population stabilisation. Linking population growth with fast depleting natural resources, she said, the assault of man on nature had greatly increased since the days of Malthus. She then said that population growth was a function of poverty and that there was a nexus between poverty, population and environmental degradation.

Regarding Policy Framework, she said that the policy so far had been governed by essentially negative considerations of reducing fertility. She said that fertility would not decline by family planning alone but by economic and social transformation. She then put forth the following seggestions for consideration:

(1) Improving educational status of women;
(2) Strict enforcement of the Child Marriage Act;
(3) Improving the quality and coverage of family welfare services;
(4) Improved contraceptives to be made available through PDS;
(5) Funds to be made available to States/UTs on the basis of actual reduction in birth rates;
(6) Further intensification of Small Family Norm;
(7) Motivating Family Welfare staff;
(8) Involving religious heads, NGOs, etc. in implementation;
(9) System of disincentives for government employees;
(10) Withdrawal of incentives to government employees;
(11) Compulsory sterilization of beggars;
(12) Pilot studies by independent agencies;
(13) Effective targetisation; and
(14) Doctors not to discourage parents who wish to adopt terminal

method.

In the discussion that followed, issues relating to the following were raised:

(i) utility of PR Act of Rajasthan which disqualifies persons having more than two children from contesting the elections;
(ii) decentralisation of the health system;
(iii) seeking more commitment from the health personnel;
(iv) seeking the cooperation of education department in motivating people to go for family planning; and
(v) area approach to policy design.

Reacting to some of the questions raised, Dr. Giridhar said that the present policy already had some elements of area approach to policy design. He said that area approach meant planning at micro levels which was required to address the specific problems of different regions. A suggestion was also made to scrutinise the 14 issues suggested by Ms. Razdan and narrow them down to a feasible number by adopting certain criteria such as feasibility.

Other Public Policies — I

In the afternoon session of 24-8-1993, papers were presented on Other Public Policies. In the first session, two papers were presented by Prof. P.S. Satsangi on 'Public Policy Analysis and Design Methodologies and Their Applications with Particular Reference to Industrial Policy' and by Dr. J.P. Saxena on 'Analysis of Options for Energy Conservation Policy in Indian Cement Industry'. Chairman of this session was Prof. J.W. Bjorkman. The rapporteur was Dr. Sharat Kumar.

The Chairman invited Prof. Satsangi and Dr. Saxena to make their respective presentations on 'Other Public Policies'. Apart from their subject matter, the papers were also concerned with policy analysis and design methodologies.

Presenting the first paper on 'Public Policy Analysis and Design Methodologies and Their Applications with Particular Reference to Industrial Policy', Prof. P.S. Satsangi reported the findings of the exercise done on the small scale industries in Agra. The exercise was directed primarily to arrive at objectives of developing the small scale industries which have been playing quite a dominant role in country's overall development. The NGT (Nominal Group Technique) methodology was adopted to short list the more important objectives out of a set of a compiled list of descriptive and normative policy objectives collected from a workshop attended by different interested and serving groups like the entrepreneurs, the bankers and the academicians. Further the ISM (Interpretive Structural Modelling) method was used for designing policy alternatives for prevention of industrial dysfunction.

The discussion veered around to the merit and usefulness of the ISM methodology which was explained as a method which converts the mental model of the system into a structure through a matrix model on the basis of information supplied by the domain of experts. In regard to industries, during stage one, seven important features, namely, production (P), marketing (M), raw materials (RM), administration and organization (AO), socio-economic perspective (SE), credit, savings and finance (CSF) and cultural heritage (CH) were identified and agreed upon by resource persons. During stage two, the resource persons were called upon to rank the policy objectives using the Nominal Group Technique which involved asking the experts to identify a few objectives which according to them were the most important. These objectives may be listed under three heads of industrial policy objectives, national policy objectives and policy objectives of small scale industries.

Triggering questions like "which of the policy objectives has the greatest potential for positive or negative impacts on Indian industries as a whole?" were used. The positive or negative impacts so recorded were subsequently tabulated ignoring the signs. Those elements which pooled no votes or only one vote were disregarded. This reduced the policy elements from 116 to 46. The resource persons after agreeing upon the final list of descriptive integrated policy elements were asked to develop a structural self interaction matrix (SSIM) on the basis of the chosen contextual relation "affects". Each element of the descriptive ranked list was compared with another element under the relation "affects" and the group responses were symbolically put in the form of V, A, X or 0 in SSIM.

The presentation evoked a host of comments and questions. Mr. Agnihotri in his observation felt that the approach adopted for identifying dimensions in advance, has the limitation of straight-jacketing the listing of dimensions of public policy and may thus have a negative impact on final results. Mr. Batra was of the view that while the ISM methodology is quite comprehensive, it provides a static framework and thus has limited usefulness in a dynamic situation. Replying to the comments, Prof. Satsangi observed that he agreed with the point of view that ISM methodology is a static one. This does not, however, exclude the possibility of making use of other methods like the system dynamics methodology.

ISM methodology, according to him, simplifies the task of determining the more important priorities, and also helps build up linkages between different factors. At the end, a certain pattern emerges which helps appreciate the more important concerns. Mr. Karki was, however, critical of ISM methodology and he argued that this methodology is based on consensus and averaging of results. It, therefore, is fundamentally against individual initiative and promotes mediocrity. The Chairman agreed with the views of Mr. Karki as he said a lot of merit in public policy can be achieved through leadership qualities which implies being persuasive in approach and making people agree to new and progressive ideas. Prof. Satsangi in his concluding observation, however, remarked that interaction is a continuing process and that is also the strong point of the ISM methodology.

The second presentation was made by Dr. J.P. Saxena on 'Policy Options for Energy Conservation in Indian Cement Industry'. Prof. Saxena observed that success of any programme such as the one on Energy Conservation, greatly depends upon correct identification of various program plan sub-elements, specially the objectives, and consequently evolving appropriate policy options to fulfill those objectives. In a large system, different options may relate to different areas. In some cases one option may relate to one or even more than one area. Thus, these options must come from the think tank of the system involving various experts related to different areas, each associated with one objective or even more objectives out of the various objectives of the program plan. Unification of diversified options associated with various experts is essential for evolving an integrated policy.

Evolving policy for achieving the objectives, therefore, constitutes multi-criteria decision-making. Policy formulation for energy conservation in an industrial sector depends on many considerations such as: the present technological status, the new developments, quality of inputs like coal and raw materials; availability of power, transportation facilities, manpower, managerial skills, financial resources, the product, the market dynamics, the government regulations and the local factors.

The Analytic Hierarchy Process (AHP) is used for an in-depth study to decide on the weightages attached to each feature selected through the Delphi exercise. Thus Delphi method is used for identifying the important features and AHP technique is used for deciding the weightages of each feature. Integration of the Delphi exercise and the AHP is known as Delphi Hierarchy Process (DHP). Similarly, the Fuzzy Set Methodology (FSM) is a useful multi-criteria decision-making technique for systematic analysis of the importance of the various policy options and determining their ranks. The features and their weightage as found out from DHP are used for identifying and ranking of the options. Thus the proposed methodology (DHP-FSM) for policy formulations is a combination of Delphi methodology, Analytic Hierarchy Process and Fuzzy Set Methodology.

Commenting on these methodologies Prof. Sushil observed that they are better as a process than as the output. Dr. Saxena while agreeing with the observation replied that one special advantage of these methodologies lies in the fact that these help clear the understanding in complex situations.

Other Public Policies—II

The second afternoon session of 24.8.1993 was again devoted to Other Public Policies. In this session two key papers were presented by i) Dr. Y.S. Rajan — 'Science and Technology Policy', and ii) Dr. A. Cameron and Rajnish Karki — 'How a Major Public Policy Initiative Creates Impacts : The Case of Computer Hardware Industry'. This session was chaired by Prof. P.S. Satsangi. The rapporteur was Mr. Sandeep Kayastha.

Dr. Rajan's presentation can be divided into three parts—dynamics of technology, globalisation and technology, and suggestions. Dr. Rajan made the proposition that S&T policy is not just equipments, designs and technology transfer but comprises complex factors such as life styles of people, social and economic conditions, security considerations, national and international political economy. Earlier, the power of societies was measured by land and labour and followed by capital in mercantile era. However, today the power and influence of nations is technology. This is evident from the concern of developed nations for intellectual property rights, and purchase of hi-tech companies of the US by the Japanese. Today, technology has shifted from replacing manual work to improvement in the comfort and communication. The pace of development in technology in these areas is so fast that the time lag between successive technologies is coming down. The technology today has become dynamic with short cycles and requires visionary capabilities to go for such technologies. The organisations, therefore, will have to learn how to cope with dynamic and risky environment. Development of new technologies takes a long time. Thus vision, investment in infrastructure and manpower and risk taking capability are required. The transfer of technology requires strong capabilities for its absorption. The specific requirements for technology absorption are skilled manpower, production and engineering capabilities, investment and vision.

Despite Third largest scientific and technical manpower in the world and a large number of labs, the technology has not grown in harmony in India. The efforts to commercialize technology developed by labs have not generally shown encouraging results. He attributed the factors for poor commercialization and technology absorption capability of industry and labs to the lack of interaction between scientists and industry, inability to identify key people, low mobility for scientists in industry and labs, poor development of skills at lower levels and mismatched development of sectors.

The globalisation process, which has been going on for thousands of years, has got a new fillip due to transport and communication technologies supported by flow of people, goods and information. Technology is not only a cause of globalisation but it is also affected by globalisation. With the increase in competition in the domestic and global scene, the transnational companies need allies all over the world. This has also helped in transfer and spread of technologies. The technology collaboration and transfers from the countries can be useful only when these are acquired before the maturity stage. Since after this standardization takes place any one can get the technology, the benefits of technology acquired are minimal. In 60's and 70's India got technologies which were in maturity stage and were moving towards standardisation stage.

To capitalise R&D, Dr. Rajan suggested that the capabilities of labs and industry should be matched, R&D should be the concern of top management on continual basis, lower staff should be trained, scientists' recruitment policy should encourage young people and not discourage them, and the decentralisation and debureaucratisation of procedures should take place. Industry should take the lead in R&D and not just become importers of matured technologies. Currently, most of the expenditure on R&D is borne by the government. This scene has to change. The threats to the acquiring of technology will be IPR and dual use of technology. Since most new technologies will have dual purpose, it will be difficult for India to get these technology. Thus special emphasis is required to enter into this area and develop these technologies indigenously. Dr. Rajan praised the efforts of Indian scientists in developing critical technologies and pointed towards positive signs of development of technologies in the country. Technology has to solve two basic problems of India—poverty and unemployment.

The second presentation of the session by Dr. Rajnish Karki and Ahmad Cameron was based on their paper pertaining to impact of the 1984 computer policy on the hardware industry up to 1990. The authors outlined how that computers grew in 50s and 60s in selected research labs and universities of the country. The computer hardware was dominated by IBM which leased obsolete computers to Institutions.

According to the authors, the concern for development of indigenous capabilities took place in 1971 when IBM refused the PM to give a particular computer. Soon thereafter a committee recommended establishment of Central Electronics Limited, SCL, and CMC. The vacuum created by the exit of IBM was filled by these institutions, ECIL and some private companies. This development initiated and created a sound infrastructure in the country.

The 1984 policy was affected by the 1983 electronics policy which slashed customs and excise duty. The dependence of industry on foreign manufacturers and suppliers grew. The 1984 computer policy regulated the clearance through inter-ministerial standing committee, reduction in import duty on peripherals, liberal import of computers by academic and research institutions, and recognition of software as a separate industry. The growth of industry in this era was analysed based on global computer technology trends, growth of computer technology in the country, human resource development, growth of Indian economy, infrastructure development, end-user needs and application areas and computer policy.

The new policy boosted the use of computers in wider areas in government and commercial organisation by linking of districts with computers, and use of computers in railway reservation, Indian Airlines (IA), ONGC etc. Computer technology saw major changes in this era. The computer moved from universities and research institutes to business, manufacturing and communication. The shortfall in computer manpower increased in this era. The universities offered new courses to meet the demand of the business and industry.

The new policy increased the number of players in hardware industry. The industry became competitive, new products were introduced, the prices fell and sales picked up. This changed the user types. The computer went into the hands of new users in business and industry as compared to scientists and engineers. During this period, the growth of the hardware industry was four times the growth of industry is general.

The authors concluded that the policy definitely played an important and promotional role for the hardware industry. It created new users, attracted new players, competition grew, prices came down, and manpower requirement was met by private sector.

The computer policy has integrated the Indian hardware industry with the global market. New products are now introduced simultaneously in India. The price differential between Indian and foreign products is little. The authors believe that the policy has put industry where it should have been. The corporate sector has responded favorably to the policy. The private sector could avoid failures by going in for well established systems. The policy has also benefited the customers. However, the authors feared that the industry might have reduced itself to the screw driver technology and the industry would not have prospered if they had gone for proprietary products.

It was pointed out by the audience that lessons from Computer Policy cannot be generalised to other areas. The PM himself had taken keen interest in this policy and he was able to push it on account of the large majority his party had at that time. The computer policy looked only into the hardware but ignored the manpower development which led to sub-standard private training institutes. The chairman felt that a consensus approach like in education policy is better suited for proper implementation. The authors said that in dynamic environment, where new technologies are being introduced in every two years, consensus approach would be difficult.

Policy Analysis and Design Methodologies—I

The presentations on 25-8-1993 were related to Policy Analysis and Design Methodologies. In the first session, three key papers were presented by i) Prof. P.K.J. Mohapatra - 'System Dynamics Modelling for Public Policy Analysis', ii) Prof. Sushil—'Policy Analysis and Design Using Flexible Systems Methodology', and iii) Dr. C. Subhash—'Emerging Long-Term Energy Policy from the Broader National Goals and Priorities in the S&T Policy of India'. This session was chaired by Prof. K. Vizayakumar. Dr. Rajnish Karki was the rapporteur.

Prof. Mohapatra's paper introduced application of system dynamics methodology to public policy analysis. System dynamics approach developed by Forrester, uses the information available from 'mental models' of the experts and the principles of cybernetics, to develop a mathematical model of the system. Computer simulation is used to approximate dynamic behaviour of the system. The paper presented two case studies (Indian tea industry, and Energy requirement of Indian transport sector) in which system dynamics approach was applied successfully to generate public policy options. It was suggested that computer simulation and application of cybernetic concepts help cover inadequacies of expert opinions, to capture the enormously complex dynamics of public systems and design suitable policies.

Prof. Sushil's paper presented a pioneering effort at designing a new methodology for systems analysis. The 'flexible systems methodology'

attempts to use one or more techniques in various combinations in accordance with the requirements of the system. Two reasons for adopting flexible systems approach are: the techniques of systems are clustered at two extremes i.e.'hard' techniques like linear programming which uses quantitative data, and 'soft' techniques like delphi which use qualitative data; the dynamics of any real system comprises various combinations of both quantitative and qualitative information. The flexible systems removes this anomaly by integrating the quantitative and qualitative tools according to the requirements of the system being analysed. The steps in applications of flexible systems methodology are: define the objectives of systems analysis, conceptualisation of the system, cluster quantitative and qualitative tools in a fuzzy manner, match attributes of the systems with the tool-clusters, selection of tools for use, integration of tools, and using integrated tools to model and analyse the problem situation. The flexible systems methodology was applied successfully to two public policy situations (agricultural waste management,and energy policy).

Prof. Subhash's paper presented a perspective on appropriate energy policy for the long-term, which relies on renewable sources of energy. Defining the primary source of energy vector, he hypothesised that hydrogen would be the energy vector of the next century. For facilitating use of this renewable resource of enormous potential, he highlighted the need to give strong push for required research.

During the discussions, the following questions and issues were raised : How the systems approach takes care of changes in one or more variables, and the alliances/interrelations among variables? The model once developed is like a machine and it cannot be modified, therefore scope for the likely changes and interrelations in variables have to be provided for during the design.

"Integrated systems methodology" was suggested as a better title for flexible systems methodology [FSM]. The suggestion was considered to be inadequate by the author, as FSM involves not only integration but also critical consideration of whole spectrum of 'soft' and 'hard' techniques.

It was pointed out that choosing a set of techniques and then integrating them is complex, and it may not be possible for practitioners to achieve, due to lack of familiarity with the large number of techniques and time/effort required. This limitation is sought to be removed by developing an expert system for choosing and integrating the techniques; and work on such an expert system is already in advanced stages.

FSM tends to integrate techniques which are vastly different even at the paradigm level. This was responded by explaining that certain overlaps can be found even among the most different techniques, and FSM takes advantage of such overlaps for integration.

The issue of predictability of system dynamics models was also raised. Predictability was stated to be a limitation of any model and the problem is compounded in public policy applications as process of public policy making has not been yet modelled.

It was concluded that use of hydrogen as a major energy resource is far from being economically viable, mainly due to high costs of producing frozen hydrogen and serious limitations in storage. The problems were acknowledged as real but at the same time enormous potential of hydrogen as a long term renewable source was stated to be undeniable. Therefore, there was urgent need to give a strong push to required research.

Policy Analysis and Design Methodologies—II

In the second session of 25.8.1993, four papers were presented by (i) Prof. K. Vizayakumar—'Environmental Policy Analysis : System Dynamics Approach', (ii) Dr. A. Vij—'Role of Models in Public Policy Analysis and Design', (iii) Mr. S.K. Batra—'Policy Guidelines on Vocational Training for Advanced Technology by International Labour Organization' and iv) Mr. V.K. Agnihotri—'An Integrated Approach to Public Policy Design'. This session was chaired by Prof. Sushil. The rapporteur was Mr. Shailendra Mendiratta.

Dr. Vizayakumar in his presentation discussed two case studies in which he had applied System Dynamics Modelling in Environmental Policy Analysis, one at the macro level for the analysis of pollution and environmental deterioration, and the other at the micro level for modelling and analysing the environmental impacts in a coal mining area. Both case studies showed the impact on various objectively identifiable indicators as a result of different policy initiatives. The presentation brought into focus the usage of modelling techniques and its power in evaluating different policy alternatives.

The second presentation by Dr. Vij surveyed the range of available modelling techniques and presented a study involving the two-way integration of two different techniques—Input/Output modelling and System Dynamics modelling. These were used to analyse possible policy initiatives in the energy sector.

The two presentation underlined the need to integrate academic thinking with practical policy making to the considerable advantage of both. Use of integrated models as effective tools for the analysis of public policy was illustrated.

In the discussion which followed, an issue was raised, whether the

System Dynamics modelling produced counter-intuitive behaviour at any stage. Both the above mentioned speakers were of the view that while no counter-intuitive behaviour was shown by the results of the modelling exercise, in some of the cases the results were certainly striking, quantifying the intuitively understood relationships. In some cases the results revealed behavioural patterns which led to further theoretical analysis of the model and resulted in better conceptualization of the policies and their impact.

Another issue agitated was whether System Dynamics modelling was adequate to represent the lesser or non-visible and non-quantifiable factors. It was argued that the technique did take in its ambit the conceptualized, and to that extent, visible factors, as well as non-quantifiable factors. In the case study presented, for example, counter-pressure exerted by pressure group was a non-quantifiable factor which had been accounted for in the model.

The other two presentations by Mr. Batra and Mr. Agnihotri outlined policy design methodologies including different steps to be taken while formulating a public policy.

Mr. Batra drew his example from the field of Training in Advanced Technology. He introduced the idea of formulation of a meta-policy framework which would be applicable across national boundaries in a region as a whole, and which would provide a framework within which independent policies would be framed by individual nations, resulting in greater harmony in the policy initiatives in the region.

Mr. Agnihotri suggested what he termed a Logical Processual Framework giving in minute detail the steps involved in framing of a policy and fitted in perspectives the different methodologies presented in many of the other technical sessions.

In the discussion that followed, an issue was raised as to whether some objective indicators could be suggested for proper timing of policy initiatives to take place. It was stated that though Stafford-Beer's Viable System Model did suggest indicators for timing of policy interventions, the situation in India was that public policy was formulated in response to a host of factors including, at times, political events. Ripening of political opinion appeared to be the major factor governing timing of public policy announcements.

Some recommendations emerged as natural corollaries to the discussions. These were:

1. There is need for greater integration between academic research and public policy making as well as for increasing use of modelling techniques in the analysis and design of public

policies.

2. With the broad objectives of having better designed and clearly expressed public policy documents, it would be appropriate to have a checklist on the lines of the Logical Processual Framework of items to be covered and processes to be undergone which may provide a guideline to policy makers and authors of policy documents.

Plenary Session

In the plenary session held on 25-8-1993 at 2.30 p.m., the reports of various sessions were presented by rapporteurs and resolutions were adopted. This session was chaired by Professor A.M. Khusro.

ANNEXURE

LIST OF PARTICIPANTS

Agnihotri, V.K.
Joint Director, Lal Bahadur Shastri National Academy of Administration, Mussoorie - 248 179 (Uttar Pradesh)

Batra, S.K.
Senior Consultant, Tata Consultancy Services, Gulab Bhavan, Rear Block, 6, Bahadur Shah Zafar Marg, New Delhi-110 002

Bjorkman, (Prof.) J.W.
Professor of Public Policy and Administration, Institute of Social Studies, P.O. Box 90733, 2509 LS the Hague, (Netherlands).

Cameron, (Dr.) Ahmed
Head, National Informatics Centre Training Unit, Lal Bahadur Shastri National Academy of Administration, Mussoorie - 248 179.

Dey, S.C.
Additional I.G. of Forests, Ministry of Environment and Forests, Paryavaran Bhavan, CGO Complex, Lodi Road, New Delhi-110 003

Dharmarajan, K.
Joint Secretary, Ministry of Urban Development, Government of India, Nirman Bhavan, New Delhi - 110 011.

Giridhar, (Prof.) G.
Indian Institute of Health Management, 1, Prabhu Dayal Marg, Sanganer Airport, Jaipur - 550 065.

Gulati, (Prof.) Ashok
Director, National Council for Applied Economic Research, Parisila Bhavan, 11, Indraprastha Estate, New Delhi-110 002.

Karki, (Dr.) Rajnish
Reader, Faculty of Management, Lal Bahadur Shastri National Academy of Administration, Mussoorie - 248 179.

Kashinath, B.
Assistant Professor, CEMPRES, Lal Bahadur Shastri National Academy of Administration, Mussoorie-248 179.

Kayastha, Sandeep
Asstt. Professor, Faculty of Management, Lal Bahadur Shastri National Academy of Administration, Mussoorie-248 179.

Khusro, (Prof.) A.M.
Editor, Financial Express, Express Building, 9-10, Bahadur Shah Zafar Marg, New Delhi - 110 002.

Krishna, Sudhir
Deputy Director (Sr.), Lal Bahadur Shastri National Academy of Administration, Mussoorie - 248 179.

Kumar, (Dr.) Sharat
Reader, Faculty of Economics, Lal Bahadur Shastri National Academy of Administration, Mussoorie-248 179.

Mahanty, B.
Department of Industrial Engineering and Management, Indian Institute of Technology, Kharagpur-721 302.

Mohapatra, (Prof.) Pankaj K.J
Department of Industrial Engineering and Management, Indian Institute of Technology, Kharagpur-721 302.

Mehta, (Dr.) Dinesh
Director, National Institute of Urban Affairs, 11, Nyaya Marg, Chanakyapuri, New Delhi - 110 021.

Mendiratta, S.
Deputy Director, Lal Bahadur Shastri National Academy of Administration, Mussoorie - 248 179.

Mukherjee, (Dr.) Amitava
Professor, CEMPRES, Lal Bahadur Shastri National Academy of Administration, Mussoorie - 248 179.

Mukherjee, (Dr.) Neela
Professor, Faculty of Economics, Lal Bahadur Shastri National Academy of Administration, Mussoorie -248 179.

Rajamani, R.
Secretary to the Government of India, Ministry of Environment and Forests, Paryavaran Bhavan, CGO Complex, Lodi Road, New Delhi - 110 003

Ramachandran, (Dr.) H.
Professor, CEMPRES, Lal Bahadur Shastri National Academy of Administration, Mussoorie-248 179.

Razdan, Rajni
Joint Secretary, Department of Programme Implementation, Government of India, New Delhi.

Rajan, (Dr.) Y.S.
Adviser, Department of Science and Technology, Government of India, Technology Bhavan, New Mehrauli Road, New Delhi - 110 016.

Sanwal, Mukul
Joint Secretary, Ministry of Environment and Forests, Paryavaran Bhavan, CGO Complex, Lodi Road, New Delhi - 110 003.

Satsangi, (Prof.) P.S.
Director, Dayalbagh Educational Institute, Dayalbagh, Agra 282 005

Saxena, (Dr.) J.P.
Director, National Council for Building Material, H-14-D, DDA Flats, Saket, New Delhi 110 017.

Saxena, (Dr.) N.C.
Director, Lal Bahadur Shastri National Academy of Administration, Mussoorie-248 179.

Subhash, (Dr.) C.
Reader, Department of Futurology, Devi Ahilya Vishwavidyalaya, Indore.

Sushil, (Prof.)
Department for Management Studies, Indian Institute of Technology, Hauz Khas, New Delhi-110 016.

Vij, (Dr.) A. K.
Manager, Computers and Systems Engineering, Engineers India Ltd., 1, Bikaji Cama Place, New Delhi-110 036.

Vizayakumar (Prof.) K.
Department of Industrial Engineering Management, Indian Institute of Technology, Kharagpur - 721 302.

INDEX